Buying Property in Thailand

Essential Guide

Limitation of Liability/Disclaimer of Warranty

Although the author and publisher have used their best efforts in preparing this book, they make no representations or warranties with respect to the accuracy or completeness of the contents of this book and specifically disclaim any implied warranties of merchantability or fitness for any particular purpose. No warranty may be created or extended by sales representatives or written sales materials. The material in this publication is of the nature of general comment only and neither purports nor intends to be advice. Each individual situation is unique and the advice or strategies contained herein may not be suitable for every situation. Readers should not act on the basis of any information mentioned, included or provided without considering (and if appropriate taking) appropriate, and if necessary, professional advice with due regard to their own particular circumstances. The author and publisher expressly disclaim all and any liability to any person, whether a purchaser of this publication or not, in respect of anything and of the consequences of anything done or omitted to be done by any such person in reliance, whether in whole or part, upon the whole or part of the contents of this publication. Neither the author nor publisher shall be liable for any loss or profit or any other commercial damages, including but not limited to special, incidental, consequential or any other damages. Designations used by companies to distinguish their products are often claimed as trademarks. All brand names and prod-uct names used in this book are trade names, service marks, trademarks or registered trademarks of their respective owners. The author or publisher is not associated with any product or vendor mentioned in this book. To avoid embarrassment some names of actual companies or individuals have either been omitted or have been changed. No part of this publication may be reproduced, stored in a retrieval system, or transmitted, in any form or by any means without the prior written permission of the publisher, nor be otherwise circulated in any form of binding or cover other than that in which it is published and without a similar condition being imposed on the subsequent purchaser.

A complete guide to buying resort property in Thailand

Rodney Waller

2012

The Essential Guide to

Buying Property in Thailand

8 STEPS to success

Lara: Wouldn't it have been lovely if we'd met before?
Zhivago: Before we did? Yes.
Lara: We'd have got married, had a house and children. If we'd had children,
Yuri, would you like a boy or girl?
Zhivago: I think we may go mad if we think about all that.
Lara: I shall always think about it.

— *Boris Pasternak*

Contents

Introduction and purpose of the book

STEP 1: What to buy in Thailand?
1. The property purchase procedure 5
2. What can a foreigner buy? 9
3. Condominium freehold 11
4. Freehold 15
5. Leasehold 17
6. Leasehold with a share of freehold 21
7. Leasehold with option to purchase the freehold 23
8. What is the purpose of investment? 26
9. Investing for capital appreciation 30
10. Investing for rental Income 37
11. What is your exit strategy? 43
12. Location and property type 45

STEP 2: Land
13. Land measurement 51
14. Land title 52
15. Land scams 55
16. Land title investigation 57
17. Land title insurance 59
18. Access? 62
19. Electricity? 66
20. Water and sewage disposal? 69
21. Zoning and building regulations 72
22. Size matters 78
23. Flat land or hillside? 81
24. Subdividing land 83
25. Serviced land plots 85

STEP 3: Buying completed properties
26. Buying completed properties 89
27. Working with property sales agents 90
28. What to look for when viewing properties? 94
29. Managed development or stand-alone property? 101
30. What is included? 104
31. What are the monthly costs? 106
32. Aspect and adjacent land 109

33. Who is the seller and what is the reason for sale?   111
34. Surveys and Structural Engineers   114
35. Comparing properties   118
36. Taking over utilities and services   124

STEP 4: Building your own property
37. Building your own property   129
38. The construction process   131
39. Management and organisational structure   135
40. Working with architects   145
41. Build Quality   151
42. Surveying land   154
43. Choosing a construction company   157
44. Quotations and the BOQ   169
45. Variations   173
46. Building Permits   177
47. Staged payments   180
48. Construction Guarantees   183
49. The construction agreement   189
50. Financial considerations   194
51. Planning for rainy seasons   199
52. Retaining walls and drainage   203
53. What sells?   206
54. Mechanical, electrical and plumbing   215
55. Pest control   219
56. Know what you want and be prepared   221
57. Delays and penalty clauses   224
58. Snagging   230
59. Scheduling and sequencing   236
60. Registering your property   239

STEP 5: Off-Plan property
61. What is "off-plan" property?   243
62. Risks and benefits of buying off-plan property   246
63. Mitigating risks   250
64. Mitigating risks (differing expectations)   252
65. Mitigating risks (market risk)   256
66. Mitigating risks (exchange rate risk)   260
67. Mitigating risks (non-completion)   263
68. What are you actually buying?   279
69. What else are you buying?   283
70. What to look (out) for?   287

71. Guarantees 294
72. Customisation 297
73. Payment schedules 302
74. Reservation agreements and deposits 306
75. Negotiating with developers 311
76. Guaranteed rental returns 319
77. Management and maintenance 326
78. Sinking funds 337
79. Rules and regulations 340
80. "Flipping" 342
81. Snagging 344

STEP 6: Legal and tax considerations

82. A practical approach 347
83. Invest in a lawyer 350
84. Appoint your own lawyer 353
85. Legal fees 355
86. Power of Attorney 358
87. Arbitration and mediation 361
88. Paying deposits 366
89. Due diligence? 371
90. Thai companies 375
91. Nominee shareholders? 380
92. The Foreign Business Act 383
93. Thai companies and corporate income tax 385
94. Personal income tax 386
95. Ownership structures 387
96. Who is the seller? 391
97. Transaction costs on purchase 394
98. Minimizing taxes upon sale 398
99. Taxes upon sale (leasehold) 401
100. Taxes upon sale (condominium freehold) 404
101. Taxes upon sale (freehold) 407
102. Corporate structure or personal name? 411
103. Inheritance 420

STEP 7: Financial considerations

104. Paying for your property 425
105. Currencies and exchange rates 430
106. Using finance to increase gains? 434
107. Mortgage financing for Thai property? 438
108. What is escrow? 448

STEP 8: Renting out your property

109. Renting your property? 453
110. Understanding rental demand 455
111. Short-term or long-term rental? 462
112. Being prepared for property rentals 465
113. Design tips for rental properties 470
114. Property management 480
115. Rental management 483
116. Additional services 488
117. Marketing, bookings and administration 491
118. Who is responsible for each task? 495
119. Setting rental rates 505
120. Marketing 513
121. Rental agreements 526
122. What to do after a booking is confirmed? 535
123. Taxes on rental income 536

Conclusion **541**

Dedicated to my father, James Edward

The author would like to express a special thank you to Crawshaws Solicitors (www.crawshaws.com) for providing general assistance and valuable information for Step 6 on the subject of legal and tax.

Introduction and purpose of the book

For the unprepared, buying property in Thailand is fraught with hazards. The purpose of this book is to provide the reader with an understanding of the potential challenges that present themselves to property buyers.

Possession of the relevant information will help potential property buyers to deal in an informed way and to discuss issues with a level of familiarity with sellers, property agents, construction companies, rental agencies and, in particular, lawyers and tax advisors. In short, the information contained in this book will prevent you from being unduly influenced by obviously unsound or inappropriate advice, and help to prevent others taking advantage of you.

A knowledge of the issues that are relevant to evaluating and buying properties will also allow you to make informed choices that meet your own objectives and needs, instead of relying excessively on the advice of sellers or agents who clearly have their own agendas.

With regard to specific outcomes, information related to the dangers involved in buying off-plan property or the criteria for choosing a construction company to build your dream property could not only save you money, it could literally save you from sleepless nights and financial disaster. In this way, just as Thai kickboxing is a form of physical self-defence; information could be considered self-defence for your financial future and lifestyle. To put things another way, a purchaser without any knowledge of the issues involved in buying Thai property is virtually guaranteed to be deceived, inappropriately advised or "ripped off" in some way; he might as well paint a target on his back or hang a sign around his neck saying "ATM – please take my money – no card needed!"

I firmly believe in the principal of seeking wisdom from those who have already done what you want to do. Accordingly, this book seeks to share the practical advice and experience of investors and property owners that have already bought property and have learnt the hard way by making mistakes.

Where appropriate, information is presented in the form of a checklist. The book is also arranged into short chapters (with some exceptions) that allow readers to quickly look up information of particular relevance. The combination of short chapters and checklists is deliberately designed for the book to be of practical use "in the field". For instance, the checklists presented in the "Renting out your property" section provide a list of tasks related to property and rental management that can be used to design and implement a rental strategy. Without such checklists, items often get overlooked. In addition, when prices are mentioned in Thai Baht, the equivalent in US Dollars *at the time of writing*[1] is noted for convenience and where it is considered helpful, a summary is included at the end of a chapter.

> **Important Tips are also presented in this shaded format for the purpose of highlighting key information or issues.**

However, while this book does contain a lot of technical detail, it is designed to be a no-nonsense, common sense guide. One suggestion for reading this book is as follows: readers should browse through the 12 chapters in Step 1 because they contain fundamental information; afterwards, readers can go directly to the relevant Steps of interest, for example, Step 3: Buying completed properties, Step 4: Building your own property, or Step 5: Off-plan property.

As the book is arranged to allow readers to skip to relevant chapters, readers should be forewarned that some of the information is necessarily repeated when it is relevant to more than one chapter.

It is also important to say what this book is not. This is a book about helping foreigners to buy, build or rent out property in Thailand's resort areas; it is therefore not an appropriate book for investors looking to buy commercial properties or properties in Bangkok. This is also not the right book for those looking to buy fractional ownership[2] or for foreigners planning to "own" property in some way through a Thai spouse or partner[3]. I am not a great believer of losing control over an asset from the outset or assuming ownership in the name of others for the sake of convenience (unless you are making a gift).

Finally, before we start, some words of wisdom (and warning):

Smile more.

Don't leave your brains at home!

And enjoy the book…

---

[1] Approximately 30 Baht = 1 US Dollar (US$).

[2] The joint ownership of a real estate asset, usually though a corporate structure.

[3] Normally, when buying freehold land, a foreign spouse must usually sign a declaration at the Land Department stating the funds belonged to the Thai spouse prior to marriage, i.e. the land is not the common property of the couple.

STEP 1
What to buy in Thailand?

1
The property purchase procedure

The procedure for purchasing property can be divided into ten distinct steps:

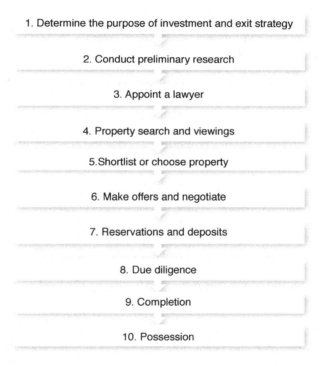

1. Determine the purpose of investment and exit strategy

2. Conduct preliminary research

3. Appoint a lawyer

4. Property search and viewings

5. Shortlist or choose property

6. Make offers and negotiate

7. Reservations and deposits

8. Due diligence

9. Completion

10. Possession

It is important to be familiar with these steps for two reasons. First, it allows buyers to proactively prepare for each step in advance. Second, by defining each step, buyers can ensure that relevant action is taken for each stage before moving prematurely to a subsequent stage. It also ensures that none of the steps are overlooked.

Following is a brief explanation of each step:

1. Determining the purpose of the investment and the exit strategy should always be the starting point because the answers influence the majority of subsequent decisions related to the purchase of property, including what to buy, where to buy and how to structure the purchase.

2. Conducting preliminary research is concerned with achieving a fundamental understanding of Thai property law (as it relates to foreign ownership), i.e. what a foreigner can and cannot own. It is important to come to terms with this basic information prior to commencing a property search so as to enable the buyer to ask relevant questions and communicate effectively with lawyers, agents and sellers. Part of the preliminary research should also be to narrow down the property search to a specific resort, area and location.

3. Appoint your own lawyer. It is advisable to appoint a lawyer at this early stage – in advance of viewing properties or making offers – for two reasons: firstly, once engaged, your lawyer is on hand to offer advise during the entire process of viewing, negotiating and purchasing. Secondly, once you have identified a property you wish to purchase, it is possible to move more quickly with a purchase if a lawyer has already been engaged. (While the sequence of steps outlined above makes logical sense and is recommended, it is also possible to continue with steps four, five and six before engaging a lawyer. In other words, some property buyers prefer to view properties, choose the one they wish to proceed with and commence negotiations before appointing a lawyer).

4. Property search and viewings. This includes working with property agents and discusses what to look out for during the viewing of properties.

5. Shortlisting and choosing a property requires properties to be evaluated and compared according to your investment objective and personally chosen criteria.

6. Making offers and negotiating requires a familiarity with the full range of issues that can potentially be negotiated with property owners or developers.

7. Reservations and deposits. Once a property has been chosen and a price has been agreed with the seller, the next step is usually entering into some form of reservation agreement and the payment of a deposit. The seller often requests a deposit as a demonstration that a purchaser is serious, in return for taking the property off the market and agreeing not to sell it to another party for the duration specified in the reservation agreement.

8. Due diligence. Sometimes step seven is skipped entirely, if a purchaser prefers to proceed with due diligence before putting any deposit money down. The risk is that the deal could be lost if a second purchaser comes along and pays a deposit to reserve the property before the first interested purchaser has completed due diligence. Whichever sequence is preferred, due diligence is an essential step to perform for all property purchases and one that should not be skipped under any circumstances.

9. Completion. Once due diligence has been completed and findings are satisfactory, seller and purchaser can then proceed to completion, which involves the signing of contracts, full payment of the purchase price (less any deposit or reservation fee already paid) and the transfer of property ownership.

10. Taking possession of the property involves the handover of keys, together with any other relevant documentation and guarantees. It is also where the purchaser needs to check and confirm that the fittings and fixtures detailed in the sales agreement remain in the property.

These ten steps provide a conceptual framework for property buyers to move through the process of purchasing a property. It also provides a framework for much of the information contained in this book. With this in mind, the following chart duplicates the ten steps listed above, together with references to the key chapters relevant to each step.

Steps	Key chapters
1. Determine the purpose of investment and exit strategy	What is the purpose of investment? (Chapter 8) What is your exit strategy? (Chapter 11)
2. Conduct preliminary research	What can a foreigner buy? (Chapter 2) Land title (Chapter 14) Zoning and building regulations (Chapter 21) Building your own property (Chapter 37) What is off-plan property? (Chapter 61 - 62) Ownership structures (Chapter 95) Understanding rental demand (Chapter 110)
3. Appoint lawyer	Appoint your own lawyer (Chapter 84) Legal fees (Chapter 85)
4. Property search and viewings	Working with property sales agents (Chapter 27) What to look for when viewing properties? (Chapter 28) Mitigating risks of non-completion (Chapter 67)
5. Shortlist or choose property	Comparing properties (Chapter 35)
6. Make offers and negotiate	Who is the seller and what is the reason for sale (Chapter 33) Negotiating with developers (Chapter 75)
7. Reservations and deposits	Paying deposits (Chapter 88)

Steps	Key chapters
8. Due diligence	Surveys and structural engineers (Chapter 34) Due diligence (Chapter 89)
9. Completion	Transaction costs on purchase (Chapter 97) Minimising taxes upon sale (Chapter 98) Corporate structure or personal name? (Chapter 102) Inheritance (Chapter 103) Paying for your property (Chapter 104) What is escrow? (Chapter 108) Taking over utilities and services (Chapter 36)
10. Possession	What is included? (Chapter 30)

2
What can a foreigner buy?
(Essential)

There is a general perception that Thai property law is complicated. Actually, the opposite is true: the laws relating to foreign property ownership in Thailand are quite clear. Foreigners can buy and own "freehold condominiums". Foreigners can buy and own buildings and structures, such as villas (as distinct from the land on which they sit), and foreigners can take leases on land or property. Foreigners cannot own land.

Where things get complicated is in the methods and legal structures employed by lawyers (on behalf of foreign clients) to circumvent or "get around" the strict rules on foreign ownership. The most obvious of these is the use of Thai companies (see chapter 90) by foreigners to buy land. These methods and legal structures are legal (it would be more accurate to say they are not illegal if set up in accordance with the law), though they might not be in the true "spirit of the law" intended.

The ownership laws together with the legal structures used to circumvent them appear to provide a balance of convenience for both sides: foreigners get to buy properties in Thailand; Thailand benefits from purchase money coming into the country, increased employment in the construction industry and increased tourist revenue from visiting property owners (especially in the retirement segment). In addition, since Thai companies are used as the vehicle through which land (and other property) is "owned" by foreigners, it acts as a face-saving mechanism in that Thai companies are, for the purposes of the law, Thai "persons" or entities and foreigners cannot therefore be considered as direct landowners in Thailand. Whether or not these laws will change over time is another matter. The only thing that can be said with certainty is that these legal structures have been used in various forms for many years.

The most important issue for potential property buyers is to understand the different forms of legal ownership. Only with such knowledge (together with an understanding of land titles and ownership structures) can a buyer properly understand what is being offered to him. The starting point of this understanding is the necessity to look beyond physical property descriptions – such as villas, apartments, townhouses – and to start understanding property ownership in terms of *legal rights*. Legal ownership rights are the most fundamental issue to get to grips with if you want to safely buy property in Thailand.

As will become evident in chapter 95 about ownership structures, it is the interplay between the type of legal ownership and the various possible holding structures that on the surface making Thai property law appear complex. However, being familiar with the different forms of legal ownership and what foreigners can and cannot own provides the foundation for understanding everything that follows. Therefore, each of the different types of legal property ownership – condominium freehold, freehold and leasehold (and leasehold variations) – are discussed in the following five chapters.

It should be noted that whether you are buying property in Koh Samui, Phuket, Pattaya, Krabi or Hua Hin, the underlying legal principles are the same. In other words, wherever you buy the fundamental forms of legal ownership are condominium freehold, freehold, leasehold, or some combination thereof. The only difference is the availability of each of the different types of legal ownership in each resort area. For example, Phuket has a reasonable supply of both luxury villas and condominium freehold properties; Koh Samui has a high proportion of top-end luxury villas but an extremely limited supply of condominium freehold properties[4]; while Pattaya – due to different building regulations – is dominated by a large and growing supply of condominium freehold units[5] with a reasonable supply of luxury villas.

Summary

- Foreigners can buy and own "freehold condominiums".
- Foreigners can buy and own buildings and structures, such as villas (as distinct from the land on which it sits).
- Foreigners can take leases on land or property.
- Foreigners cannot own land.

---

[4] For example, in 2007, of all the condominium freehold units launched in Thailand, only 3% were in Koh Samui.

[5] 12 new projects comprising 4,239 units were launched just in the last six months of 2010.

3
Condominium freehold

In a *physical* sense, a condominium is a building[6] that is divided into parts, whereby each part comprises an individual condominium unit, together with co-ownership of common property (i.e. land and property for the common benefit of the co-owners[7]). Therefore, each condominium owner has title to his or her own *personal* property[8] and co-ownership of the *common* property by way of an undivided interest in the co-owner association or "juristic person".[9]

It is in this way that condominiums differ from other apartment buildings. With apartment buildings, buyers only receive an interest in their separate unit and no shared interest in the common area, unless given such an interest by the developer. Apartment owners also have no say in the management of the building or common areas; the developer decides the standards of building maintenance and sets the management fees for owners without any oversight by the owners.

However, when speaking of condominiums in Thailand, we are not speaking of "condos" in the general sense that is used, for instance, in the United States. In Thailand, we are referring to a special legal type of freehold that foreigners (or foreign owned companies) can directly and legally own in Thailand, just as they would own a freehold property in their own country. Hence the term "Condominium Freehold" title.

Due to the fact that condominiums are a special form of property that foreigners can own, many aspects of condominiums are governed by legislation contained in The Condominium Act, which clarifies the law for property developers and provides a degree of "consumer protection" for condominium buyers. Indeed, recent amendments to the Condominium Act in 2008 were aimed at providing further protection for purchasers of condominium units from developers.

---

[6] Any building that is "contiguous" could technically become a condominium, i.e. it can include "vertical" condominiums and "horizontal" condominiums.

[7] The land upon which the condominium building is built, car parking areas, building entrance, internal access roads, utilities, and common facilities such as swimming pools, tennis courts, clubhouses, gyms and saunas.

[8] The title represents rights of ownership to the unit's volume, i.e. the height, length and width, including interior partitions; it does not extend to the external walls or structure of the condominium building.

[9] The Condominium Juristic Person is the legal entity established to own, manage and maintain the common property. Owners also have the option (if elected) to become *active* members of the juristic person committee, which oversees the work of the property manager.

As mentioned in the previous chapter, foreigners and foreign entities[10] are prohibited from acquiring a direct freehold interest in land in Thailand. As each condominium unit carries with it a proportionate ownership of land, foreign ownership is strictly controlled, which means developers of condominiums must follow certain procedures and comply with certain regulations in order to obtain condominium title for their properties.

The general rule is that only 49%[11] of the registrable area[12] of a condominium project can be allocated to foreign purchasers. For example, if there is a development comprising 100 condominium units (and all are of the same size) then 49 can be directly owned by foreigners. When the 49% quota has been used, it is still possible for foreigners to purchase the other units, although such purchases must be made on a leasehold[13] basis or through the operation of a Thai company (since a Thai company has the same rights as a Thai person). Therefore, in cases where there is insufficient interest from Thai nationals, a condominium project could for all practical purposes be completely sold freehold and leasehold to foreigners.

It should be noted that as leasehold is perceived as an inferior form of ownership in relation to freehold, the units comprising the "freehold" quota for foreigners tend to be in higher demand and are often the first units to sell.

> **Important tip:** Prior to purchasing a condominium unit, it is important to check the ratio of foreign ownership. If there are remaining units within the 49% foreign ownership quota, these can be purchased freehold by foreigners; if no foreign quota remains, the remaining units can only be purchased leasehold or through a Thai company. The difference in legal title and ownership rights are substantially different.

Many of the laws relating to the way condominiums must be structured date back to 1979 and the process for developers to obtain condominium title can be quite cumbersome. For instance, to ensure compliance with the law, condominium

---

[10] Including Thai companies with more than 49% foreign ownership.

[11] As condominium owners receive an interest in the common property, which includes the land on which the condominium is built, foreign ownership is limited to 49% because foreigners cannot own freehold land. Condominium Act (No. 3), B.E. 2542 (1999) raised the foreign ownership limit to 49% (from the previous 40%).

[12] 49% of the total sellable area of the condominium units in the condominium building at the time the developer applies to register the condominium with the Land Department.

[13] Since voting rights are associated with ownership they remain with the owner of the unit, not with the *lessee* (leasehold purchaser), unless the lessee obtains an irrevocable proxy from the freehold owner. If a large proportion of units are sold leasehold, whereby the developer retains the freehold along with the respective voting rights and control, it can disturb the "democratic" voting system.

title cannot be issued until the building has been completed and inspected. For a developer, this means title transfer to the purchaser cannot be guaranteed until the condominium title is approved toward the end of construction. This is an important concern because without proper certification as a Thai condominium, in the eyes of Thai law, it does not qualify under the Condominium Act to provide freehold title to foreigners.

From a "consumer protection" angle, there are several benefits for condominium purchasers. For instance, purchase contracts for the sale of a condominium unit by the developer (but not for a resale) are standardised and are required to be in the form established by the Ministry of the Interior. Further, the Condominium Act says that any provision in a contract of sale that is inconsistent with the "benchmark" terms and conditions and that is not in favour of the prospective buyer will be unenforceable. This largely protects purchasers from unfair contractual terms.

Furthermore, the amendments to the Condominium Act in 2008 specifically addresses the situation where developers make promises in marketing materials and then fail to deliver on such promises. In other words, laws now exist to cover the integrity of marketing materials so as to avoid misrepresentation to buyers. The Condominium Act says that advertisements and brochures used by a condominium developer to sell condominium units are deemed to be incorporated into the sales contract, and any inconsistencies between marketing materials and the sales contract will be interpreted in favour of the buyer[14]. For example, if the marketing brochure states that certain facilities will be included in the finished project, this promise is incorporated into the sales contract even if it is not written into the contract as a specific term.

There are other significant benefits for purchasers of condominium property. In contrast to non-regulated developments, condominium units receive a five-year structural guarantee and a two-year non-structural defects warranty, regardless of the terms of the developer's contract (condominium laws confirm that contracts between the developer and purchaser shall not contain unfair contract terms that limit liabilities arising from the fault of the developer for defects).

The Condominium Act Amendments also provide provisions relating to the management of condominiums, together with penalties for violations of the Condominium Law.

---

[14] Developers must maintain copies of their condominium marketing materials and advertisements and submit a full set to both the Land Department (at the time of registering the condominium) and the Condominium Juristic Person (upon transferring the common area).

Buying a condominium freehold unit is therefore one of the easiest ways for foreigners to acquire direct property ownership in Thailand, and it is the most clear, straightforward and unambiguous ownership type. For these reasons, condominium freehold property units tend to be the form of property ownership most favoured by foreigners. The certainty relating to condominium title also facilitates re-sale where the freehold "foreign-quota" units tend to command higher re-sale prices.

In relation to location, it should be noted that while there are numerous condominium developments in the resort areas of Phuket, Pattaya and Hua Hin, there are fewer opportunities in Koh Samui where the condominium market is less developed.

It is worth noting that while condominium ownership is more certain and regulated, this does not obviate the need to engage a lawyer to act on your behalf (see chapter 84). Many standard risks remain for which due diligence and legal representation are essential. There is also the issue of inheritance, and choosing an ownership structure to hold the condominium; just because a condominium can be owned in a personal name doesn't mean it is the most suitable choice. For more on this see chapter 102.

Summary

- A condominium comprises title to an private apartment unit, together with co-ownership of common property.
- Condominium freehold is a special legal type of freehold that foreigners can directly and legally own in Thailand.
- The Condominium Act clarifies the law related to condominium freehold properties and provides a degree of "consumer protection" for buyers.
- Only 49% of the registrable area of a condominium development can be allocated to foreign purchasers.
- It is still possible for foreigners to purchase the non "foreign-quota" units, although only on a leasehold basis or through a Thai company.

4
Freehold

What does "freehold" mean?

Freehold is the most complete and absolute ownership interest that can be held in property. Freehold is where land or property belongs to the owner indefinitely (as opposed to a 30, 90 or 999 year lease) and therefore represents absolute ownership of real property.

In Thailand, with the exception of "condominium freehold" discussed in the previous chapter, the most common forms of freehold generally relate to the purchase of land or villas, i.e. land, or structures built on the land.

While it is true that foreigners can own condominium freehold and structures (buildings or villas), Thai law contains no provision for foreign individuals or foreign companies to own a direct freehold interest in land (put simply, foreigners cannot own land in Thailand). Indeed, the attitude that foreigners have no right to own Thai land is buried deep in the Thai official consciousness.[15]

There are some exceptions, which are as follows:

- Foreigners investing at least 40 million Baht (US$ 1.3 million)[16] in authorized Thai securities or government bonds are allowed to buy, subject to certain conditions, up to 1 Rai[17] of land for residential purposes.

- Exceptions are permitted under the Petroleum Act for approved projects, banks and financial institutions that have become foreign owned or other promoted companies authorised by the Board of Investment (BOI), under the Industrial Estate Act or with written permission from the Interior Ministry.

As readers might note, these exceptions are hardly relevant to the average buyer of property in Thailand!

To circumvent the laws designed to restrict foreign ownership of land, many lawyers will assist foreigners in setting up a Thai company as a vehicle for

---

[15] The idea of foreign land ownership is not popular among Thai people and it is prohibited as a matter of principle.

[16] *Exclusive* of the purchase price of the land (or land and house).

[17] 1,600 square metres (see chapter 13)

owning land, whereby the foreigner does not technically "own" the Thai company (which again would not comply with Thai law) but indirectly controls it through voting rights associated with the shareholding structure. In other words, the Thai company, which is considered a Thai person or entity, *owns* the land, and the foreigner *controls* the company.

However, while Thai companies are a practical, time-tested solution for foreigners to participate in land ownership (provided they are properly set up and in compliance with Thai laws), they cannot be considered a guaranteed, secure investment long-term. This is discussed further in chapter 92.

Almost all foreign purchases of land in Thailand are therefore done through leasehold ownership (see next chapter) or *indirect* freehold ownership through a Thai company, or some hybrid of the two such as "leasehold with a share of the freehold (where the freehold is owned by a Thai company).

To fully understand freehold ownership, of particular relevance are chapter 90 on Thai companies, chapter 91 on nominee shareholders, chapter 92 on the Foreign Business Act and chapter 95 on ownership structures.

Summary

- Freehold is the closest thing to absolute ownership of property.
- In Thailand, foreigners can own condominium property, and structures (buildings) on a freehold basis.
- Foreigners cannot own a direct freehold interest in land.
- Land ownership by foreigners is therefore done by leasehold or through a Thai company that *owns* the land while the foreigner *controls* the company.

5
Leasehold

What does "leasehold" mean?

Leasehold is an interest in land or property whereby the leaseholder does not actually own the land or property (in the sense of freehold) but is granted the right of *exclusive possession and use* of the land or property. In other words, the leaseholder gets to *use* the land or property, while the owner retains *ownership*. With regard to terminology, the owner of the freehold land or property granting the lease is termed the "lessor" while the owner of the lease is termed the "lessee".

The right to possession and use is for a specified period of time in return for payment of a consideration (rent) and the terms are recorded in a "lease agreement". It is possible to take a leasehold interest over any type of property, such as land, apartments, townhouses or villas. If the lease relates to land, the agreement would generally be a Land Lease Agreement or "LLA". If the lease concerns an apartment, the agreement would generally be an Apartment Lease Agreement or "ALA".

However, a lease is not just a contractual agreement; it is also a registrable legal interest against the freehold title document. Once registered, the lease becomes a *lien* upon the title deed[18], which serves as notice to anyone who attempts to purchase the underlying land[19] that the lease exists and that by purchasing the land they would be subject to the lease. As a legal interest, it also means the lease can be bought and sold.

In Britain, under historic common law, it is possible to see leases for 999 years (essentially nominal leases of property for life), while in Asia 99-year[20] and 50-year[21] lease terms are common. In the case of Thailand, the current legal maximum period stipulated for a lease is only 30 years (and any longer term will be reduced to 30 years)[22]. Naturally, the longer the leasehold period, the longer the property can be used and enjoyed and the more attractive it is to purchasers, which translates into a higher "rent" or purchase price for the lease.

---

[18] In Thailand, long-term leases of land can only be registered on land with *Chanote, Nor Sor Sam Gor* or *Nor Sor Sam* title (see chapter 14).
[19] Or loan money against it.
[20] Such as Singapore and Malaysia.
[21] Such as Philippines and Hong Kong.
[22] A proposal has been submitted to the Thai government to extend the registration period up to 60-years.

The relatively short period specified by Thai law for leasehold property has therefore led to the creation of potentially confusing contractual leasehold arrangements designed to "extend" the lease term. Land offices in Thailand refuse to register leases for more than 30 years, although they do allow private agreements to contain lease "renewals". Consequently, great efforts are made by developers and their lawyers to provide purchasers the opportunity to acquire longer leasehold periods.

> **Important tip:** When buying leasehold property in Thailand, it is common to come across the *30+30+30-year leasehold structure.* Salespeople for property developments – including some high-end international brand names (no names mentioned) – often present these leasehold structures as "90-year leases". Beware: they are not as simple or straightforward as they are portrayed. The 30+30+30-year leasehold structure simply means the leasehold period is for an initial lease term of 30 years (which complies with Thai law) together with two options to renew, each of 30 years duration.

While such leasehold arrangements are often marketed as 90-year leases, purchasers must understand that only the first 30 years is *legally registered* and therefore guaranteed, while the two options to renew are *contractual* in nature, i.e. they are promises to renew[23]. To help explain this difference, it should be noted that in Thailand leases longer than 3-years should be registered at the Land Office[24]. Once registered, the lease is shown on the back of the land title paper, which protects the terms of the lease and the tenant's rights for the duration of the lease. It also means that if the freehold is sold or transferred to a third party, the lease remains in existence and the new owner is bound by its terms.

This means that the first 30-year lease can be registered at the Land Office and the lease is then noted on the freehold land title document, while the second and third 30-year "renewals" are *contractual* in nature, i.e. they are "non-lease rights". In other words, the renewal clauses are governed by the legal principle of "privity of contract", which means the contract is only binding on the parties who signed the contact. The renewal clauses therefore only bind the *original* parties to the lease agreement, i.e. the original freehold owner and the lessee.

---

[23] They are unsupported in case law and the Thai Supreme Court has yet to have an opportunity to decide upon their validity. Therefore, 30+30+30-year leasehold structures should only be purchased by buyers that find such uncertainty acceptable. In some cases, buyers might be better off considering a "right of superficies" instead of a lease.

[24] Failure to register the lease will result in the lease only being valid for an initial three-year period. In other words, a long-term lease is not enforceable beyond three years *unless* it is registered.

Thus, a potential problem arises with these contractual renewals if the freehold land is sold or transferred. The question arises whether the new freehold owner is bound to honour the contractual renewals; bearing in mind the new owner was not a party to the original contract. The Supreme Court has ruled that in such cases that only "real lease rights" (i.e. legally registered leases) will transfer and follow the freehold title of the land to the new owner, which means that "non-lease rights" (such as contractual renewals) do not transfer. Contractual renewals are therefore only enforceable against the original freehold landowner; if the freehold land is sold, they are no longer enforceable against the new freehold owner, unless the new freehold owner signs a renewal agreement with the lessee (hence the creation of *protective leasehold structures,* see next chapter).

Indeed, it should also be noted that few people have actually got to the stage where these 30-year leases become renewable. In addition, leasehold renewals are not *automatic;* the renewal of a lease is an active process that requires the involvement of both parties to the lease agreement in order to execute a new lease agreement and register the new lease at the Land Department. In other words, if the parties take no action at the end of the 30-year period, the lease agreement will simply end. Some developers have attempted to facilitate this process by "pre-authorising" the necessary documents ready for submission 30 years later; however, if such documents are signed by an authorised director on behalf of a company, this presupposes the director will still be around in 30 years (and that the Land Department is still using the same forms).

Important tip: Without getting into complex legal terminology, the main point to understand is that the 30+30+30-year leasehold structure is not equivalent to a 90-year lease. Options to renew should not be treated as *automatic* guaranteed rights and when property sellers mention that you are getting a 90-year lease this is not giving you a true or complete picture. Some agents or salespeople might genuinely be unaware of the difference; while others are deliberately trying to mislead you.

Important note: It is also imperative to note that a long-term lease is for all intents and purposes a rental contract where payment for the whole term is made in full at the beginning. This means it is not a fixed asset but a contract that can be terminated prior to the expiration of the lease due to breach of contract by the lessee. It is therefore *essential* that the particular terms of the lease agreement are carefully checked to ensure the terms of the lease are not unfairly to the advantage of the lessor, such as would be the case where the contract can be easily breached by the lessee.

With the complications associated with setting up Thai companies to own freehold property (see chapter 91), leasehold ownership does however provide an easier way to own property in Thailand since leases can be registered directly in a foreigner's personal name. However, it does not necessarily follow that registering a lease in a personal name is the optimal structure (it might be useful to consider the alternative leasehold ownership structures, see chapter 95).

Finally, it is important to note that leases are personal in nature, which means a lease terminates upon the death of a lessee (a succession clause is usually inserted into the contract stipulating that the lessee's rights and obligations will be assigned to the lessee's heirs[25]). Therefore the issue of inheritance also needs to be considered (see chapter 103).

Summary

- A lease is a right to *use* property, while the freehold owner retains *ownership*.
- All property can be leased, including land, apartments, townhouses and villas.
- A lease can be registered by a foreigner in his or her personal name.
- The maximum period stipulated for a lease in Thailand is 30 years.
- A 30+30+30-year leasehold structure is not the same as a 90-year lease; the first 30 years is a legally registrable lease, while the second and third 30-year periods are *contractual* options to renew that are unenforceable in the case where the freehold land is sold.
- A lease is a rental contract, which can be terminated prior to the expiration of the lease due to breach of contract by the lessee. The terms of the lease must therefore be carefully checked.
- Leases are personal rights that terminate upon the death of the lessee, which means the issue of inheritance needs to be considered.

---

[25] Or unless the heirs of both lessee and lessor are included as parties to the agreement (if they have reached the age of legal maturity).

6
Leasehold with a share of freehold

As should be clear from the previous chapter, as only the first 30-year lease of the standard 30+30+30-year leasehold structure is actually "guaranteed", the crucial element in relation to subsequent renewals (of the second and third 30-year lease terms) is the owner of the freehold title (the lessor). It is the freehold owner who holds the power to grant lease renewals.

An innovative approach to provide leaseholders (lessees) with additional security and a greater degree control over their own lease renewals is the "leasehold with a share of the freehold" structure, which falls into the category of *protective leasehold structures*. This is commonly used by off-plan developers of multiple apartments sitting on one piece of freehold land owned by a Thai company.

The general idea behind this ownership structure is that, upon completion of the development, a 30-year lease will be registered for each apartment in the name of the respective purchaser (lessee). Then, additionally, each lessee receives shares in the Thai company[26] owning the freehold land, together with collective control over the company through voting rights (see chapter 90 on Thai companies for a more detailed explanation). The company is set up in such a way to enable lessees to retain control over subsequent lease renewals. In this way, the purchaser of an apartment technically becomes both lessee and, to some degree, lessor (or more accurately, joint-lessor).

In order to provide an example of how this works in practice, a property developer sets up a Thai company to own the freehold land on which an apartment project will be built (essentially a "project landholding company"). The Thai company is typically be set up with a two-tier share structure of common shares and preference shares, with the preference shareholders controlling the company through voting rights.

Purchasers of each individual apartment enter into contractual agreements with the developer for a 30+30+30-year lease and for ultimate ownership of shares in the Thai company that owns the land. These agreements usually include an Apartment Lease Agreement (ALA) and a Share Sale and Purchase Agreement (SSPA). Upon completion of the development, each purchaser registers ownership of the initial 30-year lease for his or her respective apartment. Then,

---

[26] Or a foreign company owning the controlling shares in the Thai company.

supposing there are seven apartments, each purchaser then receives one seventh of the controlling shares of the Thai landowning company, effectively exercising control over the company together with the other 6 purchasers.

A clause in the company documentation then requires a 95% vote to *prevent* the renewal of a lease. As each owner has more than 5% of the shares, it is technically impossible for a 95% vote to be raised against the lessee (unless the lessee votes against the renewal of his own lease together with all the other lessees!). In this way, the structure provides each purchaser with (a greater degree of) control over the renewal of the second and third 30-year lease terms[27]. This structure also facilitates the complete hand-over of the land and apartments to purchasers and for the property developer to exit the project.

With the "leasehold with a share of the freehold" structure, the key issues are that:

(a) Contractual agreements are properly worded and the company structure is properly set up to achieve the desired level of control over lease renewals.
(b) Upon completion of the apartment development the shares in the Thai landowning company are actually transferred to the new owners.
(c) The Thai company has not been used for other unknown purposes during construction or taken on debts or obligations that the new owners are not aware of (but will become responsible for).

These issues highlight the need to engage professional legal advice.

Summary

- As only the first 30 years of the 30+30+30-year leasehold structure is guaranteed, the crucial issue is control over the renewal of the second and third 30-year lease terms.
- With a "leasehold with a share of the freehold" structure, in addition to legal registration of the initial 30-year lease, purchasers also become part owners of the freehold, which grants control over lease renewals.
- It is crucial to ensure the landowning company is properly set up to provide effective control over renewals.

---

[27] However, note the comment in chapter 5 that the renewal of a lease is an active process; lease renewals are not automatic.

7
Leasehold with option to purchase the freehold

Due to the fact that only the first 30-year lease of 30+30+30-year leasehold structure is "guaranteed" by way of legal registration on the title document, *leasehold with the option to purchase the freehold* is another innovative contractual structure designed to provide purchasers with greater security and control over the underlying freehold land.

This ownership structure is generally referred to as leasehold with the option to purchase the freehold, although technically it would be more accurate to say "leasehold with the option to *transfer* the freehold".

With this method, the purchaser enters into the standard 30+30+30-year leasehold structure, although the purchaser is able to maintain control over any transfer of the freehold through the right to designate a new freehold owner. While the previous chapter discussed how a purchaser technically becomes both lessee and joint-lessor, with this arrangement the purchaser becomes lessee with the ability to control who becomes the lessor.

Should Thai law change in future to allow foreigners to own land directly, the right to transfer the freehold thus gives the lessee the right to specify *himself* as the new freehold owner, thereby transferring legal ownership of the freehold title to himself. The owner would then become the owner of both freehold and leasehold, thus guaranteeing ongoing ownership of the property. This is why this arrangement is often referred to as "leasehold with the option to purchase freehold."

This structure operates on similar principles to discretionary trusts that are used to control assets and keep the taxman at arms length. The leasehold owner can decide who becomes the freehold owner in a similar way that trustees of a discretionary trust decide who becomes a beneficiary of the trust. Until such time as the beneficiaries are determined, the trustee maintains effective control of the assets.

However, it should be noted that if the foreigner is expecting to transfer the freehold into his own name, the "option to purchase the freehold" only becomes an option if Thai law changes to allow foreigners to directly own freehold land. Until such time, therefore, it is not really an option at all.

This technicality is resolved by allowing the lessee to transfer the freehold land to himself *or to another entity over which he has control.* The option to transfer the freehold is therefore suitable for those who wish to have greater control over the freehold but do not wish to go to the trouble of setting up a Thai company to buy the property on a freehold basis; instead, they purchase on a leasehold basis – that can be purchased in their own name - and take "ownership" of the freehold at some point in future by transferring it to a Thai company of which the lessee is the controlling shareholder.

It should be noted that an option to purchase or transfer the freehold is not as secure as actual ownership of the freehold; until such time as the freehold is purchased, the option remains just that: an option, not true freehold ownership. In other words, purchasers should not be under the illusion that this structure is equivalent to direct freehold ownership.

To better understand how the structure might be used in practice, the following points demonstrate how the leasehold owner maintains an option to purchase the freehold through four key elements:

(1) The lessor (owner of the freehold) grants a lease to the purchaser (lessee) with an initial term of 30 years and two options to renew of 30 years each.
(2) The lessor (usually for no additional consideration) grants the lessee an option to receive transfer of freehold title or to designate a new freehold owner at any time during the Lease Term (the "option to transfer the freehold").
(3) Upon registration of the first 30-year lease, the lessor hands over the title deeds for the lessee's safekeeping for the entire lease term.
(4) The lessor also provides to the lessee a signed power of attorney (a "Transfer Power of Attorney") to allow the lessee, on behalf of the lessor, to transfer freehold ownership from the lessor to a transferee designated by the lessee (at any time during the lease term).

It should be noted that not all "options to purchase" provide this level of security. A variation on this structure is where a person enters into a lease agreement for a specified period of time and pays rent on a *monthly* basis, with the contract providing the lessee the option to purchase the freehold at any time during the lease term. In this case, it would be highly unusual for title deeds to be handed over or a Transfer Power of Attorney to be provided, which are the documents that effectively provide the ability to transfer. Without these documents, any desire to transfer the freehold is purely a contractual claim. However, for reference, with this contractual option to purchase, the most relevant negotiation points are:

(a) Whether the purchase price is established at the date of contract or whether it is to be determined at the time the option is exercised.

(b) If the purchase price is to be determined when the option is exercised, an independent means for determining the price must be established and stated in the contract.

(c) It must be determined whether the monthly rental payments that have already been paid will be deducted from the purchase price when the option to purchase is exercised.

Summary

- Leasehold with the option to purchase the freehold gives the lessee control over the freehold through the right to transfer the freehold.
- If Thai law changes to allow foreigners freehold ownership of land, the lessee can transfer the freehold to himself.
- Alternatively, the lessee has the right to transfer the freehold to an entity under the lessee's control, such as a Thai company.
- This structure should not be perceived as an equivalent to direct freehold ownership.

8
What is the purpose of investment?
(Essential)

Before you buy or build a property in Thailand, an essential question to ask yourself is: what is the purpose of the investment? The answer to this question is crucial because it should influence subsequent decision making at each stage of the property purchasing process. For example, are you buying a property as a:

- Primary residence
- Source of rental revenue
- Holiday home
- Place for retirement
- Investment for capital appreciation

Once a purchaser has identified his or her primary objective, the answer should determine subsequent decisions ranging from the type of property purchased, its location, the legal ownership structure, and even the choice of décor and furnishings. In addition, it is important to remain consistent with the objective from beginning to end (unless the objective subsequently changes). There are all too many examples of people who have invested money in Thailand and it turns out to be a disappointment due to their failure to remain consistent with the original purpose. Examples include investors building one-bedroom pool villas for rental only to find out later that most rental demand is for two or three-bedroom villas. Or investors with a buy-hold-sell strategy who buy what they believe is a dream property *according to their own taste,* only to discover Mr. Market's idea of a dream property is something quite different.

The purpose of this chapter is to discuss some of the primary investment objectives to assist readers to consider and clarify their own objectives. The objectives of buying primary residences, rental properties, holiday homes, and retirement homes are mentioned in this chapter. The objective of pure investment – either for capital appreciation or rental income – is discussed in more detail in the two subsequent chapters.

Primary Residence

This is the easiest category of all. If you are buying or building a property as a primary place of residence, there are no boundaries! You simply buy or build whatever you want and furnish the property to your own taste, restricted only by your budget and imagination (and building regulations). The only caveat is if you plan to sell one day in the future, bear in mind not to go too crazy. There is only a limited market in Thailand for pink medieval castle-looking homes with purple bedrooms!

When buying property as a primary residence, management fees become especially relevant. For instance, if you buy a property within a development where payment of a monthly management and maintenance fee is required, such payments might be perfectly manageable when the property is generating rental income although they can soon become a burden when the property is your residence and no rental income is coming in.

Rental Property

If your main objective is to buy or build a rental property, there are a number of considerations. Firstly, location is crucial (see chapter 110). If you are planning to rent to tourists, most want to be on or near the beach; others prefer to be close to the action (restaurants and bars); while others want to be by the beach *and* close to the action. Some consideration of target segments and price points is also necessary. Secondly, it is wise to research the optimum unit size and the other requirements of the rental market segments targeted in order to determine the kind of property to buy or build, such as a one-bedroom apartment, two-bedroom private pool villa or five-bedroom villa with garden (this is often a matter taking advice from rental agents). Thirdly, décor and furnishings must be suitable for rental purposes (see chapter 112). Not only should the décor be visually stunning but also *durable*. Rental properties, like hotel rooms, get hard use and guests are unlikely to take care of your property as if it were their own home.

Holiday Home

If you are looking to buy or build a holiday home, the main question is whether you are planning to rent it out when you are not using it. If the answer is yes, then the same considerations mentioned above for rental property apply. In particular, when furnishing the property, your own particular taste in interior décor must be tempered with an eye towards the rental market. One couple I know furnished their villa entirely to their own personal psychedelic taste, which could only be described as an Austin Powers film set. When the property was advertised on rental agents' websites, it was no great surprise when rental enquiries were few and far between! It must also be remembered that rental properties are no place for Aunt Mildred's antique bone china or crystal sculptures. Objects in rental properties have a habit of getting broken or leaving the country in a suitcase wrapped in towels (your towels!).

There must also be a consideration of security. If the property is in a remote area and you plan to use it only a few months each year, some form of security and property management is highly advisable. It might be wise to have live-in staff or engage a security company.

Retirement home

If buying or building a retirement home, the main considerations are usually ease of access and proximity to friends, golf courses, restaurants, supermarkets, hospitals or other amenities. The question of timing is important, i.e. whether retirement is imminent or at some point in the future. If it is some point in the future, and if the property will be offered for rental in the meantime, the same considerations for rental properties and holiday homes (above) apply.

Combined objectives

As might be evident, sometimes the purpose of investment doesn't fit neatly into any of these categories; it is often a combination of more than one objective. For example, the objective might be to buy a dream holiday home on a tropical island and to rent it out to tourists while you are not using it; or it could be to buy a rental property for occasional use as a holiday home, then ultimately use it as a residence in retirement. In such cases, it is necessary to assess the importance of each objective and assign a "weighting" to each objective, which will then provide some guidance on the location and type of property you purchase.

Summary

It is important to clarify *why* you are buying or building a property and act consistently with this objective at each stage of the purchasing process. Below is a summary of the key considerations for each of the most common objectives:

Primary residence:
- Buy or build what you want and furnish according to your taste.

Rental property:
- Location is key.
- Must consider target market.
- Take into consideration the optimal size and type of property for the rental market.

Holiday Home:

- Will the property be rented out when not in use?
- Furnish with the rental market in mind.
- Live in staff or security?

Retirement:

- Proximity to friends, golf, shopping, hospitals.
- Timing of retirement?
- Will the property be rented out prior to retirement?

Combined objectives:

- Evaluate relative importance of each objective
- Assign "weighting" to each objective to provide guidance on property type and location

9
Investing for capital appreciation

Without going too deeply into investment or financial jargon, the two main investment objectives are usually capital appreciation or rental income (or a combination thereof). Capital appreciation is discussed in this chapter, while investing for rental income is addressed separately in the next chapter.

Capital appreciation basically means buying or building a property with the aim of selling it later for more money than was originally invested. The difference is the capital appreciation or profit (before taxes). If the prime objective for buying or building property in Thailand is investing for capital appreciation, the considerations are totally different from those discussed in the previous chapter. The colour of the bedroom curtains is less important; instead hard data and ratios become the defining factors.

There are several different measures used by investors to compare competing "deals". One of the most common ratios is return on equity (ROE), which is basically a measure for calculating or estimating profit as a percentage of the money or "equity" invested. The calculation is as follows:

$$ROE = (profit/equity\ invested)\ x\ 100.$$

ROE is commonly used to calculate investment returns in countries where mortgage financing is widely available to provide leverage for investments. For example, suppose you are purchasing a property for $100,000 with $80,000 provided by a bank in the form of a mortgage and the remaining $20,000 is the investor's equity. If, after one year, the value of the property increases by 20%, the $100,000 property is now worth $120,000. If it is then sold, the profit is $20,000 after repaying the mortgage to the bank.

The ROE (without taking into account interest expenses, costs or taxes) is as follows:

$$ROE = (20,000/20,000)\ x\ 100 = 100\%.$$

Using mortgage financing (leverage) from the bank, the investor has made a 100% return on equity[28]. In other words, he has doubled his money.

---

[28] See also chapter 106 on the effect of mortgage financing on investments.

In Thailand, which is notable for the widespread lack of mortgages and financing for foreigners (with some exceptions, see chapter 107), most properties are therefore purchased by foreigners with 100% cash, i.e. without financial leverage to boost return on equity. This means capital requirements are higher in Thailand while investment returns expressed as a percentage of capital employed tend to be lower, unless there is mania phase causing a substantial rise in prices.

It also means investment calculations are more straightforward. Again, suppose you purchase a property for $100,000 and there is no mortgage financing available. The equity required by the investor is $100,000. After one year, the value of the property increases by 20% so the $100,000 property is now worth $120,000. If it is then sold, the profit is $20,000. The ROE (without taking into account any costs, expenses or taxes) is as follows:

$$ROE = (20,000/100,000) \times 100 = 20\%.$$

The absence of mortgages for foreigners buying properties in Thailand also means that many investment strategies that depend on financial leverage, commonly employed in more developed financial systems, are not suitable strategies for Thailand. As a consequence, most investors in Thailand's resort property markets tend to be either on the property development side or are "incidental" or "mixed-purpose" investors, i.e. they make a lifestyle decision to buy a dream villa where they can spend more time in the tropics, although expect to make a profit when selling later.

When investing for capital gains, there are two primary strategies. Either the investor must time his entry and exit to profit from the momentum of market sentiment (in other words, buy low and sell higher), or buy an undervalued property, i.e. buy a property below market value and sell it at market value.

Timing the market is a more challenging than meets the eye because there are so many influencing factors that affect property markets, demand and prices at any point in time. There are also plenty of political, economic and natural calamities that could change the landscape at any time. However, there are clues that hint at opportunities and the underlying logic is to buy property when property demand and prices are low but about to rise, or when they are already rising and sentiment is expected to continue improving.

As this book is being written – just a few years after the military coup in 2006, a global economic crisis that started in 2008 and recent political unrest in Thailand's capital Bangkok – the resort property market in Thailand is currently in one of the worst downturns for years. The question is whether the market will improve and, if so, within what timeframe.

While comment on the future direction of any market is beyond the scope of this book (and in any case would only be an opinion, informed or otherwise), one comment that can be made (notwithstanding unforeseen political events in Thailand) is that resort properties represent "discretionary expenditure" rather than first homes for residential purposes. This means resort property markets tend to improve after primary markets worldwide recover to the point where property buyers are confident the worst of the global recession is over, their jobs and first homes are safe, and there are marked signs of improvement. For this reason, there is usually a time lag between the recovery of primary markets and the recovery of resort markets.

In addition, just as it helps to successfully rent out a property if it is in the right location and is the optimal size for rental demand, the same is true of successfully investing for capital appreciation, which requires careful study of the market to ensure you buy (or build) the right type of property in the right location, i.e. that you buy or build what the market wants and what will sell. In a market that is trending upwards, the best investments are typically the best properties in prime locations[29]. For shrewd investors, the best strategy is often to buy the optimal sized and priced property in a given market for which there is proven demand. The approach of supplying existing demand will save you a lot of time and effort.

Studying the supply and demand dynamics of each market and recognising market "segments" is therefore crucial. Each of the resort markets – Phuket, Koh Samui, Pattaya, Hua Hin – have different supply and demand dynamics and different segments within each market can do well at different times. For instance, it is possible to invest in one-bedroom 3.5 million Baht (US$ 116,000) apartments in Pattaya, or three-bedroom 30 million Baht (US$ 1 million) pool villas on a hill overlooking the sea in Phuket, or five-bedroom luxury beachfront villas at 55 million Baht (US$ 1.83 million) in Koh Samui.

There are defined market segments with defined price bands and it is essential to conduct your own research and speak with property agents to become familiar with them. For instance, prices for apartments, in general, are capped by villa prices. If a private villa can be purchased for 12 million Baht (US$ 400,000) and the asking price for an apartment is also 12 million Baht, buyers often prefer to buy a villa, which in the absence of a distinguishing feature places a cap on apartment prices (there are of course exceptions due to location or branding). The key is to remember that money is made by applying the right strategy, to the right market, at the right time.

---

[29] However, it also pays to remember that the more expensive a property, the smaller potential market there is for the property, i.e. fewer buyers can afford it.

With a buy and hold strategy, it should be remembered that the property must be held for a sufficient amount of time for the value of the property to appreciate. Therefore, the issue of on-going management and upkeep of the property are of paramount importance. Any potential capital appreciation can be completely lost (or at least offset) by age depreciation if a property is allowed to fall into a weathered, worn or tired-looking condition.

The value of a property can be increased during the holding period if the property can be turned into a successful rental property with demonstrable rental income. In addition to a property, the buyer will become the owner of a business with a proven rental record.

To buy an undervalued property, on the other hand, requires a familiarity of the market or sufficient research to be able to recognise an "undervalued" asset. With this strategy, money is made when you buy and realised when you sell[30].

The most fundamental point to remember in any business, including property investment, is that something is worth only what someone else is prepared to pay for it and that price is determined only at the point where the interests and expectations of buyer and seller coincide.

So how do you recognize a bargain or undervalued property? There are three issues that an investor should keep in mind:

The first issue to note is that *asking prices* of property, particularly in resort areas in Thailand, may not serve as the clearest indication of value. For instance, a luxury villa that was listed on the market for 30 million Baht (US$ 1 million) last year and has an asking price of 22 million Baht (US$ 733,000) this year does not necessarily mean it is now a bargain. Last year's price could have been simply plucked out of the air by an irrational or optimistic agent, or by a seller wishing to try his luck and test the market by advertising a premium price. I know of one sea-view apartment that was advertised at 25 million Baht (US$ 833,000) while the one next-door, only marginally smaller, had just sold for 11.5 million Baht (US$ 383,000).

Secondly, investors should consider the role of independent property valuations. Valuations are fundamentally based on a combination of three calculation: a cost approach, an income analysis, and an estimated market value. The cost approach is basically a "bricks and mortar" calculation, which determines the value of the land and the construction costs of reproducing or replacing the property, less

---

[30] Alternatively, a problem is identified that can be readily resolved.

allowances for physical depreciation. This basically gives you a "book value". Sometimes an estimated mark-up – such as 30% or 40% - is added to estimate a sales value. The income approach, on the other hand, estimates the value of a property in relation to its capacity to earn rental income[31]. A market estimate is concerned with comparing recent property transactions for similar properties in the same area. Such comparables inherently reflect prevailing market sentiment (and greater emphasis is therefore placed on this market estimate).

With the ongoing global recession, current comparisons in a climate of such a low number of property transactions in resort markets can pose a challenge. Without a sufficient number of comparable recent transactions it is difficult to accurately estimate a current market value. In a more transparent market with a consistent level of transactions and readily available and reliable transactional information, market prices can be quickly assessed. For instance, if the apartment next door sold last week for US$ 3,000 per square metre, it is quite easy to estimate the value of your apartment.

However, Thailand's property resort markets present a dual challenge: firstly, it is difficult to get reliable transaction-relation information (since many properties are sold "off-shore" or through the sale of shares), and secondly, in the current market most property agents would consider themselves lucky to complete one or two disparate land or property sales each month. Therefore, reliable values based on recent sales of comparable properties often don't exist to enable accurate property valuations. In addition, an insufficient number of transactions makes it impossible to extrapolate or predict a trend. The only thing that can be reliably said is that a property should be undervalued if it is below the combined "replacement" cost of land and construction costs (less an allowance for physical depreciation).

The third issue that should be understood is that undervalued properties need to be discovered on a deal-by-deal basis because *property prices depend on the individual circumstances of the seller*. This is especially so in Thailand's resort markets where there is a general absence of mortgage financing and 100% cash purchases are the norm.

To illustrate the point, if a plot of beach land has been in a Thai owner's family for generations and he is not desperate for money, and if a neighbouring plot sold for 21 million Baht (US$ 700,000) per Rai last year, he will want 22 million Baht (US$ 733,000) per Rai, regardless of what is happening in the global economy, and will just hold out until someone is willing to pay it. On the other hand, if a

---

[31] Or the present worth of net rental income that could realistically be achieved over the life of the property.

British expat was asking 20 million Baht (US$ 665,000) for his villa last year and desperately needs cash to cover mortgage payments or failed investments in the UK, he is more likely to be motivated to accept a lot less, perhaps even 12 million Baht (US$ 400,000). Thus, the individual financial circumstances of the seller are a key factor influencing the purchase price.

With the general absence of mortgages for foreigners, there are usually no affordability issues in Thailand for foreign property owners. In other words, foreign property owners are not struggling to repay Thai mortgages on their resort properties because they have no mortgages! The fact that most purchases were made in cash means that selling prices are determined by how much the owners need access to that cash to cover other liabilities or living costs. Therefore, whether properties come onto the market and their asking prices depend on the overall wealth or "financial health" of the foreign owner. If an owner's wealth has collapsed in the global crisis, and money is required to cover losses at home, the owner might need to sell. If an owner's wealth remains largely intact, there is no pressure to sell, especially at the bottom of the market. Prices in Thailand clearly, therefore, depend on property owners' individual circumstances.

This is how we must look at the market; instead of painting it with a broad brush, we need to understand the market on a deal-by-deal basis. If an investor is looking for undervalued property, selective bargains are available in those cases where owners must sell properties to cover investment losses in their home countries, which makes them "motivated sellers".

Within Thailand, the principal resort destinations are considered to be Phuket, Koh Samui, Pattaya and Hua Hin. While Pattaya and Hua Hin attract a number of Thai buyers for condominiums and villas due to the proximity to Bangkok, the luxury resort markets of Koh Samui and Phuket are almost entirely comprised of (and dependent upon) non-Thai or foreign buyers. For this reason, Koh Samui and Phuket are more influenced and exposed to whatever is happening in the global economy. Foreign economies are currently severely affected by recession, which leads to the possibility of uncovering more undervalued properties in these locations.

There are also opportunities to buy undervalued property where property developers are suffering cash flow problems. However, this avenue should only be pursued in relation to completed properties where there is no risk of non-completion[32]. Off-plan pre-construction developments or developments that have not yet been completed can be particularly high risk (see chapter 67).

---

[32] Unless you are willing to take over ownership of the project (together with all liabilities) and complete it yourself.

It should be mentioned that even the best planned capital appreciation investments can be undone (or enhanced) by foreign exchange movements (see chapter 105).

Summary

- Investing for capital appreciation means buying property with the aim of selling it later for more than was originally invested.
- The two primary strategies are timing entry and exit to profit from the momentum of market sentiment, or purchasing an "undervalued" property and selling at market value.
- Resort properties represent "discretionary" expenditure and there is usually a time lag between the recovery of primary markets and an improvement in resort markets.
- If a buy and hold strategy is employed, the issue of on-going management and upkeep of the property is of paramount importance.
- "Asking prices" do not serve as the clearest indication of value.
- Independent valuations should take into account property replacement cost, income earning capacity, and recent sales of comparable properties.
- Undervalued properties must be discovered on a deal-by-deal basis since transaction values depend on the personal financial circumstances of the seller.

10
Investing for rental Income

> **Important tip:** Before beginning a discussion on rental income, investors should note that if they have built a new villa or taken possession of a new property, once the property has been rented out – just like driving a new car off the garage forecourt – it is no longer be possible to sell it "as new" at that premium showroom-like price. The decision to rent out a new property therefore needs be taken carefully[33].

If your objective is investing for rental income, the most common ratio used to compare potential investments is "rental yield", which is the rental revenue received (or expected) in one year divided by the purchase price of the property[34]. In other words, it could be considered the annual return on investment, expressed as a percentage. Thus:

$$Yield = (annual\ rental\ income\ /\ purchase\ price) \times 100$$

To provide an example, suppose you spend $US 750,000 to purchase a villa and the villa is rented out at $US 300 per night for 150 nights per year, the yield would be as follows:

$$Yield = ((300 \times 150)/750,000) \times 100 = 6\%$$

The yield is a helpful way to compare and analyse properties because it quickly identifies which properties present better value. However, to allow an accurate yield calculation, the source and quality of the input data is important. First, annual rental income needs to be estimated. If the property has a rental record, these numbers can be useful, although bear in mind they could also be unreliable if they have been "doctored" by a seller to make the property look better.

The best way to estimate rental figures is therefore to perform your own research (on similar properties in the same area). Speaking directly with property owners is perhaps the best source of information. It is also helpful to speak with rental agents to get their professional opinions. Alternatively, information can be gleaned from rental property websites; however, keep in mind these rental figures will be "published rates" rather than actual rates (see chapter 119).

---

[33] In China, for example, most property buyers prefer to buy new properties so when investors take possession of a new property they lock it up and leave it unoccupied so they can still sell it later as though it were "new".

[34] Or *total capital expenditure*, which is the purchase price of the property plus fixtures, fittings and furniture.

A conservative method to estimate annual rental revenue is to take the average nightly rental rate and multiply it by 100 days. This assumes the property will be rented out for 100 days out of 365 days in the year (which is an occupancy rate of only 27%). If you market the property professionally, this should be a conservative estimate; if the investment makes sense at this level, it will certainly make sense at higher occupancy rates.

For example, if the nightly rate for a villa is $US 300[35] and the purchase price is $US 600,000, the yield based on 100 days occupancy is as follows:

$$Yield = ((300 \times 100)/600,000) \times 100 = 5\%$$

It is important to note that the yield calculations have so far been concerned with "gross yields". In other words, calculations have been based on *gross* rental income without subtracting any costs, expenses or taxes. To calculate "net yields", daily rates need to be reduced by a percentage reflecting rental management costs and taxes[36].

For the purposes of illustration, suppose rental management costs and taxes work out to be 25% of the daily rate, then a nightly rate of $US 225 should be used instead of US$ 300 to calculate the net yield (i.e. US$ 300 less 25%). This is the "after-costs" revenue that should be generated by the property. Plugging these figures into the formula, we get the following net yield:

$$Net\ Yield = ((225 \times 100)/600,000) \times 100 = 3.75\%$$

As is evident, there is a significant difference between gross and net yields.

Looking at the other number used in the calculation – purchase price – it should be noted that if money is spent on a property following purchase to prepare it for rental, these costs should technically be added to ensure yield calculations are based on actual investment, rather than just the purchase price. For instance, if after you buy a property and it is necessary to renovate or make structural repairs, these costs should be included. If the property is purchased unfurnished, the cost of furniture should also be included. This has the effect of reducing the yield but provides a more accurate yield calculation since it is based on the actual investment.

---

[35] To get a more accurate yield calculation, investors should estimate the different rental rates for low, mid, high, and peak seasons (typically Christmas, New Year and Chinese New Year) and use the appropriate weighted average nightly rate for the yield calculation (see chapter 119).
[36] See chapters 114 - 117 and chapter 123.

Yields also allow you to monitor your investment. Suppose that three years after you have purchased a property, the yield is calculated based on *current* rental income and the *original* purchase price, this provides an indication of how much the rental yield has increased or decreased since purchase.

Alternatively, if the calculation is based on *current* rental income and a *current* valuation of the property, it allows you to monitor your investment and can indicate an opportune time to sell. In general, an increasing yield means a stronger rental market, or a falling property market with falling valuations, or both. Falling yields, on the other hand, means falling rental rates (often through an increasing supply of rental properties), or a rising property market with increasing property valuations, or both.

Some property analysts suggest investors buy property with 7-10% yields, and sell when yields fall below 3%, which is usually when prices are high, yields are low, and the general retail public are buying. Such advice is applicable when buying in principal cities where most property sales are for primary residences and when transparent transaction information is available, together with transaction volumes sufficient to indicate trends. However, with resort properties, since the purchase objective is often not *pure* investment (in the sense that the owner typically wants to use the property as a holiday home for part of the year), it becomes a question of what yield an owner is content with. In addition, with the right property in the right location, yields on resort properties can be quite stunning. For instance, I know of a villa that rents for an average of $US 600 per night for 250 days per year (in the second and third years after completion). The villa was purchased for $US 480,000, which equates to a gross yield of 31%[37].

Yield = ((600 x 250)/480,000) x 100 = 31.25%

However, not every property owner has the same success. If you buy the wrong type of property, at the wrong time in the market cycle, at an over-inflated price, the yield calculation looks very different!

> **Important tip:** Always keep in mind that the level of rental income generated by a property is a major factor determining the *value* of your property.

Once the decision to rent out a property has been made, one key decision to make is whether to accept short-term or long-term rentals. In terms of investment returns, what we are speaking of here is the difference between daily, weekly,

---

[37] This means the property only needs to be rented out for 3.2 years for the property investment to be recouped.

monthly or annual rental rates. Short-term rentals to tourists are generally charged on a nightly or weekly rental basis and the advantage is higher pro-rata rental rates. However, higher rates come with the responsibility to provide professional property and rental management services (see chapters 114 - 118), for instance, meet-and-greet, airport transfer, guest introduction to the property, housekeeping and cleaning, all of which are generally included in the rental rates.

Long-term rental, on the other hand, is generally for periods in excess of several months, charged on a monthly (or annual) basis. The advantage of accepting long-term rental is that you no longer need to actively market or manage the property. The tenant takes care of the property (and typically pays the utility bills according to usage[38]). The disadvantage is that pro-rata rental rates tend to be lower relative to short-term rates.

To maximise rental returns, it is important to buy or build a property where there is proven rental demand. Location is key and it doesn't take much time to speak with a selection of rental agents to discover what types of properties in which areas rent for most days of the year at the highest rates. Beachfront properties generally command the highest rental rates, then sea-view properties, followed by properties that are "close to the beach". It is important to find a niche in demand that can be met, which means providing a property with the optimum number of rooms to a particular segment of tourist demand.

If part of your reason for investment is for rental income, a positioning strategy is essential (if your property is not differentiated by a unique location, style or design, or if it does not appeal to a defined niche market, then you are competing with all the other offerings in the marketplace *based only on price,* see chapter 110).

There are many niche markets and you might consider targeting one or more of them. For instance, there is a particularly strong rental market for Korean honeymoon couples for which one-bedroom private pool villas are ideal. Travelling together as several couples is also popular and therefore three and four-bedroom pool villas with large living, dining and outdoor areas are popular. Three or four bedroom villas are ideal for vacationing families, while two-bedroom apartments or villas are ideal for young families. To provide an example of a more specific niche, a property developer in Phuket built one-bedroom "Jacuzzi apartments" in close proximity to the main bar and entertainment area!

These market segments are mentioned purely to help investors consider the rental market in terms of a market positioning strategy. A consideration of market

---

[38] Electricity bills can be particularly high in tropical resorts due to the use of air-conditioning.

segments should take place during the process of evaluating potential properties, rather than considering rental opportunities only after a purchase.

It is important to recognise that maximising rental returns concerns the interplay between rental rates and *occupancy levels*. Indeed, occupancy levels are perhaps the most crucial factor. For instance, a 9-bedroom villa commands higher rates but might not rent out consistently throughout the year, whereas a 3-bedroom villa rents at a lower nightly rate but is more likely to receive a higher number of enquiries and rent out for a higher number of days annually.

For example, if the daily rate is set at U$ 1,000, the property might only achieve 20% occupancy, which is 72 days each year, with total revenue of US$ 72,000 as follows:

$$1,000 \times 72 = 72,000$$

However, lowering the rate to US$ 600 per night could increase occupancy to 50%, which is 183 nights each year and results in total revenue of 109,800:

$$600 \times 183 = 109,800$$

Important tip: These calculations demonstrate the importance of occupancy levels vis-à-vis rental rates. Property owners would do well to consider this relationship; too many rental property owners are preoccupied only with achieving the highest rental rates.

Another factor to consider when investing for rental returns is the length of the season. In Phuket, for example, the season is generally considered to be 7-9 months between the months of tropical rain, while Koh Samui has a 10-11 month season since it usually rains for only 4-6 weeks each year between October and December (see chapter 51). The length of the season can make a significant difference to rental income.

Another crucial factor influencing the success of a rental property is the quality and professionalism of property and rental management services (see chapter 118). Indeed, without truly professional rental management staff looking after both your property and guests, investors should be careful about making long-distance investments in rental properties.

Summary

- If your objective is investing for rental income, the most common ratio used to compare investments is "rental yield".
- *Gross* yields are based on gross rental income without subtracting costs, while *net* yields are based on rental income less rental management costs and taxes.
- In addition to allowing property comparisons, yields also allow investments to be monitored after purchase.
- To maximise rental returns, it is important to buy or build a property where there is proven rental demand.
- Maximising rental returns concerns the interplay between rental rates and *occupancy levels*.

11
What is your exit strategy?
(Essential)

Before you buy property in Thailand, it is essential to have an idea of your exit strategy.

Formulating an exit strategy for each property you buy just takes a few minutes of careful consideration. However, it should influence many decisions you subsequently make in relation to the property. Here are some general examples of exit strategies:

- Buy land – build – sell
- Buy land – build – rent
- Buy completed property – hold – sell
- Buy completed property – rent – sell
- Buy completed property – rent – own use upon retirement
- Buy off-plan property – sell or 'flip' for profit before completion
- Buy off-plan property – rent – sell

In addition to an exit strategy, it is also wise to have in mind some sort of timeframe. For example:

Timeframe	Plan of action
-	Buy land
6 months	Designing, planning and preparing to build
12 months	Construction
36 months	Rental property
Total 54 months (4 ½ years)	Sell for capital gain before property begins to look "tired" and significant renovations are required

The exit strategy and timeframe should in turn influence a number of important decisions. For instance, it should influence the manner in which the sale and purchase contract is drafted with the inclusion of certain contractual clauses. For example, if the strategy is to purchase "off-plan" property and exit the investment by selling at a profit before completion (see chapter 80 on "flipping"), the agreement must contain the relevant "assignment clause" that gives you the authority to transfer ownership of the asset before taking formal possession.

Knowing in advance your exit strategy will almost certainly influence the choice of ownership structure or asset holding vehicle for the property (see chapter 95). For example, if the strategy is to *buy - hold - sell,* ownership of the property should be structured to make the sale as quick, easy and tax-efficient as possible. Instead of purchasing a leasehold property in your own name, such an exit strategy might dictate the use of a Thai or offshore company structure to simplify the transfer process and mitigate taxes upon sale.

Alternatively, if the strategy is to *buy land - build – rent,* it might dictate an offshore company ownership structure through which the rental business and banking can be conducted (although be sure to seek professional legal and tax advice to ensure compliance with Thai laws).

The timeline for an exit strategy is also useful to periodically monitor the investment. Due to the changing business and political environment, it is also important that exit strategies, time lines and asset ownership structures have built-in flexibility. For instance, a *buy - hold - sell* strategy for the purpose of capital appreciation might become *buy - hold - rent* due to an unfavourable sales environment. A *buy - rent - sell* strategy with a 3-year timeline might be extended to 5-years if yields and property values are rising; or a *buy - rent - retire* strategy might become *buy – rent – sell* if the market price has increased to the point when you would consider taking profit to re-invest, or if currency exchange rates have moved significantly in your favour. Finally, a *buy - hold - sell* strategy might morph into a *buy - hold – own use for retirement* in Thailand if you fall in love with the country.

Summary

- It is essential to formulate an exit strategy before you buy property, together with a timeframe.
- The exit strategy and timeframe should influence a number of decisions that are subsequently made in relation to a property investment.

12
Location and property type

Now that we have a fundamental understanding of what type of properties foreigners can buy, together with our investment objective and exit strategies, we should now be in a position to consider the *type* of property to buy.

When buying resort property, the basic choices are simple: beachfront, sea-view, mountain-view, inland or a property linked or catering to a pastime, for example, a marina property or property adjacent to a golf course.

If buying a property as a permanent residence or for retirement then the choice depends entirely on personal preference and budget. However, if you are thinking in terms of rental income or capital appreciation, it is necessary to consider a positioning strategy or niche. It is also necessary to consider *scarcity*. Land with beach frontage and beachfront properties are more expensive because they are more sought after and because they are in scarce supply. Indeed, in the most popular resort destinations, prime beachfront land and properties are rarely on the market or they only become available at premium prices.

For instance, in Wongamat/Naklua, undoubtedly recognised as the most prime area in Pattaya, beachfront condominium properties were selling for an average of 124,124 Baht (US$ 4,130) per square metre in 2010, as opposed to 55,318 Baht (US$ 1,840) per square metre in the Pratumnak area, which is dominated by sea view projects and within a short drive to the beach, or areas farther away from the seashore where the average selling price is 34,597 Baht (US$ 1,150) per square metre[39].

Properties with amazing sea views, especially those with sunset views in prime locations are also relatively scarce and therefore command higher prices and rental rates. There will always be a market for prime beachfront and sea-view properties, and prices reflect their scarcity. In Phuket, for instance, many real estate agents consider 65 million Baht (US$ 2.5 million) as the starting point for the high-end market, while in Koh Samui, villas at one internationally branded beachfront resort have asking prices of between 70 million Baht (US$2.33 million) and 205 million Baht (US$6.83 million).

---

[39] Condominium Focus, Pattaya Update – January 2011, Raimon Land, www.raimonland.com

Golf properties or marina properties, on the other hand, command a premium by catering to a defined market segment. Whether they make good investments or rental properties is purely determined by the supply and demand dynamics for such types of properties.

However, if a property is not beachfront, or it does not have a sea view, or if it is not located in a golf or marina development, it must have some distinguishing factor or "unique selling point" to be a successful rental or investment property; if not, it falls into the general non-descript category where it competes with all the other general non-descript properties for sale and for rent. Expressed in marketing terms, a "4-bedroom luxury villa with 180° panoramic sea-views where stunning sunsets can be enjoyed from the infinity pool" gets more attention than a "4-bedroom villa with pool for rent".

Property investors must also consider the issue of *proximity*. In major cities, proximity to subway stations and schools are key sales propositions. With resort properties, it is proximity to the beach, restaurants, bars and entertainment areas. Location or *proximity* is a key distinguishing factor.

The point of this discussion is to make sure investors consider their positioning strategy in terms of *scarcity* and *proximity*, especially if investing for rental income or capital appreciation. Scarcity and proximity play a significant role in determining the purchase price of a property.

It is also worth bearing in mind that circumstances change and evolve over time. Several decades ago, the sons of landowning Thai families often inherited the "productive" coconut plantation land, while daughters inherited the "unproductive" beachfront land. Ironically, with the phenomenal increase in the value of beachfront land, daughters often became richer than sons! This is the case on some of Thailand's best-known islands. The situation temporarily reversed after the tsunami that hit Indonesia and the west coast of Thailand in 2004. In the months following this sad event, interest in beach land and beachfront properties diminished, while enquiries for hillside properties increased. With the apparent increase in turbulent weather, sea levels and natural disasters (more recently the case of Japan's Tsunami in 2011), the wisdom of making long-term investments or sinking retirement money into beachfront property must be questioned.

Only after there has been a consideration of location should attention turn to the different property types, for instance, villas, pool villas, apartments, penthouse apartments, duplex apartments and townhouses. Each of these property types has its own merits, although a purchasing decision needs to be taken in line with the investment objective, in addition to a consideration of the various forms of legal ownership (condominium freehold, freehold, leasehold). To clarify each physical property type, their respective descriptions are as follows:

Property type	Description
Villa	A freestanding building or buildings sitting on its own separate area of land
Pool villa	A freestanding building or buildings sitting on its own separate area of land with a private pool
Apartment	A room or suite of rooms designed as a residence and generally located in a building occupied by more than one household
Penthouse	An apartment on the top floor of a building, often with a roof terrace
Duplex	An apartment having rooms on two floors connected by an inner staircase
Townhouse	One of a row of apartments sharing common dividing walls

Summary

- When buying resort property, the basic choices are simple: beachfront, sea-view, mountain-view, inland or a property linked or catering to a pastime, for example, a marina property or property adjacent to a golf course.
- Land with beach frontage and beachfront properties are more expensive because they are more sought after and are in scarce supply.
- Properties with amazing sea views, especially those with sunset views in prime locations are also relatively scarce and therefore command higher prices and rental rates.
- Golf properties or marina properties command a premium by catering to a defined market segment.
- Investors consider their positioning strategy in terms of *scarcity* and *proximity*.
- Only after there has been a consideration of location should attention turn to property types.

L STEP 2
Land

13
Land measurement

In the United Kingdom, Europe and the United States, land area is generally measured in acres, hectares or square metres. In Thailand, while square metres are used for measuring floor areas of villas and apartments, the unit of measurement used for land is "Rai". For instance, when speaking with agents or browsing property brochures, prices for land are generally stated "per Rai", for example, "3 Rai of land for sale at 10 million Baht per Rai" or "4-bedroom villa for sale with 1 Rai of land".

To put things in familiar terms, one Rai is equal to 1600 square metres, 0.395 Acres or 0.16 Hectares. One Hectare is 6.25 Rai and one Acre is 2.53 Rai. Other units of measurement in relation to land are "Ngan" which is 400 square metres and "Wah" which is 4 square metres. The table below can be used for quick reference:

1 Rai	= 1600 square metres (or 4 Ngan)
1 Ngan	= 400 square metres (or 100 Wah)
1 Wah	= 4 square metres
1 Rai	= 0.395 Acres
2.53 Rai	= 1 Acre
1 Rai	= 0.16 Hectares
6.25 Rai	= 1 Hectare

As a national land survey has not yet been completed in Thailand, most land cannot be accurately mapped in relation to neighbouring plots and this has the potential to cause disputes when land and titles change hands.

When viewing land, the seller or agent will often mention the size in Rai or Ngan, then vaguely point out the boundaries; for instance, "from that big palm tree to the pile of coconuts in the corner!" If you proceed by making an offer, and certainly prior to purchase, it is essential for measurements to be checked to make sure the land is the same size as promised (it is also crucial to check that the piece of land you are buying is the same as the piece of land that has been shown to you; stranger things have happened!).

It is also important to find out how many separate land "titles" comprise the piece of land that you are interested in. For example, the land size might be referred to as 6 Rai, although this could be made up of 3 separate land titles of 2 Rai each, and even different grades of land title, as will be discussed in the next chapter.

These issues are part of the due diligence process (see chapter 89).

14
Land title
(Essential)

When buying land in Thailand, knowledge of title deeds and land ownership laws is fundamental. Land titles are the most common evidence to prove land ownership, rights of possession and other interests in land[40]. In Thailand, there are various types of land title that each provides a different level of security for the owner. It is therefore essential for foreign purchasers to be familiar with the various categories of land title and to confirm the land title for any land they might be interested to buy. When looking at completed properties, this also includes the land on which properties sit.

Chanote

The most secure type of land title in Thailand is called *"Chanote"*, or *Chanote Tee Din*, otherwise known as a land deed. This is land that has been accurately surveyed using a global positioning system (GPS) to set the area and boundaries of the land and plot them against the national land survey grid. The common sign of Chanote land is the existence of numbered concrete posts in the ground marking the boundaries. A person with their name shown on a Chanote land deed has the legal right to the land and can use the deed to confirm this right to government authorities. For reference, a copy of a *Chanote* land title document is shown on the next page, with an overlaid English translation[41].

---

[40] Land titles only serve to evidence rights to land and thus do not serve as evidence of ownership of the structures or buildings built on the land.
[41] Reproduced with the permission of Satayu Publishing Co., Ltd.

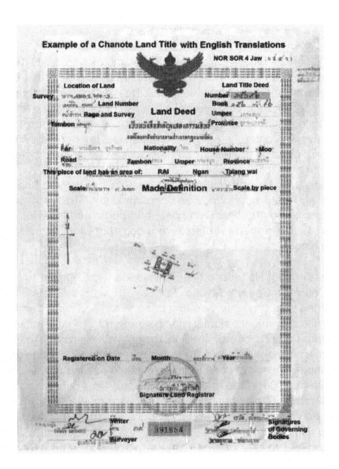

Example of a Chanote Land Title with English Translations

Nor Sor Sam Gor

In the absence of GPS surveying, there are other (lesser) official land titles that can be used to prove ownership and possession. The second most secure land title is *"Nor Sor Sam Gor"*, otherwise know as a *Confirmed Certificate of Use*. Land with Nor Sor Sam Gor title is also commonly marked out with marker posts against the national survey, although these have not been plotted by GPS. This type of land title certifies that the person on the certificate has a *confirmed right* to *use the land*. It implies that all requirements to issue the title deed have been met and that the title deed is pending. Nor Sor Sam Gor land may be sold, leased and used as mortgage collateral.

Nor Sor Sam

The third level of land title is called *"Nor Sor Sam"*, or *Certificate of Use*. This is basically the same as Nor Sor Sam Gor (Confirmed Certificate of Use), except that not all formalities required for certifying the right to use the land have been performed; Nor Sor Sam Gor title does not therefore provide the same clear-cut ownership rights as land with Chanote title. As a result, before any legal act concerning the land can take place – such as sale, lease or transfer – a public notice of intent must be posted for 30 days to allow anyone to contest it.

To summarize thus far and make things easy to remember, Chanote land is land whose area and boundaries are confirmed by GPS; Nor Sor Sam Gor is land marked out by farmers with posts and pegs; and Nor Sor Sam land is land marked out by farmers with posts and pegs but with a higher likelihood of neighbourly disputes!

Below these three levels of land title, there are a whole host of others existing in Thailand, such as *Sor Gor Neung, Por Bor Tor Ha* and *Por Bor Tor Hok,* that each conferring various rights, use and possession associated with the land in question. While they might potentially be upgradeable, most of these do not give the owner a right to build, or even the right to apply for planning permission to build a structure of a permanent nature. To avoid unnecessary risk and complications, foreigners should therefore confine themselves to dealing only with land that is Chanote or Nor Sor Sam Gor, as these are the only titles over which a registrable right of ownership or lease can exist. Transactions involving Nor Sor Sam land should only be undertaken under strict supervision of your lawyer.

If you are looking to buy land, or any property with land involved, the first thing to check (and double-check) is the grade of land title. If a seller or sales agent mentions the land title, make a note and then ensure this is thoroughly researched during due diligence. It is quite common for sales agents to have no hands-on knowledge of the relevant land documents. It is equally common for sales agents to believe land is of a certain title, yet in reality it is of a different title or, in some cases, it is still in the process of being upgraded. Checking land titles is a matter for lawyers. It is strongly advised not to buy land without full due diligence being carried out on the land by a competent law firm, which includes a title investigation (see chapter 16).

15
Land scams

Many foreigners have heard generally about the dangers of financial loss associated with buying property in Asia and are apprehensive about getting bogged down in an unsavoury property transaction. Many, however, are not familiar with the specific details of how problems can arise. The purpose of this chapter, therefore, is to provide examples of the type of land transactions that could lead to unwanted consequences and complications for purchasers. It should, however, be noted that the incidence of "bad" property deals as a percentage of all transactions is very small; nonetheless, it is better that readers are aware of the nature of such deals to allow preventative measures to be taken.

Selling land the seller doesn't own: This is where a "seller" tries to sell you land of which they pretend to be the owner for the purpose of taking deposits or purchase money from you.

Selling land subject to an ongoing dispute or claim: In this case, the seller is in a dispute with another, or subject to a competing claim for the land, and is trying to cash out and pass the problem onto a buyer.

Selling land with no access: This is the simple case where a piece of land has no access, or is subject to a dispute concerning access, and the seller is attempting to sell the land as though no access problem exists.

Selling land different to that shown: This is where a seller takes you to see a nice piece of land and then presents you with title documents belonging to a different piece of land.

Selling land smaller than stated: In this case, the seller takes you to see a piece of land, waves his arms around vaguely and expansively, giving you the impression of a land size that does not correspond with the size stated on the title documents.

Seller is not the owner but has an option on the land: While this is technically not a "scam" in the true sense of the word, it is the case where a "seller" misleads you by saying he is the owner of the land, although in fact he has only an *option to purchase* the land. The potential buyer should be aware that this is not the standard sale and purchase scenario and the "option holder" is often trying to use your money to buy the land before selling it to you, thereby pocketing the difference.

Selling land that floods during rainy season: During the dry months, a piece of land might look ideal for building a dream vacation home. However, during the heavy rains characteristic of the monsoon season, low-lying land can turn into a lake; land adjacent to klongs[42] can flood; even sloping hillside land can be deluged by fast flowing streams that seem to materialise from nowhere, taking chunks of land with it! Getting an accurate fix on a piece of land's height above sea level is helpful for low-lying land but it is only part of the picture; it is also necessary is to take notice of the height of a piece of land in relation to the contours of surrounding land. The land might be well above sea level but if neighbouring land is higher, it might still flood. Perhaps the best way to avoid becoming the owner of a Grade A piece of swampland is to speak with locals who will be quite familiar with which areas are prone to flooding during the rainy season!

These are just some of the examples that a buyer may encounter. The term "scams" is not technically correct in all cases since some of the examples might be inadvertent and without the seller having any intention to mislead. It is true that in some cases Thai sellers are not acting in bad faith when trying to sell a lesser claim; they are just doing what everyone else is doing, which is acting informally and disregarding applicable laws. In addition, taking an option on land and selling for profit using the buyer's money is a valid investment strategy, although one that could become problematic for the buyer. The term "scams" has therefore been used here in the sense that a seller is typically selling problems or giving you less value than you are paying for; any "discrepancy" then becomes the buyer's financial loss. It is also possible that a buyer is placed in a situation that can be difficult, if not impossible, to reverse or resolve.

The success of each of these scams relies on the buyer: (a) not engaging their own lawyer and (b) not performing thorough due diligence. If due diligence is not properly performed, there are a number of worst-case scenarios, all of them different, except for one thing in common: they are all bad!

The good news is that most (if not all) of these potential scams can be thwarted by engaging a competent lawyer (see chapter 84) and by being careful not to hand over any money until due diligence has been completed. Buyers should also consider escrow-type arrangements to protect the handover of any deposits or part payments (see chapter 108).

As the due diligence process helps purchasers to avoid these types of problems, it is reasonably safe to assume that money is generally lost by those trying to cut corners; buyers trying to *save money* by not engaging their own lawyer; buyers that are unwilling to pay the full legal expenses required to conduct extensive due diligence; and buyers who trust what they are told by sellers or their agents without making the effort to double-check. This is the source of the oft-heard expression "buyers leaving their brains at home because they are on holiday!"

---

[42] Concrete channels built for drainage.

16
Land title investigation

The title of the land that you purchase determines the security and value of your investment. Therefore, it is essential to perform a thorough check of the land title to make sure you are buying what you think you are buying. This is the role of the *land title investigation,* which is part of the due diligence process. Indeed, title investigations should be considered the most fundamental check to perform before any property purchase involving land. This includes land, land and villas, apartments sitting on shared land (and even off-plan property purchases where a land title investigation should already have been performed by the developer and other purchasers).

A title investigation should also be the first thing recommended by your lawyer. In some cases title investigations are quoted separately and in addition to a review of sale and purchase documents; in such cases, don't be tempted to save money by excluding this element of due diligence.

> **Important tip:** Remember, property title is proof of ownership; therefore the quality of the title determines the fundamental security of your investment.

In performing a title investigation, a full title search will be undertaken, which in Thailand requires verification of title back to its origins as possessory title "Sor Kor 1". The lawyer will also check both front and back of the title deed to confirm the actual ownership (making sure the owner or seller has the right to sell) and the title of the land (such as *Chanote or Nor Sor Sam Gor*). In addition, a proper translation of the documents should also highlight any other ownership rights, endorsements, liens, or encumbrances that might exist over the property. The investigation should also confirm the shape, area and orientation of the property in relation to roads, streams or other public property. Access documents will then be checked to ensure you have the appropriate legal access rights to the property.

The ultimate objective is to ensure you are buying land that has a clear title unencumbered by any claims and not subject to any dispute with neighbouring landowners. If the title investigation does uncover any issues, you can then make a choice – under the guidance of your lawyer – whether or not to proceed with the purchase. Alternatively, based on the findings of the title investigation and due diligence, you might want to re-negotiate the purchase price with the seller.

If there is an issue that cannot be easily resolved, it is better to walk away and find another property[43].

To allow for cases where issues might be found during the due diligence process, the reservation agreement should contain a "subject to satisfactory due diligence" clause, which should provide the legal basis for the refund of any deposit paid (see chapter 89).

---

[43] Identifying and solving problems is an investment strategy in its own right, although it is better suited to property markets with transparent and secure legal systems. In Thailand, with its opaque legal system, buying into problems can sometimes mean getting dragged into a quagmire that is difficult to exit.

17
Land title insurance

Title insurance is basically indemnity insurance against financial loss from defective land titles[44].

Market practices and property registration systems in Thailand can present considerable challenges in establishing clean title to property. As with any titling system that is still in the process of evolution, combined with reforms related to farmers' land grants, it is often accompanied by a level of fraud and the improper issuance of land titles. A form of deeds registration system is maintained by land offices throughout the country but there is no state guarantee of title. In other words, the government does not compensate owners who lose their land as a result of inaccurate or incorrect information being held in government registers. Thus, fraudulent title upgrades or transfers of land by government officials acting beyond their authority could result in the annulment of upgrades or property being returned to the State (or rightful owner) without compensation. For this reason, land title insurance is a useful risk management tool.

> **Important tip:** When purchasing land, buyers must either rely on title information provided by sellers or engage a lawyer to conduct a title investigation. However, despite holding title documentation and deeds, there is no *absolute* guarantee of title and no availability of land title insurance *within* Thailand. However, there is one title insurance company, headquartered in Hong Kong, which might be able to provide coverage for Thailand[45].

While the vast majority of titles are correctly issued (and foreign investors must therefore keep their concerns in perspective), it does not disguise the fact that, in a minority of cases where title deeds have been improperly or illegally issued, they could potentially be revoked. This means that just because land titles have been issued does not always mean they are *legal*, which is difficult concept for many foreigners to grasp.

There are various reasons why land titles could be subject to conflicting claims or where titles might have been illegally or improperly issued, although these generally fall into 4 categories:

---

[44] It is principally a product that is sold in the United States due to the comparative deficiency of its land record laws.
[45] www.firstam.com.hk

- Physical problems – for example, unknown or undeclared rights of way, incorrectly defined boundaries, or the encroachment of buildings onto adjoining land.

- Financial problems – for example, unknown or unregistered mortgages or undisclosed persons having contributed to the original purchase price.

- Legal problems – for example, lack of due process in title upgrade, discrepancies in land description, incorrectly filed or stamped documents, missing signatures, undisclosed or missing heirs.

- Fraud, forgery or duress[46] – for example, government officials acting fraudulently or outside the scope of their powers such as when development rights are granted on forestry land[47].

Most issues and conflicting title claims can be picked up by lawyers conducting thorough due diligence, although this is not always the case. The consequences of any of the potential title defects mentioned above are uncertainty of ownership, a drawn out legal process and legal expenses for the purchaser. With the absence of a government guarantee of land titles, in case of any loss, the only other possible alternative is taking legal action against your legal advisor in negligence, although this is usually difficult to establish and is only of value anyway if the law firm is adequately backed by professional indemnity insurance, which most are not.

The purpose of land title insurance is therefore to protect landowners' financial interests in real property against loss due to title defects, liens or other matters. Indeed, title insurance policies are typically no-fault based, which means the fact of a claim against a title or a loss is sufficient to make a claim on the policy. If there is a problem subsequent to a land purchase, the insurer will typically assist in defending the legal action and ultimately reimburse the policyholder for the actual monetary loss incurred, up to the amount of insurance cover provided by the policy (generally the value of the property[48]). This is a much better recourse than suing a lawyer in negligence.

---

[46] Interestingly, this category accounts for the highest percentage of claims in Asia (and can influence the other three categories of claim).

[47] In Thailand, the two primary instances where land documents are unlawfully issued are in relation to the falsification of land claim documents that form the basis for the first issuance of land documents, and encroachment (usually of forestry land), which is the unlawful intrusion upon the rights or possessions of another.

[48] Policyholders also have the option to take out endorsements to cover any increase in a property's value.

Title insurance is therefore something that should be considered by land purchasers, particularly purchasers of larger pieces of land[49]. It is advisable to involve the title insurance provider prior to engaging a law firm and commencing due diligence on the land; title insurance companies prefer to get involved at an early stage and are selective about which lawyers are engaged to conduct due diligence.

---

[49] For smaller land plots the costs, as a percentage of the purchase price, are often considered prohibitive.

18
Access?
(Essential)

Successful property investing is not just about buying land or property; it is also about making sure you have both physical and legal access to the land or property.

When viewing land or properties, you should always be making a note of the physical access. In Europe or the US, good quality roads are taken for granted. In Thailand, a good quality five metre wide concrete road is usually the best that you can hope for; equally common are steep, potholed, overgrown dirt tracks barely wide enough for a car to pass.

If a property has a concrete access road, the next question to ask is whether it is a "government" road (public road) or a privately owned road. If it is a public road, this means the local government is responsible for its upkeep and maintenance. If, on the other hand, it is a "private" road, such as a road put in by the developer of a project, there might be maintenance fees to consider. The level of such fees, together with any associated terms and conditions need to be carefully examined as part of contractual due diligence.

If access to the property is by a dirt road, or a combination of concrete roads interspersed with sections of dirt roads, these might provide a tolerable access route in the summer months. However, during the rainy season, these dirt roads might be literally washed away, which means the road to your property becomes impassable and access to your property disappears. This is bad enough if the property is a primary residence; in the case of a rental property, it tends to throw a very large spanner in the works of your rental business!

I am familiar with several 20 million Baht (US$ 665,000) hillside villas that in the summer months appear to be sound investments. However, during the rainy season a 200-metre stretch of dirt road that forms part of the only access road is literally washed away, turning into a combination of metre-deep crevasses and moguls complete with protruding boulders, which becomes impassable even by 4WD.

> **Important tip:** When viewing properties where the access road is a dirt track, property owners or salespeople sometimes mention that a concrete road is "planned", either by the government or by a private consortium of landowners. Such claims are often a sales tactic and therefore need to be substantiated.

Government plans (or rumours of government plans) for the construction of new roads are not to be relied upon and can take years to eventuate, if at all. If there is mention of neighbouring landowners "clubbing together" to build a new road, such plans tend to be even more unreliable; neighbours rarely come to an agreement over financial contributions or responsibilities. Some landowners do not have the financial means, while others will claim they don't in the hope that the other landowners will pay for the road! In the meantime, nothing happens.

If a seller promises to put in a road prior to completion, or within a certain time after completion, it is prudent to put a value on road construction (based on a formal quotation) and include it in the contract either as a condition precedent of the sale or as a separate part of the purchase price to be paid once the new road has been completed (within a specified time limit). In this way, and in the worst case, you can use that portion of the purchase price to engage your own contractor.

As is evident, the type of physical access to a property in Thailand is a serious consideration. However, in addition to the *type* of road, the *gradient* of the access road is also an important consideration. What many property buyers fail to realise is if they want a dream property with panoramic sea-views, they must usually drive *upwards* to get to it! The question of gradient is therefore a relevant concern. For instance, does the road have a nice, gentle gradient to the property or is it a steep, heart-thumping journey?

I am familiar with a beautiful, apartment development with stunning sunset views but parts of the access road are built almost at a 45° angle, complete with sharp bends to make the journey really exciting! In summer, a normal saloon car can negotiate the access road with relative ease (and a bit of practice). However, during the rainy season, when mud and sand wash down off the hillside, gaining access to the property becomes perilous and is a trip only for those with nerves of steel. Remember: extreme access is no access at all, especially from the perspective of rental guests. If you are buying such an apartment for your own use, with practice and a good 4WD, you might get used to such an extreme entrance to your property. If you are considering the rental market, however, a group of tourists renting a car and driving in Thailand for the first time would be horrified at having to negotiate such a steep access road to get to their "dream vacation home". Furthermore, once local taxi drivers get to know the access road, they might refuse to take guests back to the property. This will certainly not encourage referrals or repeat bookings!

With regard to re-selling such a property, I have literally witnessed cases where potential buyers decided not to buy the property from the vantage point of the car park *before they even got to the apartment!* In other words, luxury furnishings and Gaggenau ovens will not save you if buyers experience fear just getting to the property.

The issue of gradient is not only relevant for people considering the purchase of land and property; it is also relevant for those planning to build property. If access roads are excessively steep or treacherous, material suppliers might not be able to deliver; alternatively, they might increase delivery costs or charge "danger money" or deliver only half-loads, which also translates into higher costs. Similarly, if water is supplied by truck, drivers will sometimes refuse to deliver (see chapter 23). Having said that, with proper master planning and engineering, there is often a way to reduce the gradient by spreading it over a longer distance.

> **Important tip:** If you are considering the purchase of land with a steep access road, contact concrete companies and water delivery companies and ask them to test the gradient (in advance of the purchase). This might require some form of payment, although it certainly advantageous to know in advance whether key deliveries can be made.

Once *physical* access has been considered, the next element to investigate is *legal* access. By this, we are speaking of either owning an access road to the property, or ensuring legal servitude to the property by foot and by vehicle, which generally means a road owner granting right of passage to another. In such cases, right of servitude is typically required from the nearest government or public road to the boundary of the land. Suffice to say, legal access rights should be stated on the land title document (as distinct from scraps of paper signed by neighbours!).

Issues of access and servitude are issues properly dealt with by your lawyer. Do not become one of the rare statistics where a buyer purchases a beautiful, expensive property and only later realises he doesn't have access to it, except by air...

Summary

- Successful property investing is not just about buying land or property; it is also about making sure you have access to the land or property.
- The first issue to check is *physical* access; for instance, is there a concrete road to the property, or is access via a dirt track that can be washed away during the rainy season.
- The next issue is whether the access road is a government (public) road, or a private road that might involve maintenance fees.
- The *gradient* of the access road is another important consideration.
- It is also necessary to investigate legal access, which is ensuring ownership or legal servitude to the property.

19
Electricity?
(Essential)

Once land title and access have been considered, the next item on the list is utilities, i.e. electricity, water and sewage disposal. Utilities are an important issue to consider *prior to purchase* because if any utility is missing (or requires upgrading) it is going to cost you money; in some cases, a lot of money.

The most important utility – and potentially the most costly in terms of new installations – is electricity, which is the subject of this chapter, while water supply and sewage disposal are discussed separately in the following chapter.

With regard to electricity, therefore, the first thing to check is whether there is an existing electricity supply to the land. All other things being equal, land prices tend to be higher if there is an existing electricity supply, or if electric has been brought to the boundary of the land.

The second thing to check is whether an existing electric supply is single-phase or three-phase[50]. Three-phase electricity is superior because it is more efficient for high loading, i.e. running multiple air-conditioners together with swimming pool pump systems. Single-phase electric is often sufficient to power a residential property, although if many electrical appliances are used simultaneously you might sometimes experience dimming lights or water pumps struggling to work properly due to unstable or insufficient power. Single-phase electricity is often used by developers to provide a temporary supply of electricity to a site during construction.

If there is no electricity supply to the land, then it will need to be installed, which involves two main questions: whether 3-phase electricity is available in the area, and what is the distance from the nearest electricity supply (public electricity network) to the perimeter of the land[51]. Installation costs for a new electricity supply usually comprise the cost of a transformer plus the cost of running wires and poles (or underground cables) from the nearest electricity supply to the

---

[50] Electrical service is transmitted in the form of an alternating current whose magnitude and direction reverse cyclically about 60 times per second. If you put a voltage meter on a single-phase line and could slow it down to produce a graph, the line would look like a child's drawing of a wave moving up and down. Three-phase electricity is just like having three single-phase lines that are out of sequence by one third of a cycle so that the waves rise and fall one after another in sequence, providing a more stable electricity supply.

[51] It might also be necessary to obtain permission from adjoining landowners if electricity cables must cross their land, which is an entirely different (and potentially costly) issue.

land. To provide an indication, a recent quotation for the installation of a 500 KVA high voltage transformer to supply electricity to a small apartment building was 1.4 million Baht (US$ 46,600), which included more than 400,000 Baht (US$ 13,300) of cabling[52]. Due to the high costs of a new electricity supply, whether or not there is an existing supply becomes a crucial question. If there is no existing electricity supply, it is prudent to obtain at least two independent quotations for installation so that these estimations can be considered as part of the investment calculations (or used in negotiations with the seller of the land).

The third issue is to confirm whether the electricity supply is government or private. The former is usually preferable because this means a direct, metered electricity supply from the government, billed at government rates, which are typically in the region of 3.8 – 4.2 Baht per kW. A private supply is simply where a third party sits between you and the government system, which means the third party meters the electricity and bills you at a higher rate, which includes a profit mark-up. In the case of serviced land plots or a property development, the "third party" is usually a property developer or property management company that owns the common areas and utilities infrastructure. For instance, while the government electricity rate might be 4 Baht per kW, you could be billed with a 30%, 50% or even 100% mark-up by a property developer or management company, which means 5.2, 6 or even 8 Baht per kW. Over the long term, this can make a significant difference to utility costs.

It is also worth mentioning the option of solar power, which is usually available in the form of solar roof panels, although its use has not become widespread primarily due to the high initial costs of the panels and their installation.

Solar panels are certainly worth looking into for powering lights, appliances and for providing hot water, although solar power might need to be run in concert with traditional sources of electricity in order to power air-conditioning units and other high-load appliances or equipment.

---

[52] The longer the distance, the thicker the cable required.

Summary

- Due to the costs of installing a new electricity supply, confirming the existence of an existing electricity supply to land is a crucial issue to consider *prior to purchase.*
- The second issue is to check whether an electricity supply is single-phase or three-phase.
- The third issue is to confirm whether the supply is government or private, and to check the rates per unit.
- If there is no existing electricity supply, two independent quotations for installation should be obtained so costs can be factored into investment calculations or used in negotiations with the seller.

20
Water and sewage disposal?

In Thailand, there are generally three main possibilities for water supply: government-metered supply, deep-well water and delivery by truck.

Being connected directly to the government water network is generally the optimum solution,[53] which means a direct, metered supply to your property at "government rates", which are generally between 10 Baht (US$ 0.33) and 22 Baht (US$ 0.75) per unit (1,000 litres)[54], depending on the region. However, in a similar manner to electricity, if water is supplied *privately*, such as when water is invoiced through a property developer or property management company, bills can be expected to marked up with an appropriate percentage or "administration fee" (the supply of water is another profit opportunity).

For deep-well water, it is necessary to check whether a deep well already exists on the land *and whether it is operational*. If not, it is necessary to engage a company to conduct tests and bore a well deep enough to ensure an adequate supply of water. It should be noted that while some companies guarantee to charge only if water is found, others offer no such guarantee (in other words, holes are bored, no water supply is established and you still receive an invoice for the work). For this reason, details of the contract need to be ascertained before work commences. The cost of establishing deep-water wells depends on the depth at which water is found, which can be 20 metres or 200 metres. In addition, costs are sometimes influenced by the type of subsoil, i.e. rock is generally more expensive to drill through than clay.

Once a water supply is confirmed, there is also the cost of a pump to consider, together with the additional cost of a filter system to treat the water, depending on its quality and colour[55]. If deep-well water is the chosen method of water supply, it is advisable to get quotations in advance of any land purchase so the costs to be factored into your budget.

Truck water delivery simply means that water is delivered to your property by truck, which means you need underground or aboveground water storage tanks.

---

[53] Unless in times of drought when supply becomes "selective".
[54] 1 unit is one cubic metre, 1,000 litres (1m).
[55] A lab test is usually conducted on the water.

For an average-sized 3-bedroom villa, a storage capacity of 8,000 – 16,000 litres[56] is generally considered sufficient. To provide an example of costs, truck water deliveries in Koh Samui are approximately 500 Baht (US$ 16.65) for 6,000 litres or 230 Baht (US$ 7.65) for 2,000 litres, although water quality differs according to source[57].

An alternative option for providing *some* of your water needs is the use of rainwater collection systems. These can be added to a property or designed into the architecture of a new house by a competent architect, landscape design company or rainwater storage specialist.

The possibility of seasonal water shortages should be mentioned. If there are water shortages, this can affect all the methods of water supply: some areas on government supply will not receive water; deep-water wells might need to be bored deeper; and truck water might not be available. For instance, in 2010 Thailand experienced one of the worst droughts in its history, which significantly affected water supplies in some provinces, including island resorts. A little background research on historical water shortages (or the expectation of future supply issues) should be taken into consideration when designing a water supply system.

Finally, there should be consideration of sewage disposal. Either the land or property is connected to the government sewage system (if one exists) or an underground septic tank system is required, which might periodically require emptying by pump.

As you can see, there is more to utilities in Thailand than at first meets the eye! Due to the terrain and the typically under-developed infrastructure in certain resort areas, it is necessary to consider the different types of supply. It is also necessary to evaluate the potential cost-impact of arranging a water supply when purchasing land before a price is agreed with the seller.

---

[56] Basic household water requirements have been estimated at around 50 litres per person per day, excluding water for gardens (by Peter Gleick http://en.wikipedia.org/wiki/Peter_Gleick).

[57] For example, deep-well water or water from a reservoir.

Summary

- There are three general possibilities for water supply in Thailand: government-metered supply, deep-well water and delivery by truck.
- A government water supply is generally the optimum solution since it means a direct, metered supply to your property at government rates.
- If a deep well exists it is necessary to check *whether it is operational*. If not, a private company must be engaged to conduct tests and bore a well deep enough to ensure an adequate supply of water.
- The use of rainwater storage systems should also be considered.

21
Zoning and building regulations

Any investor looking to purchase land to build on (or to "land bank" as an investment) needs to be familiar with local zoning laws.

Zoning is an internationally accepted system for controlling development and refers to land being divided into different zones or sections, which are each reserved for different land uses, such as residential, commercial, industrial or agricultural. Each zone is usually colour coded and is subject to a different set of rules specifying what can and cannot be built land on land within each zone. To provide an idea what zoning looks like and how it works, here is the zoning map for Koh Samui[58].

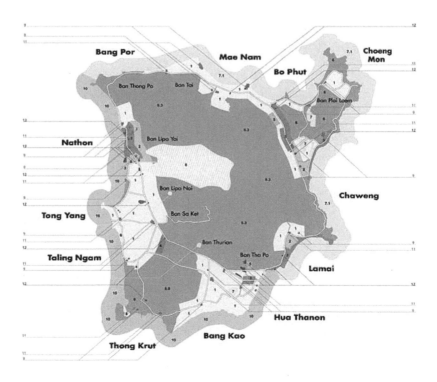

---

[58] Courtesy of Siam Map Company: www.siammap.com

1 Low density residential area	**7** Kept open for the public use
2 Medium density residential area	**8** Reserved forest area
3 High density residential area	**9** Educational institutes
4 Industrial and warehouse area	**10** Tourism and fishery
5 Specific industrial area	**11** Religious area
6 Agricultural area	**12** Government offices and public utilities

The zoning laws that became effective in Koh Samui as of the 25th July 2006 introduced 12 specific zones, as identified in the key. For example, Zone 1 is "low density residential", Zone 2 is "medium density residential", Zone 3 is "high density residential", and Zone 8 is "reserved forest area". Each of these different zones has specific rules or "building regulations" that determine what construction is permitted. These rules specify not only the type or purpose of buildings that are permitted, but also restrictions concerning size, height and density. For example, in relation to Zone 1:

Zone numbers 1.1 to 1.20 are low-density residential areas. And land in these zones shall be used mainly for residential and tourism purposes. Land may be put to other purposes in these zones. But, any land used for other purposes mustn't exceed 15% of the land in each of these zones. Constructions prohibited in the yellow zones include: factories; gas and petrol storage facilities; animal breeding; industrial; entertainment venues; slaughterhouses; silos; waste disposal; or junkyards.

In these zones the following rules apply:

a) *The total area of any buildings, except hotels, must not exceed 2,000sqm and the height of any building must not exceed 12m.*

b) *Where the land is used for residential purposes, including hotels, apartments, and bungalows, the surrounding space must be at least 40% of the whole.*

c) *Where the land is used for acceptable purposes other than residential, it shall have a surrounding space of at least 20% of the whole.*

d) *Where the land borders a public canal or public water source, the land 6m from the edge must not be used (except for the construction of water transportation facilities or public utilities).*

e) *The land 10m from the coast must not be used (specific exceptions exist).*

f) Where the land is within 50m from the coast, no building should exceed 6m in height. And its total area must not exceed 75sqm, and the surrounding space must be at least 75 % of the whole (specific exceptions exist).

It is common to find building regulations featured in magazines in graphical form as follows[59]:

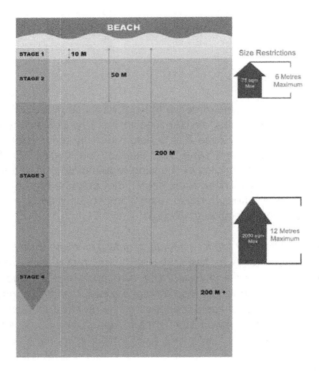

It is also useful to keep in mind that a 6-metre restriction generally means a single-storey house, while a 12-metre restriction means anything from a single-storey house to a three (or sometimes four) storey property.

Each of Thailand's resort area has its own zoning map, together with different sets of building regulations. If you are planning to buy land, it is necessary to get access to an up-to-date zoning map and to become familiar with the various rules and building regulations for each zone.

---

[59] Reproduced with the permission of Satayu Publishing Co., Ltd.

In addition to zoning and building regulations, it is also necessary to become aware of any "special rules" that might relate to specific areas. One such rule is referred to as the "80 metre rule" where no construction is permitted on land (in certain provinces) that is 80 metres above MSL (mean sea level) in order to protect green hillsides and hilltops. There are other special rules that might apply to building in other provinces above 150 metres, or restrictions related to building on land with a slope of more than 25° (where no groundwork, excavations or landfill are permitted).

Further, it is not only useful to understand building rules and regulations; it is also advantageous to understand how they are applied in practice. For instance, the application of a 12-metre height restriction to a sloping hillside often allows the total height of a property to be above 12-metres if separate terraced structures are each within 12m.

Important tip: When purchasing land, it is important to become familiar with existing zoning laws, building regulations and any special rules relevant to the area of interest. It is crucial to take appropriate legal advice and to keep abreast of any *proposed* rules that might impact land use in future. Remember, if zoning and building regulations change, these changes could impact the value of land.

The Town and City Planning Act and the Building Control Act are the two main pieces of legislation governing construction of residential properties in Thailand. Keep in mind that when developing property a number of restrictions may apply, which might include some or all of the following, depending on the province:

- Height of the structure
- Width of the structure
- Distance from the beach and/or shore
- Proximity to another property
- The use of the structure (residential, commercial, industrial)
- Building lot size
- Angle of slope of land
- Height of land above sea level
- Type and colour of roof

If you are planning to build, it is important to consider in advance the type and size of the property you want to build and to ensure the land you buy has the appropriate zoning and building regulations for a build permit to be granted. It is not unknown for investors to buy land without first confirming the applicable zoning regulations and are either unable to build on the land or must build a smaller structure than intended. Similarly, if you are planning to build an apartment complex where the floor areas and financial forecasts are based on a Floor Area Ratio (FAR)[60] of 60% of the land area, only to find out that the relevant zoning laws allow an FAR of only 40%, the viability of the whole project can be put into question.

It pays to remember that the same building regulations also cover adjacent land within the same zone, i.e. your neighbours. Thus, if you buy land with a 12-metre height restriction to build your dream single-storey villa, don't be surprised if a three-storey property is built next door[61]. For this reason, it is not only useful to be familiar with the zoning and building regulations for their relevance to your land but also for their relevance to the land around you (particularly in front of you). In Thailand, you can't legally protest about your neighbour blocking your views if they are in compliance with the regulations!

As each colour-coded zone is reserved for a different land use and corresponding restrictions dictate the type of properties that can be built, zoning significantly influences the price of land. When buying land, it is therefore important to ensure you are paying a price that corresponds to its zoning. In other words, don't take the word of a landowner or salesperson; make sure to double-check the appropriate zoning and restrictions with the help of your lawyer.

It also pays to keep abreast of any proposed changes to zoning laws and building regulations because it is essential that decisions are based on up-to-date information. All good architects and lawyers should be familiar with the various building regulations and can therefore be a good source of advice.

Finally, while zoning and building regulations are strictly adhered to by Land Department Offices when applying for build permits, they are not set in stone. In other words, there are occasions or circumstances where "special dispensations" are granted to build a property that might not strictly follow the letter of the law.

---

[60] FAR is the maximum floor area of the buildings relative to the size of the land.
[61] However, just because a neighbour has built a 12-metre high, three-storey property, don't assume you can also; it is possible that the two plots of land are located in different zones and subject to a different set of regulations.

Summary

- Any investor looking to purchase land to build on (or to "land bank" as an investment) needs to be familiar with local zoning laws.

- Zoning refers to land being divided into different zones or sections, which are each reserved for different land uses.

- Each different zone has specific rules or "building regulations" that determine what construction is permitted.

- It is also necessary to become aware of any "special rules" that might relate to specific resort areas.

- If you are planning to build, it is important to consider in advance the type of property you want to build and to ensure the land you buy has the appropriate zoning and building regulations for a build permit to be granted.

- As each colour-coded zone is reserved for a different land use, and corresponding restrictions dictate the type of properties that can be built, zoning significantly influences the price of land.

22
Size matters

Unless you are land banking, the size of the land you are looking for should primarily be driven by what you intend to do with it, instead of what is offered to you. This sounds obvious, although it is surprising how many people, when they are on holiday on a tropical island, depart from this principle.

To provide a general idea of size, if your objective is to build a villa, one Rai (1,600 square metres) of land is sufficient to build a large size four or five bedroom pool villa with a large garden for children to run around in. Two Rai (3,200 square metres) is suitable for a sprawling luxury villa with plenty of privacy and enough garden space for children to get lost in. Alternatively, a good sized three or four-bedroom pool villa can be built on ½ Rai (800 square metres) of land (or as little as 500 square metres) with a limited garden area[62]. On a more economic level (and subject to local building regulations), it is possible to fit four small villas on one Rai or less (although guests will possibly hear neighbours sneezing!).

Subject to local building regulations and zoning laws, it is also feasible to build a small apartment complex on as little as ½ Rai or one Rai. A small resort, depending on the number of rooms or villas, usually requires upwards of one or two Rai, while large resorts generally consider upwards of twenty Rai.

> **Important tip:** The key point is that location should be determined by your investment objective (see chapter 8) and land size should follow the architectural requirements of the property you are planning to build.

Land requirements should be discussed with a competent architect, so that the optimum land size can be determined prior to any land hunting expeditions. I am surprised at the number of people who buy land and only start thinking what to do with it afterwards. Indeed, land is often bought simply because it was offered to the buyer as a "special deal", rather than the land purchase following a pre-defined strategy. The most successful approach is to determine your investment objective, identify the size of land you need, and then look for land in locations that have the appropriate zoning and building regulations. Knowing what you want in advance also helps property agents to shortlist land meeting your requirements and saves a great deal of time driving around, which is the norm in the absence of a clear brief.

---

[62] Sometimes it is better to buy a larger plot than is required to prevent future construction occurring too close to your property.

Important tip: It should be noted that, all things being equal, the smaller the piece of land you buy, the higher the price "per Rai", and the larger the piece of land, the lower the price on a "per Rai" basis, which is consistent with the principle of *economies of scale*. For example, if you buy 10 Rai of land, the price might be 8 million Baht (US$ 265,000) per Rai, while a 1 Rai plot of land in the same location might cost 10 million Baht (US$ 333,000).

With regard to beachfront land, the five key determinants of price are as follows:

1. Location (and access)
2. Quality of the beach (i.e. powder sand, stone or mud and rocks)
3. Suitable (year-round) swimming
4. Tidal beach (i.e. does the tide go out, leaving a 100 metre walk to get to the water?)
5. Beach frontage (the width of the land in direct contact with the beach), i.e. land with 80-metre beach frontage will be more expensive than land of the same size, in the same area, with 50-metre beach frontage.

However, prices for beachfront land tend to behave in a special way. Prices for small land plots are expensive, while larger land plots try to extrapolate their value from the value of the land immediately adjacent to the beach with beach frontage. For instance, a 2 Rai plot of beachfront land with 50-metre beach frontage might command a price of 20 million Baht (US$ 665,000) per Rai, while an adjacent 20 Rai piece of beach land, also with 50-metre beach frontage, might also be asking for 20 million Baht (US$ 665,000) per Rai, despite the fact that only a small proportion of the land plot is technically adjacent to the beach, while the land further back, which would normally command only 8 million Baht (US$ 265,000) per Rai, has attempted to derive its value from the "beachfront" land. In such cases, the best way to commence price negotiations is to offer the market value for beachfront land for the several Rai immediately adjacent to the beach, and a proportionately lower figure for the large area of land behind the "beachfront" land.

Beachfront land in prime locations is so scarce and highly sought after that the price for small plots has soared to astronomical heights. For example, one land plot came up for sale in a special zone with building regulations that allow 12-metre high construction immediately adjacent to the sea wall. The plot measured just over 50 Wah (200 square metres) with an asking price of 30 million Baht (US$ 1 million). If it makes any sense to extrapolate the pro-rata price per Rai, it equates to approximately 240 million Baht (US$ 8 million) per Rai!

Summary

- Land acquisition should follow a pre-determined strategy, with location determined by your investment objective, and land size determined by what you plan to build.
- In general, the smaller the size of the land, the higher the pro-rata price per Rai, while the larger the size of the land, the lower the price on a per Rai basis.
- Asking prices for large pieces of beachfront land often attempt to derive their value from the market price of the land immediately adjoining the beach, as though the whole plot were "beachfront" land.

23
Flat land or hillside?

Apart from views, there is another key point to consider when deciding between flat land and hillside land: *it costs more money to build on hillside land*. While this point may seem obvious, it is surprising how many land purchasers fail to consider this fact until after a purchase. In other words, it becomes obvious, but only later!

To provide an example, suppose you have found ½ Rai (800 square metres) of flat land for 5 million Baht (US$ 165,000) and plan to spend 10 million Baht (US$ 333,000) to build a villa on it, which just fits inside your budget. You are then shown a ½ Rai plot of steep, sloping hillside land with a better view for 4 million Baht (U$ 133,000) and prefer the hillside plot because total costs will be 1 million Baht (US$ 33,000) lower. However, this is often a false assumption because building the same villa on steeply sloping land will generally be more expensive due to the extra engineering and structural work required (unless cost or design cuts are applied to the villa). For example, instead of 10 million Baht (US$ 333,000), the build cost on the steeply sloping land might be 12 million Baht (US$ 400,000), which takes the project 1 million Baht (US$ 33,000) *over* budget. Thus, despite land costs being lower, total costs are higher due to the gradient of the land.

Indeed, for hillside properties, engineering and structural work might sometimes account for 30-40% of construction costs, particularly if the land is steeply sloping or if a topographical survey reveals difficult terrain for foundations. Topographical surveys are essential for hillside land, as they will determine the precise extent of structural work required.

The fact that a property is to be built on a steep hillside could also translate into increased construction costs due to higher delivery charges from material suppliers and concrete companies (as mentioned in chapter 18). In addition, if water is supplied by truck, drivers might refuse to deliver due to the danger of negotiating steep gradients.

Once you are aware of the construction implications between flat land and hillside land, it is possible to factor the relevant costs into investment calculations in advance, rather than trying to compensate for them later.

Summary

- It costs more to build on hillside land than flat land, due to the additional structural and engineering work involved.
- Steep hillside land might also present a challenge in relation to material deliveries and the supply of trucked water.
- If buying hillside land, topographical surveys are essential, as they will determine the extent of structural work required.
- Recognising the additional costs in advance allows them to be factored into financial plans prior to land acquisition.

24
Subdividing land

If you are buying land and plan to divide it into smaller plots for re-sale, or if you are planning to build several villas for sale individually with a separate plot of land, you will encounter the issue of subdivision. Subdivision is the act of dividing a piece of land into two or more plots, which creates new property lines and individual land titles.

It is helpful to be aware of the procedures relating to the subdivision process set out in the Land Allotment Act[63]. To summarize the law, land under a single land title can generally be subdivided into a maximum of nine plots every three years. This means that if the land you have purchased has just been subdivided, you must wait three years before you can apply again for subdivision (being Thailand, there are of course exceptions). To subdivide land into more than nine plots at a given time requires a developer's licence, which generally takes in the region of two years to obtain.

In addition to the act of subdividing, consideration must also be given to the ownership structures for the subdivided land plots. For instance, if Thai companies are the chosen holding entity for individual plots of land, it is essential they are set up in compliance with Thai law (see chapters 90 and 91).

When subdividing land, it is highly recommended to seek the advice of a lawyer competent in this area of the law in order to make sure relevant checks are made on land documents and that subdivision documents are correctly submitted.

---

[63] The primary purpose of the Land Allotment Act is to set minimum standards related to the infrastructure and utilities of housing developments, such as minimum widths for internal project roads and minimum sizes for green areas and common areas.

Summary

- Subdividing is the act of dividing land into two or more plots to create new land titles.
- Land can generally be subdivided into a maximum of 9 plots each 3 years.
- To subdivide into more than 9 plots requires a developer's licence.
- Careful consideration must be given to ownership structures.

25
Serviced land plots

If you intend to build a property but prefer not to go through the whole process of buying land (or subdividing), securing access, putting in infrastructure, and bringing electricity to the site, a compromise is possible: purchasing a serviced land plot. Serviced plots become available when a developer has bought a large piece of land, subdivided the land into plots (usually), settled the issue of access and put in both infrastructure and utilities. Individual plots of land are then offered for sale with full infrastructure and utilities for buyers to build their own properties.

Apart from the obvious advantage of avoiding the hassle of subdivision and the installation of utilities, serviced plots often come with the option of pre-existing architectural drawings (which saves money on architectural fees), custom property design services and construction services.

In cases where the developer also provides construction services, it is often possible for the developer to work on lower margins (than would be the case with off-plan properties) because none of the developer's money is tied up in land or materials (assuming the land is paid for in full and construction proceeds on the basis of pre-paid staged payments). In addition, economies of scale are often available on professional fees, such as architectural services or submission fees (although ensure you have engaged your own lawyer, see chapter 84).

With regard to disadvantages, perhaps the principal disadvantage relates to the possibility of restrictions on architectural design or construction materials due to the objective of ensuring consistency within the development[64]. Another potential limitation accompanying the purchase of a serviced plot is where a developer makes it a condition of purchase to be the appointed contractor for any construction.

With regard to the price of serviced land plots, since a developer has added value to the land by subdividing, putting in infrastructure and installing utilities, serviced plots are typically sold at a premium to the cost of land, infrastructure and utility connections if you were to do it all yourself (the difference being the developer's profit). However, this is not always the case. Sometimes developers

---

[64] Such restrictions can also be an advantage in that they also apply to neighbouring plots and provide some protection from excessive development.

sell land at cost in the expectation of making a profit on construction. Occasionally, developers sell land at cost in order to recover a proportion of the money invested in land so that the proceeds can be used for construction, whereby the developer can achieve a higher profit by selling completed properties.

One of the key considerations in relation to serviced plots is on-going management fees for the maintenance of common areas, which includes roads, drainage, landscaping and any other facilities provided. Further, since the developer has taken the trouble to bring services and utilities to the land, utility bills are usually invoiced with a profit margin (see chapter 29, which highlights the difference between buying stand alone properties and properties within a managed development). Serviced plot owners could also find themselves contractually tied into property and rental management services.

Before making a decision, it is therefore important to read the contractual small print and weigh up the advantages and disadvantages in light of your own objectives.

Important tip: Just because a developer has bought and subdivided land, arranged access and put in infrastructure does not mean buyers of serviced land plots should dispense with the usual due diligence of investigating land titles and access rights.

Summary

- The advantage of serviced plots is that land has already been subdivided and both infrastructure and utilities have been installed.
- Purchasers generally pay a premium price for serviced land plots because a developer has added value to the land.
- Developers might also provide architectural design and construction services.
- Disadvantages include possible restrictions on design and materials, ongoing management fees for the maintenance of common areas, and higher unit costs for utilities.

STEP 3

Buying completed properties

26
Buying completed properties

When speaking of buying a "completed" property, we are simply referring to property that *exists*, as distinguished from "off-plan" property (see Step 5).

Completed property falls into two categories: new property, which is purchased from a builder or developer, or property purchased in the secondary ("re-sale") market, which has had previous owners. The purpose of the following 10 chapters is to provide practical advice about what to look out for when buying completed properties, which includes villas, apartments, penthouses, duplex apartments, townhouses or condominiums.

The principal advantage of buying a completed property is risk-related: the property is actually standing there; therefore, you know what you are getting and how much you will have to pay for it, as opposed to an "off-plan" property investment, which technically is only a paper asset until completed and transferred (and where there is always the risk of non-completion). Buying property on the secondary market is also a far easier way of getting into the property market than buying land and building your own property.

The main disadvantage of purchasing a completed property, if it could be considered a disadvantage, is that unless you are buying at a distressed price or below market value, you are generally paying the retail price for the property, as opposed to the development costs, i.e. the combined cost of the land and construction.

However, risk still exists in relation to purchasing completed properties and it is wise to stand back from the euphoria of a deal in order to recognise these risks. The fundamental risks relate to land title, access rights and utilities (which have already been discussed in chapters 14 - 20) and for this reason due diligence must be carried out prior to purchase (see chapter 89). There is also the issue of structural defects, which is why a structural report is recommended when buying a re-sale property (see chapter 34).

27
Working with property sales agents

If you are buying property in Thailand, you will probably need to enlist the help of property agents to view a selection of their property listings. It is also likely that you will encounter salespeople working for property developers.

In the United States, it is common to have "sellers agents" and "buyers agents". Sellers agents work on behalf of the seller, while buyers agents advertise the fact that they work in the best interests of the buyer. In Thailand, however, there are rarely such distinctions. Property agents, with a few notable exceptions, tend to work in the best interests of themselves! For instance, in relation to price, most property agents will not be overly concerned whether a property sells for 15 million Baht (US$ 500,000) or 14 million Baht (US$ 465,000). A deal is a deal and it pays the rent. While the difference for the buyer (and seller) is 1 million Baht (US$ 33,000), the difference in commission for the agent personally might only be 15,000 Baht (US$ 500), a sum not worth jeopardising a deal for in order to negotiate a better deal for either the buyer or seller. Indeed, the better the deal negotiated on behalf of a buyer, generally the less commission an agent will receive from the seller.

As a property purchaser, it is unlikely property agents will expect a commission from you on a sale. Property agents in Thailand generally receive their commission from the seller, which is typically between 3% and 5%, although in some cases it can be as much as 10% when "sub-agents" are involved. Logically, the source of an agent's income generally indicates that their loyalty is to the seller. Since it is theoretically impossible to work simultaneously in the best interests of both buyer and seller, agents are not generally working for the purchaser or representing the purchaser's best interests. In relation to land title, for example, if an agent suspects there might be an issue with the title or rights of access, such suspicions are often not mentioned in the hope a deal will go through, with the assumption that it is your responsibility as the buyer to discover any such problems during the due diligence phase (which indeed it is). There is also the (infrequent) practice whereby the seller of a property specifies the minimum amount they are happy to receive for the property, and the agent tries to sell the property for a higher price with the aim of keeping the difference. This is clearly not in the interests of the buyer.

It is also necessary to be also aware of property developers masquerading as independent property agents. These are developers that are building properties for sale but also operate an "independent" property agency marketing a wide range of properties, in addition to their own. Their salespeople will show you the range of properties, although their main agenda is to sell their own; information and advice is therefore presented (or skewed) accordingly. There is nothing sinister about the practice, so long as you are aware of the agenda and come to your own conclusions.

Remember, a salesperson's job is to sell. This means information is presented in a manner designed to show properties in a positive light or, in some cases, more of a luminous glow! Facts are communicated selectively; attention is generally not drawn to things you should be worried about. While there are salespeople and agents that conduct their work ethically, many are inherently biased in the information, advice and opinions they provide. When dealing with salespeople, therefore, buyers would be wise to bear in mind that salespeople make their living by earning commissions; that it is in their interests to make a sale rather than advise a client otherwise; and while there is a fine line between advising a buyer that a particular property is unsuitable and crossing the line in order to secure a commission, most opt for the latter.

In addition, it should be noted that the average salesperson is not generally a practicing specialist in Thai property law. Or a specialist in property taxes. Or an expert on the Thai economy, the political environment or market trends. Many are knowledgeable, but knowledge is not equivalent to expert, professional advice. While the resources are available that would allow sales agents to educate themselves, many prefer not to. For instance, I once asked the head salesperson for a property developer a straightforward question related to the leasehold status of the apartments he was selling (bearing in mind leases were the only product the company was selling). His reply was, "I have no idea". When I asked if he could find out from his company's lawyer, to his credit he agreed and we arranged to meet the next day. When we met the next day, he said, "I still don't know, but here is a two page letter from the lawyer". In other words, he hadn't bothered to read the information himself and will still be none the wiser when another client asks the same question!

The reason I mention this example is not to denigrate property agents or salespeople; it is simply to remind property buyers not to be overly dependent on property agents or salespeople for information and advice. Certainly they should not be relied upon for negotiating best terms or prices on your behalf; *buyers must take ultimate responsibility for their own best outcomes.*

> **Important tip:** The biggest mistake a prospective investor can make is to treat the information and advice provided by salespeople as undisputed truths. Equally it is a mistake to rely on advice provided by salespeople in order to avoid paying professional fees for legal and tax advice. In sum, *we should not treat salespeople as our advisors.*

It should also be remembered that while property agents and salespeople usually disappear after the completion of a property transaction, it is the buyer who takes possession of the property, together with any associated problems. It is important to understand at the outset the distinction between a property salesperson's role and responsibilities and the role and responsibilities of a purchaser or investor. Understanding the respective roles should help to prevent us making decisions based on questionable information.

The role of property sales agents is to show you properties meeting your criteria and to provide property-specific information. Unless you have engaged a "buyers agent" who is genuinely working on your behalf as a buyer, it is your job as a buyer to conduct your own research and to verify and evaluate information provided by salespeople. It is also the buyer's job to negotiate terms and prices (through the agent if necessary); it is the buyer's job to take appropriate professional advice and to appoint a lawyer to ensure proper due diligence is carried out. In other words, we should not be unduly influenced by the agendas of other participants in the sales process or cut corners at the insistence of others against our better interests.

It is also good advice to work only with reputable agents and to keep your wits about you. It also helps to know exactly what type of property you are looking for and to communicate this information to sales agents in advance, which gives them time to prepare a list of properties that are suitable, instead of wasting time viewing properties that are not. However, take care when giving a specific budget to property agents: agents generally show you only the properties that are close to your budget (or just above) in order to secure the maximum commission, rather than properties that cost significantly less that might also be suitable.

To get access to a potentially wider choice of properties, together with a different perspective, it is worthwhile contacting at least two different property agents. In addition, a useful source of "supplementary" local information is the owners of local restaurants, bars and businesses. They are often able to provide information and insights that are generally not available through more formal channels (although all information should be verified).

Summary

- Property agents in Thailand generally receive commission from the seller, which indicates that the agent's loyalty is also to the seller.
- Remember, a salesperson's job is to sell, which means facts are communicated selectively and attention might not be drawn to things you should be worried about.
- The average salesperson is not generally a practicing specialist in Thai property law, property taxes or market trends.
- The sales agents role should be to show you properties that meet your criteria and to provide property-specific information.
- It is the buyer's job to verify information provided by salespeople, negotiate terms and prices (through the agent if necessary) and take appropriate professional advice.

28
What to look for when viewing properties?
(Essential)

This chapter is designed to serve as a checklist of information that buyers should note when viewing properties. Buyers can determine for themselves the points that are most important according to their own individual circumstances. However, while some points are aesthetic in nature, others are fundamental to a property's value and should therefore bear upon the decision whether or not to proceed (many of these points are the subject of separate chapters). Fundamental points are noted with an asterisk (*) and should be noted on the first viewing of a property, while items of aesthetic importance can be noted on subsequent viewings, once the choice of properties has been narrowed down.

Checklist

Is the property for sale on a leasehold or freehold basis? This question is of fundamental importance as it influences the question of legal ownership and potential ownership structures (see chapter 95). If the property is leasehold, note the number of years remaining on the (first 30-year) lease and the existence of any options to renew.

What is the title of the land? Recall from chapter 14 that prudent foreigners should confine themselves to dealing only with land that is *Chanote* or *Nor Sor Sam Gor,* as these are the only titles over which a registrable right of ownership or lease can exist.

What is the land plot size and floor area of the property? These are useful figures when comparing properties (see chapter 35).

What is the asking price and estimated rental figures? These figures can be used to calculate yields (see chapter 10). If the seller is able to supply historical records, then this could make things easier, although bear in mind these figures might not be "accurate" and are sometimes inflated to make the property appear to be a better investment.

How many bedrooms and bathrooms does the property have? This question is not only relevant to the size of your family or number of in-laws, it is also relevant if you plan to use the property for rental income, where an optimal-sized property needs to be considered for the target market.

Does the property have adequate storage space? This is an often-overlooked issue, although it is particularly important for a rental property where a storage room is needed to keep spare linens and towels (see chapter 113). Storage space is also useful for storing sun loungers and outdoor furniture during rainy seasons or when not in use, or for personal belongings that you want to leave at the property for future visits.

*Is the property a stand-alone property or part of a managed development? (See chapter 29). If it is part of a development, carefully define the "common areas" and the "private areas" that belong exclusively to the owner of the property.

If part of a managed development, what are the management and maintenance fees? This is an important question because these bills will need to be paid on a monthly basis whether the property is used or not. Usually they are charged on a square metre basis.

What is the age and general condition of the property? Remember that properties often require renovations or repairs after 4-5 years.

*Location. Make a note of the proximity to beaches, restaurants, schools, hospitals, supermarkets, golf courses, airports or whatever is important to you. Don't take a salesperson's word for any distances involved; drive or measure them yourself (a salesperson's "5 minutes to the beach" is often overly optimistic or has been measured by Superman!) Note also the location of nearby temples, which are interesting as tourist attractions, although during celebrations the noise tends to keep local residents (including rental guests) awake late into the night.

*What type of access does the property have? Is the road a concrete road or dirt track? Is it a government or private road? What is the gradient? (See chapter 18)

*What is the visual aspect and are there any vacant, adjacent land plots? Recognise the premium value of views and the potential for obstructions or development on surrounding land (see chapter 32).

Note the directions North, East, South and West in relation to the property. It is nice to sit around the pool deck or on a balcony to watch the sun setting in the West. It is also useful to work out which areas of the property will receive sunlight in the mornings, and which areas will be in the shade during the afternoon (for this reason it is helpful to carry a compass with you).

What is the method of wall construction? Note whether walls are cavity or single-skin; clad with stone, tiled or rendered? This not only provides an insight into build quality but also insulation value and noise reduction.

What is the floor finishing? Are floors finished with Italian marble, Terrazzo, hardwood, homogeneous tiles, or brushed concrete?

What is the roof finishing? Note whether the roof is of concrete tiles, terracotta tiles, or thatch (which requires changing every few years?) Is the roof insulated to reduce air-conditioning bills? If possible, visit the property during a heavy rainstorm; it is the best time to find out if the roof leaks!

What renovations or repairs are required? Part of the visual inspection should be to keep an eye out for cracks in floors and walls, or discolouration from water damage, both of which might indicate structural problems (see chapter 34 about home surveys and structural engineering reports). In addition, advice should be sought on the condition of the electric wiring and plumbing system.

Does the property have existing structural guarantees or defects warranties? Make a note of the company providing the guarantees and whether they are *transferable.*

Is there any termite damage? Termites are horrible little creatures that burrow into your house by eating through wood or concrete and tend to make their homes behind skirting boards, doorframes and kitchen cupboards, where they eat the house from the inside. Pay particular attention to skirting board damage or a hollow sound if skirting boards are tapped. If the house has termites, it means a pest control company must be engaged to eradicate them[65], which usually involves spraying the property on a monthly basis (see chapter 55). Repairs will also be required to any damaged areas.

Who are the utility and service suppliers and what are the rates? (See chapters 19 and 20). Note whether the electricity supply is three-phase or single-phase and whether it is a government or private supply. Is the water supply government or private, from a deep well or delivered by truck? Is the property already connected with telephone, Internet and satellite TV?

Does the property have fans or air-conditioning units? If the property only has fans and you can't live without air-conditioning, the cost of installing new air-conditioning units must be taken into account. Sometimes properties have air-conditioning in the bedrooms and fans in the living room. Another relevant question is the brand of the air conditioning units and whether the company has maintenance services in the area (if not, it could take several days for engineers to fix them).

---

[65] Pest control should be considered a standard part of maintaining a resort property. Ideally, pest control is about keeping termites and other insects out; not dealing with them only when damage becomes apparent.

What is the type and quality of doors and windows? If the windows and doors are of wood, it is helpful to find out the type of wood and whether it is prone to expanding, contracting or splitting over time. This is especially relevant for beachfront properties where doors and windows are directly exposed to the elements. Aluminium powder-coated windows and doors tend to better withstand extreme weather, although there are significant differences in quality, from heavy-duty Sun Paradise double-glazed windows to single-glazed, lightweight, inexpensively manufactured windows that leak during storms. In addition, expansive concertina doors might look great on a sunny afternoon with a cool breeze, although the low quality brands tend not to look so good after heavy winds! Remember that the quality of windows and doors also has a bearing on security.

Are doors and windows fitted with mosquito screens? If the property is in a location that is attractive to mosquitoes, mosquito screens are a valuable benefit; relative to the cost of doors and windows, they can be quite expensive to install. If there are no mosquito screens, make a note if doors and windows have the requisite tracks pre-installed for mosquito screens to be fitted later.

Quality and appearance of the kitchen and appliances. A beautiful kitchen is an important selling point for any property. Make a note whether kitchen worktop surfaces are granite (durable) or MDF-covered chipboard (less durable). Are cupboard doors hardwearing, high-gloss melamine or MDF-covered chipboard? Look inside the cupboards for signs of wear and tear. List the appliances, as any missing appliances – such as ovens, dishwashers or microwave ovens – will need to be added at your cost. Note also the brand of kitchen appliances. This is not a study in superficiality; if the developer or previous owner has invested in good quality appliances, it is likely that good quality materials and accessories have been used throughout. If the kitchen is fitted with a Gaggenau oven, the property is likely to have been built to a similar standard. The inverse is also true: if money has been saved through the installation of inexpensive kitchen appliances, it is also likely that money has been saved elsewhere on materials. If a kitchen is in a poor state, a replacement kitchen can cost anywhere from 250,000 Thai Baht (US$ 8,300) to 2.5 million Baht (US$ 83,000), or more.

Bathroom accessories. For the same reason, it is also worth noting the brands used for bathroom accessories, such as showerheads, taps, bath faucets, towel rails, washbasins and toilets. High quality brands such as Grohe not only tend to last longer but often indicate that a similar quality of materials has been used throughout. Lower quality "Made in China" models tend to discolour or require earlier replacement.

Is the property furnished? It is important to note whether the property is being sold in a fully furnished, semi-furnished or unfurnished state. If furniture is included with the property, make a note whether it is also included in the purchase price or if it is additional to the purchase price. The quality and state of wear-and-tear of the furniture should also be noted, together with paintings, art objects, curtains and blinds, and any built-in furniture, such as wardrobes. If the property is to become a rental property, if anything is missing or needs replacing, it adds to capital expenditure.

Audiovisual equipment. Note the number of TV's, DVD players and music systems and check whether these will remain in the property after sale.

Garden lights, sensor lights and alarm system. Security is an important element, especially for remote properties, and an existing system might save the effort of having a system installed. Check the operational details of the system; does it just make a loud noise or is linked to a company with a 24-hour response team.

Lighting plan. This should include checking whether lighting is adequate, together with a walk-through of the property to check which light switches turn on which lights. It might sound ridiculous but, in Thailand, you might be glad you did it (see chapter 54)!

Swimming pool. Is the swimming pool private or communal? Who takes care of the pool management and what are the monthly fees? If the property is part of a managed development, are the fees included in the monthly per square metre cost or are they additional?

Car Parking. How many car parking spaces does the property have? Is it covered or uncovered parking? If the property is part of a managed development, are the parking spaces allocated or unallocated?

Who is the seller and what is the reason for sale? This information is important in that it influences the property ownership structure, the manner in which the property is transferred, and can also provide insights into the best way to proceed with price negotiations (see chapters 33 and 96).

What type of beach? This is a key question for beachfront properties or properties near the beach, especially for rental properties. Is the beach swimmable or is it one that requires a hundred metre walk to reach waist-deep water? Are there dangerous currents? (Some beaches in Phuket have dangerous rip currents during winter months that have resulted in drowning)

It is advisable to take a camera with you to each property viewing. Photographs can be extremely useful to jog your memory, especially if you have returned to your home country after a vacation or in the case where you have viewed so many properties that all the details have blurred together into an amorphous mental blob!

Finally, before signing anything, it is recommended to view a property at different times of the day and on different days of the week; the same property can become noticeably different at different times. For instance, in the case of noise levels, a property might be an oasis of tranquillity during the week and like a discothèque at the weekend. If practical, it is also worthwhile viewing a property in different seasons. Seasonality is especially relevant to access roads that could be washed away or underwater during rainy seasons. It is also relevant to beaches – a beach might look amazing at high tide in the winter months, and decidedly less attractive at low tide in the summer when the sea disappears to leave a 100 metre wide beach of rocks and dead coral.

The chart on the next page provides a practical checklist for property viewings (with asterisks (*) marking the items of fundamental importance):

Property Viewing Checklist	Notes
*Leasehold or freehold?	
*Land title?	
*Plot size and floor areas?	
*Asking price?	
*Estimated rental figures?	
*Number of bedrooms/bathrooms?	
Storage space?	
*Stand alone property or managed development?	
Management and maintenance fees?	
Age and general condition of property?	
*Location or proximity to beaches, restaurants, etc.	
*What type of physical and legal access? Gradient?	
*Visual aspect, vacant adjacent land plots?	

Property Viewing Checklist	Notes
Note North, South, East, West (sunset)	
Wall construction?	
Floor finishing?	
Roof finishing?	
Renovations or repairs needed?	
(Transferable) structural guarantees?	
Termite damage?	
Electricity supply and rates?	
Water supply and rates?	
Waste water disposal?	
Telephone, Internet, cable TV?	
Fans or air-conditioning?	
Type and quality of windows and doors?	
Mosquito screens or tracks?	
Kitchen and appliances?	
Bathroom accessories?	
*Furnished or unfurnished (including artwork)?	
Audio-visual equipment?	
Garden lights, sensor lights, alarm system?	
Check lighting plan	
Private or communal swimming pool?	
Car parking, covered, allocated?	
*Who is the seller, and what is the reason for sale?	
Type of beach?	

29
Managed development or stand-alone property?

One of the most basic choices when buying property is the choice between buying a "stand-alone" property and a property within a managed development. A managed development is simply a development where infrastructure has been put in for multiple properties, maintenance costs are shared among owners and a range of property management services are provided. In contrast, a stand-alone property is just that – a property that stands alone (in the sense that it is not part of a managed development). Both have their advantages and disadvantages, which should be considered according to your objectives and circumstances.

Advantages of managed developments

The main advantage of buying a property within a managed development is that security[66], maintenance and upkeep of common areas (such as lifts, swimming pools, gardens and roads) are provided whether or not you are in residence.

In addition to common area management services, a range of management and maintenance services are usually available in relation to privately owned properties. In other words, properties can be serviced and owners can arrive to find their property ready for immediate occupancy. Further, in the case of rental properties, management companies often provide *rental* management services such as airport transfer, housekeeping and cleaning services (see chapter 118). Rental management is either provided for a monthly set fee, or a percentage of rental income, or both.

As a management company is usually in charge of invoicing for the supply of utilities (water, electricity, telephone, Internet, satellite TV), payments are often consolidated into one monthly invoice, which obviates the need to pay each of the companies separately.

Disadvantages of managed developments

One disadvantage of buying property within a managed development is that *all* costs and maintenance fees for the upkeep of a development are shared. This might also include contributions to a "sinking fund" whereby property owners pay regular contributions that are set aside for future major repairs and renovations.

---

[66] If you are not resident in Thailand, security can be of particular importance.

In addition, since utilities are provided through the management company, utility bills are often inflated by a profit margin for the management company. When buying property within a managed development, it is important to check the terms and conditions of the management contract in relation to the extent of services provided and the management and maintenance costs, which are usually invoiced on a "per square metre" basis (see also chapter 77).

Important tip: Once you have purchased a property within a managed development, it is not typically something that you can later opt out of. This means if you move in as a full time resident, monthly management fees can become a burden. They can also become a burden if a property is seldom rented out, whereby sufficient rental income is not generated to cover the fees.

Potentially the most significant disadvantage concerns the management company itself and the quality of the services provided. If a development is not properly managed or services such as pool cleaning, gardening or security are not provided to an adequate standard, it will quickly lead to problems, either for owners or their rental guests, which ultimately will have a negative effect on the value of your investment. It is therefore wise to check the management contract for a collective termination clause (by a majority vote of the owners) that might allow a change of management company. If there are any doubts as to a management company's competence, it is advisable to seek out other owners in the development to get their opinion of the management company and the quality of services provided.

Advantages of a stand-alone property

The advantages of a stand-alone property are the inverse of those of a managed development: no monthly management fees; no sharing of communal area expenses or sinking funds; no mark-up on utility bills (unless the supply is through a private third party). In other words, owners own their property and are masters of its destiny.

Disadvantages of a stand-alone property

The main disadvantage to consider with a stand-alone property is the absence of security, which is a key consideration, especially in remote areas. Similarly, there is no one on hand for gardening, pool cleaning or to prepare the house for your arrival, which means unless these services are separately contracted or a management company is engaged, you get to spend the first week of each vacation performing maintenance, repairs and housekeeping!

It should also be noted that tropical homes left unattended for long periods rapidly deteriorate. For this reason, at the very minimum, stand-alone properties require some form of airing and cleaning programme. If you have a pool and garden, pool maintenance and gardening services are also essential if you don't want to arrive to find a plot of primary jungle with a green rectangular swamp in the middle.

For larger properties, a common solution is to have a live-in maid or private staff. With the low salaries in Thailand, this type of arrangement could work out to be less expensive than paying the monthly invoices associated with a managed development. However, if your visits are infrequent, there is the issue of ensuring staff are properly performing their duties in your absence.

The alternative is to engage a professional property management company to manage and maintain your property. There are a number of management companies in each of the primary resort areas, many of which are under western management. Property management companies generally have a list of services from which to choose, from simple cleaning and airing to full property and rental management services and it is a matter of choosing a level of service to suit your circumstances (see chapters 114 -118 for a more detailed discussion on rental management).

Summary

- A managed development is where infrastructure has been put in for multiple properties, maintenance costs are shared among owners and a range of property management services are provided.
- The main advantage of managed developments is that security and maintenance of common areas (such as lifts, swimming pools, gardens and roads) are provided.
- One disadvantage of a managed development is that all costs and maintenance fees for the upkeep of the development are shared. There might also be a "sinking fund".
- Check the management contract for a collective termination clause (by a majority vote of the owners) that might allow a change of management company.
- The advantages of a stand-alone property are no monthly management fees; no sharing of communal area expenses or sinking funds; and no mark-up on utility bills.
- The disadvantage of a stand-alone property is the absence of security and, unless services are separately contracted or a management company is engaged, no one is on hand for gardening, pool cleaning or to prepare the house for your arrival.

30
What is included?

In legal terms, the contents of a property are either classified as "fixtures" or "fittings". A fixture is an item that has been *annexed* to a property to such an extent that it has become part of the property and cannot be removed without causing significant damage (to the building or land). A fitting, on the other hand, is something that is easily removable from the building or land, such as an object or personal possession.

Generally speaking, items that are "fixed" to the property (fixtures) are assumed as *going with the property* upon sale, while items that are not fixed to the property (fittings) cannot be assumed to *go with the property,* which means they are open to discussion and require clarification with the seller. It is not uncommon for buyers, upon taking possession of their new dream property, to find half the treasured objects (that created the initial "Wow" factor) have disappeared. This could either be because the buyer assumed they would remain in the property and never bothered to check, or because the seller took the opportunity to remove them in the absence of any formal obligation not to. This is not just the case with beautiful art objects, lamps or DVD players; it can extend to missing air-conditioning units, curtains, appliances or towel rails. One buyer took possession of a property to find most of the door handles missing!

Since there are no absolute, hard and fast rules for what constitutes a fixture or fitting, it is best to make clear which items are included with the sale of the property, and which items the seller plans to remove prior to sale. This should be considered a three-step process.

Chapter 28 contained a checklist of things to pay attention to while viewing properties. As part of this checklist, notes should have been taken with regard to furniture, curtains and blinds, artwork, appliances, audio-visual equipment (DVD players, TV's), air-conditioning units and any other relevant items, including car parking spaces. When the decision has been taken to proceed with a particular property, and before making an offer, the first step is therefore to confirm with the seller (or sales agent) precisely which items go with the property *and are included within the purchase price.* If the desired items are not included in the purchase price, the additional cost must be determined.

Once the details have been agreed, the second step is to ensure that all the items forming part of the sale are specifically mentioned in the sale and purchase contracts[67]. If necessary, photographic "evidence" can be included in the appendices.

The third step is to ensure that, upon taking possession, the items in the property are cross-referenced with the items in the contract. Treating fixtures and fittings in such a detailed and diligent manner not only clarifies the intentions of the buyer and seller, it is also helps to avoid disagreement and disappointment.

Summary

- Since there are no hard and fast rules for what constitutes a fixture or fitting, it is best to make clear which items will be included with the sale of the property, and which items the seller plans to remove.
- All the items forming part of the sale should be specifically mentioned in the sale and purchase contract.
- Upon taking possession, the items in the property should be cross-referenced with the items in the contract.

---

[67] It should be noted that if the purchase price is broken down into house and furnishings, it is wise to consult with your lawyer or tax advisor due to the tax consequences.

31
What are the monthly costs?

No property purchase or investment decision should be made without a complete summary of transaction costs and ongoing monthly bills and management fees. Transaction costs in relation to the purchase of property include legal fees, transfer fees and taxes. Legal fees are discussed in chapter 85, while transfer fees and taxes are covered in chapter 97.

This chapter is concerned with the ongoing monthly fees related to the running and management of a property. If you are buying a property as a primary residence or holiday home, estimating monthly costs is important to allow proper budgeting. It is not uncommon for property buyers to get so caught up in the excitement of a purchase that the issue of ongoing costs is overlooked. When they are considered later, the costs can become an unanticipated burden. In some cases, purchasers put their life savings into a resort property, only to find they don't have enough left to cover the monthly costs.

If, on the other hand, you are investing in property for rental income, a detailed summary of the monthly costs is essential to manage cash flows and estimate net rental yields (see chapter 10). With rental properties, knowledge of the monthly costs also allows the break-even point to be determined, i.e. how many nights the property must be rented out to cover costs and break even (see chapter 119).

The following table is intended to provide a checklist of the most common costs associated with the management of a property.

Service description	Monthly cost
Electricity	
Water	
Telephone	
Internet	
Cable or satellite TV	
Garden maintenance	
Pool cleaning and maintenance	
Pest control	
Security	
Cleaning and airing	
Property inspection and maintenance	
Wastewater management	
Common area management fees	
Sinking fund	
Insurance	
Accounting fees	
Rental management (fixed costs)	
TOTAL MONTHLY COSTS	

With regard to utilities, estimating monthly costs is either a matter of noting fixed monthly service fees, or finding out the cost per unit and estimating consumption. It is helpful if the previous owner is able to provide historical information, which they are normally happy to do (unless it reflects too badly on net rental income!). Remember, utility bills tend to be higher when a property is rented out (due primarily to the use of air-conditioning).

In the case of garden maintenance, pool cleaning and maintenance, pest control, security, cleaning and airing, property inspection and maintenance, and wastewater management, these fees can be estimated by discussing the requirements with a professional property management company.

If the property is part of a managed development, there are usually common area management fees, which are typically calculated on a per square metre basis according to the floor area of your property. For example, fees within an apartment complex could range from 25 Thai Baht (US$ 0.83) to 45 Thai Baht (US$ 1.50) per square metre per month.

It is quite possible that some of the abovementioned services – such as garden maintenance, pool cleaning and maintenance, and security – are provided by the management company and the costs are therefore included in management fees. In addition, it is also common for utilities and services to also be invoiced through a management company, based on consumption. It is important to check carefully which services are included and which are not included in the management fees. For instance, I am familiar with one property development where management fees include gardening, security, cleaning and maintenance of the common areas; however, pool cleaning and maintenance are excluded and invoiced separately. Further, it is important to check whether there are fees payable towards a sinking fund, which is money paid into an account to cover future major renovations and repairs to common areas and facilities.

With managed developments, it is important to make a distinction between *common* areas and the *private* area of your property. Management fees generally cover cleaning and maintenance of the common areas but not the cleaning and maintenance of your property, which is private. Likewise, pest control is often part of the management company's duties, although for common areas and not within private areas (which requires access to private property). In addition, it is often the case that insurance covering the building structure and common areas is arranged by the management company, while insurance for the contents of individual properties need to be arranged separately by the owners (if you plan to rent out a property, make sure this is covered by the insurance policy).

With regard to accounting fees, these are payable when it is necessary to prepare personal income tax or corporate income tax returns.

Depending upon how you set up the property and rental management services, there is typically some combination of fixed and variable costs. Since this chapter is concerning with the ongoing monthly costs for property management (and not *rental* management), at this stage it should suffice to include only the fixed costs associated with rental management.

32
Aspect and adjacent land

A British couple bought a stunning private villa on a hillside with beautiful panoramic sea views. Within three years after purchase, a low-rise apartment block had been built directly behind the villa, and another one directly in front. Not only had they lost their privacy with tenants looking down on their property from the apartments behind, they also lost part of their sea view due to the apartments in front. In addition, with the villa being surrounded by almost continual construction noise for three years, holiday rentals were made impossible, rental income was reduced to zero, and the combination of these factors significantly reduced the market value of their property.

When buying property, especially resort property, unobstructed sea views or the element of privacy can account for a significant part of the purchase price. In cities, the premium commanded by a good view is mentioned to be in the region of 20% of the purchase price; it is possibly much higher with resort properties.

Important tip: When viewing properties, it is essential to recognise the premium price represented by the view and to evaluate the risk posed to that premium. If a property is bordered by an open expanse of land with mature coconut trees waving gently in the wind, don't assume it will stay that way forever; if your property has unobstructed sea views but the land plot in front has building regulations that would allow structures to obstruct the view, that vacant plot poses a risk to the future value of your property.

In Thailand, except for the registration of easements, there is no system for recording restrictive covenants directly over land titles to protect your property from the potential impact of construction on adjacent land; any limitation could only be set out contractually between the parties. In other words, there is no direct enforceability over land, only the threat of civil contractual penalties, and if the land is sold to a third party privity of contract is broken[68].

Therefore, when buying property it is essential to be familiar with the zoning laws and building regulations for the area in which you are buying property (see chapter 21). It is also important to investigate the ownership of adjacent land, together with any potential plans for development that could have a future impact on your property. It is possible for your lawyer to make relevant enquiries at the land

---

[68] The contract is only binding on the parties who originally signed the contact.

office, although bear in mind that such enquiries might only uncover development plans that have been *submitted;* in other words, plans that are still on the drawing board might not be discoverable through formal enquiry. Thus, vacant land with the potential for future construction should be identified as a risk, although there are various degrees of risk. If adjacent land is semi-agricultural and in the hands of local "ancestors", the planning process to upgrade the land and obtain the necessary permits for construction could take many years. If, however, the land title is Chanote or Nor Sor Sam Gor and is in the hands of a property developer, it may only be a matter of months[69]. To err on the side of caution, if the land title is anything other than agricultural land or primeval jungle, assume the worst and accept that it is likely to be developed at some point in the future[70].

Important tip: In the excitement of viewing a property, it is crucial not to get tunnel vision, where your focus is entirely on the property to the exclusion of what is going on around it. By including the surrounding land as part of your due diligence, you will at least be aware of the potential risks posed by future construction and can take decisions conscious of these risks. Be aware also that properties sometimes come onto the market for the very reason that the owners have become aware of planned construction on adjacent land.

What happens on an adjacent land plot can and will affect the value of your property, either through obstructing the view, affecting rental income due to construction noise, or through its impact on the attractiveness of the local area. Therefore, to secure the long-term value of your property, choose a property that is not only attractive today but whose premium price is protected from the negative impact of future development.

Summary

- When buying property, especially resort property, unobstructed sea views or the element of privacy can account for a significant part of the purchase price.
- It is important to investigate the ownership of adjacent land, together with any potential plans for development that could have a future impact on your property.
- What happens on an adjacent land plot can and will affect the value of your property, either through obstructing the view, affecting rental income due to construction noise, or through its impact on the attractiveness of the local area.

---

[69] Especially if the land has recently been cleared of vegetation ready for construction.
[70] Even agricultural land is not averse to the odd illegal structure!

33
Who is the seller and what is the reason for sale?

Two more items on the checklist to investigate are "who is the seller?" and "what is the reason for selling?" In Europe or the United States, the answers to such questions tend not to be as important as in Thailand, or they are only important to the extent that the information might be useful in price negotiations. However, in Thailand these questions are highly relevant because the answers can determine the fundamental attractiveness of a property and, indeed, whether the wishes of buyer and seller can be made to coincide.

In relation to the question "who is the seller?" what we are really establishing is the *nature* of the seller, i.e. whether the seller is a person, a Thai company or an offshore company[71]. This is a key piece of information because the current ownership structure influences the manner in which the property is transferred and the buyer's choice of ownership structure. It also influences how and where the purchase price is paid, together with the transaction fees and taxes payable (see chapter 96 for a more detailed discussion).

For example, if the current "owner" of the property is a Thai company, a purchaser typically has the option of taking over the Thai company by way of share transfer, or transferring the assets "out of the company" into a new Thai company or ownership structure. The seller usually prefers a buyer to take over the Thai company because it requires a simple transfer of shares, reduces transaction costs (stamp duty) and allows the seller a clean and simple exit strategy. A buyer, however, might be unwilling to take over an existing Thai company due to the risk of undisclosed liabilities, and the issue of tax liability on gains made by the previous owner, which would also be technically assumed by taking over a company[72]. However, transferring the property "out of the company" involves higher transaction costs (property transfer fees and taxes) and an unwelcome corporate tax liability for the seller.

If, on the other hand, the property is currently owned in an individual's personal name, the property must be transferred to the new owner, which has personal income tax implications for the seller. Consequently, the seller might try to pressure the buyer into officially declaring a lower purchase price in order to reduce his tax burden, which might then become a sticking point.

---

[71] Or an offshore company with a controlling interest in a Thai company.

[72] The property will remain on the company books at the original purchase price and if, upon eventual re-sale, a subsequent purchaser wishes to transfer the property "out of the company", the seller is now liable to income tax on both his gains *and* the gains made by the previous owner.

Sometimes land and structures (such as villas) are held separately; for instance, a Thai company might own the land, while the structure is held in a personal name. This involves the decision whether to transfer both land and structure to a new ownership structure, or to take control of the Thai company through share transfer and thus transfer only the structure.

Alternatively, the current ownership structure might be a two-tier corporate structure. For instance, a Thai company might own the property, and in turn an offshore company, such as a BVI (British Virgin Islands) or Hong Kong company, owns the controlling shares of the Thai company. In such cases, the seller might want to dispose of the property by selling the offshore company, while the buyer might be unwilling to assume the inherent risks of buying an offshore company, together with the ongoing administrative costs involved.

As is evident, the current ownership structure of a property (i.e. the "seller") can be a defining factor influencing a purchase decision. If a seller demands a particular method of transfer as a condition of sale, and the seller is not in agreement, the answer to the question "who is the seller?" can in fact become a deal breaker. For this reason, details of the current property ownership structure should be considered part of the initial research. It is also necessary to find out the seller's preferred method of transferring the property, and whether the seller is flexible. These issues should certainly be considered prior to making offers or paying a deposit. Professional legal and tax advice should also be taken at a suitably early stage to determine which method of transfer and ownership structure is in your best interests.

The second question, "what is the reason for sale?" is also useful information because the seller's motives and circumstances could have a bearing on purchase price negotiations (or the manner in which the purchase price is paid). For example, if the seller is leaving Thailand and needs money urgently, he might be willing to accept a lower price. Likewise, if a divorce is involved, a lower price might be considered for quick settlement (subject of course to due diligence). On the other hand, if the seller is wealthy, making a "low-ball" offer will be a waste of time. Alternatively, if the seller is an investor whose most important objective is to confirm a deal at the current price, it might be possible to pay an initial deposit, with payment of the balance spread over an extended period of time.

It should be noted that if the *real* reason for selling is that the seller has just discovered major renovations are needed, or the foundations are faulty and the property is in danger of imminent collapse, you might not get a truthful answer about the reason for sale! For this reason, engaging a structural engineer to conduct a survey prior to purchase is prudent, which is the subject of the next chapter.

Summary

- Details of the current property ownership structure should be considered part of the initial research.
- The current ownership structure influences the manner in which the property is transferred, the buyer's choice of ownership structure, the manner in which the purchase price is paid, and the transaction fees and taxes payable.
- The reason for sale is useful information because the seller's motives and circumstances could have a bearing on price negotiations.

34
Surveys and Structural Engineers

As mentioned in chapter 26, the main advantage of buying a completed property is that the property *exists,* in contrast to purchasing property "off-plan", which is the contractual promise of a property. The main risk associated with completed properties – apart from issues related to land title and access – is structural soundness, i.e. that the property might have structural issues and require major renovations. This is where a professional survey is indispensable. Indeed, it is only logical that a buyer should want to learn as much as possible about the condition of a property and any need for major repairs *before* a purchase decision is made.

Buyers need to understand that just as there are wide differences in professionalism and the workmanship provided by different construction companies, there is consequently a wide range of different properties in terms of build quality. This is particularly the case in Thailand's resort areas where many properties are built on steeply sloping hillsides or beachfront land.

Most buyers believe that if a property has major structural damage, it is easy to spot. It is true that the most obvious evidence of an unsound property is (non-cosmetic) cracks appearing in walls and floors, or water damage to paintwork, and both should be visible during a property viewing (unless the property has been recently repainted). However, some structural problems are not as easily visible, and the fact remains that most buyers are not trained, experienced home inspectors or structural engineers.

To protect their investment, most property buyers rely on a combination of a walk-through visual inspection and an indemnity clause in the sales contract. In such cases, an indemnity is legal terminology whereby the seller guarantees that the property is sold in good structural condition and if structural damage is later discovered that the seller was aware of but failed to disclose, the seller agrees to indemnify the buyer for the cost of repairs or losses suffered as a consequence. Indemnity clauses have their usefulness but buyers should recognise that they are *reactive* in nature. In other words, they address the issue of structural damage *after the fact,* and their successful enforcement requires legal action. The burden of proof also rests on the buyer to prove the seller was aware of the structural damage and failed to disclose this information.

As mentioned, having to enforce your rights in court is *reactive* in nature; it is far better to be *proactive* in relation to the structural soundness of your property. Surely it is better to be aware of any structural issues *before* you buy an asset or start to negotiate the purchase price?

Important tip: A visual inspection by the average property purchaser or a contractual indemnity clause should not be considered substitutes for a professional home inspection survey. It is important that a survey takes place as part of the due diligence process *before* signing contracts. This is the only way to provide peace of mind and to *proactively* secure the long-term value of the property.

In theory, surveys should be conducted when buying re-sale properties *and* new properties; being new is no guarantee of structural soundness, particularly in Thailand's resort areas. With the various levels of professionalism of property developers, new properties can also be unsound if structures or drainage systems have not been properly designed; it is just harder to spot. In fact, during recent heavy rain, a brand new beachfront hotel collapsed. There were also reports of a new luxury villa collapsing at one of the world's most famous branded resorts. In the case of new properties, without a technical survey you are in effect relying on a builder's or property developer's "structural guarantee" (which in the case of cash-strapped builders or underfunded property developers is not worth the paper it is written on).

The role of a survey is to assess the physical condition and structural soundness of a property by means of a thorough professional examination of the physical structure and major mechanical systems. This generally includes a professional inspection of the foundation and structural components, such as retaining walls, drainage systems, roofing and swimming pools, together with plumbing, electrical and air-conditioning systems. To properly perform the survey, a property surveyor therefore needs to be familiar with all the elements of home construction, materials and systems, how they all function together and what leads them to fail.

Property surveys are a standard part of the process of buying property in more developed property markets, largely due to the need of banks and financial institutions to assure the value of the properties serving as collateral for loans. In Europe and the United States, there is an entire profession of chartered surveyors providing the formal certification of properties. In Thailand, in the absence of an equivalent profession or recognised professional body, a wide range of professionals can be engaged to inspect properties, ranging from general contractors to architects. However, property buyers should confine themselves to experienced structural engineers or reputable property inspection companies.

A property survey generally requires between three to five hours to perform, depending on the size of the property and complexity of any problems. After the survey, a detailed inspection report should be provided, describing the main components of the property and identifying existing or potential problems with the use of photographs. Such reports should also recommend any necessary remedial work.

Once structural problems have been identified, a potential purchaser has two options: to walk away from the deal or to use the report as a basis to continue negotiations. In the case of walking away from a purchase, it is important that any deposit or reservation fee paid to secure the property is refundable "subject to satisfactory due diligence findings and the satisfactory findings of a property survey" (see chapter 89).

> **Important tip:** In the case where, despite the identification of problems, a buyer wishes to proceed with the purchase but on more favourable terms, the recommendations provided in the inspection report can be used as a basis for a construction company to quote for the remedial work. Then both the report and the quotation provide the formal basis to renegotiate the purchase price. Alternatively, the seller can be requested to carry out the necessary repairs (under the supervision of a structural engineer) prior to purchase, and this can be made a condition of the contract.

While a property survey adds to transaction costs, from a strategic point of view the inspection will be worth its cost many times over if a major problem is identified and you are able to negotiate a discount with the seller to cover the cost of structural repairs, or if you pull out of a bad deal based on the findings of the survey instead of becoming the proud owner of a structurally unsound property!

Summary

- Apart from issues related to land title and access, the main risk associated with completed properties is structural soundness, i.e. that the property might have structural issues and require major renovations.

- While some structural problems are easy to spot, many are not easily visible, and the fact remains that most property buyers are not trained home inspectors or structural engineers.

- Enforcing contractual indemnity clauses is *reactive* in nature, while structural guarantees are often not worth the paper they are written on.

- It is better to be *proactive* in relation to the structural soundness of a property by being aware of any structural issues *before* making a purchase decision; this is where a professional survey is indispensible.

- If structural problems are identified, a potential purchaser is presented with two options: to walk away from a deal or to use the report as a basis to continue negotiations.

35
Comparing properties
(Essential)

If you are buying a property for your own residential use and fall in love with that "must have" property, comparisons with other properties are largely irrelevant. In most other cases, comparing properties on a more formal basis helps buyers and investors to determine which one offers the best value.

Price per square metre

A good starting point is to compare properties using the ratio of price to size. The most common calculation is "price per square metre" (PSM), which tells you how much property you are getting for your money. The price per square metre ratio is calculated simply by dividing the asking price of the property by its size in square metres.

In relation to property *size*, the most common measurement is Net Floor Area (NFA) or Net Accommodation Area (NAA), which is the floor area of the property excluding common areas (shared landings, stairs, corridors and balconies). These details are normally indicated in the sales literature or they can be calculated from floor plans. To provide an example, if a property has an asking price is 15 million Baht (US$ 500,000) and the Net Floor Area is 160 square metres, the price per square metre is 93,750 Baht (US$ 3,125).

15,000,000 / 160 = 93,750

If a similar property is on the market for 16.5 million Baht (US$ 550,000) with a Net Floor Area of 190 square metres, the price works out to be better overall value at 86,840 Baht (US$ 2,895) per square metre.

16,500,000 / 190 = 86,840

When calculating price to size ratios, the general rule to bear in mind is that the smaller the property, the higher the price per square metre; and the larger the property, the lower the price per square metre (all other things being equal). Price per square metre allows a quick comparison between properties of different prices and sizes. It is an ideal measure for apartments, condominiums, townhouses and penthouses, where gardens and swimming pool areas tend to be part of the *common areas* rather than part of the private unit you are purchasing.

It should be noted that when comparing land and villas, Net Floor Area should include salas and balconies, but not swimming pools or garden areas. Due to the nature of tropical homes and the "outdoor living" design concept, floor areas are often calculated including these "outdoor living areas" (it is also a tactic used by property developers to make properties appear larger for advertising purposes).

Thus, while price per square metre calculations provide a useful comparison for built-up floor areas, they don't take into account the overall size of land or garden. Therefore, when comparing land and villas, it is also helpful to compare plot sizes.

Yield

Another measure used to compare potential property investments is "yield", which is the estimated annual rental income expressed as a percentage of the asking price (or purchase price). The formula[73] for calculating yields is:

Yield = (Annual Rental Income / Purchase Price) x 100

To provide an example, suppose the asking price of a villa is US$ 750,000 and the villa is rented out for an average of 150 nights per year at the rate of US$ 300 per night. This means total annual rental income is 150 x 300 = US$ 45,000, and the estimated yield is as follows:

Yield = (45,000 / 750,000) x 100 = 6%

The yield can also be worked backwards in order to estimate a "fair value" for a property or to compare the purchase price of properties based on rental expectations. Based on research or the advice of a trusted property agent, it is first necessary to estimate the average yield for the area in which the property is located, then a purchase price can be estimated that reflects the property's earning capacity using this formula:

Purchase Price = (Annual Rental Income / Rental Yield) x 100

Using the numbers from the previous example:

Purchase Price = (45,000 / 6) x 100 = 750,000

(On a calculator, it can also be computed as: Purchase Price = 45,000 / 6%)

---

[73] This is the calculation for *gross* yield as opposed to *net* yield, which takes into account costs, expenses and taxes. For a more detailed explanation of yields, refer to chapter 10.

For instance, if the average yield for the area is 6% and the asking price for the property is US$ 800,000, the calculation would indicate the property is "overvalued".

Price per square metre and yields are useful ratios for investors concerned with investment returns. However, for property purchasers with different priorities, such ratios might be useful, although there are many other factors that explain price differences or help to justify higher prices. These are discussed below.

Material specifications

An important factor influencing the price of a property is the specification of materials used for construction. Properties with imported marble tiles, Italian kitchens and high-end European bathroom accessories generally command a higher price per square metre than a property built with local materials or with accessories and appliances imported from China.

Age and condition

The age and condition of a property is another pertinent influence on price. New properties obviously command higher prices than comparable properties in the secondary market. In addition, it should be noted that properties often require renovations, repairs or repainting after several years, especially if subject to frequent rental use or exposed to tropical conditions.

Location and proximity

Location, or more specifically *proximity,* has a significant influence on price. Properties in locations that are considered to be "prime" are more sought after and in higher rental demand, both of which support higher values. The most obvious "proximity" is proximity to the beach; beachfront properties are limited in supply and in high demand. Proximity to nightlife, restaurants, schools, hospitals, supermarkets and golf courses also contribute in various degrees to price premiums. In addition, proximity to an airport (provided a property is not adjacent to the control tower or directly under the flight path) means shorter transfer times to a vacation property, which is of quantifiable economic value.

Valuations

When comparing properties, professional valuations or *appraisals* have a key role to play (although be careful about *who* the valuation company has been engaged by and for what purpose). Valuations have already been discussed in chapter 9, although it is worth repeating the three main methods of valuing properties here:

- The *cost approach* determines the value of a property by estimating the cost of the land together with the construction cost of replacing the building at current prices, less an allowance for physical depreciation. This basically gives you a "bricks and mortar" or "book value" calculation. The underlying principle is that the value of one property equals the replacement cost of another[74]. A market value can then be extrapolated from these figures by adding a profit margin of, for instance, 30% or 40%, depending on market conditions.

- The *income approach* is suitable for income producing properties, such as rental properties. The basic premise is that a property's ability to generate rental revenue determines its value, just like the valuation of a business. There are two possible sub-approaches: Direct Capitalisation, which uses only one year of net income for the calculation and which is suitable in stable market environments; and Discounted Cash Flow, which is the present value of net rental income to be realistically achieved over the life of the property, used where future income is expected to fluctuate.

- The *market approach* is perhaps the best and clearest analysis because it is concerned with comparing recent property transactions for similar properties in the same area. The premise is that a property's value is derived from the value of recently transacted property, which inherently reflects prevailing market sentiment.

Branding

If a property is within a resort managed by an internationally recognised hotel or management company, "branding" becomes a factor influencing the purchase price. For instance, a stand-alone villa might have an asking price of 20 million Baht (US$ 665,000), while a comparable villa within a branded resort could be priced at 30 million Baht (US$ 1M). What justifies such a price premium?

A brand is more than just a trademark used to differentiate a company from its competitors. In many respects it is a form of guarantee (depending, of course, on which brand!). Top brand names represent a certain level of quality

---

[74] The drawback with this approach is that if property prices decline, while construction material costs rise, the cost approach can sometimes provide a higher figure than what might be considered fair market value.

in workmanship and construction materials. It also represents a certain level of design excellence and uniqueness, together with a certain standard of management, maintenance, facilities and service. Indeed, the classic definition of a "branded" property is usually reserved for residences managed by top-end international hotel operators where hotel facilities on the same site are at the disposal of property owners.

Branded residences bring the tangible asset of professional property management and the high standards associated with an experienced and recognised hotel company (as opposed to an inexperienced developer attempting to learn the ropes). The quality and standards of property management reflect on the brand and, for this reason, the interests of both the brand and property owners are aligned, as opposed to a non-branded resort where the use of inexperienced, poorly trained property management is often a way to cut operating costs and increase short-term profit margins.

The brand and reputation of a recognised company also guarantees a level of marketability. A pre-existing level of brand awareness translates into a certain level of rental demand, which in turn often means the ability to guarantee a rental return on the property. It is at least partly the reason why branded properties tend to maintain or increase in value. Again, as a property purchaser, it is up to you to evaluate what the price premium represents and whether it makes financial sense for you.

Aesthetics

Resort properties are by definition *lifestyle* purchases; dream vacation homes rather than primary places of residence near to places of work. Therefore, the price component of aesthetics – visual attractiveness, design attributes, natural beauty, and the "Wow" factor – tends to be more exaggerated. It is hard to define the exact premium for a property designed by a top architect or the increase in price attributable to the sound of waves lapping the beach as you sleep; or the contribution made to a purchasing decision by a beautiful sunset or palm trees swaying peacefully in a cool sea breeze. But asking prices will somehow find a way to reflect these aesthetic attributes. Property agents will put a premium price on a property that reflects how the market might respond to such attributes. As a purchaser, it is up to you to decide the value of these aesthetic attributes, and whether the premium is justified.

The circumstances of the seller

It should be recalled from chapter 9 that asking prices of properties and the prices at which deals are concluded depend to a great extent on the individual financial circumstances of the seller[75]. While it is advantageous to evaluate properties using scientific methods or ratios to determine which properties offer the best value, we must also approach the market and understand it on a deal-by-deal basis.

When comparing properties, it is essential to conduct your own independent research and to get your own feel for prices in the area. Only then will you really understand if asking prices are undervalued, reasonably priced or inflated. Remember, asking prices, especially in the secondary market, are often just that – *asking* prices; in other words, prices that sellers are asking or *hoping* for. It is up to you to recognise what is a fair price and the onus is therefore on you, rather than the property agent, to find the sellers "bottom price".

Summary

Properties can be compared in many different ways, combining subjective opinions with scientific methods. When evaluating properties, potential purchasers should consider the following:

- Price per square metre
- Yield
- Material specifications
- Age and condition
- Location and proximity
- Valuations
- Branding
- Aesthetics
- Circumstances of the seller

---

[75] They should also contain an element that reflects the desirability or *marketability* of the current ownership structure (see chapter 102).

36
Taking over utilities and services

An issue that is often overlooked by property buyers is the transfer of ownership of utilities, services and management fees. Indeed, sometimes these matters are only brought to the new owner's attention when services are suspended.

Admittedly, taking over utilities and services it is not the most important issue on a buyer's mind; however, in Thailand, adding it to your checklist could save a great deal of inconvenience. For instance, if the electricity supply to your property is suspended for non-payment, sweltering indoors for a few days without air-conditioning can be an inconvenience; for a rental property, it can be a disaster.

Therefore, when ownership of a property is transferred, there are four issues to consider:

The first issue is to make sure the previous owner has paid all bills up to the date of handover. In the case where bills or management fees have been paid in advance, or payment has been made on a monthly or quarterly basis whereby the dates do not correspond with the handover date, it is often necessary to come to an agreement with the seller to settle any difference.

Second, it is necessary to go through the list of utilities and services (see chapter 31) and decide which services will be terminated and which ones will be taken over and transferred into your name (or into the name of a Thai company, depending on the asset holding structure). In the case of government utilities, such as electricity, it is often the case that the buyer and seller (or those granted power of attorney on their behalf) must attend the relevant department to transfer the account. This usually requires signed copies of passports or, in the case of a Thai company, updated company documents.

The third issue is to make sure any deposits for services that have been paid by the seller are taken into account (although the onus is usually on the seller to bring these to the buyer's attention).

The fourth issue is to make sure the correspondence address is changed with each service provider to ensure bills are received. For instance, management companies often send invoices by email so it is usually a matter of advising the management company of your email address, while government utilities generally require a postal address. It should be noted that government services tend to be suspended like clockwork if bills are not paid on time; in fact, suspension is perhaps the *most reliable* facet of their service!

> **Important tip:** With regard to the transfer of utilities and services upon purchase of a property, it should be noted that such transfers are generally *not* considered to be within the remit of conveyancing work done by law firms. Therefore, *do not assume* that the transfer of utilities will be handled on your behalf by your lawyer as part of the sale and purchase process; it is usually handled by the buyer and seller (or by agents with a power of attorney) at the time of handover (or shortly thereafter) when both are present to make the change.

I am familiar with one example where a villa had been purchased by a foreign buyer who *assumed* the electricity supply had been transferred at the same time as the transfer of the property. He continued to pay the electricity bill each month (which was delivered to his mailbox) and two years later, following significant renovations to the property, he planned to upgrade the current electricity supply from single-phase to three-phase. At the electricity office he found out he was powerless to do anything because the electricity meter and account were still in the name of the previous Thai owner. He anticipated the account transfer would be a simple task; in reality, it took several months to track down the previous owner and for the account to be transferred.

In practice, if the matter of transferring utilities and services is brought up during the sales process, the property agent can often liaise with the seller on your behalf and arrange for the accounts to be transferred. If documents are required from the seller, it is highly recommended that they are requested during the sales process, when the seller is focussed on the sale. During the sales process the necessary documents can be prepared, signed and stamped ready to submit immediately upon handover. If they are requested afterwards, when the seller has received payment of the purchase price in full and is off on holiday to celebrate, the process of transferring utilities and services could encounter all manner of delays, particularly if the seller needs to be present to sign documents (and has failed to arrange power of attorney).

In the case where a property is a stand-alone property, each utility and service provider generally requires individual attention. However, if a property is part of a managed development, the process of taking over utility bills is often simplified because bills are typically consolidated by the management company into a single invoice, which therefore just requires notification of the date of transfer and the new owner's details.

For services that don't require a formal account transfer or are contracted when needed, it is necessary to make sure the relevant contact details are received from the seller, which will save time searching for companies or contact details when you need them. This is often the case with truck water delivery companies, sewage disposal companies, insurance companies, pool and garden management companies. Finally, it is good practice to keep all the invoices and contact details for each utility or service provider together in one folder quick for reference and for ease of transfer on eventual sale of the property.

Summary

- When a property is purchased, it is necessary to go through the list of utilities and services and decide which services will be terminated and which ones will be taken over and transferred into your name.
- Any documents required from the seller should be prepared, signed and stamped during the sales process ready for submission immediately upon handover.
- It is necessary to check that the previous owner has paid all bills up to the date of transfer; any deposits for utilities or services paid by the seller should also be taken into account
- Ensure all correspondence addresses are changed to ensure bills are received.

STEP 4
Building your own property

37
Building your own property

People who decide to build their own properties generally fall into three categories: those who are unable to find a suitable property in the secondary or off-plan market; those who have always dreamed of building their own home; and investors intending to profit by building a property at land plus construction costs and selling at retail price. Regardless of the motive, building your own property in Thailand is not a decision to be taken lightly; if not approached in the correct manner or if the risks are not fully appreciated, it can soon turn into something distinctly less than the dream.

As noted in chapter 8, the *purpose* of investment should influence both what you build and where you build. If you are building a property as a permanent residence or as a place for retirement, you can build wherever you want, subject only to personal taste (and building regulations). However, if the purpose is wholly or partly for rental income, it is critical to build in a location where there is rental demand and consideration must be given to designing a property that meets the requirements of the rental market, especially in relation to the floor area and number of bedrooms.

There is also the question of whether to buy an existing property that can be renovated, or to build a property "from scratch", i.e. a new-build. One benefit of renovating an existing property is that utility supplies (water and electricity) are typically already in place. In addition, it might not be necessary to submit an application for a build permit (depending on the scale of renovations). Buying an existing property reduces the amount of construction required and therefore lowers both construction costs and the duration of build. However, if you are paying the market price for an existing property, it is often more cost effective to buy land and build a new property[76]. In addition, the issue of structural soundness must be considered; unless an existing property is thoroughly checked before purchase (see chapter 34), it could create problems later on. Buying an existing property to renovate might also restrict your creativity; it is certainly not the same as having a blank canvas to give expression to your wildest design visions.

When building your own property, there are a number of things to consider. Even to get to a point where you can start construction, it is necessary to have a general understanding of the topics covered in Step 2 in relation to buying land

---

[76] Unless you buy at a price that is below the "replacement cost".

for construction, such as land titles (chapter 14), ensuring access to the land (chapter 18) and arranging utilities (chapters 19 and 20). It is also necessary to be familiar with zoning and building regulations (chapter 21) and to ensure what you plan to build on the land is permissible. Subdivision (chapter 24) might also be a consideration.

Once you get to this point, there are still a multitude of issues ahead. These include working with architects, obtaining build permits, determining the most suitable management and organisation structure, getting quotations, choosing a construction company, considering build quality and specifications, variations, interior design and landscaping. Each of these topics is discussed in the following chapters.

Before committing yourself to the path of building a house in Thailand, it is crucial not to underestimate the scope of issues involved. Remember, it is not something you can start and stop later if you are not enjoying it! It is equally important not to approach such a challenge casually, which is almost a guarantee of failure or financial loss.

The task of building your own property needs to be approached methodically. Only if it is carefully planned and approached with full awareness of the issues and risks can you expect to get what you want, at a cost somewhere near your initial estimate, and actually enjoy the process! It is also necessary to prepare psychologically and emotionally. From the outset, especially if you are dealing directly with local builders, you must be prepared to deal with culture shock, absurd situations, the most elementary and childlike mistakes, and inevitable delays.

For those who dream of building a home, it can ultimately be a rewarding and enjoyable experience. For those building for investment, it can be financially rewarding. But lets not beat around the bush: get it wrong and it can be a source of frustration on an unimaginable scale. The unprepared will be elevated to levels of stress they didn't know existed! Suffice to say that building a property can be a rewarding experience, and buying a completed property is much easier!

So again, at risk of repetition, building your own property is not a decision to be lightly taken. However, if the decision has already been made, especially if this is your first time, the following chapters should be helpful.

38
The construction process

The purpose of this chapter is to identify the sequential steps involved in building your own property, which are as follows:

1. Determine management and organisational structure

2. Select architect

3. Design process: concept design, construction drawings and specifications

4. Involve specialist contractors at design stage

5. Obtain build permits and relevant licences

6. Engage project manager (PM)

7. Short list construction companies for tender

8. Put the project out for tender

9. Review and evaluate quotations

10. Select most suitable construction company for the job

11. Preparation of construction contracts

12. First payment or mobilisation fee

13. Commencement of construction work

14. Staged payments according to construction progress

15. Completion of property

16. Snag list

17. Arrange occupancy licence

18. Final payment to construction company (less retention)

19. Connection of services

20. Installation of furniture, curtains and blinds

21. Insure completed property

Identifying each separate step allows the steps to be followed in a logical and systematic manner. However, the precise order can be modified depending on the choice of management and organisational structure. For this reason, the choice of management and organisational (chapter 39) is the first step because it dictates the order of subsequent steps. This step is basically determines your level of involvement in the project, how construction will be supervised, whether a project manager is engaged and, if so, the potential range of services the project manager provides.

Step 2 is the selection of an architect, while steps 3 and 4 are the design stages, where concept designs for the property are developed, with input from the various specialist contractors. The contractors involved at this stage might include kitchen contractors, landscape designers, security companies, audio-visual and intelligent lighting companies. The reason for their involvement at this early stage is because their input influences the design and development of architectural plans.

Once plans for the property have been finalised, these then need to be submitted to obtain the appropriate building permits or licences (Step 5). Architects, project managers or construction companies should be able to assist with obtaining the necessary permits. While many proceed with construction before receiving a build permit – based on the assumption that it is a procedural formality – it is better to err on the side of caution and obtain the necessary permits before starting construction; construction should only start when the permit is in your hand, not based on promises by officials or contractors, no matter how imminent the issuance of a build permit might appear.

Step 6 is engaging a project manager or project management company (this step can be omitted if a project manager is not engaged). Depending on the level of involvement desired, it is possible to directly engage a construction company, and then engage a project manager to oversee their work; or engage a project manager to supervise the entire project from start to finish (including the work of the construction company).

> **Important note:** At which stage should a project manager be engaged? Some owners prefer to work with an architect to design and develop concept plans, and to meet project managers only after a full set of drawings is available; others select and appoint the construction company themselves, then engage a project manager to oversee their work. Owners preferring minimal involvement involve a project manager at the outset: experienced project managers can provide valuable design ideas and recommend suitable

> materials; supervise the architectural design phase[77]; oversee the tender stage and assist in the selection of a construction company; and then supervise the project to completion. (If a project management company is engaged at this stage, it will therefore become step 1 instead of step 6).

Steps 7 and 8 involve the short-listing of construction companies for the project, providing each with a full set of plans and specifications, and then handling the correspondence with each company to assist them to quote on the work. If a project manager is engaged, they will be able to assist by recommending construction companies and dealing with all the paperwork and correspondence associated with the tender stage.

Steps 9 and 10 include the evaluation of quotations and the selection of a construction company, while Step 11 involves entering into a contractual relationship with the construction company, usually through a construction agreement. The construction agreement should clarify to the greatest extent possible the expectations and respective obligations of both parties. It should therefore include all relevant documentation, such as land title documents, build permits, architectural and structural plans, material specifications, the bill of quantities (BOQ) and any quotation documents.

Construction typically commences within a defined number of days following the first payment or "mobilisation fee", (steps 12 and 13)[78]. After construction has commenced, it is important to ensure that subsequent payments are only made pursuant to the completion of certain stages of construction (step 14), as specified in the contract and verified by an architect, project manager or an independently engaged engineer.

At "completion" of the property (step 15) it is necessary to perform a snag list (step 16), which is a thorough check of a property to ensure everything is working properly and to identify defects that need to be rectified. The contract usually states a specific time limit for the performance of "snagging" by the customer and the rectification of defects by the construction company.

An occupancy licence otherwise referred to as a "blue book" is a document that provides the property with an official residential address (step 17), which is often arranged with the assistance of your lawyer, project manager or construction company.

---

[77] Some project management companies have in-house architectural services.
[78] It should be noted that many construction companies arrange a Buddhist blessing ceremony on the land before they start in order to drive out bad spirits and bring the project luck. Don't neglect or underestimate the important role of such beliefs in Thai culture.

The final payment to the construction company (step 18) is typically made on practical completion of the property, after rectification of the defects identified in the snag list. This payment should be less the amount of retention, which is the withholding of a specified percentage of the construction contract for a certain period of time to cover the cost of defects arising after completion.

Step 19 is the connection of services such as telephone, Internet or satellite TV, if these haven't already been arranged as part of the construction agreement.

Step 20 is the installation of furniture. Sometimes furniture and interior décor is within the remit of the project manager. If not, it is something that needs to be arranged separately. Due to potential sun damage, curtains and blinds should be installed at the same time, or immediately after the installation of furniture.

Finally, the property and its contents should be insured (Step 21) or, in the case of renovations, the insurance policy should be modified to reflect its new value as a completed, furnished property.

39
Management and organisational structure
(Essential)

The decision as to the most appropriate management and organisational structure is perhaps the most important decision you will make in relation to building your own property. While "management and organisational structure" might be a grand-sounding title, what we are really talking about is the issue of *supervision;* construction workers will be building your house and someone must supervise them. Without adequate supervision, quite simply, you will not get the quality of workmanship that you desire or expect; indeed, your property might not get finished at all.

There are many well-trained, competent and conscientious Thai workers. However, there are just as many (if not more) who lack any hint of conscientiousness; who take no pride in their work; and who will do the absolute minimum quality standard they are allowed to get away with. In addition, while in many other countries things are built with the intention of creating a long-lasting asset; in Thailand there is a general acceptance of "impermanence", where things are built almost as temporary structures without a view to the long-term; a mentality of *throw it together and if it doesn't work properly it can be fixed later* (by someone else!).

For these reasons, an unusually high degree of management supervision is required. While architectural drawings provide the design of a property, someone must ensure the work is carried out according to the drawings; while engineers provide detailed structural drawings and material specifications, someone must check that specifications are being adhered to; while the construction schedule details the order of work, someone must order materials on time and ensure workers keep to the schedule in order to ensure a timely completion. In other words, there must be supervision and leadership in relation to all aspects of construction; otherwise you will simply not get what you want.

These are not issues that can be checked periodically or at the end of the project; these are issues that require management and supervision on a daily basis. Concrete is poured and walls are built in a matter of hours. If something is built to the wrong specification or in the wrong place, someone must be there to check and correct it. Indeed, I have heard many developers and project managers comment in jest that "things are built in the morning and taken down in the afternoon!" For these reasons, supervision needs to be as close to "real-time" as possible.

Proactive management and supervision is especially important for things that are difficult to correct, such as concrete structures. Once concrete has set, the only way to change it is to break it up and start again. This is also true for many of the materials used; once they have been used, they cannot be re-used and must be replaced. Each mistake also has the potential to affect the completion date, especially if materials need to be re-ordered, which requires tasks to be postponed until they arrive.

Remember, if workers are left to their own devices and mistakes are made, they will not take responsibility for them; they will simply grin at you. Depending on the choice of management and organisational structure, any cost involved in rectifying work or replacing materials will either be at the construction company's expense, or it will be at your expense, in which case it adds to overall construction costs.

It is these factors that make the choice of management and organisational structure such a critical issue. Fundamentally, it is the quality and effectiveness of supervision that determines whether a project is completed according to the original design and intent; whether a property is built to a good quality standard; whether a project is finished within budget; and whether it is finished by the scheduled completion date. The key question, therefore, is who will be responsible for this level of supervision?

The purpose of this chapter is to outline the various *conceptual* alternatives for managing and supervising a construction project. It should be noted that the various alternatives differ significantly in terms of their demands on you and your time. Ultimately, the choice depends upon several considerations: your own construction experience; the time you have at your disposal and are willing to commit to the project; your Thai language skills; your ability to understand and deal with Thai culture; and your ability to cope with frustration and stress! Readers planning to build a property should consider these attributes carefully as the various management structures are discussed.

The alternatives presented start with the one that is least demanding of your time (i.e. more "hands-off") and progress through alternatives that demand increasing involvement and place increasing demands on your time (i.e. more "hands-on").

1. The Project Manager

The first management and organisation choice is to engage a professional project manager (PM). This could be an individual or a project management company[79]. The management and organisation structure will appear as follows:

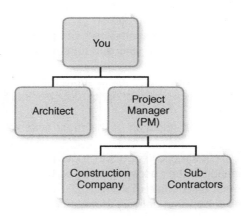

With this structure, concept plans, drawings and material specifications are worked out with the architect, with a pre-defined level of involvement of the project manager. In some cases, professional project management companies offer architectural design services, effectively making them a one-stop shop for your project.

Thereafter, the project manager is engaged to manage the project from beginning to end, taking the drawings and turning them into the reality of a property, including all aspects related to construction. The project manager will coordinate architects, engineers, general construction companies and any other trades or companies required for a project, such as mechanical and electrical engineers, landscape designers, kitchen contractors and interior design companies.

The project manager or project management team can assist you with a range of services, including design advice, the selection of materials, putting the project out for tender, selecting the most suitable construction company, and thereafter supervising construction to ensure engineering specifications, workmanship and material quality standards are maintained. Depending on the expertise and resources of a project manager or project management company, the following is a list of services that could potentially be provided:

---

[79] These are sometimes referred to as construction superintendents, project engineers or construction supervisors.

- Concept and design advice
- Architectural services
- Structural engineering, mechanical and electrical drawings
- Material selection
- Obtaining necessary build permits and licences
- Putting the job out to tender to various construction companies
- Review and evaluation of quotations
- Keeping an accurate documentary record of correspondence and reports with all contractors and sub-contractors throughout the project
- Help to establish budgets and make suggestions for reducing the scope of work or "value-engineering" to reduce or keep construction costs within budget
- Recommendation or selection of the most suitable construction company for the job
- Preparation of construction contracts, together with the discussion and co-ordination of their acceptance by both parties
- Putting together a schedule of work
- Ordering and scheduling delivery of materials
- Checking and testing materials
- Checking invoices and paying construction companies, sub-contractors and suppliers
- Overseeing and supervising construction
- Tracking project budgets and verifying stages of construction for staged payments
- Selection and engagement of sub-contractors such as landscape gardeners, interior designers and kitchen design contractors
- Maintaining an up-to-date central control system for architectural design and engineering drawings, and their distribution as required
- Discuss variations and arrange quotations for new work or changes to work
- Prepare a comprehensive interior and exterior snagging list upon completion and coordinate the rectification of faults
- Check guarantee and warranty documents
- Assist with purchase, delivery and installation of furniture

The range of services for which a project manager is engaged is entirely up to you. The key point is that your level of involvement can be minimised, which means this management and organisation structure is ideal for those who do not live in Thailand, or who have neither the time nor inclination or the necessary construction experience to manage a project themselves. Involvement could perhaps be limited to input on interior design, paint colours, kitchen design and the selection of appliances!

Prior to choosing a project manager, it is important to meet several different project management companies to compare their expertise, professionalism and the potential range of services. It is also important to choose a project manager that is familiar with high quality construction standards and has a track record of managing projects of the desired standard. In addition, as the project manager is often the sole point of contact for the remainder of the project, it is imperative to choose one with whom you can effectively communicate.

> **Important tip:** Construction guarantees (discussed in chapter 48) and liability are also important issues to consider. Construction companies normally provide structural guaranties and defects warranties on their work. However, it is also wise to ensure the project manager (or project management company) is contractually accountable for work that is being supervised, which requires relevant warranty clauses to be included in the project management agreement..

If the project management company presents you with their "standard project management agreement", it is important that this is checked by your lawyer, with particular regard to any exclusions of liability. I am familiar with cases where construction problems have been discovered where the project manager states the problem is the fault of the builder, while the builder blamed the project manager because the work had been performed according to the project manager's instructions. For this reason, the issues of responsibility and liability need to be addressed at the outset.

If a capable and experienced project manager is engaged, a project can generally proceed without your involvement, and you can relax in the knowledge the project is being professionally supervised. However, even with a capable project manager, it is still advisable to visit the site on a regular basis. There is a big difference between looking at an architects drawing and walking through a semi-built house; it is only when you are on site that you get a feel for the size and dimensions of a property and how it will be used. Being on site during construction is the best perspective from which to suggest design improvements. It is also far more cost-effective to make changes during construction than making changes at the later stages of completion (although the impact of "variations" must be considered, see chapter 45).

With regard to project management fees, these are calculated according to the scope of services and charged either at a monthly rate for the duration of the project, or a monthly rate plus a percentage of the build cost[80]. However, it

---

[80] Bonuses are sometimes agreed based on cost savings.

should be noted that while a project manager should streamline the construction of your property, the additional project management costs are easier to justify on larger properties or projects. In other words, a project manager's fees might be harder to justify on a project with a low build cost.

2. The Construction Company

The second organisational alternative has no project manager and involves directly engaging a construction company to build your property. In diagrammatic form, the management and organisation structure is as follows:

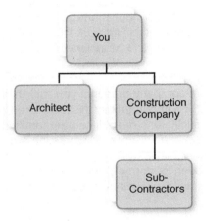

Conceptually, without a project manager, you must either supervise the work of the construction company yourself, or choose a highly professional construction company.

As the person overseeing the work of a construction company, you need to be able to read architectural and engineering drawings and be familiar enough with materials, construction methods and standards of workmanship to be able to spot errors and recognise the difference between good and bad workmanship. The level of communication with the construction manager must also be such that you are able to effectively communicate any changes or requirements. You must also have the time and commitment to be able to consistently supervise construction through to completion.

If you have neither the time nor inclination, or lack the qualifications, experience or familiarity with construction materials required to supervise construction work, you are effectively trusting the construction company to supervise its own work. Full responsibility is given to the construction company to carry out work according to the architectural drawings; to use the quality and grade of materials specified; and to complete the project on time and within budget. These are tall orders for a construction company in Thailand.

It must also be recognised that there is an inherent conflict of interest in having a construction company perform the work and at the same time supervise its own quality standards, without cutting corners. Construction companies often attempt to cut costs once a tender price has been agreed. Cutting costs can be done simply by changing the specification of "hidden" materials, such as the substitution of 16mm steel reinforcement bars with 12mm steel reinforcement bars. It can also be done by using visually equivalent but less durable materials or omitting materials entirely. For this reason, choosing a construction company with professional integrity becomes especially important (chapter 43 discusses the issue of choosing a construction company in more detail).

In summary, if you use the "construction company" management structure then either (a) there is no one supervising the construction company or (b) you become the de facto project manager or supervisor yourself, and if you do not have the time to visit the site on a regular basis, or your knowledge and construction experience is inadequate to oversee construction work, refer to (a)!

3. Managing Principal Contractors and Finishing Contractors

The third management and organisational structure recognises the distinction between structural work and finishing work, and contractors are separately engaged for each. In diagrammatic form it looks like this:

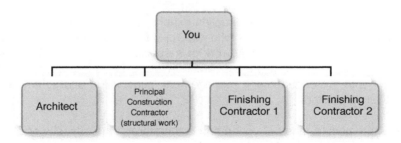

Thai construction companies have extensive experience building steel and concrete structures (foundations, superstructures and roof structures) and most are therefore relatively competent in structural work, provided a competent engineer has provided the correct specifications. In contrast, relatively few building companies are competent in finishing properties to "luxury western standards".

Due to the distinction between structural and finishing work, a commonly used approach by property developers (and individuals building their own properties) is to engage a primary contractor for structural work, and then separately engage specialist contractors for the various finishing works, such as plumbing, electrical, carpentry, tiling and painting.

As is evident, this approach requires a higher level of management and involvement because each contractor must be separately engaged and their respective work separately scheduled and supervised. Such a task should not be underestimated; indeed, many would consider it a challenge of a mentally and emotionally sadistic nature unless you are experienced in managing both construction sites and Thai workers. To be involved in the construction of your own property to this degree requires not only experience in construction methods and materials but also the ability manage and coordinate the work of various contractors and to communicate effectively with the workers. If you do not possess these qualities or attributes, it is strongly suggested that a professional construction company is engaged to oversee all construction work (see option 2 above) or, better still, engage a project manager (option 1).

In relation to guarantees and warranties, with this management structure it is also necessary to secure a separate guarantee from each contractor to cover their respective area of work. The potential downside is that if the work of one contractor detrimentally affects or influences the work of another, it is a challenge to make anyone ultimately responsible for guaranteeing anything!

4. Self Build

This "organisational structure" is included for the sake of thoroughness and is for people with sufficient construction experience or specialised knowledge of a particular trade (or trades) who plan to build all or part of the property themselves, subcontracting only work of a specialist nature. It is basically a full-time commitment to a project, which involves the ordering of materials together with the engagement, management, supervision and scheduling of specialist contractors.

This is the most "hands-on" option and is therefore at the opposite end of the spectrum to the "hands-off" approach of engaging a project management team. Diagrammatically it appears as follows:

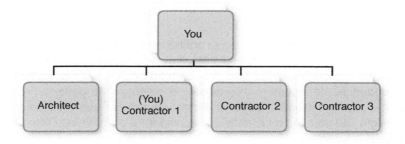

Building your own property is often chosen as a means to keep construction costs as low as possible or because being involved in the work is a passion in and of itself. However, it should be born in mind that potential cost savings are traded for an immense commitment of your time and labour, together with, inevitably, a degree of frustration and stress. To manage a construction project at this level necessitates the supervision of every detail, which usually requires a good command of the Thai language, an understanding of Thai culture and the ability to cooperate effectively with Thai workers.

Overview

As is apparent from the four above-mentioned alternatives for managing construction of your property, each differs greatly in terms of your time commitment and level of involvement. Without wishing to sound dramatic, choosing a management and supervision structure that is appropriate to your personal circumstances will define the success or failure of a project. In other words, if you are non-resident or do not have time to oversee work on site, hiring a project manager or project management team is the most suitable option. The only alternative is to find a highly competent construction company, which is not easy.

Similarly, if you have no construction knowledge or experience, a project manager is essential. Without a professional, independent party working to safeguard your interests, how can you know if the construction company you have engaged is following the plans or performing work to the required standard? Arriving to take possession of a newly completed property, how do you know if the structure has been correctly engineered?

In addition, if you have no Thai language ability or the patience and personal qualities required to deal directly with Thai construction managers or workers, it is recommended to engage a project manager or construction company managed by someone who speaks your language.

Generally speaking, the more involved you become in a project, i.e. the closer you move towards option 4, the more stress and frustration you are exposed to. This aspect of the decision should not be underestimated. If you choose an organisational structure that fits your personal characteristics and circumstances, building your own property can be a pleasurable experience. Choosing a structure that demands management experience, knowledge and patience you don't possess can lead to financial loss or elevate your stress levels to a point where you might find yourself reluctantly auditioning for a part in *One Flew Over the Cuckoos Nest Part II.*

Summary

The 4 fundamental organisation and management structures for building your own property are as follows:

- Engage a project manager or project management team that can assist you with a range of services and supervise a project from beginning to end.
- Directly engage a construction company to build your property, which means, unless you are qualified to supervise construction work, the construction company is effectively supervising itself.
- Engage various contractors for structural work and finishing work, which requires their respective work to be separately scheduled and supervised.
- Self-build, which is a full-time commitment to a project and involves building all or part of a property yourself, subcontracting only work of a specialist nature.

40
Working with architects

For most people, watching as your dream home takes shape at an architect's office is one of the most exciting aspects of building your own property. However, for some, the decision is not about which architect to use but rather *whether to use a professional architect at all*. For instance, while investors building multi-million dollar luxury homes usually seek the most competent and creative architects, those building modest properties on a tight budget often attempt to convey their ideas directly to a builder whose in-house "architect" will attempt to cobble together a functional abode.

Investors intending to build their own properties (on a budget) would do well to bear in mind that saving money on architectural fees has consequences: if you engage an average architect, you are likely to get an average looking property, whereas if you engage an innovative, experienced architect, you are more likely to get an innovative property. Fees charged by architects tend to be highly correlated with the quality and creativeness of their work; top architects command higher fees because their creativity and vision can literally transform an ordinary idea into a work of art. Further, by combining vision with the latest materials and the creative use of space, talented architects can dramatically increase the value of a finished home, justifying their fees many times over.

For instance, if your construction budget is 12 million Baht (US$ 400,000), an average architect could give you a home worth 15 million Baht (US$ 500,000) at market price; whereas a home designed by a top architect might command 18 million Baht (US$ 600,000), all other things remaining equal. In this sense, architecture could be considered the construction equivalent of alchemy! In addition, a well-designed property will maintain its value, while a poorly designed property or one that quickly goes out of style can assist price depreciation.

This chapter therefore proceeds on the basis that engaging a talented professional architect is a key stage of the property construction process. However, a word of advice: when dealing with an architectural firm, make sure the lead architect is personally involved in the work, rather than the work being farmed off to an office trainee after the initial meeting.

Professional architects offer a wide scope of services, which can generally be broken down into five stages[81].

The five stages are:

1. Concept design
2. Design development
3. Construction drawings and specifications
4. Bidding or tendering
5. Construction phase

Each of the stages is discussed below:

Stage 1: Concept Design

This stage comprises the initial brainstorming meeting where ideas – both practical and completely unrealistic – are shared with the architect. The architect assesses these ideas and presents his or her own ideas and recommendations. Through a process of evaluation and elimination, and with the assistance of doodles and sketches, the ultimate aim is the creation of concept design illustrations. The concept design stage often involves several meetings, culminating in a draft master plan with floor plans, sectional drawings, elevation drawings, and 3D renderings if requested.

Stage 2: Design Development

This stage is where the concept drawings from the previous stage are modified, developed and improved. It is also the stage where specialised contractors should be consulted and involved, such as structural engineers, mechanical and electrical (M&E) engineers, kitchen contractors, interior designers, security consultants, landscape designers, audio-visual and intelligent lighting contractors. Their input at this stage is important in order for their recommendations to be integrated into a coherent design. Basic material selections are also made at this stage. At the end of design development, a detailed set of drawings will be prepared and their compliance with local zoning laws and building regulations should be verified.

---

[81] After reading chapter 39, it will be noticed that some services offered by architects overlap with the services offered by project management companies. If you are planning to engage a project manager, it is therefore necessary to decide which company is responsible for each task in order to avoid duplication of work and fees.

Stage 3: Construction Drawings and Specifications

When all desired changes have been incorporated into the design development drawings, the next stage is concerned with producing detailed construction drawings and material specifications for final approval. Once approved, these drawings and documents can be used for the tendering stage. They include site master plans, floor plans, sections and elevations. These drawings differ from those created in the previous stage in that they are fully dimensioned, materials are often detailed on the plans and key areas are enlarged. Depending on the scope of work agreed with the architect, this stage might also include a range of 3D perspectives and presentation boards showing examples of the building materials, finishings and colours.

Stage 4: Bidding or Tendering

At this stage, construction companies are invited to tender for the project and quotations (usually accompanied by a bill of quantities or BOQ) are submitted and reviewed. The architect then works with the construction companies to answer any questions and to ensure any in-house drawings are in accordance with the overall design concept. At the end of the tendering stage, the construction company considered most suitable for the job is chosen.

Important tip: It pays to bear in mind the respective roles and responsibilities of architects and construction companies. It is the architect's job to visualise and conceptualise a design for your property, not to accurately estimate how much it will cost to build. Accurate build costs can only be determined by receiving formal quotations from construction companies. In other words, architects often get carried away with their creativity without consideration to the confines of your budget!

Stage 5: Construction Phase

At this stage it is usual for the appointed construction company (or project manager) to take over responsibility for construction work, together with the ordering of materials and administration related to the project. However, some larger architectural firms also offer project management services. At a minimum, architects should make periodic site visits during the construction stage to ensure work is proceeding in accordance with the overall design concept and objective.

Fees

There are typically separate architectural fees for each of the stages mentioned above. Total fees therefore depend on the number of stages the architect is engaged for; for instance, some stages, such as the tendering stage, might be overseen by the architect or by a project manager or you might prefer to manage this part of the process yourself.

Payment for architectural fees, at least for the first stage, is generally requested in advance. Thereafter, invoices are usually issued as work progresses through each stage; alternatively, you could be billed monthly according the percentage of work completed. If, during the design process, there are substantial changes in the size, complexity or scope of work involved, architects normally reserve the right to adjust fees correspondingly. Some architects also invoice you additionally for costs or expenses incurred, such as travel expenses, presentation materials, printing or delivery costs.

> **Important tip:** It should be noted that additional services – such as tasks outside the agreed scope of services or changes made to previously approved designs – are often billed at an hourly rate (or a lump sum). For this reason, it prudent to take time to check plans and drawings to ensure all required changes have been incorporated *before you approve the drawings.*

If you are working on a budget, one way to save architectural fees and still get an innovatively designed property would be to engage a talented architect for the initial creative stages, i.e. Concept Design and Design Development, then reach an agreement with a more "generic" architect (with lower fees) to produce construction drawings. Another option is to select a construction company with in-house architectural services and to arrange for the construction company to produce the more functional construction and mechanical system drawings (based on design development drawings provided by the "concept" architect)[82]. It is also a possibility to make the provision of detailed construction drawings a condition of awarding the project to a construction company and to ensure any associated fees are included in the tender price.

Marketing materials

If you are building a property in order to sell upon completion (or prior to completion), it is often useful to request presentation materials, such as 3D renderings, for marketing purposes and meetings with potential purchasers.

---

[82] Although refer to the comments in point 1 of Chapter 41 on Build Quality.

A limited number of renderings are often included as part of the architectural design package, although this should be confirmed in advance. A set fee is generally charged for each (additional) perspective. Due to the specialised nature of the work involved, such fees can be relatively high when compared to architectural fees.

In addition to architectural firms, there are other companies that specialise in the generation of three-dimensional (3D) renderings or perspectives, based on drawings supplied by the architect (usually AutoCAD). Indeed, talented modellers can create 3D perspectives that are so lifelike it is difficult to tell them apart from a photograph of a property.

It is worthwhile mentioning that if you are planning to use materials supplied by an architect for promotional or commercial purposes, make sure permission to use the materials is granted in the contract. This is because commercial use of materials is often excluded, with files and perspectives remaining under proprietary ownership of the architect.

Computerised 3D modelling is another useful sales tool. It is difficult to get a feel of size and scale purely from two-dimensional drawings, whereas 3D computer modelling software allows you to view the architectural design of a property in three-dimensional form, allowing it to be rotated and viewed from all angles. More advanced software allows potential buyers to take a "walk through tour" of the "fully furnished property" as though it were already built. 3D computerised modelling can also be an indispensible tool in the process of designing your property. Indeed, architects often use 3D presentation materials in client meetings during the design process.

Architects generally use CADD (Computer Assisted Design and Drafting) software, such as AutoCAD, which is professional software widely used in the industry[83], while another more "consumer friendly" software is Google SketchUp[84]. If you want to use these three-dimensional electronic files for commercial purposes, permission usually needs to be obtained.

---

[83] With the sophistication of computer software, scale models are generally only used by property developers.
[84] http://sketchup.google.com/

Summary

- Architectural services can generally be broken down into five stages:
  - Concept design
  - Design development
  - Construction drawings and specifications
  - Bidding or tendering
  - Construction phase
- Total architectural fees depend upon the number of separate stages an architect is engaged for.
- It might be possible to save on architectural fees by engaging a talented architect for the initial creative stages, and then to reach an agreement with a more "generic" architect to produce construction drawings.
- If you plan to sell the property prior to completion, marketing materials should be considered in advance.

41
Build Quality

Good quality construction is one of the most fundamental factors underpinning the long-term asset value of your property. It also plays a crucial role in the avoidance of structural problems and ongoing repairs. While a poorly constructed property will show premature signs of ageing and can quickly and significantly depreciate in value, a well-built property is an enduring asset.

Construction quality is a function of three primary components:

1. The quality of architectural, structural and engineering drawings
2. The quality and specification of materials
3. The quality of workmanship and on-site supervision

Each of these components needs to be carefully managed throughout the construction process and is discussed separately below:

1. The quality of architectural, structural and engineering drawings

It is only by working with competent architects and engineers that you can achieve good quality architectural, structural and engineering drawings.

As discussed in the previous chapter, drawings pass through several stages until final construction drawings are prepared. If you have engaged a competent architect to provide a full set of drawings for your project – from concept design drawings to structural and engineering drawings – there is a greater probability that the drawings will be correctly specified because the architect is working independently and the architect's services are fee based rather than construction-related; in cases where a construction company's in-house architect produces structural drawings, the temptation exists for corners to be cut on material specifications because, once a contract price has been agreed, any reduction in materials or specifications means a wider profit margin for the construction company.

For instance, the main materials used for structural work are concrete and steel bars. If engineering specifications are modified to reduce the weight of steel used in foundations, columns and beams, it can produce significant savings. This would be impossible to spot unless you are a qualified engineer or an experienced project manager has been engaged to supervise construction.

While *professional* construction companies do not cut corners, less professional companies might be tempted. For this reason, in cases where a construction company produces construction drawings, it is worthwhile having them reviewed by an independent architect or engineer. It is also important that a qualified engineer signs off the drawings and a copy is kept for your records. This is useful documentation related to structural guarantees and warranties.

2. The quality and specification of materials

The second issue influencing the overall quality of construction is the choice of materials. Simply stated, it is possible to use cheap, low quality materials or durable, expensive materials (while expensive materials are not always the most suitable or durable, price is often an indication of quality). For instance, floor and wall tiles can cost 300 Baht (US$ 10) per square metre or 3,000 Baht (US$ 100) per square metre. Rain shower systems can be purchased for 8,000 Baht (US$ 265) or 30,000 Baht (US$ 1,000). The difference is usually a combination of material quality and the location of manufacture; products might be manufactured locally in Thailand or imported from Europe or China.

Advice should therefore be taken from architects, project managers and construction companies in relation to the selection of materials. The advice of interior designers might also be helpful, especially for finishing materials. It should be noted that construction companies are not always the best decision makers in relation to the choice of materials; indeed, materials that are obviously of poor quality to an architect or project manager might not be obvious to those directly involved with the construction of your property. The inverse is also sometimes true: architects might specify materials (for aesthetic reasons) that the construction company knows are unsuitable for the purpose, based on practical experience. With key materials it is often best to discuss the choices with all the parties involved and to evaluate opinions from the various perspectives.

The key point to consider is that if your budget allows, try to avoid using the very cheapest materials; not only do they tend to look cheaper, they also tend to fail earlier, which increases maintenance costs and leads to premature ageing of the property. Indeed, potential buyers often form their impression of a whole property from the poor choice or failure of one material. All other things being equal, properties of a higher quality construction standard should command a higher purchase price; whereas properties built to low quality standards generally command a lower price. The relationship is unambiguous.

> **Important tip:** If you are working to a budget, a sensible balance needs to be struck between design, quality and cost. However, it is important to recognise that quality standards and specifications should remain *consistent* throughout the property; i.e. the use of expensive, high quality materials in one part of a property will be denigrated by the obvious use of cheaper materials elsewhere.

It is also worth bearing in mind those areas of a house that are most important from the perspective of function and potential re-sale (see chapter 53, "What sells?").

3. The quality of workmanship and on-site supervision

The third issue is that of implementation: taking architectural drawings and material specifications and turning them into a property. This is where choosing the right construction company for the job (chapter 43) and ensuring proper supervision of the work is of crucial importance (chapter 39); it has already been noted that vastly different levels of workmanship exist between different construction companies, between different groups of workers within the same construction company, and between different individuals within a work group.

Fundamentally, the most important decision is to choose a construction company with experience in the construction of *luxury properties built to western standards,* especially in relation to finishing works, such as plumbing, electrical work, carpentry, tiling and painting.

Summary

- Good quality construction is one of the most fundamental factors underpinning the long-term asset value of your property.
- Construction quality is a function of three primary components:
  - The quality of architectural, structural and engineering drawings
  - The quality and specification of materials
  - The quality of workmanship and on-site supervision
- Each of these components needs to be carefully managed throughout the construction process.

42
Surveying land

Before any construction begins, it is good practice to have the land surveyed.

For the purposes of general residential construction, there are three basic types of survey – land survey, topographical survey and soil survey – each of which provides different information about the land.

Land survey

A land survey is a rudimentary survey, which establishes the precise boundaries of the land or subdivision. Land surveys are useful in that they enable the location of planned buildings to be confirmed in relation to land boundaries. If land has Chanote title, the location of the concrete pegs will be checked.

The purpose of such a survey is to basically check that you are building in the right place; that structures will not encroach on neighbouring land; and to ensure that construction adheres to local building regulations. If there are any discrepancies between the drawings and the actual land boundaries, it is better to find out before construction begins rather than after; if a property has been built in the wrong place and the mistake is discovered later, few builders are going to say "terribly sorry, let us take it down and build it again in the right place at our own expense!"

Arranging a basic survey should be standard procedure for any construction company worth their salt. I am familiar with a recent example where a construction company started building for their client and when a survey was later conducted at the client's request (who was doubtful of the measurements), it was discovered that the building was in the wrong place and in breach of building regulations. The work had to be dismantled and started again.

In concept, an architect is engaged to design a property and a construction company is engaged to build it. However, *ultimate* responsibility for making sure the buildings are in the right place is yours; you will be the owner of the property when it is complete and the builder is unlikely to take responsibility for mistakes. For this reason, you should insist that a professional land survey is undertaken prior to construction. In addition, the construction agreement should contain detailed provisions to ensure the construction company is contractually responsible both for conducting a survey and for ensuring the property is in compliance with building regulations.

Topographical survey

The next level of survey is a topographical or contour survey. This is a more detailed survey that accurately plots the features and three-dimensional surface shape or "contours" of the land. Topographical surveys are performed by surveyors who walk across the land and take readings at different points using optical survey instruments (theodolites). The readings and measurements are then presented either as contour lines on a site plan or as a three-dimensional map or model.

Topographical surveys are useful because identifying the gradient and shape of the land allows the foundations and super structure of a property to be appropriately engineered. Architects can design a beautiful home but it is a contour survey that fits the design to the precise contours of the land.

The level of detail required of a topographical land survey depends on the particular land plot and the architectural design. This might range from a boundary and level survey, which provides the basic "lie-of-the land"[85], to a fully detailed topographical survey that plots contours at half-meter intervals and includes all significant aboveground features. A contour survey should be considered essential for hillside land because gradients substantially influence the cost of foundations and structures. However, a contour survey performed on less obviously or dramatically sloping land is also advantageous; land gradients can be difficult to estimate by visual inspection alone. For example, during a visual inspection of a small land plot, the gentle gradient was assumed to amount to no more than two metres from top to bottom. After precise measurement, it was found to be more than five metres; enough to require alterations to garden levels and architectural plans.

To provide another example, architectural plans for a hillside house were completed without a topographical survey. After a detailed topographical survey was conducted at the request of the construction company, the height difference between the drawings and the actual land contours was significant enough to require an additional storey in the concrete substructure, which translated into an additional one million Baht (US$ 33,000) in build costs. If a topographical survey is conducted at the outset, such costs become a subject for discussion with the architect and construction company; however, if conducted after a construction agreement has been signed (or after construction work has commenced), it usually becomes a source of disagreement and a significant variation.

---

[85] Often used for initial feasibility studies

Soil survey

A third level of survey is a soil survey, which is the process of taking soil samples and mapping soil types and depths over a given area. This information is then used to design foundations and substructures suitable to the soil type. In Thailand, particularly on hillsides or areas strewn with boulders, one of the most important tasks is to identify the location, type and depth of rock substrata. If rock is found on a site, the question arises whether to remove it or build foundations on top. Sometimes, it is possible to incorporate rock formations into the architectural design of a property[86]. The discovery of rock formations on a site often requires the re-engineering of foundations.

Summary

- *Land surveys* establish the precise boundaries of the land.
- *Topographical surveys* accurately plot the three-dimensional shape or "contours" of the land.
- *Soil sampling* maps soil types and depths in order to assist the design of foundations and substructures.
- The more detail and information that can be ascertained through various land surveys, the better equipped the architect and construction company are to design and build a property.
- Detailed survey information also allows more accurate cost estimates for excavations and structural work.

---

[86] Large rocks can also be "shaped" through the use of expanding mortar, which is inserted into drilled holes.

43
Choosing a construction company
(Essential)

Once the choice of management and organisational structure has been made (chapter 39) and architectural drawings have been confirmed, it is time to shortlist construction companies for the tendering process and ultimately determine the most suitable construction company for the project. The purpose of this chapter is to outline the criteria for selecting a construction company. Before proceeding with the discussion, however, four things should be kept in mind during the selection process:

First, the construction company plays a primary role in the quality of your finished property.

Second, once engaged, you will be working with the construction company for many months (typically 4 months or more for a renovation and usually in excess of 12 months for a new-build) and the chosen construction company will be largely responsible for the level of stress you experience during this period!

Third, clients and builders have different perspectives and expectations of a project, particularly in relation to costs, and these different perspectives need to be understood at the outset. A builder understands his role in the following way: the client provides money and the builder provides the service (combining materials and labour) of building a property. Thus, if construction takes longer than anticipated or costs are higher than expected, the builder will attempt to recover the money through variations or cost savings. A client, on the other hand, generally sees the builder as agreeing to build a property for a certain price; therefore, if it ends up taking longer or costing more, this is largely irrelevant because both the scope of work and the price have already been contractually agreed, and it is the builders job to perform according to the contract. In other words, while the client sees costs as fixed (notwithstanding legitimate variations), construction companies typically see cost as a moving target (or ever-increasing budget). The client must therefore flesh out as much detail as possible about the job in advance, making sure there are no "information gaps" that a construction company could later take advantage of to increase the contract price.

Fourth, when you sign construction contracts in countries with developed, transparent legal systems, and a construction company fails to perform its obligations, there is recourse through the legal system. In other words, the threat of legal recourse hangs over the construction company during the performance of the contract and the construction company is keenly aware of its obligations, together with the consequences of failing to meet them. In Thailand, with its opaque legal system, when you engage a construction company, you are effectively putting your (financial) fate in their hands. In the event that a construction company fails to meet its obligations, the only alternative is a protracted legal battle with an uncertain outcome; a process that clients generally avoid at all costs. Construction companies understand this and operate accordingly; the threat of legal consequences is too remote to bear on performance.

In addition to these four points, and for those unfamiliar with building in Thailand, a general misunderstanding should be cleared up, i.e. the misunderstanding between what constitutes a good building company and a bad building company. Many believe that when you engage a good builder you get what you want, and when you engage a bad builder you get what you want but the process is not as smooth; the quality standard is lower than expected and things take longer than anticipated. Let me help to dispel this misunderstanding: with a good builder (and a bit of luck), you get what you want, on time, plus you get to enjoy the process. With a bad builder, work often stops half-way, leaving you with a choice of financial loss or legal action; in the case where the builder does complete the work, it costs significantly more than budgeted, it takes a year more than expected, quality is substandard, and the process is such a nightmare that you no longer have any desire to live in the property upon completion. I hope that helps to clarify things!

It should now be evident, choosing the right construction company is an issue of fundamental importance both to your finances and your mental health! It is easy to find construction companies through advertisements in local property magazines, through Internet searches or through the recommendations of architects and project managers. The most important step is to sort the good from the bad and invite only the most suitable to tender for the work.

With regard to the number of companies invited to tender, one or two tenders is unlikely to yield best results. If the property is a modest sized villa, tenders from the three most suitable construction companies should be sufficient; due to the time and resources required to prepare and submit a detailed quotation, it would not be justifiable to put the job out to five, six or ten construction companies. However, if the property is a high-end luxury villa, inviting more companies to tender would be justified and it would be wise to seek the advice of an architect or project manager during the process.

It is also worth mentioning that the tender process is not just about getting alternative prices for the construction of a property; it is also an excellent means to get to know more about the different construction companies, i.e. how they operate, how their responses are organised and how well they communicate.

In addition to prices, construction companies should be assessed against a number of criteria before they are shortlisted or selected for the job. The 8 most important criteria are listed below and then discussed in more detail:

1. Financial Stability (Solvency)

2. Quality of Workmanship

3. Internal Organsiation

4. Communication

5.Service

6. Experience

7. Size

8. Integrity

1. Financial Stability (solvency)

Confirming the solvency and financial health of a construction company is the number one concern. It is not hard to understand that the bankruptcy of a construction company during construction has a less than positive influence on your property. But what *precisely* are the consequences? Rather than experiencing them firsthand, it is instead preferable to consider the consequences and guard against them. Here are five potential consequences:

First, any money paid to the construction company is usually gone and is unlikely to be recovered. The question is, what did you get in return? If you have only paid a deposit or mobilisation fee to the construction company and the company becomes insolvent before construction commences, the deposit is usually lost (or written off) with nothing in return. While distressing, bankruptcy prior to commencement is often the "cleanest" outcome (depending on the size of the deposit), as we will see.

If bankruptcy occurs *during* construction, the question concerns the proportion of completed work relative to the percentage of the contract price paid. For this reason, it is important to avoid financially over-reaching by making sure payments are always made correspondingly to the progress of construction (see point 6 of chapter 50 on "Financial Considerations"). For example, if you have paid 60% of the value of the construction contract but construction progress is only at the 40% stage at the time of bankruptcy, regardless of any other consequences there is already a loss incurred equivalent to the shortfall[87].

Second, if you are not willing to write off the financial loss and wish to pursue legal action against the construction company, this will involve a potentially lengthy legal dispute (with an unknown outcome) and ongoing legal costs.

The third issue is a tricky one. Assuming the construction company's insolvency breaches and terminates the construction agreement, you must now find another construction company to take over and continue work on the project. This raises several issues. Construction companies are notoriously reluctant to take over the work of another construction company. When you find one that is willing to do it, it is necessary to go through the quotation process all over again, although with additional complications; the value of work already done must be assessed and the balance of work outstanding must be calculated. In addition, the new quotation will usually contain a premium due to the risk, uncertainty and reluctance of the new construction company to take over another's work. Guarantees will also be affected. For example, if the structure of the property has been completed by the first construction company prior to its bankruptcy, the new construction company will not guarantee the work of the previous one, which means the property will be without a structural guarantee; any structural guarantee you might have had will be with a bankrupt company and so is effectively worthless. The absence of a structural guarantee could prove to be a challenge to resale and insurance cover for the property might be affected.

Changing construction companies part way through construction is also time consuming. The fourth effect of bankruptcy, therefore, is usually a significant delay to the completion of your property. Cash flow forecasts will need to be revised, taking into account potential loss of rental revenue and exchange rate risk (see chapters 50 and 66).

---

[87] It is unusual for construction to get *ahead* of staged payments and for this reason it is unlikely to result in a net gain.

The fifth issue is security. A semi-finished property without workers on site is exposed to property damage and the theft of materials. In addition, if the original construction company became insolvent and was unable to pay workers' salaries, it is not uncommon for workers to return to the site and take things to recover what is owed. This means materials purchased and paid for according to the previous construction contract (and taken into account in the new quotation) can go missing, whether stored for use or even if already installed as part of your house! Specifically, we are referring to cases of vanishing air-conditioning units, roof tiles, appliances, even the removal of electrical wiring for its copper value.

By now, we should have a more accurate picture of the calamitous consequences of a construction company's insolvency. It is an experience to be avoided at all reasonable cost and underlines the importance of establishing a construction company's financial credentials prior to including the company in the tender process[88].

However, establishing a company's financial health is no easy task. In fact, short of full disclosure and a complete financial audit, it is an impossible task. Which public or private construction company is going to open their books unreservedly to a prospective client? It might be possible to request bank statements or financial records, although without a cash flow analysis and a full disclosure of financial obligations, they are meaningless. Thus, in the absence of a full audit and unequivocal financial statements, it is crucial to take a more practical approach in order to recognise the potential signs of poor financial health. Most people who engage a construction company to build their property mistakenly believe all will be well if staged payments are made on time, in accordance with the terms of the agreement. If the construction company promises to keep client accounts separate, how can things go wrong?

The answer is quite easily. A construction company's financial stability depends on the sum parts of all of its various contracts and obligations. Company management might promise to keep separate client bank accounts but if the company has several ongoing jobs, each on staged payments, and money is needed for materials on one job to reach the next payment stage, more often than not funds will be "borrowed" from another account to pay for the materials with the intention of paying them back later. But what happens if the client, for whatever reason, fails to make that next payment? Suddenly, the prospect of both jobs coming to a halt is a possibility. With regard to getting your house built on time (or at all), any question of illegality, breach of fiduciary duty or breach of contract is largely semantic once a construction company becomes insolvent.

---

[88] It might also be necessary to re-establish a company's solvency prior to signing contracts.

To gain an insight into the financial health of a company, it is therefore necessary to understand the scope and obligations of the company before committing your money. The alternative is simply hoping for the best, which is what most clients inadvertently do!

> **Important tip:** A key action to take is to visit the other sites that the construction company is currently operating to look for "tell-tale" signs. One glaringly obvious sign of a financially challenged construction company is a shortage of workers (or the total absence of workers) on site. If this is explained away by a public holiday or "the day after payday", visit the site on another day or various other days.

When a site is not active, it is generally due to one of four main reasons: either there is a land title issue or a legal dispute; the client has requested the project to be put on hold or is not keeping up with staged payments; the construction company is unable to procure labour or is waiting for delivery of materials; or the construction company is unable to meet its payment obligations for materials or salaries. It is your job to figure out which one of them is the *actual* cause.

It is sometimes the case that a financially challenged construction company is actively looking for new work in order to use the initial payments to bolster short-term finances and complete other jobs. Once they have caught up with work on other jobs, they often plan to use the proceeds to start the new project. For this reason, it pays to have a healthy dose of suspicion about companies when tender prices come in significantly below the quotations of other companies. It might be due to an innocent calculation mistake or due to items missing from the bill of quantities (an experienced architect or project manager will pick up such mistakes or omissions). However, less innocuously, a low quotation might have been submitted specifically for the purpose of securing a contract and bringing in a much-needed short-term cash injection into the company's depleted coffers (their ability to complete the job at that price is irrelevant).

These types of financial juggling acts are commonplace among the less professional, poorly financed or poorly managed construction companies. It is therefore crucial to be sensitive to the risks. It is also important to use common sense and trust your instincts. If you are investing your own money, you owe it to yourself to perform some basic checks and research. It is possible to make both formal and informal research. Thailand's resort areas are small, which means, among locals at least, everyone generally knows everyone else's business. It doesn't therefore take much effort to ask around for unofficial snippets of information in relation to a construction company. Some of the information garnered might be malicious or misinformed but if it is your money at stake it is your job to verify it. Sometimes, where there's smoke there's a smouldering fire (or an implosion waiting to happen!).

> **Important tip:** Don't work with construction companies that you suspect are in financial difficulties; otherwise they might well be using your hard-earned money in an attempt to solve them. This is true for small and large companies alike. Likewise, don't work with companies you have a "bad feeling" about; without meaning to sound like a witch, there is often a factual source for such vibes!

2. Quality of Workmanship

There are many different construction companies. Some are excellent; others average; some are below average. Some construction companies are suitable for Thai-style houses using local materials and construction methods, while others are capable of building luxury properties to top quality western standards. The question is, which construction companies are suitable for your project?

> **Important tip:** If you plan to build a Thai-style property with local materials, most builders will usually fit the bill. However, if you are planning to build a luxury villa to the top European quality standards, you must find a construction company that (a) recognises the quality standards involved, and (b) is capable of achieving such standards. *If not, the construction company will be learning on your job and you (or your project manager) will become the teacher!*

There is no better way to evaluate a construction company's suitability than to make site visits to a construction company's previously completed jobs, in addition to jobs that are currently in progress. There is no shortcut.

While on site, it is necessary to pay particular attention to the quality of finishing, particularly floor and wall finishing, tiling, bathroom fittings, and overall attention to detail. In addition, notice whether the site is tidy and well managed. I recently visited a site during the finishing stages of a project, which was being supervised by a very strict project manager who demanded that workers stop work at 5pm every day to clean up their workspace. The site was immaculate. In addition, once floor tiles had been laid, shoes were no longer permitted inside the house! However, not all sites are like this one; at the other extreme, I have seen sites that look like natural disaster zones, which is a clear reflection of management quality.

For each site or project, it is also important to confirm the actual role of the construction company. Are they the main contractor, or have they just been engaged for structural work, M&E or finishing work? Sometimes a construction company's sales manager will take you to one of "their" sites although it later transpires they were only responsible for foundations and structural work; not the crucial finishing work[89]. In addition, if the property you plan to build has special features or uses special materials, ascertain the construction company's experience with such features or materials (for example, Terrazzo floors, frameless glass balustrades, cantilevered balconies, spiral or central beam staircases, infinity pools with Jacuzzis or waterfall features). Most construction companies at a certain standard of professionalism will be able to adapt to any new materials and construction techniques, although it is reassuring to know a construction company's expertise in advance. In other words, it is much easier to work with a construction company that has already done what you want to do than with one that must reinvent the wheel!

3. Internal Organisation

It is important to gain an insight into a construction company's internal management and organisation. For instance, some building companies technically consist of only one person, who gets work done through engaging sub-contractors as they are required, while other companies employ staff "on the books", paying them monthly salaries. Then there are companies with the full gamut of resources, hundreds of workers and an organisational chart to match. It is imperative to understand a company's management structure and resources to determine the degree of control the company has over its workers *because a builder is only as good as its workers.*

The next question is how jobs are *supervised* internally. Is one gang of workers assigned to each job and left to their own devices, or is a project manager assigned to each job to oversee and supervise the workers? How often does the project manager visit the site: daily, twice a week or weekly?

A level of understanding related to a company's internal organisation and supervision is of considerable importance. As discussed in chapter 39, if the chosen management and organizational structure is to directly engage a construction company, there is an inherent conflict of interest in having a construction company perform the work and at the same time supervise its own quality standards. Someone *within* the construction company must therefore be responsible for that supervision; it is up to you to ascertain how each company manages its projects and how the required level of supervision is provided.

---

[89] This distinction is also made in chapter 39 concerning management and organizational structures (see alternative 3: Managing Principal Contractors and Finishing Contractors).

4. Communication

With the complexity of building a property and the multitude of ongoing changes and decisions that are typically made during the process, communication with the construction company is a key factor to consider. If you are unable to communicate effectively with the construction company, what hope is there that you will get what you want?

If you want your property to be a "hands-off" construction project (as discussed in chapter 39), then it is advisable to engage a professional project manager who speaks your language. If you are planning to directly engage a construction company, it is necessary to consider whether it is under Thai or foreign management; if you are unable to communicate effectively in Thai, it is necessary to find a construction company with management that speak your native language or a common language. In addition, when construction commences, there is usually a single point of contact through which all communication proceeds. It is important to confirm who this will be; more often than not, it is not the well-educated, straight-talking salesperson with whom you have been working with up to the point of signing the contract!

However, communication is not just about language; there must also be some level of *cultural* understanding. This is an important distinction. Cross-cultural communication is fraught with misunderstanding; instances where the same words are used but understood in completely different ways, if at all. Most misunderstandings in construction are related to quality standards. For example, quality standards to an American property investor who is staying at the Four Seasons will be vastly different to those of a Thai project manager who lives in a home with a tin roof. The level of communication required for the successful completion of your dream property transcends language and understanding; it also concerns cultural context and this needs to be born in mind at all times.

5. Service

Building dream homes, particularly at the finishing and furnishing stages, is a highly subjective process, and ideally one that requires a service-oriented approach from a construction company. Architectural designs and drawings might look great on paper, although when construction starts there are invariably design or material changes you will want to make. The process of making changes is facilitated if the construction company's management team has time to spend with you to discuss alterations and to answer questions as work progresses.

During initial meetings, therefore, prospective construction companies should be evaluated with regard to whether they are receptive, responsive and likely to provide the desired level of service. An opinion needs to be formulated in advance because the level of service provided by a construction company will make the difference between getting a property you are happy with and one you are forced to settle with.

One of the best ways to ascertain whether a construction company is service-oriented is to speak with its previous clients; a company with nothing to hide should not hesitate to put you in contact with its previous clients and since the level of service is crucial in the context of residential property construction, it is worth making the time and effort to perform the necessary research.

6. Experience

When selecting a construction company, ideally you want to be working with a construction company and management team that not only have construction experience *but construction experience in Thailand.* There is a notable difference between building properties in the United Kingdom, Germany or Singapore, and building properties in Thailand. While the fundamental concepts remain the same, the cultural learning curve and operational environment are quite different. In other words, it is unwise to engage a construction company with no operating experience in Thailand; it is preferable to work with a construction company with an established network of material suppliers and third party contractors, instead of a construction company that is still trying to figure out which suppliers and contractors are reliable, and which are not. Construction companies that have operated in the local environment for a number of years with completed properties under their belt have generally been through the "weeding out" process and have arrived at a point where their core suppliers and construction teams are established. Further, unless the "new kid on the block" is able to poach workers from their competitors, they typically end up employing itinerant workers or contractors that have been "let go of" by competitors (usually for inferior performance[90]).

Remember, inexperienced construction companies and management are still in the process of building a core team of professional tradesmen and your property will therefore become a "lab test" for testing their competence.

---

[90] Unless work has dried up, construction companies work hard to hold on to their best teams.

7. Size

A construction company's size is also an important consideration. It is necessary to find the right balance between, on the one hand, the company's resources and ability to do the job, and on the other hand, the level of dedication, responsiveness and service you expect. In other words, the management team of a small company might be entirely focused on your project because it is their main source of revenue; they will always make themselves available to answer queries or to discuss changes, even though they might not have the same resources or equipment of a large company. Conversely, a large construction company might have in-house engineers and architects, their own machines and equipment, and hundreds of employees at their disposal, but their focus is likely to be on the larger projects or developments within their portfolio, which naturally accounts for the bulk of their revenue.

I recall the experience of building a luxury villa, where it was possible to walk around the site and consistently spot mistakes that should have been noted and taken care of by the construction company's project manager. The fact is the designated project manager was managing several sites and most of his attention was demanded on bigger projects; consequently, he didn't have enough time to supervise work on the villa, which was considered "low-priority".

To get to the point, you want your job to be treated as a priority, not like a pimple on a dog's hind leg (hardly noticed but occasionally needs to be scratched!). For this reason, the size of a construction company and the scope and size of its current projects are relevant considerations. If your job is worth 5 million Baht (US$ 165,000), and a construction company's other jobs mainly comprise 50 million Baht (US$ 1.65 million) projects, you don't need a supercomputer to work out the construction company's priorities.

8. Integrity

The question of integrity is simply concerned with whether the construction company's management will do what they promise. During the initial meetings with a construction company, all manner of promises are usually made in relation to "customer satisfaction", "making your job a priority", "building your property to the highest standards" and "providing top quality service". However, when the construction agreement has been signed, it is not only important that work is carried out in accordance with the agreement but also in the *spirit* of the agreement, which includes these general promises even if they were not formalised.

An area where integrity plays a crucial role is in relation to "variations" (see chapter 45). Variations usually refer to changes made after construction has commenced. Since variations impact the overall cost of construction, these changes must be quoted and agreed before the relevant work proceeds. While a construction management team operating with integrity will assist you with these changes and charge a fair price, a team lacking integrity will use variations as an opportunity to make additional money, often overcharging "captive" clients for the work involved[91]. The worst-case scenario is where a construction company submits a low quotation for a project, omitting certain items in the expectation of charging for them separately as variations.

Integrity is an important factor in the selection of a construction company and is another factor that is best ascertained through discussions with the company's previous clients. If the integrity of a company is in question, move on.

Summary

Apart from price, construction companies should be assessed against a number of criteria before being shortlisted for tender. The 8 most important criteria are:
- Financial Stability (Solvency)
- Quality of Workmanship
- Internal Organisation
- Communication
- Service
- Experience
- Size
- Integrity

---

[91] For this reason, there needs to be a clause covering the calculation of variations in the Construction Agreement.

44
Quotations and the BOQ

During the tender stage, quotations should ideally be received from several construction companies. Construction companies can present quotations in various ways.

One method is to submit a price per square metre (of floor area), for example, 25,000 Baht (US$ 830) or 45,000 (US$ 1,500) Baht per square metre. However, while quotations presented on this basis might be suitable for large condominium developments, this method is not suitable for individual properties because it lacks sufficient detail to reflect the actual cost of materials and labour. In fact, such lack of detail is often a deliberate ploy to avoid having to accurately assess construction costs or for the purpose of overcharging by obscuring the details, using what appears to be a legitimate calculation. Construction companies quoting on a price per square metre basis without providing any further detail should be avoided.

A more professional manner of submitting a tender is to provide a quotation together with a bill of quantities (BOQ), which is a detailed breakdown of the materials and labour required for the construction and completion of your house. A BOQ scrutinizes a job down to the finest detail, listing the material quantities and specifications required, virtually to the individual nail and screw. It also includes the labour hours involved for each task.

When a construction company completes a BOQ, it is typically submitted with a summary sheet, which provides sub-totals for each of the main sections, together with the total price including overhead and profit. A standard BOQ is generally broken down into the following sections:

- *Preliminary Work,* which generally includes site preparation, surveys and any demolition work required
- *Structural Work,* which includes excavation, formwork, steel reinforcement and concrete works
- *Architectural Work,* which generally includes brick and block walls, roof work, wall finishes, floor finishes, ceiling finishes, doors and windows, staircases, painting and sanitary fixtures.
- *Mechanical and Electrical (M&E) System Work,* which includes the main electrical power system; lighting sockets, switches and fixtures; telephone and other communications systems; hot and cold water supply, sanitary

systems and waste water pipe systems; rain-water recycling systems; air-conditioning systems; and swimming pool pump systems.
- *Overhead Fees and Operating Profit,* which are usually a certain percentage added on top of the total sum for the above categories.

To provide an idea of the level of detail, here is an extract from the "Structural Work" section of an actual BOQ:

Item	DESCRIPTION	UNIT	QTY.	MAT.	LAB.	UNIT RATE	AMOUNT
D	**Precast concrete slab. (Safe load DL+LL>150 kg/m2)**						-
22	50mm.thick precast concrete slab in floor [Pool deck and Terrace]	Sq.m.	62.00	300	100	400	24,800.00
23	Wire mesh [dia.4mm.@ 0.20 x 0.20m.]	Sq.m.	62.00	55	30	85	5,270.00
							-
	Waterproof System					-	-
24	Waterproof coating to swimming pool	Sq.m.	92.00	250	80	330	30,360.00
25	PVC. Water stop 6" in infinity pool.	m.	43.00	185	50	235	10,105.00
		Total for CONCRETE WORK					401,088.75
	TRADES FW FORMWORK						
E	**Formworks**						
8	Formwork to sides of pad footing.	Sq.m.	56.00	225	140	365	20,440.00
9	Formwork to sides of pier	Sq.m.	39.00	225	140	365	14,235.00
10	Formwork to sides of column.	Sq.m.	32.00	225	140	365	11,680.00
11	Formwork of Infinity swimming pool.	Sq.m.	142.00	225	140	365	51,830.00
12	Nail	Kg.	125.00	48	-	48	6,000.00
		Total for FORMWORK					254,705.00
	TRADES RE STEEL REINFORCE-MENT						
F	**Reinforcement SR-24 [14 Days Standby price]**						
8	6 mm.dia. in pier	Kg.	108.00	25.75	5	31	3,321.00
9	6 mm.dia. in column.	Kg.	120.00	25.75	6	32	3,810.00
10	Wire	Kg.	8.00	48.00	-	48	384.00
		Total for STEEL REINFORCEMENT					311,230.08

A BOQ has a number of advantages. First, it is completely transparent in that it allows you to examine the specifications and the quantity of materials, together with the labour rates for each part of the construction. This transparency allows an architect or project manager to check through a BOQ to ensure everything is included.

Second, the provision of such detailed information allows quotations from different construction companies to be easily compared. As each section has a sub-total, it is easy to evaluate which companies are more expensive for certain types of work. Similarly, labour rates can indicate which companies are more expensive for specific tasks. Detailed material specifications also allow a project manager or architect to check that specified materials are both suitable and comparable. If one construction company is less expensive than another, the difference can be quickly explained in terms of material specifications, quantities or labour rates.

Third, and in relation to budget, if you need to reduce the overall cost of a project, a BOQ allows you see where money is being spent and to determine the sections of the BOQ where costs can be cut by changing materials or reducing specifications. Depending on the size of the desired reduction, cost cuts might only require the substitution of various materials or it might be necessary to go back to the architect to redesign the property.

If a construction company has been engaged to complete the property from start to finish, including such facets as landscaping, kitchen design and furniture, the construction company is unlikely to have the "in-house" expertise to perform all the various specialised tasks, which means they are subcontracted to third parties. In the BOQ, these items are either listed as "provisional costs" or they are noted in accordance with the subcontractors' quotations. Whichever manner is used to insert these costs into the BOQ, an operating profit is generally added by the construction company for arranging the work. An alternative way to cut costs, therefore, is to directly engage landscaping contractors, kitchen design companies and interior design companies,[92] which reduces overall costs by the amount of operating profit added by the construction company.[93] A similar method for reducing costs is to purchase materials directly and supply them to the construction company (although the issues of quality, delivery and responsibility for on-site storage must also be considered).

It should be noted that the summary page submitted with a BOQ usually contains a section for "Provisional Cost" items (PC), sometimes referred to as "Provisional Sums" (PS), which are *estimates* for unconfirmed work. In other words, (a)

---

[92] This works well so long as you are prepared to take responsibility for organizing, scheduling and supervising the respective work.
[93] Refer also to chapter 59 on "Scheduling and sequencing".

work that cannot be entirely foreseen or detailed, (b) work for which the costs are unknown at the time, or (c) items about which a final decision has yet to be made (at the time tender documents are submitted)[94].

> **Important tip:** Special note should be taken of PC items because they are sums entered into the BOQ only to "get things moving" and, as the name suggests, they are *provisional*. As work proceeds and the exact materials and construction methods for PC items are confirmed, these sums will change to reflect the true costs. Remember, if materials or equipment are chosen for PC items whose cost exceeds the provisional sums, the difference will be added to the contact price.

It is unusual for the first draft of a BOQ to be accepted from a construction company. Usually there are questions, revisions and material changes that lead to revised drafts until a final draft accurately reflects the architect's drawings and specifications.

> **Important tip:** The BOQ from the construction company ultimately selected for the job should form part of the Construction Agreement (see chapter 49), usually as an appendix. This acts as a formal control on materials and specifications throughout the project.

Summary

- For individual properties, quotations based on a price per square metre lack sufficient detail to reflect the actual cost of materials and labour.
- A bill of quantities (BOQ) scrutinises a job down to the finest detail and should include all the materials and labour required for the construction and completion of your house
- The BOQ format allows quotations from different construction companies to be easily compared.
- Take special note of "Provisional Costs" because they are estimated figures for unconfirmed work and are likely to change later with the effect of increasing the contract price.
- The BOQ from the selected construction company should form part of the Construction Agreement.

---

[94] Sometimes PC items are value estimates given by the architect or by the client so that all construction companies submitting a tender use the same values for these items to effectively remove them as an item of differentiation in the bids.

45
Variations

Before a contract price is agreed and a Construction Agreement is signed, it is important to check the bill of quantities (BOQ) with a fine-toothed comb because after signing the contract (and commencing construction), any changes are treated as "variations".

A "Variation" is basically any change of design or materials that is made in relation to the construction of a property[95]. Such changes can be the result of a change of mind by the client; a change instituted by the architect or construction company; or a requirement of a local government authority. Examples of variations include changing the specification of floor tiles, enlarging the size of a window, changing the kitchen layout, substituting paving slabs for wooden decking, adding a balcony, upgrading wooden doors and windows to PVC doors and windows, moving walls to change the layout of a room, changing bathroom fixtures and adding built-in wardrobes.

As variations involve changes to previously agreed drawings and specifications, and because these changes have financial consequences, variations are potentially a major source of conflict and disagreement between clients and construction companies. For this reason, there are three important issues to consider in relation to variations:

1. Procedures
2. Pricing
3. Impact on completion date

1. Procedures

The construction agreement should set out a clear procedure for dealing with variations and, to avoid potentially disruptive misunderstandings and disagreements, it is essential that the procedure is carefully followed. In the absence of a clause setting out a procedure for variations, construction companies might refuse to carry out the changes or they could make things unnecessarily difficult.

---

[95] Providing the change does not significantly deviate from the plans and specifications to which the building permit relates.

The relevant variation clause in a construction agreement usually begins by stating that the "work to be done or materials used may be varied at the request of the Employer; at the request of the construction company; due to the requirement of a local government or statutory authority relating to the work (if such requirement could not have been foreseen by the construction company); or due to other matters that could not reasonably have been foreseen by a construction company experienced in working in Thailand".

Contracts then typically continue by setting out procedures for both the client and construction company to deal with variations. These procedures usually require notice in writing (a "Variation Order") to be submitted and approved *before any variation work commences*. The notice should provide a full description of the proposed variation, together with the difference in price and it should be signed and agreed by both parties.

2. Pricing

The relevant clause relating to variations should include an agreed method for pricing variations and a procedure for the payment of variation work.

> **Important tip:** Clear procedures for variations are important because variations have operational consequences for the builder and financial consequences for both parties. If a chosen material is less expensive or a design change reduces the amount of labour or materials required, the variation should result in a reduction in the overall contract price. If, on the other hand, the new materials are more expensive than those stated in the BOQ or a design change increases the amount of work, variations add to overall costs.

As mentioned in chapter 43, a construction company will sometimes win the tender for a job with a low quotation and then attempt to profit through variations. In order to protect yourself as the "employer", it is prudent to stipulate a rate in advance at which variations will be carried out; for instance, "the construction company agrees the price of any variations will be at the rate of cost of materials plus 15% operating profit". This should help to prevent quotations being submitted that are substantially higher than standard contract rates. If a quotation for a variation appears excessive, there should also be a provision for the client to provide an alternative, independent quotation or for some other method to be used in order to establish a fair "cost price" for materials and labour.

There must also be a procedure for the payment of variation work. For example, payment might be required in advance of variation work being carried out or the difference in cost might be taken into account at the next staged payment.

3. Impact on completion date

The Construction Agreement should contain a provision for adjusting the completion date as a consequence of variation work. Since variations, by definition, require changes to construction, any effect on the progress of construction needs to be provided for. Indeed, significant variation work might have to be put on hold while the details and cost of a variation are worked out and agreed by the parties.

> **Important tip:** When a construction company provides a quotation for a variation, it should be accompanied by an estimate of the additional time required to complete the work, *together with any consequence to the scheduled completion date.* This is important because changes to the contractual completion date might impact penalty payments if the Construction Agreement contains a penalty clause.

Dealing proactively with regard to completion dates and penalty payments is important. All too commonly, clients *informally* request variations, the price difference is agreed but no mention is made of the impact on the completion date; when the construction company finishes work three months behind schedule, and the client draws attention to the penalty clause, the construction company then uses the variations as an excuse, whether or not they had an impact on the completion date. Construction companies also benefit by having clearly defined procedures for variations; advising clients of a change to the scheduled completion date due to variation work, in accordance with the contract, *prevents* penalty fees being charged to the construction company.

It should be noted that there are some circumstances where additions or amendments might fall outside the ambit of "variations", such as where changes are made that are beyond the scope of work; or where such an excessive number of changes are made that individually fall within the scope of variations but collectively lead to a point where a construction company finds it impossible to work with you![96] Just beware that should a construction company find itself in a contract where it is no longer making money, the company might find it to their advantage to argue that such changes demand a significant increase in contract price or an amendment to the Construction Agreement. Even if things do not reach this point, constant or excessive changes often lead to a lowering of effort by the construction company and a loss of momentum (it might help to refer to chapter 56, "Know what you want and be prepared!").

---

[96] In the US, this is termed "abandonment" or "cardinal change".

It is also important to pay attention to provisional sums (PS) or provisional cost items (PC). As mentioned in the previous chapter, it is possible for unconfirmed items in the BOQ to *become variations by stealth*. For example, if the precise cost of an item on the BOQ is unknown *and has been under-estimated*, when the time comes to confirm the costs, the actual costs could be considerably higher than provisioned for. In other words, the contract price has increased by stealth.

Summary

- A "Variation" is any change of design or materials made in relation to the construction of a property after the BOQ has been agreed or after the Construction Agreement has been signed.
- Due to their operational and financial impact, variations are a potential source of conflict between clients and construction companies.
- The construction agreement should set out a clear procedure for dealing with variations and it is essential that the procedure is carefully followed.
- The contract should also provide an agreed method for pricing variations to prevent quotations that are excessively higher than standard contract rates.
- When a quotation is provided for a variation, any impact on the scheduled completion date should also be noted (particularly in relation to penalty payments).

46
Building Permits

Obtaining a building permit (construction permit) is a key stage in the process of building your own property[97]. A building permit is evidence that a property adheres to the rules and restrictions specified by local zoning laws and building regulations, together with any other special rules relevant to the area where you are building (see chapter 21). In addition, in the case where an individual person builds a house on a plot of land, a building permit issued in the name of that person is often *assumed* to be proof of ownership. When transferring the house, this document is therefore requested as "supporting" evidence of ownership.

Under Thai law you cannot begin construction until a building permit has been issued, although in practice there are numerous occasions when building permits are obtained after the event.

Important tip: While many people do in fact start construction before a building permit is issued – based on the assurance that the issue of a build permit is imminent or based on the assumption that the process is a mere formality – it is strongly advisable to wait until you have a building permit before starting construction.

The Town and City Planning Act and the Building Control Act are the two most important pieces of legislation governing the construction of residential properties in Thailand. Under these acts the following responsibilities are enforced:

- Awarding Building Permits
- Enforcing the Building Control Act
- Property Developments
- Zoning Regulations

The Building Control Act is set up to govern the construction of buildings, placing restrictions on their size, shape and height, which are specific to certain areas or zones. Building permits are regulated by the Building Control Act and issued under the Town and City Planning Act. Generally, the following documents need to

---

[97] It is also necessary to consider a building permit when you plan to modify the structure of an existing building.

be submitted to the Land Department Office to obtain a building permit, although individual requirements vary from province to province[98].

- Land title deed that allows for purchase, sale or transfer
- Architectural drawings
- Land Development Permits (obtained before the land sale), i.e. the Land Trade Licence and Land Distribution Licence
- Infrastructure permits such as water, electricity and housing construction permits
- Sub-division licence (if more than nine plots of land are being developed)

Upon submission, the documents and drawings are checked to ensure the proposed construction complies with the zoning laws and building regulations for the particular area and, as mentioned in chapter 21, an assessment will include some or all of the following:

- Height of the structure
- Width of the structure
- Distance from the beach and/or shore
- Proximity to another property
- The use of the structure (residential, commercial, industrial)
- Building lot size
- Angle of slope of land
- Height of land above sea level
- Type and colour of roof

Building permits require between several weeks and several months to be issued. For this reason, it is important to plan ahead when scheduling construction. If a construction company has already been engaged, they are often eager to start, even prior to the issue of a building permit. As the ultimate owner of the property, responsibility for the compliance of your property with building regulations is *yours*, which means it is unwise to give in to pressure from a construction company to prematurely commence with construction.

---

[98] It is therefore necessary to contact the local Land Department office for precise requirements. Construction companies and architects typically assist their clients with building permit applications.

In the case of a Condominium development, which requires a condominium licence, once a building permit has been obtained an official from the Land Department will attend the development to ensure compliance with the plans and zoning laws. When the building is 90% complete, the developer will usually file an application for the condominium licence, which is issued if the building is in compliance with the plans and zoning laws.

Summary

- It is advisable to wait until a building permit has been issued before starting construction.
- A building permit is evidence that the property you are building complies with local zoning laws and building regulations.
- Building permits can take several months to be issued so it is important to plan ahead when scheduling construction.

47
Staged payments

When engaging a construction company to build your property, confirming the construction payment schedule is a key factor. Payment Schedules A and B below provide two alternative examples of a construction payment schedule.

Payment Schedule A

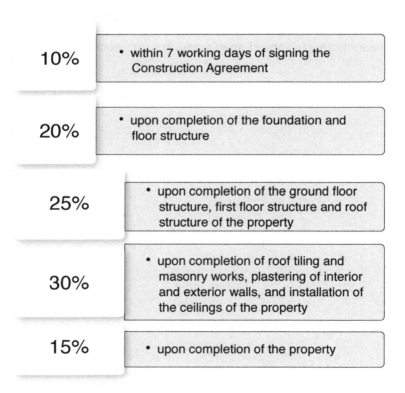

10%
- within 7 working days of signing the Construction Agreement

20%
- upon completion of the foundation and floor structure

25%
- upon completion of the ground floor structure, first floor structure and roof structure of the property

30%
- upon completion of roof tiling and masonry works, plastering of interior and exterior walls, and installation of the ceilings of the property

15%
- upon completion of the property

Payment Schedule B

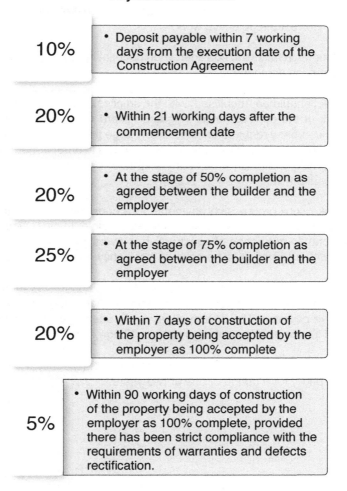

10%	• Deposit payable within 7 working days from the execution date of the Construction Agreement
20%	• Within 21 working days after the commencement date
20%	• At the stage of 50% completion as agreed between the builder and the employer
25%	• At the stage of 75% completion as agreed between the builder and the employer
20%	• Within 7 days of construction of the property being accepted by the employer as 100% complete
5%	• Within 90 working days of construction of the property being accepted by the employer as 100% complete, provided there has been strict compliance with the requirements of warranties and defects rectification.

In terms of construction, it is evident that Payment Schedules A is more precise since it specifies the actual work that needs to be performed to reach a staged payment. Payment Schedule B, on the other hand, specifies construction progress in percentage terms, which is open to interpretation and requires independent verification.

However, note that than Payment Schedule B has a retention payment. Retention is a sum that is withheld at the end of a job for a certain period to ensure the completion of defects that might arise after handover of the property. The holding of retention motivates a construction company to return to the property to perform repair work; if the construction company fails to make good on defects within a specified period, the retention sum should cover the cost of engaging another contractor to correct the defective work.

There are four main factors to consider when negotiating the payment schedule with a construction company:

First, a project should be "mobilised" with the smallest possible initial payment, with the bulk of the contract price weighted toward the end, if possible. If a construction company requires an excessively large percentage of the contract price at the outset or in the initial stages, and is *unable* to order materials without payment, working with such a company might not be the wisest choice (see point 1 of chapter 43).

Second, make sure progressive payments to a construction company mirror the progress of construction work as closely as possible. In other words, never allow payments to get ahead of construction to avoid the risk of financial loss associated with a construction company's insolvency (see chapter 43).

Third, it is a good idea to engage a project manager, architect or independent engineer to assess and certify the completion of each stage prior to making the respective payment. The document generally used to verify each stage of construction for the purposes of payment is a "Stage Completion Certificate".

Fourth, keep a retention sum at the end of the project (typically 5% or 10% of the contract price) for a period of one or two years.

48
Construction Guarantees

When you are at the stage of selecting a construction company, an important consideration is that of construction guarantees. The type of guarantees offered and the respective guarantee periods are key criteria for comparing construction companies.

To allow construction companies to be compared in relation to guarantees, it is helpful to clarify the various kinds of guarantees that are relevant to the construction of a property. These include:

1. The snag list or "snagging"
2. Defects warranty
3. Structural guarantee
4. Return to site policies and procedures
5. Statutory guarantees
6. Manufacturers or specialist guarantees.

1. The Snag List or 'snagging'

The snag list is not essentially a guarantee, although it plays an important part in the rectification of defects prior to the handover of your new property (for a full discussion of snagging, see chapter 58). With a newly built property, there will inevitably be defects that have been overlooked or areas that have been left unfinished. Snagging is the process of listing these defects so the construction company can rectify them before formal acceptance of the property.

Even though the snag list generally covers relatively minor problems that are easily rectified, it is helpful to understand in advance a construction company's procedures for dealing with snagging and defects. It is also important to ensure these procedures are included in the construction agreement in order to avoid misunderstandings. Such procedures should outline the association between the rectification of items on the snag list; practical completion; the final payment; and payment of retention.

2. Defects Warranties

The defects warranty comes into effect on completion and handover of a property and covers any defects discovered within a specific period of time after handover. A defect in this instance refers to any omissions or faults that become apparent in the property that are *not of a structural nature* (defects of a structural nature are covered by the structural guarantee, which is separate and in addition to a defects warranty)[99].

The standard length of time for a defects warranty is one year from the formal acceptance of completion of the work (or handover of the property), although other time periods are also common, such as six months or two years. In the case of "condominium freehold" property, the minimum requirement for a defects warranty is set at two years.

It is worth mentioning that properties should generally be built to withstand various weather conditions such as tropical storms, heavy rain, strong winds and conditions associated with the rainy season (see chapter 51). I have lost count of the number of times I have heard architects and builders claim that certain weather conditions are *"extreme conditions"* or *"freak weather"* or *"unexpected phenomena"* or *"acts of God"* in order to avoid responsibility for poor design or construction. Rainy seasons, wind and rain are anything but "unexpected" phenomena; they come around quite reliably on an annual basis and properties should therefore be built to withstand tropical storms, strong winds and torrential rain.

Only recently a roof section of a newly completed beachfront villa lifted up under heavy wind allowing rain to blow inside and causing the collapse of a ceiling. The builder claimed it was due to "unusually severe weather". Wind coming off the sea? Rain? Unusual? Incredible! I recall another example where rain running off a hill caused the collapse of a "retaining wall". *"Freak weather"* insisted the developer! Rain in Thailand? Freak weather conditions? Is it possible that the retaining wall was not correctly specified or built to retain the soil behind it?

Yet another example occurred recently during the recent heavy rain, where a hole in a newly completed roof allowed rainwater to leak into the house and cause extensive damage. The builder's response: *"This year the rain is not normal"*. You can't make these stories up. Can you imagine the construction company's marketing literature: "we build houses to withstand only *normal* rain!"

---

[99] Damage or defects arising as a result of the property owner's negligence or from normal wear and tear are generally excluded.

To avoid these "excuses" for poor design and construction, it is wise to speak with your lawyer to ensure an appropriate clause is inserted in the construction agreement or guarantee documentation to make the builder responsible for building a property that is able to withstand such *unexpectedly freak* weather!

3. Structural Guarantees

Structural guarantees cover issues related to the *structural integrity* of a property. In contractual terms, this is usually specified as foundations, foundation beams, pilings, concrete columns and beams, concrete floor slabs, support beams, load bearing walls, non-load bearing walls, roof beams, roof steel structure and load bearing parts of the roof, external rendering, ceilings, floors and load bearing parts of the floors, staircases and internal floor decking (where these fail to support normal loads), retaining walls, below ground drainage, driveways and footpaths.

Structural guarantees should generally cover all material and labour costs involved in correcting a structural problem and are often specified to last for a five or ten year period. In the case of condominium freehold property, the standard contract provided by the Ministry of Interior provides for a minimum period of five-years in relation to structural guarantees.

4. Return to site policies and procedures

All construction companies offer some form of defects warranty or structural guarantee; however, it is the procedures, terms, conditions and return to site policies that serve to differentiate them. This is where careful attention to detail is required.

Each construction company has a different procedure for the notification and submission of claims. In addition, there are often differences concerning the type of defects covered under defects warranties and structural guarantees. For instance, some companies include "all materials and labour", while others note that "labour is included and materials are excluded", or vice versa. Any other exclusion related to the guarantees should also be noted.

It is crucially important to check and compare the details of the guarantees provided by different construction companies, negotiating modifications where necessary. It is also important to ensure that guarantees and warranties are described in as much detail as possible in the construction agreement; anything that is not sufficiently clear leaves room for interpretation, which means room for a construction company to reject a claim and refuse to perform the work.

Another crucial difference between construction companies is the timing and manner of the response to work falling within a guarantee. For instance, a defects warranty might contain the provision that "the construction company agrees to put right any defects within 28 days of receiving notification of the defects". If there is no specific mechanism for informing the construction company of a defect and no specific time limit for effecting the work, builders will drag their heals in returning to site and it can take forever to get work done. Few builders jump at the prospect of taking workers off a new site to put right problems on a previous job, which creates no new income. For this reason, should rectification work not be performed within the specified time limit, there should be a provision in the contract to engage another contractor to do the work, whereby the original contractor can be invoiced.[100]

It should be noted that standard contracts used by construction companies often differ in the manner in which claims are evaluated or the procedures used to determine if a claim falls within a guarantee. For instance, if you claim that work is defective or that a property requires remedial work of a structural nature, and the construction company disagrees, what then? Unless a specific procedure is outlined, arguments generally continue to a point where the relationship breaks down and hope no longer exists for unenforced remedial work. The usual solution is to provide for an independent engineer or expert appraiser to assess the work, issue a formal report and for parties to be bound by the findings. If this solution fails, it is useful if the construction agreement has a dispute resolution procedure to provide for resolution of the dispute by mediation or arbitration (see chapter 87); without a properly outlined dispute resolution mechanism, the only other course of action is legal action.

It is strongly recommended that a competent lawyer is engaged when the construction agreement is being prepared. When a problem arises several years later, it is too late to change the wording of contracts!

Ultimately, however, the integrity of the builder is usually the factor determining how quickly things get put right. It is also worth remembering that guarantees are only of any value if the company standing behind them remains in business and is financially capable of performing the work; otherwise they are not worth paper they are written on. Due to the overriding combination of integrity and solvency, the time and effort spent selecting a construction company that is financially sound and acts with integrity is time well spent (see chapter 43).

---

[100] This is the case with "condominium freehold" properties, where buyers may hire a contractor to perform the work and then request the cost to be reimbursed by the developer.

5. Statutory Guarantees

Condominium freehold is a special form of property that foreigners are allowed to own directly on a freehold basis (see chapter 3). Many aspects of condominiums are governed by legislation, which provides owners with a level of "consumer protection". In the special case of Condominium Freehold property, the new owner automatically receives a five-year structural guarantee and a two-year non-structural defects warranty under Thai law, regardless of the terms included in the developer's contract.

6. Manufacturers or Specialist Guarantees.

In addition to defects warranties and structural guarantees, it might also be necessary to consider manufacturers guarantees or guarantees associated with specialised equipment. For example, manufacturers of split air-conditioning units generally provide a one or two year parts and labour warranty on the interior unit and a five or six year warranty on the exterior compressor unit. Companies fitting PVC or aluminium windows and doors typically provide a guarantee ranging from one year up to ten years. Another important guarantee relates to swimming pool pump systems. Manufacturers of electrical appliances, specialised acoustic systems, alarm systems and kitchen appliances also generally provide some form of warranty.

It is useful to check whether guarantees are "manufacturers guarantees" or "contractual guarantees". For instance, if you have a contract with a construction company to build your house and in turn the construction company enters into a contract for the installation of specialist equipment, the guarantee is often contractual in nature (with the construction company), which affects the manner in which a guarantee operates.

The important point is to make sure you are in possession of all the relevant guarantee and warranty documents at the time of the handover of the property and to keep them in an easily accessible place. If you are renting out the property while residing in another country, it is advisable to store these documents locally in Thailand with your lawyer or property management company.

Summary

- The type of warranties and guarantees, together with the terms and conditions associated with them, are key criteria for comparing construction companies.
- It is important that guarantees and warranties are described in as much detail as possible in the Construction Agreement.
- Since condominium freehold properties are covered by legislation, purchasers automatically receive statutory guarantees.
- It is helpful to compare construction companies in relation to the following six categories of guarantee:
  - The snag list
  - Defects warranty
  - Structural guarantee
  - Return to site policies and procedures
  - Statutory guarantees
  - Manufacturers or specialist guarantees.

49
The construction agreement

Most people believe the main purpose of a Construction Agreement (or indeed any contract) is to act as a basis for legal action in court. While this is certainly one of the purposes, the primary purpose of a construction agreement should be to avoid disputes in the first place by making an agreement that is as detailed as practicably possible in order to reflect what has been agreed between the parties. In other words, the agreement is meant to clarify the relationship between the parties so that it can be referred to when there is a misunderstanding.

When the Construction Agreement has been signed, it is generally too late to change it. It is also more difficult to negotiate amendments later because commitments and obligations have started and the balance of negotiating power has changed.

> **Important tip:** It is strongly recommended to spend more time considering, discussing and negotiating the details of a construction agreement before rushing into the commencement of a project. Think twice, act once, and never be pressured by a construction company into starting construction without a properly drafted Construction Agreement in place, even with a tight deadline.

Unbelievably, some people even build properties without a written contract! The construction company is engaged by agreeing a price and commencing work. In other words, the construction company is trusted to perform in accordance with verbal promises. However, with communication being what it is – fraught with misunderstanding – it is impossible for a construction company to meet your expectations unless they are properly defined; this is not to mention the inevitable changes that will be made after work has commenced, which, without a clearly defined procedure, is virtually a guarantee of conflict.

A competent lawyer should be instructed to draft (or review) the agreement with the chosen construction company because it needs to be customized to the project and to individual circumstances. However, the purpose of this chapter is to discuss the standard contents of a Construction Agreement, which are summarised below:

A. Identification of the land.
The land should be identified in the agreement by its Chanote number, size and address. Usually the Chanote document will be included in the annexes.

B. Parties

The parties to the agreement – the "Employer" (or "Client") and the "Construction Company" (or "Builder") – should be clearly identified by name, address and contact details. If the party is an individual, a signed passport copy should be attached as an annex. If the party is a company, updated company documents and a copy of the signed passport of the directors should be attached.

C. Contract price and payment

The total contract price (and currency) should be stated, together with precise details of "staged payments" (as discussed in chapter 47). A separate clause should cover any retention payment, stating the percentage or sum withheld and clarifying the basis on which it becomes payable. The method of payment can also be stipulated if, for example, payment is required to a specific bank account.

D. Commencement Date

The commencement date should be noted, either as a specific date or a specific number of days following the first payment to the construction company. For instance, "the Builder shall commence the work on December 10th 2012 or within 7 days of receipt of the first payment, whichever is the latter".

E. Completion Date

It is important to state the completion date and a procedure for accepting completion of the Work, which is particularly relevant to the issues of snagging and defects (see chapter 58). The contract might specify, for instance:

"When the Work is completed, the Builder shall notify the Employer and the Employer shall then have Thirty days in which to issue a written acceptance or notify the Builder in writing that the Work is not complete. In the event that within Thirty days the Employer does not notify the Builder either way, it shall be deemed that the Employer accepts completion of the Work. If the Employer notifies the Builder that the Work is not complete, the Builder shall have Thirty days in which to complete the Work".

F. Extension of Time

The contract should contain a provision to cover delays, whether due to weather conditions or significant variations, and how they are dealt with.

G. Late Completion Penalty

A penalty clause usually provides for a financial penalty (calculated on a daily or monthly basis) to be paid to the Employer by the construction company for late completion or handover of the property. Fundamentally, a penalty clause provides a "financial incentive" for the construction company to complete the property on or before the specified completion date; without a penalty, there is no deterrent to the construction company for letting the completion date drift (see chapter 57). The late completion penalty should also be designed to compensate for costs and losses as a result of late completion. The rental value of the (completed) property should be considered as a starting point for the penalty payment, which should compensate for lost opportunity costs.

H. Certification of Staged Payments
There needs to be a procedure for certifying the completion of each stage of work according to the payment schedule. If an architect, project manager or engineer has been specifically engaged to certify each stage of completion then their role needs to be detailed. There should also be a provision for dealing with late payments, how it might affect ongoing work and the completion date.

I. Approval of Materials
A clause might be needed to cover the procedure for testing and approving materials prior to use. This is often the case when a project manager is involved in overseeing the work of a construction company.

J. Materials Supplied by the Client
If you want to supply certain materials for the project, there should be a clause specifying the materials and detailing which party will be responsible for quality, delivery and on site security.

K. Warranties and Guarantees
All guarantees and warranties provided by the construction company should be carefully detailed. This should also include the procedure for the notification and rectification of defects. In addition, the construction company should warrant that construction will be carried out in compliance with local building regulations, statutory authorities and all relevant laws of Thailand.

L. Insurance
It is important to ensure the construction company has adequate insurance coverage for the project. As the owner of the land, you do not want to be exposed to liability for the actions of the construction company. The construction company should be contractually responsible for arranging an adequate insurance policy, including public liability, professional indemnity and workers compensation insurance ("all risks insurance"). It is wise to request a copy of the insurance documents.

M. Taxes and Fees
The construction agreement needs to specify which party is liable for taxes, fees and duties in association with the payment for construction services.

N. Variations
A detailed clause should cover the procedure and pricing method for variations, which are material or design changes made during construction (discussed in chapter 45).

O. Assignment
You might wish to include an assignment clause to allow the rights and obligations under the construction agreement to be assigned (by selling) to another party without the consent of the construction company, or to prevent the assignment of the rights and obligations of the construction company without your consent.

P. Security and Liability
It is prudent to include a clause to cover the issue of security. Construction companies often prefer to provide their own security for a site, particularly if tools, equipment and materials are stored on site. "Security" for smaller jobs could simply comprise a few workers from the construction company living on site in temporary accommodation huts, while for larger projects a professional security firm might be engaged. It is necessary to clarify which party is responsible for security-related costs and, most importantly, which party is accountable in the event of theft of materials (this includes materials that you might supply for construction, see "J" above).

Q. Suspension of Work
A clause is usually included to cover the event where work is suspended, for example, due to late payment or a disagreement related to variations. The clause must also provide a procedure for the recommencement of work once the issue has been remedied.

R. Termination
In the event that one of the parties is in breach of contract, becomes bankrupt or otherwise wishes to terminate the contract, there must be a termination procedure, which generally covers the refund of payments and any entitlement to damages. Usually there are two separate clauses, which cover termination by the client and termination by the construction company.

S. Dispute Settlement and Arbitration
The contract should ideally provide a procedure for referring disputes to arbitration or mediation in order to resolve disagreements more efficiently and without the need to instigate legal action (see chapter 87).

T. Notice
Notice clauses are for the parties to provide correspondence addresses for any issue relating to the contract. If you are not residing in Thailand or do not have a reliable correspondence address, it is common to use the address of your appointed lawyer in Thailand.

U. Annexes

A number of drawings and documents should form part of the construction agreement including architectural drawings, floor plans, master plans, structural drawings, mechanical and electrical drawings, material specifications, a copy of the BOQ, land title documents, company documents and passport copies. These documents are normally attached as annexes or appendices of the construction agreement.

In addition to the standard clauses summarised above, construction agreements should be customised to meet the specific requirements of your project. The beauty of contacts is that you can put anything you want in them so long as it is legal and the other party agrees! It is true that all kinds of promises are made by construction companies in order to secure a job, but their actions rarely match their promises. One of the most common problems is that builders start a job and then move workers off to another site because it is a "higher priority", which leaves your job at a standstill for weeks or even months. Sometimes a skeleton staff of three unskilled workers is left behind to make it appear that the job is still "in progress" – one sweeping up, another walking around with a hangover wondering what to do, while the third is fast asleep in a corner.

To avoid this kind of problem and the delays that are the obvious consequence, it is often a good idea to ask the builder how many workers need to be on site at each stage of construction. Armed with this information, a clause can then be inserted into the contract specifying the minimum number of workers that must be on site; if the number of workers falls below the *minimum* number for a predefined period, a financial penalty could be applied (or it could be considered a breach of contract). Naturally, such a clause would need to be drafted by a lawyer to reflect the specific circumstances of a project, although such a clause would certainly send a clear signal to a construction company that you are serious!

With regard to the *execution* of contracts in Thailand, it is normal practice to initial every single page of the construction agreement, including annexes, and to sign the signature page. This is to confirm that you have read, understood and agreed to all contents.

Finally, while it has already been mentioned that construction agreements should be as detailed as possible for the purpose of *avoiding* disputes, in reality the best way to avoid disputes with a construction company is to maintain a good working relationship with the key people (if you are working directly with Thai people this includes understanding their culture and way of doing things). When you have good relationships, it is possible for issues to be openly discussed and resolved as they arise; only when relations break down does the contract become legally significant.

50
Financial considerations
(Essential)

To ensure the successful completion of a construction project, it is important for cash flows and finances to be carefully planned. It is surprising how many people start construction of a property and realise only towards the end that they are running short of funds because they had simply not taken everything into account. This is one of the worst outcomes because completion then depends on cutting costs where it really matters – on finishing work such as interior décor, furniture, fixtures and fittings, and landscaping,

This chapter discusses 8 primary considerations to take into account to ensure the completion of your property, which are as follows:

1. Check BOQ
2. List specialist contractors and other costs
3. Check funds
4. Financial cushion
5. Prepare for making payments
6. Staged payments
7. Variations
8. Contingency planning

1. Check BOQ

The first consideration is to make sure all the requirements of the project are included in the BOQ and there are no omissions. As mentioned in chapter 45, once the BOQ has been approved and contracts have been signed, any changes or additions will be treated as "variations".

2. List specialist contractors and other costs

The second consideration is to identify all the other costs related to finishing the project. This includes the work of specialist contractors and all aspects related to the interior décor and furnishing of the property (particularly if the property needs to be in a rent-ready condition). In addition, the costs involved with the management and administration of your property for the first six months after completion should also be included in your calculations. This includes accounting fees, marketing costs and the *fixed costs* associated with property management (as distinct from rental management, which are generally *variable* costs that are covered by rental income, see chapter 118).

The chart below lists some of the items that might need to be included in the overall financial budget:

Expense item	Cost
Kitchen design contractor	
Kitchen appliances, equipment and utensils	
Audio-visual system and electrical appliances (TVs, DVD players, speaker systems)	
Utility and service connection costs (electricity, water, sewage, telephone, Internet, satellite or cable TV)	
Intelligent lighting systems	
Alarm systems	
Interior design and furniture (including mattresses and spare beds)	
Artwork	
Built-in wardrobes	
Outdoor furniture (such as sun loungers, dining tables and umbrellas for pool decks, terraces and balconies)	
Curtains and blinds	
Pest control	
Landscaping, which includes "hard" landscaping such as retaining walls and water features; and "soft" landscaping, which refers to plants and trees	
Garden and exterior lighting	
Entrance gate (automatic or manual)	
Bed linen and towels	
Legal fees, accounting fees and taxes	
Marketing and advertising costs	
Fixed property management costs (6 months)	
Total:	

It should be noted that costs related to furnishing a property are the costs that are most frequently overlooked, especially for fitted wardrobes, mattresses, bed linen and towels, and outdoor furniture.

For expense items that are not included in the BOQ, particularly those involving specialist contractors, it is necessary to arrange separate quotations to ensure they become part of your overall financial budgeting. If one or two items on the list are forgotten it may not be a big deal; if several major expense items are overlooked, they could account for a noticeable shortfall.

3. Check funds

The third step is to ensure you have sufficient funds available to cover the full contract price with the construction company, all work to be performed by specialist contractors and all the items listed in point 2.

4. Financial cushion

The fourth consideration is to make sure you have a financial "cushion". This is essential. Although it sounds like common sense, *this is the most common reason that properties don't get finished (or are finished with budget cuts)*. It is sensible to set aside an extra 10-20% of the contract price to ensure you have liquidity for cost overruns or variations. 10% should be considered an absolute minimum.

There are always unforeseen costs that arise during a construction project: materials that need to be substituted at a higher cost; items that have been overlooked by the architect and the construction company; or changes that you will want to make as construction progresses (variations). If you are already stretching the limits of your financial resources, any additional costs are going to create problems. Alternatively, if financial constraints prevent you from making modifications, they will become a source of frustration.

Important tip: If you have added up the financial requirements of the project and the sum total is already close to the limit of your financial resources, you should cut 10-20% of the costs right now, before you start.

5. Prepare for making payments

The fifth consideration is to send money to Thailand in advance to cover the full contract price with the construction company, the additional work to be performed by specialist contractors and furnishing costs.

Sending the *full* amount of money required in advance (even if the construction contract is payable according to a staged payment schedule) is the most conservative approach. In this way, exchange rate risk is avoided (assuming the construction contract is payable in Thai Baht).

If a portion of the required funds is kept overseas in another currency and you plan to remit money to Thailand in accordance with the staged payments, you are exposed to currency exchange rate risk. The currency in your home country might move in your favour by appreciating in value, which means you can buy more Thai Baht at the time of transfer. Conversely, the currency you are holding could depreciate in value relative to the Thai Baht, in which case your money will be worth less and you might be facing a shortfall (which occurred to many people holding US dollar denominated funds in 2006 – 2007 and again in 2009).

I recall the example of a British couple that started construction of their house in 2008 and have subsequently put the project on hold, "pending a more favourable exchange rate". In the six-month period from the middle of 2008 to the beginning of 2009, the exchange rate of the British Pound to Thai baht fell from 67 to 48, which translates into a significant increase in construction costs if your money had been kept in British Pounds (for a more detailed discussion on exchange rates, see chapter 105).

6. Staged payments

The sixth consideration is never to allow payments to a construction company to get ahead of construction progress, as discussed in chapter 47 (in order to reduce the risks related to the insolvency of a construction company). This means making sure staged payments are clearly detailed in the construction agreement and are closely correlated to the progress of work. For example, you should be paying up to 50% of the contract price only when 50% of the work is complete, as certified by an architect, project manager or an independently engaged engineer. If you have to engage an independent professional to verify the stages of completion, it means additional costs but provides a higher level of safety and certainty to the payment process. It reminds me of the example of a property developer that was pushed to the verge of insolvency after paying the building contractor more than 70% of the contract price when the contractor declared bankruptcy having completed only 25% of the work (the Thai contractor gambled away the money). The same principle applies whether you are building a large-scale development or a stand-alone property.

7. Variations

The seventh consideration is to keep a close eye on variations. During construction, each time you make a design or material change, it is treated as a variation and variations have financial consequences. If each change you make costs more money, be sure to keep track of the extra costs and their cumulative financial impact.

8. Contingency planning

The final consideration is to have a contingency plan. If cost overruns get out of control and beyond your financial means, you must have a "Plan B" for securing additional funds. Don't wait until the last minute when you are pushed to the brink and desperately need money before speaking with the bank manager or a trusted friend; secure alternative sources of funds *in advance*.

Summary

- Poor financial planning and failing to take all expenses into account are the primary causes of the failure of construction projects.
- Running short of funds towards the end of a project is one of the worst scenarios because it means cutting costs on finishing work, which is vitally important for the rental and re-sale of a property.
- It is important to have a "financial cushion" to ensure liquidity for cost overruns or variations. This means if the financial requirements of a project are already close to the limit of your financial resources, cut costs now, before you start.
- There are always unforeseen costs that arise during a construction project.
- Have a financial contingency plan and ensure an alternative source of funds is in place in advance.

51
Planning for rainy seasons

In most countries, construction workers generally work year-round with the exception of heavy storms or sub-zero temperatures. In Thailand, while sub-zero temperatures are not a concern, it is necessary to consider the annual monsoon rains. During these "wet seasons" rain falls like a wall of water; sometimes for a few hours during the afternoon, other times it continues for days or weeks with hardly a pause.

As can be imagined, the rainy season can significantly hinder progress on construction projects. Heavy rain prevents structural work from proceeding; it is not possible to excavate foundations for retaining walls, houses or swimming pools because any excavations are likely to collapse and fill with water. Similarly, it is not possible to pour concrete, build exterior walls, carry out roofing work or perform finishing work such as rendering or painting. In other words, a significant range of tasks associated with construction must be put on hold.

It should be noted that the onset and duration of the rainy season differs for each of Thailand's resort areas. In Phuket, for example, rainfall increases sharply in May and September then tapers off in October, while in Koh Samui the heaviest rain usually falls in November and tapers off in December (see the charts later in the chapter). In addition, the onset and duration of the monsoon season changes from year to year; sometimes it commences earlier and lasts longer; sometimes it comes later and ends earlier. Some years the rainy season is barely noticeable; some years you think the rain will never stop.

However, the good news (for construction) is the timing of the rainy season is reasonably predictable, which means it can be anticipated and planned for. As indoor work is generally the only work that can proceed without being affected by heavy rain, planning around the monsoon season means scheduling the construction of a project to reach the point where all structural work has been completed and the property is considered "closed" before the onset of the wet season; in other words, the roof is watertight, exterior walls have been completed, windows and doors have been installed and interior work can proceed despite the rain.

Construction schedules differ for each property depending on several factors, such as the size, design and amount of structural work involved. To provide an example of planning construction to increase the prospects of completion without weather-related delays, suppose construction is scheduled to last 9 months and requires 6 months to reach the point where the property is "closed" (and 3 months for interior and finishing work), construction should ideally commence 6 months prior to the anticipated start of the rainy season (in the resort area where you are building), preferably with a one-month margin of error (in case the monsoon season starts earlier).

For instance, if you are building in Koh Samui where the rainy season is generally from mid-October to mid-December, construction should commence no later than February or March. If you building in Phuket, where the southwest monsoon season is generally from May to October, things are a little trickier although an ideal time to start work would be once the weather clears in November.

If construction of your property does not reach the stage where it is watertight before the onset of heavy rain, you could find that work is not just delayed but that it might need to be put on hold until the rainy season has come to an end. Therefore, if a project has not started and it is not possible to reach the stage where a property is watertight before the wet season, it might be wise to reschedule work for commencement *after* the wet season. If such planning is not practicable, knowing the approximate timing of the rainy season at least allows you to plan the ordering of materials and to schedule the order of work in anticipation of the weather. Workers can be directed to concentrate on structural and outdoor work, such as retaining walls and swimming pools, leaving indoor work to be carried out later.

While rainy seasons are reasonably predictable, which supports a certain degree of planning, it must also be recognised that the weather can at times be completely *unpredictable.* For example, the heaviest rain in a decade unexpectedly hit Koh Samui in March 2011, which caused the widespread flooding and the suspension of both flights and ferry services to the island.

For general reference, therefore, the average monthly rainfall for four of Thailand's resort areas is shown below[101].

---

[101] Source http://thailandforvisitors.com

Average Monthly Rainfall in Phuket (mm)

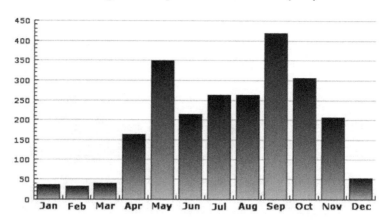

Average Monthly Rainfall in Koh Samui (mm)

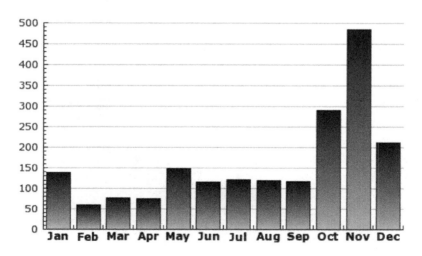

Average Monthly Rainfall in Pattaya (cm)

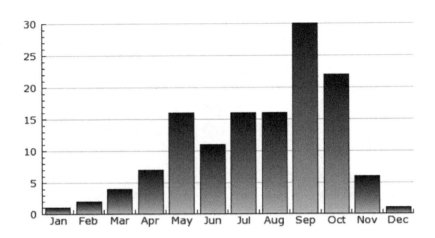

Average Monthly Rainfall in Hua Hin (cm)

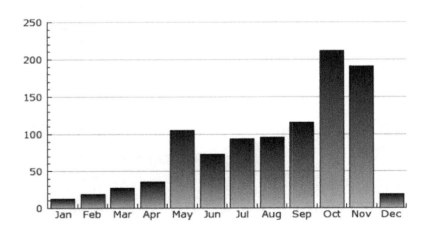

52
Retaining walls and drainage
(Essential)

It is crucially important when building a property, especially on sloping or hillside land, that the twin issues of retaining walls and drainage are properly taken into consideration. The reason for their importance is perhaps best illustrated through the use real-life examples.

A property developer bought a plot of hillside land and built a row of luxury villas. At the back of the villas, where the land was steeply sloped, a wall was built to hold back the soil. A year after completion and after heavy rain, a section of the wall simply collapsed and slid down the hill, together with a landslide of soil and rocks (which stopped within inches of the villas). The problem was traced directly to the specification of the wall: quite simply, it was a garden wall, not a *retaining wall.* This distinction, while critical, is generally not well understood by those buying land in Thailand to build tropical homes.

The example serves to illustrate that walls that hold back soil need to be designed and engineered for the job. The precise specification depends on the weight of soil it must keep in place; the type of soil; and the gradient of the slope. For this reason, a topographical survey (see chapter 42) is usually required. Retaining walls must be of the right height, thickness and shape, and contain the correct specification of steel reinforcing. In other words, retaining walls are structural walls, which play an integral role in providing the structural integrity of the property. There is no use spending 15 million Baht (US\$ 500,000) to build a luxury property if it is bowled over by a landslide due to an improperly engineered retaining wall!

Vital to the structural integrity of a retaining wall is the issue of drainage. In this context, we are usually speaking of a system of drainage channels and weep holes (holes that allow water to drain through the wall). Again, the crucial importance of a properly designed drainage system can be illustrated by another "incident":

A three-storey apartment building with a basement garage had been built on a hillside and the wall at the back of the garage was also acting as a retaining wall. During the rainy season, heavy rain had fallen on the hillside behind the apartments, which had swelled the soil and increased pressure on the wall to the point where the waterlogged soil simply burst through the wall, causing a section to collapse. This time the prognosis was twofold: firstly, the wall was not strong enough; secondly, and most importantly, there were no weep holes. Had there been adequate weep holes in the wall, together with a drainage channel inside the wall, pressure would not have been allowed to build behind the wall.

Ensuring adequate drainage on a site is crucial. Water must be properly collected and channelled away, especially on hillside land. Here is another example of "how *not* to do things": A villa was built on a gently sloping hillside. The issue of drainage had not been properly addressed and no drainage system had been installed at the back of the villa or around it. In the absence of a drainage system, rainwater had forged into own route down the hill and under the house. After several monsoon seasons, the flow of water had washed away the soil under the house, exposing the foundations until eventually one of the corner pad foundations was literally suspended in mid-air! In this case, restitution work consisted of new sub-structural foundation work, together with the installation of a drainage system to channel water around the house and down the hill. Repairs were also required to walls that had cracked with movement.

The purpose of this chapter is not to go into the mechanics of building retaining walls or drainage systems; it is merely to underline the crucial importance of these two aspects of construction and to highlight the fact that they underpin the structural integrity of a property. An architect might design a property but the issue of retaining walls and drainage systems are of a structural nature; it is the point where architectural drawings intersect with the specific features of the land. Drawings for retaining walls and drainage systems need to be prepared by qualified engineers in advance of construction and implemented by the construction company according to the drawings, with the supervision of an engineer (or a project manager if applicable).

If the issue is left to a construction company to implement, the construction company might not have the in-house expertise to properly engineer a retaining wall or properly design a drainage system. Indeed, if a price has already been agreed with a builder, this is one area where costs could be "minimised".

It is important to bear in mind that problems related to retaining walls or drainage systems often take years before they become apparent and if they do arise, significant remedial work is often required. In addition, problems of this nature are always more expensive and difficult to repair after the fact, if they can be repaired at all. Structural problems also significantly impact the market value of a property. As a property owner, it is ultimately your responsibility to ensure sufficient attention is paid to these issues and that suitable professionals are engaged.

Summary

- The twin issues of retaining walls and drainage systems are crucial because they underpin the structural integrity of a property.
- As they are issues of a structural nature, retaining walls and drainage systems must be specifically designed and engineered for the job, which means qualified engineers need to be consulted.
- Structural problems often take years before they become apparent but if problems do arise, significant and expensive remedial work is often required.

53
What sells?

During the finishing stage of construction, it is important for consistency in quality and design extends throughout the property. Using high quality materials in one area easily shows up cheap materials used elsewhere, while attention to detail in some parts of a house and a lack of detail in other parts leads to a degree of visual discomfort.

However, having noted the need for consistency, the fact is that some areas of a house are more important than others; in other words, they tend to be focal points for potential buyers and tenants. These are the elements of the house that separately or collectively create the "Wow" factor. The 5 key elements discussed in this chapter are as follows:

1. Bathrooms
2. Kitchens
3. Interior design and furnishings
4. Landscaping
5. Outdoor living areas and swimming pools

These are the five elements of a property that potential buyers and tenants pay most attention to; the elements that (consciously or subconsciously) contribute most to the overall aesthetic impression of the property. In short, these are the elements that ultimately sell or rent your property. Prospective tenants or buyers neither see nor appreciate the money you have spent on foundations or structure; they form an impression from the aesthetic design elements (unless the tenant or buyer is an engineer!). Buying decisions (except those of a pure investor) are generally emotion-based; just like food, if it is not visually appealing, people will not eat it. With property, if it is not visually appealing, people will not buy or rent it.

This does not mean you have a licence to cut corners in areas that are not immediately visible, such as foundations or structure. It simply means setting aside a sufficient budget in order for special attention to be given to these 5 key areas.

1. Bathrooms

The difference between a beautiful bathroom and an average bathroom has more to do with the design and combination of materials than the *cost* of materials. Designing beautiful bathrooms requires the application of time and thought to the task. However, if you are not well endowed in the design taste department, get help; engage an architect or interior designer to choose materials and design the bathrooms. Alternatively, find a colour combination or design concept in a luxury magazine or hotel to use as a starting point (this might appear to be a case of "replication" but it is also be referred to as "conceptual benchmarking"!).

Another alternative is to use the services of a tile company. Some of the more established tile companies provide professional, inexpensive bathroom design services[102]. In-house designers will assist in the selection and combination of tiles and create a three-dimensional visualisation of your bathroom. A set of full colour design renderings is then provided, together with material specifications, a bill of quantities and even instructions for laying the tiles. These design documents are sufficiently detailed for direct implementation by a construction company.

In relation to bathroom accessories – taps, showers, washbasins, and lavatories – the quality and brand selected will reflect on the property in general. Accessories can be imported from Italy, Germany, Japan, China, or manufactured locally in Thailand. European brands (such as Grohe or Paini) tend to be at the high-end of the quality spectrum. Chinese-made brands, on the other hand, while they might be well designed and shiny looking when new, tend to deteriorate more rapidly both in function and appearance (leading also to higher maintenance costs). Thailand has several locally made brands, such as Cotto, American Standard and VRH, that are reasonably priced and of good quality.

Bathroom lighting also requires some thought. Don't just install standard down lights by default; consider the use of soft recessed lighting, wall-mounted lamps or glass roof sections to provide natural light.

In general, bathrooms should not just be viewed as functional areas; they can become design-features in their own right with freestanding Terrazzo bathtubs, outdoor rain-showers, tropical plants, water features, TV screens incorporated into mirrors and soft music emanating from hidden speakers.

2. Kitchens

Kitchens are another key element and one of the first things that many potential property buyers take note of. A beautifully designed, well-equipped kitchen with quality appliances can play a disproportionately important role in a purchasing decision. Instead of being considered at the later stages of construction, kitchen

---

[102] Tile companies have an obvious incentive for providing design services – to sell their tiles. However, there is no obligation to buy from the same company. One example that comes to mind is Cotto, which, at the time of writing, has a design studio at the Bangkok showroom.

design should be integrated at the initial property design stages. The colour scheme and materials chosen for a kitchen should blend in with the overall design concept. It should also blend ergonomically with the other indoor and outdoor living spaces and with the incorporation of breakfast bars and islands can become an informal congregation area.

In relation to functionality, remember to consider the location of appliances and workspaces bearing in mind the movement of people within the kitchen area. Kitchens should also be well-lit and as spacious as possible within the proportions and confines of the floor area.

There are numerous kitchen design companies each of Thailand's primary resort areas although prices vary dramatically between low-end and top-end, depending on materials used, their country of origin and brand names. For instance, fitted kitchens can be installed for as little as 250,000 Thai Baht (US$ 8,300), while high-end Italian kitchens can be 2.5 million Baht (US$ 83,000) or more.[103]

Remember, if you are planning to rent out a property, it is important to select durable materials that are tough enough to withstand hard use by tenants. For example, granite should be used for kitchen work surfaces, which is hardwearing, instead of compressed chipboard laminate (MDF), which tends to chip easily and can swell if saturated by water. Similarly, durable materials should be selected for cupboard doors, such as high-gloss melamine or aluminium-edged acrylic.

With regard to appliances, when choosing between different brand names the issue of service and repairs should be a major consideration. It is often better to select a good quality local brand with a comprehensive service warranty and a local service centre, instead of a high-end international brand with non-existent service and parts that need to be ordered and imported before an appliance can be repaired. For rental properties especially, the efficiency and response time of local repair services should trump other considerations.

Useful tip: Due to frequent power cuts in Thailand, kitchen and electrical appliances *without* digital clock displays should be chosen; otherwise digital displays spend most of their life flashing and require constant re-setting.

---

[103] If you are working on a budget, a reasonable range of kitchens are designed, supplied and fitted by Homepro, the home-improvement chain.

3. Interior design and furnishings

Before discussing the intricacies of interior design, the first question to consider is whether or not to furnish a property. If you are building a property for immediate re-sale, bear in mind that some buyers prefer to furnish the property themselves (or already have their own furniture). Having said that, the market for *unfurnished* properties in resort destinations is proportionately smaller than would be expected in a major city. This is due to the nature of resort property markets: with a large proportion of potential buyers living internationally and visiting occasionally, the overriding preference is for fully furnished properties not only because of the challenge of furnishing a property while living overseas but because resort property owners prefer not to spend valuable vacation time shopping for furniture!

If you are deciding whether or not to furnish a property (for re-sale), consider also that there is a significant difference between marketing and showing a property that is sensationally furnished; and showing a property that is just bare walls (while attempting to convince a potential buyer that it will look sensational once furnished!). The fact is, most property buyers have little imagination, especially for interior design; however, most will instantly appreciate beautiful interior décor if it has been done for them.

If you decide to furnish a property, it is highly recommended to use the best interior designer or interior design company you can afford. Selecting furniture, fabrics, accessories and colour schemes is an art that requires either an innate talent or a professional eye; it is far more of an art than simply selecting pieces at retail stores and having them delivered. However, engaging a professional interior designer does not necessary cost more than selecting individual pieces at retail prices. It is often possible to provide a design concept (such as Thai, Balinese, Modern, Minimalist, Traditional) together with a budget and leave a designer to do their work (or you can be actively involved in the process). If you are building a property for use as a residence or vacation home, you can furnish to your own individual taste. However, bear in mind if you plan to rent out or eventually sell the property, the interior design concept should not be too "individual" that it fails to appeal to the general rental or property market.

With regard to furniture, one question that often arises is whether to have "built-in" wardrobes or standard "off-the-shelf" wardrobes. The obvious advantage of built-in wardrobes is that they are specifically made (by a builder or furniture retailer) to fit the allocated space. The main disadvantage of contracting a builder to provide built-in wardrobes is the limitation on materials; generally, the choice is between various types of wood. In addition, no matter how skilled the carpenter, it is difficult to build hand-made in-situ wardrobes that look better and function better than factory-built wardrobes with their perfect lines and wide range of materials and designs. The other disadvantage is cost: whether made-to-size wardrobes are provided by a construction company or a furniture retail company, prices are usually significantly higher than standard-sized factory-made furniture.

> **Useful tip:** One way to save money on wardrobes and still have them appear like built-in units is to choose a wardrobe design from a furniture retailer prior to finalising architectural drawings, then work backwards by designing and building walls exactly fitting the "off-the-shelf" wardrobes. In this way, you pay for standard sized wardrobes yet they appear "built-in".

Remember, due to potential sun damage (fading of fabrics or cracking of wooden furniture), curtains and blinds should be installed at the same time or immediately after furniture has been installed in the property (or furniture should remain unpacked until the installation of curtains and blinds).

4. Landscaping

Just as interior design is more than going shopping for furniture, landscaping is more than planting a few trees and plants around the house.

Professional landscaping makes a significant contribution to the aesthetic appearance and enjoyment of a property. It can also provide that "Wow" factor: there is a huge difference between walking into a garden that is sparsely planted with half dying plants, and walking into a lush, green, tropical oasis with scented flowers and shade provided by mature trees.

Ideally, landscape designers should be involved at the initial architectural design stages, instead of being invited towards the end of construction to fill in a few flowerbeds. Experienced landscape designers might suggest the incorporation of "hard" landscaping elements into the architectural design, for example, ornamental features, pathways, steps, or retaining walls for the purpose of creating different garden levels. Alternatively, planters might be added around pool decks and terraces, while mature trees can be strategically located to provide shade for terraces. Indeed, sometimes a single mature tree can become the focal point of the whole property and the property is designed around it!

The cost of landscaping depends on several factors, which are discussed below:

a) *Maturity of trees and plants.* If you want a garden to look mature from day one, it is necessary to buy fully-grown trees and plants. However, there is obviously a cost difference between a ten-metre tall palm tree and a two-metre tall palm tree.

b) *Density.* A garden planted with dense tropical foliage costs more than a few plants sparsely spaced at one-metre intervals. There is a general misperception that a densely planted garden gives a more luxurious impression; however, it should be remembered that overplanting is one sure way to make any garden appear smaller.

c) *The selection of plant and tree species.* Some plants and species are more expensive than others and plant species must be carefully selected according to the conditions (bright sunlight or shade; soil type; depth of planters). Plants also need to be selected to complement one another and their susceptibility to insect attack and diseases must be considered. Certain chemical compounds in plants tend to attract certain insects, for example, hibiscus and aphids are particularly susceptible to attack by mealy bugs; without due care and attention to selection, it is possible to spend money on plants only to lose them and have to replace them within months. There are numerous other considerations, for instance, trees and plants that drop leaves, seedpods and flowers (such as the delonix "flame" tree or ficus group of trees) should not generally be planted next to swimming pools; mango trees drop resin so it is wise not to put anything permanent or expensive under them; and trees with wide-spreading roots should not be planted near building foundations or pathways. Colours must also be considered: planting the perimeter of a garden with cool colours such as blue or white makes a garden appear larger; while warm colours such as red and orange should be avoided in small gardens because their effect is to make a garden appear smaller.

d) *Garden lighting.* The proper lighting and accenting of planted areas is an integral part of landscape design, especially for tropical resort properties where people spend more time sitting outside in the evening. In addition, when garden areas are lit, it has the visual effect of increasing the size of a garden; when gardens are unlit they get "lost" in the darkness, giving the impression of a smaller garden.

e) *"Hardscaping".* This is the use of retaining walls, pathways, steps, water features, drainage and watering systems that are often included as part of an overall landscaping plan. Some of this work overlaps with a construction company's scope of work.

f) *Design fees.* In addition to trees, plants and hardscaping, some landscape designers charge a separate "design fee".

g) *Aftercare.* Putting in plants and trees is just the beginning; someone needs to be responsible for the ongoing maintenance of landscaped gardens, which might include adding compost, mowing lawns, removing dead leaves and branches, and ensuring plants and trees receive sufficient water. Plants must also be monitored for diseases, parasite, fungus and insect attack, which may require the application of fertilisers, insecticides and anti-fungal agents. Maintenance is a key consideration and is normally charged at a monthly rate.

It should be noted that architects are rarely qualified landscape designers. To be a landscape designer requires specialist, in-depth knowledge of plant species and garden planning. This means that unless an architectural firm has an in-house landscaping team, a specialist-landscaping contractor generally needs to be engaged.

5. Outdoor living areas and swimming pools

When designing a property, many people tend to focus on the property to the exclusion of the outdoor areas around. However, among the most compelling reasons for buying or renting a property in a tropical location are the warm weather and "outdoor lifestyle". For this reason, outdoor living areas should receive equal design attention as indoor areas[104].

The "outdoor-living" concept should influence a property's design and layout from the outset with the incorporation of balconies, pool decks, salas, tropical gardens, outdoor Terrazzo bathtubs and rooms opening out onto terraces and pool decks through the use of concertinered or sliding doors. One friend of mine has recently completed construction of several private pool villas where one of the main selling points is an outdoor entertainment system with a five-metre projector screen that allows guests to watch movies from the pool or while seated in the lush tropical garden. It is a selling point that serves to differentiate the properties from others.

The outdoor living concept should also extend to allow guests to sit outside during the hottest parts of the day and when it is raining. Protection from the sun or rain can be provided by sunshades (or sail-type shades) or the incorporation of covered areas into a property's structural design.

It is equally important not to neglect outdoor walkways, passages and "back of the house" areas, which can be landscaped, paved, equipped with outdoor furniture and turned into alternative areas for guests to relax.

---

[104] Property developers often market the size of their properties, not in terms of square metres of internal floor area, but as "total floor space including outdoor living areas", which reflects the importance attached by buyers to outdoor living space.

Swimming pools also need to be incorporated into the overall indoor and outdoor living spaces. Remember, when a property is in use, especially by short-term rental guests, much of the activity centres around the pool deck and the rooms leading from the pool area. The property needs to be designed with this flow of activity in mind, which means ample space should be allowed for outdoor furniture, sun loungers, barbeque areas, salas, pool-area bars and outdoor showers. In addition, it should include the location of guest toilets so that guests do not need to walk through the living areas or bedrooms. The use of water features, Jacuzzis and infinity pools cascading over textured tiles to produce a waterfall effect should also be considered in combination with lighting for pools, terraces and landscaping.

An often-overlooked issue is the depth of swimming pools. I am familiar with one (tall) villa owner who asked the construction company to build a pool with a minimum depth of 1.7 metres, only later to discover that the villa could no longer be safely rented out to families with children, which significantly limited his rental market! If you want a pool that can be used by children, a depth of 50 - 60 centimetres is suitable for younger children, while up to 90 centimetres is suitable for older children. For an adult pool, a depth of 1.5 metres is usually considered the starting point (if you want a lap pool that allows "tumble turns" a depth of 1.7 metres is usually required).

Important tip: On the subject of safety, European safety standards usually require swimming pools to have an outlet drain measuring at least 50 centimetres square, which is a size that prevents small children from being pinned through suction to the bottom of the pool. In Thailand, where there is no such legislation, drain sizes tend to be significantly smaller, which can pose a danger to children. Indeed, most construction companies are not even aware of such dangers when designing pools. However, with smaller drain sizes, one way to remove the hazard is to install three separate drains; a child cannot simultaneously cover three drains and the suction power required to pin a child to the bottom of the pool is safely dispersed.

In addition, for pool decks and terraces, remember to choose tiles or materials that are non-slip and are not too hot to walk on in the sun.

With regard to construction, there are two primary construction methods for concrete pools. One method is to construct formwork for the entire pool and to pour the concrete for the whole pool (base and sides) at one time. The advantage of this method is the absence of "cold joints" in the concrete (where separate concrete sections are joined), which minimises the possibility of leaks. The challenge with this method is that there is no room for error; for instance, if the formwork moves during the pouring of concrete, it can be a disaster. The second method is to pour concrete for the base and sides of the pool separately. The base is poured first and rubber material referred to as "water-stop" is inserted around the full perimeter of the pool to create a waterproof joint between the base and sides.[105]

With regard to pool pump systems, it is important to ensure the pump is sufficiently powerful relative to the size (volume) of the pool. In addition, for operational efficiency the pump room should be located as close to the pool as possible.

Summary

- While consistency in quality and design must extend throughout a property, some elements of a property are more important than others because they are focal points for potential tenants and buyers.
- This does not mean you have a licence to cut corners in areas that are not immediately visible (such as foundations and structure); it simply means setting aside a sufficient budget in order for special attention to be given to these key elements.
- The 5 key elements discussed in this chapter were:
  - Bathrooms
  - Kitchens
  - Interior design and furnishings
  - Landscaping
  - Outdoor living areas and swimming pools

---

[105] This is a thick strip of rubber about 150mm wide, the bottom half of which is inserted into the concrete base of the pool with the other half protruding vertically into the pool wall, which is poured later. This forms a solid barrier between the base and sides to prevent leakage.

54
Mechanical, electrical and plumbing

Mechanical, electrical and plumbing (MEP) drawings are the technical drawings for the electrical, plumbing and air-conditioning systems of a property. These are detailed drawings that set out the location of lights, light switches, power sockets, air-conditioning units and fans for each room.

Unless you are a qualified electrical engineer, the particular specifications and cabling requirements will not mean much to you and should be left to professionals to oversee. However, no specialized training is required to decide the location of power sockets and light switches. Indeed, it pays to get involved in the system design process; there is nothing worse than moving into your new home and to realise after a few days of use that there is no socket in a corner to plug in a reading lamp and no socket in the sala to power a laptop. Alternatively, you might notice that light switches are inconveniently located or some rooms are insufficiently lit.

As will become evident, if you leave the decision making to others in relation to the electrical layout of your home, it will not only fail to reflect your personal preferences; in the worst case (which is not uncommon in Thailand) you will get an electrical system that fails to conform to logical, practical or ergonomic principles. To illustrate the point, an acquaintance recently took possession of a newly built 1,600 square-metre, 8 bedroom luxury villa situated on a hillside with stunning sea views. After only a few hours of moving in, they began to notice the highly unusual and impractical electrical configuration. For instance, a light switch located in the outdoor barbeque area turned on not only the lights around the pool deck but also the hall lights and kitchen lights, while a switch in a hall leading to the bedrooms turned on lights in one of the bedrooms, together with the outside lights along one side of the villa!

While M&E plans are rarely at the top of the priority list, getting involved in the design of these systems gives you an opportunity to influence their practical configuration. Remember, if using a property as a residence, you become familiar with the use of lights and switches until their operation is virtually unconscious. However, if a property is used for short-term rentals, each time guests check-in they must learn which switches operate which lights. Therefore, the configuration of the lighting plan needs to be obvious and logical (or lights need to be labelled).

Properly evaluating electrical design drawings requires you to visualise walking through the finished property, using lights and switches room by room. With regard to lighting, there are 5 considerations. The first consideration is to ensure that the lighting in each room is adequate. Remember, lighting can be provided by a single type of lights, such as halogen or LED downlights; or a combination of different types, such as downlights, recessed lighting and lamps. The location of dimmer switches also needs to be specified.

The second consideration is to make sure switches are conveniently located. The standard height is normally is 1.1 metres or 1.2 metres above finished floor level (although any measurement can be specified). Light switches are typically located inside the door as you enter a room, although for some rooms it is more practical to locate switches outside the room so lights can be switched on before entering.

The third consideration is to ensure switches turn on lights in a reasonable and logical manner. For instance, if you are entering the room on one side and exiting on the other side, a two-way switch is more convenient than returning to the same switch to turn off the lights. Switches for swimming pool lights or pool deck lights can be located in the living room or in the rooms leading onto the pool deck.[106]

A fourth consideration is to ensure that the type and location of light switches reflect the style of lighting; for instance, if lighting is provided by recessed lights or downlights, wall switches are usually the most suitable option. However, if floor lamps or table lamps are to be used, it needs to be determined whether the lamps will be operated by integrated wall switches or whether each lamp has its own switch mechanism (and thus requires a plug socket instead of a switch). Any specialised lighting systems should also be considered, such as pre-programmed "intelligent lighting" or "mood lighting" systems.

A fifth consideration is external lighting, which includes external house lights; security sensor lights; lights for entrances, walkways and car parking areas; and garden lighting, which might include feature lighting for plants and trees.

With regard to power points, it is important to ensure there are a sufficient number of plug sockets in each room: in hallways for vacuum cleaners; in living areas for lamps and laptops (consider pop-up floor sockets); in bedrooms for bedside lamps and corner lamps. In addition, if lights are needed inside wardrobes (a standard feature for off-the-shelf wardrobes) sockets need to be added in the relevant locations. Particular attention should be paid to kitchens, which need sockets for the fridge, oven, hob, extractor fan, microwave, dishwasher, washing machine, kettle, toaster and coffee machine – that's already ten sockets without

---

[106] It is also recommened that pool lights are put on a timer that switches lights off after a specific period of time.

additional sockets for blenders, juicers, music players or mobile phone chargers.

It is a useful idea is to put international or "multi-plug" sockets in convenient locations around the house, which are appreciated by international rental guests and saves them having to go out to buy travel plugs. With regard to external areas, waterproof power outlets should be located around pool terraces, seating areas and in the sala. These are particularly useful for laptop use.

With regard to precise locations, power points need to be considered in relation to furniture layout. For each room, it is necessary to determine where the main pieces of furniture will be and where power points will be needed in relation to the furniture. For example, if you have lamps on either side of a bed, check the measurements to ensure there is sufficient space between the power points to fit the appropriate size of bed (single, double, queen or king). I have seen numerous instances where power points designed for single or double beds end up hidden behind queen or king-sized beds!

Careful thought must also be given to power points required for TVs, DVD players and Wii systems, together with the relevant cables and sockets. The location of TVs and entertainment systems need to be determined, taking into account the best vantage points in relation to the location of furniture.

> **Important tip:** Light switches and power sockets are far easier and cheaper to install during construction than after a property is complete. Changing the location of a socket or adding a new socket requires cutting chases into walls, rewiring, plastering and repainting (not to mention the inconvenience caused to occupants).

In relation to plumbing drawings, the location of showers and taps are generally dictated by architectural drawings and kitchen design drawings. However, you might also need to consider outdoor taps for the purposes of gardening or car cleaning.

When the architect (or construction company) has completed the MEP drawings, it is good practice to request separate A3-sized copies for each room since A4 copies tend to be too small to see technical details. Indeed, if only one drawing is provided for each floor of the property, a magnifying glass is usually required to discern the lines and symbols![107]

---

[107] If you are not confident with technical drawings, construction companies sometimes allow you to draw the desired location of light switches, sockets and outdoor taps on the walls with a marker pen when the building has reached the appropriate stage of construction (when internal walls are complete and before plastering).

Upon completion, checking the operation of the MEP system is one of the tasks to perform as part of the snagging process (see chapter 58).

Summary

- Mechanical, electrical and plumbing (MEP) drawings are the technical drawings for the electrical, plumbing and air-conditioning systems of a property.
- The particular specifications should be left to professionals to oversee; however, it pays to get involved in the system design process.
- It is important to ensure there are a sufficient number of power points in each room; these are much easier to put in during construction than after the completion of a property.

55
Pest control

Many people's idea of "pest control" is calling a pest control company after some type undesirable insect is discovered in your house. However, while it is usually possible to deal with ants or cockroaches in this manner, one of the biggest threats in the tropics is presented by termites.

Termites are whitish soft-bodied ant-like insects that live in colonies and build nests in the ground. They usually enter a building through cracks or joints in concrete and, once inside, eat their way through skirting boards, doorjambs and wooden furniture. If left untreated for long periods of time they can cause substantial damage. As termites enter a house from the ground, the best and most comprehensive treatment is to prevent them from getting near your house and into your house *in the first place*[108]. The issue of pest control must therefore be approached in a proactive manner.

A common misperception is that engaging a pest control company to spray around your house on a monthly basis provides a comprehensive pest control solution. However, the most comprehensive solution is the installation of an underground or "sub-floor" piping system, which is pumped full of anti-termite insecticide that seeps into the soil to repel termite activity. Thereafter, the company that carried out the installation usually returns on a monthly basis to check and treat the house by spraying.

If an underground piping system is to be installed to combat termites, it needs to be planned and implemented during the foundation stage of construction. The normal procedure is for a pest control company to arrive on site after the concreting of ground beams but before the ground floor concrete is poured. The first stage is the installation of a system of PVC pipes around foundation walls, ground beams and other areas considered "high risk". Slow release nozzles are regularly spaced along the length of the pipes and an inlet valve is located at ground level on the outside of the building for the anti-termite insecticide to be pumped into the pipe system[109]. The insecticide is slowly released over time to form an effective barrier to termites around the foundations of the house. In addition, at the time of installation, the pest control company usually

---

[108] This is one of the reasons why many Thai houses are built on "stilts" rather than in direct contact with the ground.
[109] The pipe system typically needs to be re-injected with insecticide on an annual basis.

"saturate-sprays" the soil with insecticide to provide a horizontal barrier to termites before the ground floor concrete is poured.

Dealing with termites is a serious matter and one that is often overlooked by those building property in Thailand. It is also an issue about which architects and construction companies alike fail to remind you, which means you often have to be the driving force behind the integration of a comprehensive anti-termite solution into the construction of your home. In general, there are five things that should be born in mind about pest control:

First, don't underestimate the damage, both physical *and* emotional that termites can cause (it is not a pleasant experience to discover your house is being eaten from the inside by an army of small crawling insects).

Second, take a proactive approach. A monthly contract with a pest control company to spray a completed property is not equivalent to a preventative underground piping system.

Third, prevention is better than cure. Without an underground piping system, if an infestation of termites is discovered, the solution is generally the drilling of holes through your internal finished floor at regular intervals around the perimeter of your house, the injection of insecticide into the holes and then patching the holes with concrete. This is not ideal if your floor has been finished with expensive tiles or terrazzo!

Fourth, plan in advance. Contact several pest control companies, request formal proposals and compare offers as early as possible. Once a company has been chosen, their work needs to be scheduled and coordinated to fit in with the work of the construction company.

Fifth, the issue of pest control should influence the construction or design details of a property. For instance, air-conditioning condenser units should be positioned outside the main buildings and not in voids under a house (warm, moist air creates a perfect environment for termites); all ceilings should have access hatches (to enable pest control technicians to spot insect activity); and wooden skirting boards should be avoided. In addition, all wood should be removed from a site as soon as construction is finished so as not to leave food for termites.

Finally, it should be noted that pest control usually means the application of potentially harmful toxic chemicals. However, there are also companies[110] offering 100% non-toxic methods.

---

[110] For instance, www.ecopestsamui.com

56
Know what you want and be prepared

It is worth devoting a separate chapter to the issue of "knowing what you want and being prepared" because it will save you time and money at each stage of the construction of your property. If you are not prepared and don't know what you want, the inverse is true; it will cost you more time and extra money at every stage.

For example, if you know the style and size of property you want, together with the number of bedrooms and an idea of the preferred layout, it is going to take an architect much less time and effort to produce a set of plans to meet your requirements. Conversely, if you walk into an architect's office without a clear idea of what you want, it will take more time and numerous revisions before you finally arrive at a set of drawings you are happy with.

Further, once construction has started, the more you change your mind in relation to materials or design, the more variations there will be (see chapter 45) and the more delays will be introduced into the construction process. Variations and delays typically end up costing you more money and extending the completion date, which means potential losses either in terms of additional costs or lost rental income. If, on the other hand, you have taken the time in advance to select materials, colours, tiles and accessories, it is far quicker and easier for a construction company to prepare the bill of quantities (BOQ) for your house. It also ensures there are no stoppages or construction delays while materials are chosen; instead they can be ordered in advance.

Knowing in advance the exact materials and accessories you want to use offers another potential benefit. The overall contract price for the construction of a property is usually calculated by adding together material costs and labour rates, then adding a certain percentage for overheads and operating expenses, and then another percentage on top for profit. Thus, for each material listed in the BOQ, you are paying an additional percentage for overhead and profit, typically at least 15%. However, if you have taken time to independently select materials and accessories, it gives you the option of directly ordering some of the materials yourself[111]. These materials will not be listed in the BOQ; instead you will be paying cost price and saving the overhead and profit added by the construction company.

---

[111] Bearing in mind that you must be responsible for quality and on-time delivery. In addition, there are the issues of on-site storage and security.

In general, when building your own property, the best advice is to take more time in planning and preparation instead of jumping in feet first. Take time to look at other properties to determine the preferred style. Study home design and architecture magazines to assist your choice of design concept. Based on the investment objective (chapter 8), decide in advance the ideal number of bedrooms and an approximate layout. Talented architects will of course present ideas to you, although it helps an architect to have some direction as a starting point. Therefore, go to home décor centres and building material suppliers to pre-select materials, tiles and bathroom accessories. Meet kitchen design companies, furniture designers, interior designers, lighting companies, and audio-visual and electrical appliance companies. Get a formal quotation from each independent contractor in advance so they are ready for approval and the companies will be on notice to fit into the work schedule of the main construction company. Gather as much information as you can before you start. The more research you conduct and the more informed you are about various material and design choices, the more prepared you will be to make design and material decisions as the relevant stages are reached.

It is also good practice to spend more time in preparation and research before engaging the relevant professionals. Therefore, start work with the architect only when you are familiar with the different architectural styles and when you have a good idea of what you want to build; prepare to sign contracts with the construction company only when you have achieved a familiarity with the relevant materials and when the BOQ has been double-checked for material specifications; finally, sign contracts and start construction only when you are financially prepared (see chapter 50).

> **Important tip:** The more familiar you become with materials and the work of specialist contractors, the easier it will be to communicate with the professionals involved in the project, particularly the architect and construction company. Further, the more you know, the less the possibility exists for the construction company to cheat you, take advantage of you or cover up their mistakes!

Summary

- Knowing what you want and being prepared will save you time and money at each stage of the construction of your property.
- The more you change your mind in relation to materials or design, the more variations there will be and the more delays will be introduced into the construction process.
- Variations and delays typically end up costing you more money and extending the completion date, which means potential losses either in terms of additional costs or lost rental income.
- Spend more time in research, planning and preparation before engaging the relevant professionals.

57
Delays and penalty clauses
(Essential)

Delays and the late completion of construction projects in Thailand are not an unusual occurrence; they are almost *inevitable.* In fact, so few projects are completed on time that they would fall into the special category labelled "rare".

Thailand is a difficult environment for any construction company to operate in and delays are due to a multitude of reasons. Here are just some examples:

- Labour problems (such as workers failing to return after pay day or simply leaving en-masse without notice)
- Unavailable or late delivery of materials
- Delivery of incorrect materials
- Mistakes made by workers, which requires work to be taken down, new materials to be ordered and work to be redone
- Adverse weather conditions (such as heavy rain preventing work from being carried out)
- Design changes that become necessary as the project proceeds
- Variations at the request of the employer or construction company

In addition to the abovementioned issues, there are a variety of other factors that are impossible to predict or plan for. I recall one example where completion of a luxury villa was delayed because of the late delivery of doors and windows. When they did finally arrive, several weeks late, the delivery driver parked his truck outside the site on a steep access road while he got out to ask the site foreman where they should be unloaded. As they were speaking, the truck rolled down the hill, gaining speed as it went and eventually crashed into a giant boulder at the bottom, catapulting the entire cargo of doors and windows into the air. Naturally, they were all dented, twisted and damaged beyond repair!

Delays also tend to have a compounding effect. For instance, if bad weather holds up structural work on retaining walls, work on the house is unable to commence; the late delivery of materials for a key stage of construction often prevents work from continuing on subsequent stages; and the delivery of incorrect materials means an additional delay while new materials are ordered and delivered. In addition to delays of this nature, construction companies often underestimate the time required to complete the work or put themselves under pressure by agreeing a tight deadline at the outset in order to secure a contract.

In Thailand, therefore, *the key factor is not whether there will be delays but the extent of the delays and how you choose to deal with them*[112]. It pays to keep uppermost in mind the ultimate objective of getting a completed property built to a high quality standard and to this end it is essential to take a common sense approach to dealing with delays. For instance, if a project is clearly not going to be completed within the contractual deadline, the issue of penalty clauses often arises. For foreigners unfamiliar with the challenges, trials and tribulations of getting work done in Thailand, late completion penalties often appear to be the ideal method for punishing the construction company and benefitting financially from the delay. However, from the perspective of the construction company, if penalty payments become too severe – to the point of making a project unprofitable – the potential is high for relationships to break down or for potential shortfalls to be made up by cutting corners or substituting materials. Those that have engaged a construction company to build their property need to be aware of these issues and deal with them sensibly.

This is especially the case where delays have become so pervasive that completion of the property will actually result in a financial loss for the construction company. At this point, the only incentive for completing the job becomes the maintenance of their reputation. If the company has a reputation to protect, work is likely to continue; if it hasn't a reputation worth protecting, work is likely to stop. It is often as simple as that. In other words, if preventing a financial loss is a greater incentive than protecting a reputation, you could quite easily find the construction company stopping work and leaving the site.

Quality of workmanship is also at stake. If a builder must complete work by a certain date to avoid financial penalties, and the only way to meet a deadline is by rushing work or throwing additional workers on site whose capabilities are questionable, the result tends to be sub-standard work. Hurrying work in Thailand is often self-defeating in that sub-standard work must be taken down and be done again, which takes even longer. Owners that are quick to crack the whip to enforce deadlines must keep in mind the delicate balance between speed and quality. In sum, it is often better to allow more time in order to get a top quality finish: quality lasts a lifetime, even though it might take an extra month or two; completion to a high standard, especially in Thailand, should be valued more than on-time completion.

In addition, building a property in Thailand is not a precise science. There are often issues that must be dealt with on an informal basis or things the construction

---

[112] For condominium properties, the Standard Form issued by the Ministry of Interior sets out strict criteria that must be fulfilled by a developer to claim a construction extension, with a maximum extension of one year.

company might need to do that are beyond the scope of the contract, such as dealing with troublesome neighbouring landowners or government officials looking for "donations". There is also the issue of remedying items on the snag list (see chapter 58) that can either be dealt with cooperatively and efficiently, or slowly and reluctantly. If you are inflexible with a builder on deadlines or the enforcement of a penalty clause, the builder is likely to become inflexible with you on other matters. They might work to contract and do no more, charging extra to perform work that would normally be included without charge. Sometimes, if you take a hard line, you might find the project no longer runs as smoothly.

This is not to say you must forgive a construction company for any and all delays. It is just wiser to accept from the outset that there are likely to be delays and, when they occur, you must deal with them in a pragmatic manner. It is first prudent to identify the source of the delay before action is taken. If the construction company is busy with other jobs and your site has been left without workers, then you might be justified in taking a tough stance. If, on the other hand, adverse weather or material supply problems have prevented work from proceeding, and in the case where the Construction Agreement does not provide adequate guidelines, the matter should be approached with some degree of flexibility. Such flexibility includes managing your own expectations. Don't get too attached to a certain completion date or feel *personally* aggrieved if the construction company is unable to finish your house by the agreed completion date. The successful completion of a property in Thailand generally requires these issues to be approached with common sense and to be fair yet firm.

> **Important tip:** A Construction Agreement without a clearly defined penalty clause is asking for trouble and puts you at a significant disadvantage. The existence of a penalty clause at least gives you the *option* to enforce late payment penalties, or to use penalty payments as a bargaining chip in a whole host of situations that might arise.

A common example where late penalty payments can be used is in the context of variations. During the course of construction, there will inevitably be changes or additions to the approved drawings and it is possible to negotiate the cost of these changes to be offset against late payment penalties. This is a win-win situation: the client gets changes done without technically have to pay extra for them, while the construction company is able to offset the value of the work against penalty payments at construction cost.

Despite its name, the primary purpose of a penalty clause is not to punish a construction company. Instead, penalty clauses should *motivate* construction companies to complete projects on time. This is particularly important when a property needs to be complete by a fixed date due to other commitments, such as rental bookings. Consider the case where a construction company has a number of concurrent jobs where each job has a contractual penalty clause *but your job doesn't.* Imagine which jobs are going to receive most attention in the event a construction company has limited workers or resources?

In reality, if the Construction Agreement is without a penalty clause, there is nothing (except a termination clause) to prevent the construction company taking as long as it wants; in other words, the absence of a penalty clause is a licence for a construction company to take their time and, in the case of a poorly organised company, completion of your property will take a *very* long time. Here is a real life example to illustrate the point. A construction company was contracted to build a villa. The Construction Agreement stated the completion date as October 15th and contained a penalty clause. In September – when it was clear that the completion of the project would be slightly later than the contractual completion date – some variations were necessary. After negotiation, the construction company agreed to perform the variations for free in exchange for the client agreeing not to enforce late completion penalties (assuming completion would be a month late, based on the construction company's verbal assurances). Shortly after this agreement, the number of workers on the site was reduced, the pace of work slowed, and *seven months later the construction company had still not competed the job!*

This example perfectly illustrates the consequences when the motivating force of a penalty clause is removed; without a penalty, any incentive to complete on time simply disappears.

With regard to the amount of the penalty payment, the opportunity cost of rental bookings for the completed property should be considered as a starting point for the penalty clause. For example, if the average rental rate for the property is US$ 300 per night (taking into account high, low and peak seasons) and assuming an occupancy rate of 50%, the starting point for a monthly penalty payment should be in the region of US$ 4,500.[113]

Builders make all kinds of promises during the tender stage in order to secure a job but their subsequent actions rarely match their promises. They often start a job with good intentions and then, depending on their overall workload, workers are moved off to other sites, leaving your job at a standstill for weeks or even months. Sometimes a skeleton-staff of three unskilled workers is left on site

---

[113] 15 days x US$ 300 = 4,500.

just to give the appearance that the job is still "in progress": one sweeping up; another walking around wondering what to do in the absence of instructions; and the other sleeping off a hangover in the corner!

In addition to a penalty clause, therefore, it is also worth more clearly defining the "grounds for termination". For instance, if you ask a construction company at the tender stage how many workers are needed on site at each stage of construction in order to complete the project on time, it is technically possible to put these numbers into the contract, together with a clause stating if the number of workers falls below a specified minimum, it could be considered breach of contract or grounds for termination (or financial penalties could be applied). When a construction company is under pressure to complete several other jobs, this might help to keep workers on your site.

In Thailand, since delays are virtually inevitable with construction projects (even with the existence of a penalty clause), it is wise to have a contingency plan for late completion, particularly in relation to rental bookings or planned vacations (remember that late completion might also have a bearing on exchange rate risk, see chapter 66).

Important tip: If you are planning a vacation to stay in your new house upon the scheduled completion date, make sure to buy flight tickets that allow a change of date. Alternatively, make a hotel reservation in case your property is not complete. If you have advance rental bookings, make sure the rental contract provides you with the ability to refund money to guests, or to provide guests with alternative accommodation, should your property not be ready on time.

Having contingency plans will help to remove the pressure in relation to a specific completion date. Consequently, when there is less pressure to complete the property by a certain date, it will help you to deal with the construction company on a more level-headed and objective basis.

Summary

- Delays and the late completion of construction projects in Thailand are almost inevitable, due to a multitude of reasons.
- The key factor is not whether there will be delays but the extent of the delays and how you choose to deal with them.
- It pays to keep uppermost in mind the ultimate objective of getting a completed property built to a high quality standard and to this end it is essential to be flexible and to take a common sense approach to delays.
- Penalty clauses should *motivate* construction companies to complete projects on time; otherwise there is nothing to prevent them taking as long as they want.
- A Construction Agreement without a clearly defined penalty clause puts you at a significant disadvantage. The existence of a penalty clause at least gives you the option to enforce late payment penalties or to use penalty payments as a bargaining chip.

58
Snagging

With any newly built property, there will inevitably be faults, defects or things that have been overlooked or left unfinished by the construction company. "Snagging" is the process of going through a property upon completion to identify and list these defects. The list of snags or "snag list" is then submitted to the construction company for the defects to be rectified.

The snag list generally covers relatively minor problems that can be easily rectified, such as uneven plasterwork, poor paint finishing, chipped tiles or incomplete grouting; more significant alterations and design changes have generally been taken care of during the construction process, and structural issues are covered by structural guarantees (see chapter 48). The rectification of items on the snag list should, however, be considered separate to the "defects warranty" or return-to-site policy, which typically extend for six months or one year *after* completion of the property.

In addition to the primary goal of getting a properly finished and fully functional property, the process of snagging is important for several reasons. The submission of a snag list and the rectification of defects are linked to the acceptance of "practical completion" and formal handover of the property. Being linked to practical completion usually means that satisfactory rectification of the items on the snag list is tied to the release of the final payment and the payment of retention (see chapter 47). As a consequence of the snagging procedure being linked to the final payment, snagging has the potential to become a source of conflict with the construction company, if not handled correctly.

With regard to the timing of the snagging procedure, construction companies (and off-plan developers) usually issue a formal notice to advise you that the property will soon be completed and will be ready for inspection, usually with 30 days notice. Sometimes they will also provide you with a snagging document that can be used to list defects.

> **Important tip:** It is imperative not to allow yourself to be unduly pressured by a construction company to carry out snagging before work on the property has finished. It is equally important not to inspect the property if it has not been properly cleaned; dirt on floors and walls can mask cracks and defects.

In addition, don't feel pressured to conduct a snag list in the presence of the builder. If the builder walks around with you to perform snagging, they might try to hurry you and you might feel uncomfortable noting minor defects. As there is usually only one opportunity to submit a snag list, it is important that you take time to properly inspect a property (it might be of practical use to walk around the property again with the builder once the defect list has been prepared). If a defect is not listed, it pays to remember that its later rectification either depends on the goodwill of the builder or it will need to be repaired at your own expense.

In other countries, such as the UK, it is often possible to engage an inspection company or "snagging inspector" to perform the service of snagging on your behalf. A professional inspector will go through your new home, make a thorough list of defects, suggest optimal remedies and follow up with the builder to ensure all the defects are satisfactorily rectified. In Thailand, unless a qualified snagging inspector is available, you generally need to do the snagging yourself, although it might help to take a friend with you – two sets of eyes are better than one (even better if the friend has construction experience). To assist you, a snagging checklist can be purchased and downloaded from the Internet[114].

Ideally, snagging should be performed by moving into the property, which allows you to check and test every aspect and function of the property through actual use. However, this is not always possible; builders are reluctant to allow you to move in prior to submitting a snag list due to the damage that might be caused by occupants or by careless removal personnel carrying large pieces of furniture![115] If there are no outstanding payment issues and you have a good relationship with the builder, it might be possible to negotiate moving-in and submitting a snag list at a later date.

Important tip: It is important to complete the snagging process before the final payment (or retention payment) is made. In this way, you retain some degree of leverage to get defects resolved to your satisfaction.

When you have had the opportunity to thoroughly inspect your new property, the snag list should be submitted as early as possible, while the builder is still "hot" on your project and workers are in the vicinity. If weeks or months are allowed to pass before you get around to checking the property, workers have typically moved on to other jobs, which means they now have to be (reluctantly) taken off other sites to perform work on your house. This is especially the case if the

---

[114] There are many different sources. An example can be found at www.snaggingchecklist.co.uk although it is likely to be more appropriate for properties built in the United Kingdom.
[115] Builders are also reluctant to allow clients to move in before formal completion and before payment has been made in full.

construction company has received payment in full, whereby the rectification of outstanding work on your snag list now largely depends on goodwill.

There are two other reasons why defects should be identified and rectified as early as possible. First, if all the defects have been dealt with before you move in, you will not have the hassle of workman needing to gain access to your property later, which is an inconvenience when the property is occupied. Second, if you are planning to rent out the property, it is better to find and fix defects yourself, rather than running the risk of defects being discovered by tenants. If a defect affects a tenant's enjoyment of the property (especially plumbing and electrical problems), the tenant will be inconvenienced while repairs are made and will often demand a discount or refund, depending on the seriousness of the defect.

So what is the best way to perform snagging? The best approach is to perform a methodical room-by-room inspection of the property, including the exterior of the property and outdoor areas, including the pool, pool deck and terraces.

What are you looking for? The short answer is any material defect, anything that does not function properly, or any work that has been left unfinished by the construction company. For later reference, it is a good idea to photograph each defect. To provide an example of the *kind* of defects you might come across, the list below details the top ten snagging defects identified in new properties by New Build Inspections[116] in the United Kingdom[117].

- Plasterwork patching and redecoration.
- Ceramic tiling and bathroom tiling grouting incomplete.
- Architraves and skirting boards require caulking.
- External brickwork missing weep vents and requires brick acid wash.
- Block work not fully pointed.
- Loft insulation incomplete and not laid correctly.
- Extractor fans venting into roof and ceiling voids.
- Pipes not lagged in roof void areas.
- Broken roof tiles.
- Defective or scratched glazing.

One of the main things to test in a new property is the mechanical and electrical system. For instance, the operation of all lights, dimmer switches, plug sockets, fans and air-conditioners need to be checked. Each plug socket, light fitting and light switch cover plate should be checked to make sure they are level (not

---

[116] www.newbuildinspections.com
[117] These defects are not wholly representative of the defects found in Thailand due to the different construction methods used; for example, note the reference to external brickwork and loft insulation.

crooked), that they at the correct height and are clean and free from paint and plaster. Light switches should also be checked to ensure that switches operate lights according to the lighting plan (see chapter 54). The system loading should also be tested by turning on all appliances and lights simultaneously.

In the bathrooms, taps and showers should be checked to make sure they operate properly. In addition, taps, shower units and accessories, such as towel rails and toilet roll holders, should be checked to make sure they have been securely fixed. Bathrooms should also be checked for scratched surfaces, damage to sanitary fittings, loose toilet seats and leaks. It is also necessary to be aware of smells in the bathroom; poor plumbing is a common problem in Thailand and leaking pipes create damp and mouldy smelling bathrooms.

With kitchens, it is necessary to look for cracked or chipped worktops, gaps in the caulking joints, incorrectly closing cupboard doors, and loosely fitting handles and taps. In addition, the brand names and model numbers of kitchen appliances need to be checked for consistency with those listed in the BOQ (bill of quantities) or in the marketing materials (in the case of properties purchased off-plan).

Hot water systems should be checked and both baths and Jacuzzis should be filled and tested; plumbing systems for Jacuzzis and bathtubs are another common problem and if inlet and outlet pipes have not been correctly installed, they will leak or overflow into the rooms below!

Other items on the snag list are uneven floors, rough or patchy plaster, and poor paint finishes. All floor and wall tiling should be checked for chipped tiles and incomplete grouting (as noted in the "top ten" list above). Walls, floors, balconies and terraces must be also be checked for cracks[118], while internal doors, external doors and windows need to be checked for smooth operation and the proper functioning of handles and locks. Surfaces also need to be examined for chips, dents and scratches.

With regard to swimming pools, the main items to look out for are cracked pool tiles, incomplete grouting and the operation of pool lights and pump systems.

In relation to the roof, it is necessary to look for cracked or missing tiles, or any gaps where driving rain can enter the property.

---

[118] Although bear in mind that new properties need time to "settle" and it is normal for cosmetic cracks to appear. These are easily rectified and are often left several months before the builder repairs them.

Since it is often possible to submit only one snag list, it is important to be as detailed as possible. If the chosen construction company has high quality standards and invites you to perform snagging only after they have already performed their own rigorous check for defects, it is possible that only a few snags will be found. Indeed, the owner of one recently completed property discovered only six defects. With some new properties, however, it is possible to find between ten and twenty snags per room, which can mean as many as a hundred snags for an average three-bedroom, three-bathroom property!

With regard to submitting a snag list, sometimes the builder provides a standard form for you to fill in. In the absence of a standard form, the best way is to prepare your own snag list using a spreadsheet or word document. Defects should be listed in a logical order, usually room by room, in the order that you find them as you walk through the property. The list should have six columns, as follows:

- Snag Number: for the purpose of giving each defect a quick-reference number for future correspondence.
- Room and location: to make it easy for the builder to find the defect. The defects should be listed in order by room and location, rather than in a random manner.
- Description: a full and detailed description of the defect.
- Picture: pictures are useful to support the description, reduce misunderstandings and assist the builder in locating defects.
- Recommended remedy: if there are several alternative methods to rectify the defect, or a preferred alternative, a full description of the materials and construction method can be included.
- Completed: it is useful to have a column that can be ticked when you re-inspect the property to check that defects have been rectified. Alternatively, the date that each defect is rectified can be inserted if inspections are ongoing.

When you are sure all defects have been noted and the snag list is complete, print two or more copies, keeping one copy for your own records, while the others are submitted to the construction company. Depending on the level of formality required by the contract, you might wish to get a signed and stamped copy in return from the construction company as proof of receipt, or a copy might need to be sent by registered courier.

Summary

- "Snagging" is the process of going through a property upon completion to identify faults, defects or things that have been overlooked or left unfinished by the construction company.
- The list of snags or "snag list" is then submitted to the construction company for the defects to be rectified.
- Submission of a snag list and the rectification of defects are usually linked to the acceptance of "practical completion" and formal handover of the property.
- Never feel pressured to conduct a snag list in the presence of the builder. There is usually only one opportunity to submit a snag list so it is important that you take time to properly inspect a property.
- The best way to perform snagging is to conduct a methodical room-by-room inspection of the property, including the exterior of the property and outdoor areas, including the pool, pool deck and terraces. It is also a good idea to photograph each defect.

59
Scheduling and sequencing

In Thailand, it is wise to sequence each task in order to avoid complications and disagreements. It is also important, whenever possible, to schedule the work of different contractors so that the work of one contractor does not interfere with the work of another. For example:

- Architectural plans should be finalised, approved and signed off before construction companies are approached for quotations.

- The bill of quantities (BOQ) and detailed quotations must be approved before a contract is discussed with the construction company.

- All the details of the Construction Agreement need to be checked, approved and signed before the construction company delivers materials to the site or commences work on the project.

- Snagging must proceed only when the construction company has finished its work (and sends you a formal notice to advise that the property is ready for snagging).

- Third party contractors, such as kitchen contractors, should only start work when all the items on the snag list have been completed and the construction company's workers have left the site.

- Furniture, curtains and blinds should only be delivered and installed when the construction company and specialist contractors have finished their work.

- If you intend to sell the property, don't accept viewings until it is completed and furnished (potential purchasers have little imagination) and don't start marketing the property until professionally taken photographs are available.

Here are three examples to illustrate the importance of scheduling and sequencing:

- Toward the end of the tender stage, one construction company is becoming a favourite contender for the project and you are just tying up a few loose ends on the BOQ (bill of quantities) before agreeing a final price. Since it looks like this particular construction company is going to win the contract, it is *informally* agreed that materials can be delivered to the site and preliminary work can start. Shortly thereafter, a dispute arises over the contract and the contractor significantly increases the price due to an error or "unforeseen" element". You decide that this construction company is no longer competitive (or ethical) but it is too late; the construction company has already started work, which further complicates the disagreement!

- The kitchen contractor arrives to begin the installation of high quality kitchen cabinets and worktops, while workers from the construction company are still on site. Halfway through installation, cupboard doors are found to have been chipped and worktops have been scratched. The kitchen contractor guarantees that they were installed in perfect condition; the construction company dismisses any suggestion that their workers were involved in causing the damage. Kitchen components must be reordered and replaced, which adds another month to the completion date. In addition, who will cover the cost of replacing the components?

- Furniture has been ordered from a supplier and the delivery date is fixed. Unfortunately, the construction company is running behind schedule and the furniture is delivered and installed while construction workers are still on site. The owner of the house arrives at lunchtime to find workers sleeping on top of the furniture. Further, some of the furniture has been damaged and (green curry) food stains are evident from their lunch. Who foots the bill for replacing the furniture? The furniture supplier delivered and installed the furniture, leaving it in pristine condition, while the construction company disclaims all responsibility. In addition, during delivery and installation, the furniture company workers have made scratch marks on the walls and have damaged the handrail when the furniture was carried upstairs. The walls therefore need to be repainted and the handrail replaced. The construction company has indicated that this repair work will not be included in the snag list; instead, additional costs will be charged for the repairs.

It is inevitable that the work of specialist contractors must be coordinated with the work of the construction company. In such cases, it is sometimes unavoidable that personnel from different companies must simultaneously carry out work on the site. However, whenever it can be avoided, the work of the various contractors should be scheduled or sequenced so that there is no overlap. This is true for property construction in any country; it is especially relevant when planning the construction of properties in Thailand.

Summary

- It is wise to approach each task of a project in sequential order to avoid complications and disagreements between the various professionals and contractors.
- It is also important to schedule the work of different contractors so the work of one contractor does not interfere with the work of another.

60
Registering your property

Once construction of your property is complete, one of the last things to do is to register the property, which is necessary to arrange services such as telephone, Internet, electricity and the delivery of mail to the house.

Property in Thailand is registered by way of a house registration book or condominium registration book. The Thai name for registration book is "Tabian Baan" (translated literally, Tabian means "registration" and Baan means "house"). In appearance, house registration books look much like the savings account passbooks issued by Thai banks. The house registration book is an important official administrative document that is issued by the local municipality or Tessabaan. However, it has nothing to do with *actual legal ownership of a house or condominium and should not be confused with proof of ownership.* Under Thai law, the Tabian Baan or house registration book is an official document that identifies the address of the property (household) and is evidence of the registered address of the persons living at that address (it may or may not state the name of the owner and the occupants).[119]

There are two types of house books – the blue house book (Thor. Ror. 14) for Thai nationals (and foreigners with residence permits) and the yellow house book (Thor. Ror. 13) for foreigners who legally reside in Thailand but do not have residency permits. The blue book is the standard issue.

The key document for submitting an application for a house registration book is the Building Permit (see chapter 46) although various other documents may be required and procedures may vary from district to district. The process of registering and obtaining a house registration book generally takes only a few days. Your lawyer or construction company should be able to assist you with the process.

---

[119] In many cases, the house registration book can serve as a useful means of verifying your address when dealing with governmental departments, such as the transfer and registration of cars and motorcycles at the Transport Department.

STEP 5

Off-Plan property

61
What is "off-plan" property?

Before beginning a discussion of off-plan property, it is worth defining what buying "off-plan" means. Off-plan property is basically buying the rights to a "property" that has yet to be built, as opposed to buying a finished property on the secondary market. Typically it means buying property from a developer at the "pre-construction" stage. In other words, you are buying a piece of paper; the *promise* of a property. It is also common for a property developer to commence construction of a project and continue to sell units of "property" throughout construction while still referring to properties as "off-plan". In this sense, the term off-plan is used in a general sense to refer to properties that are not yet completed by the developer, either pre-construction or during construction.

When purchasing an off-plan property, it is conceptually important to understand that the developer is assuming responsibility for purchasing land; subdivision; all issues relating to access and utilities; and full accountability for construction and project management. In other words, you are technically passing full responsibility to the property developer for most of the issues discussed in Steps 2 and 4, and for reference the relevant chapter headings are reproduced below. It might be useful to return to these chapters to understand the scope of a property developer's work.

Step 2: Land
- Land measurement
- Land title
- Land scams
- Land title investigation
- Land title insurance
- Access?
- Electricity?
- Water and sewage disposal?
- Zoning and building regulations
- Size matters
- Flat land or hillside?
- Subdividing land
- Serviced land plots

Step 4: Building your own property
- Building your own property
- The construction process
- Management and organisational structure
- Working with architects
- Build Quality
- Surveying land
- Choosing a construction company
- Quotations and the BOQ
- Variations
- Building Permits
- Staged payments
- Construction Guarantees
- The construction agreement
- Financial considerations
- Planning for rainy seasons
- Retaining walls and drainage
- What sells?
- Mechanical, electrical and plumbing
- Pest control
- Know what you want and be prepared
- Delays and penalty clauses
- Snagging
- Scheduling and sequencing
- Registering your property

If you are considering the purchase of off-plan property, you are in essence consenting to pass responsibility to the property developer for all of these matters, in addition to financial planning, cash flow forecasting, marketing and sales. Indeed, for those who have no intention or inclination to get involved in the property construction process, this is one of the principal benefits. However, it can prove to be a double-edged sword; by passing responsibility to a property developer for these tasks, you are also largely or wholly giving up control over their implementation. *It is this giving up of control that is the source of most of the risks associated with off-plan property.*

To put off-plan investments in perspective, an analogy is possible with other investment types. For instance, if you invest money into your own company, you have full control over management and decision-making. This is in stark contrast to investing money in the shares of companies listed on the stock market, in which case any control over your investment is immediately given up to others. The former is reflective of building your own property, while the latter reflects the situation of off-plan property investments.

The risks and benefits associated with buying an off-plan property are discussed in more detail in the following chapters.

Summary

- Off-plan property is basically buying the rights to a "property" that has yet to be built, as opposed to buying a finished property on the secondary market; in other words, the *promise* of a property.
- When purchasing an off-plan property, it is important to understand that the developer is assuming responsibility for purchasing land; subdivision; all issues relating to access and utilities; and full accountability for construction and project management.
- By passing responsibility to a property developer for these tasks, you are largely or wholly giving up control over their implementation. *It is this giving up of control that is the source of most of the risks associated with off-plan property.*

62
Risks and benefits of buying off-plan property
(Essential)

Lets start with the benefits of purchasing off-plan property. The principal benefit of purchasing an off-plan property is that you are getting a new property built for you just by signing on the dotted line and paying the money, without any further involvement on your part (if all goes well). There is no need to look for land, deal with access issues, arrange utilities, get quotations from construction companies, or engage a project manager.

A further benefit is that properties sold at the preconstruction stage are typically sold at a discount to market value, which allows purchasers to lock in a future capital gain at the point of signing the contract. In other words, it is a way to buy properties at a lower price. An additional and consequent benefit is improved rental yields. Rental income will be based on the market value of the *finished property,* which means the *actual* yield is higher when based on the discounted off-plan purchase price, rather than the market value of the property at completion (refer to the calculations in chapter 10).

> **Important tip:** It should be understood that the advantage of improved yields only arises if the pre-construction purchase price is sufficiently below the market value of the property at the time of completion. In an upwardly moving market, buying off-plan properties can be an excellent investment strategy. However, if the off-plan price is not properly discounted or the market turns downward (or the purchasing currency weakens during construction), you could be assuming the inherent risks of buying an off-plan property without the corresponding rewards. Instead of risk-free returns you will be buying into *return-free* risks!

Buying an off-plan property from a developer also has the advantage that, once you have signed on the dotted line, the price is fixed (except in cases where the developer runs out of money and comes back to ask for more!). This is in contrast to engaging a construction company to build your own property, in which case you believe the contract price is fixed but with variations being the norm rather than the exception (see chapter 45), the property virtually always ends up costing more than you planned and budgets often go out the window.

Being able to secure an off-plan property with a reservation agreement and a small deposit also reduces the capital required by a purchaser to take control over an asset, while the remaining payments only become due according to the stages of construction, or at best, upon completion[120].

So what are the inherent risks of off-plan property investments?

The most basic risk stems from the fact that you are entering into a contract to buy a property without having first been able to view and evaluate the finished product. Architectural sketches are advertised and three-dimensional perspectives are featured in magazines well before occupation is possible; in most cases, a year or two in advance of completion. For condominium freehold units, developers are under a statutory duty not to misrepresent facts, although in the case of unregulated developments, detailed plans of the proposed development are sometimes not even available. Remember, when you buy off-plan, you are paying for a property where the end result might differ from expectations.

However, to more fully appreciate the risks for purchasers, it is necessary to understand the benefits of selling off-plan properties from the perspective of a property developer. Selling property at the pre-construction stage has two primary benefits for a property developer, both of which are fundamentally related to financing. Firstly, if a developer can sell units of property and receive deposits from purchasers before construction has commenced (with further payments corresponding to the stages of construction), the capital investment required by the developer to build a project is significantly reduced. Secondly, if the developer is able to confirm the sale of a certain number (or percentage) of units, the developer is often able to borrow money from a bank, which can be used to fund construction since, at least on paper, confirmed sales mean guaranteed inward future cash flows from the purchasers.

Taken to the extreme, an off-plan sales strategy allows a property developer to start a project with minimal investment, usually only the cost of land and marketing. In certain circumstances, a developer does not even need to buy land; if a property developer can enter into a joint venture with a landowner, whereby payment for the land can be made concurrently with property sales,[121] it is perfectly feasible for a property developer to start a project with no investment, except for marketing related costs.

---

[120] Payment of a large part of the purchase price upon completion is unusual because generally the purpose of selling off-plan in Thailand's resort areas is to use progress payments to fund construction.

[121] The property developer typically pays a premium price for the land, in exchange for the landowner's acceptance of payment in stages.

Herein lies the principal risk: that of non-completion due to an inadequately capitalised developer that is dependent upon sales to finance a project. During prosperous times, when property buyers are numerous and property prices are rising, new (and under-capitalized) property developers are attracted by the large profits to be made with minimal investment. If demand for property is strong and the company is reasonably well managed, they can succeed. However, in a declining property market or during times of crisis (which are regular occurrences in Thailand), developers that are wholly reliant on sales to finance projects are often unable to complete them and go out of business, leaving a trail of semi-finished properties and financial losses behind them.

The consequences – financial and otherwise – of a developer failing to complete a project are similar in nature to a construction company becoming insolvent during the construction of your house. These were discussed in chapter 43. In the case where you have purchased land, separately engaged a construction company to build a property, and the construction company then becomes insolvent, despite the difficulties and financial losses involved, at least you own or control the land and can engage another contractor to complete the property. However, in the case of purchasing an off-plan property from a developer, the risks are compounded because you have allowed the developer to assume responsibility for purchasing land, building the property, project managing construction, and everything else in-between. In other words, with off-plan properties you are generally the owner of nothing (depending on the circumstances) until the property has been completed and formal legal ownership of the property (and any interest in the land) has been legally registered to you. If the developer becomes insolvent during this process, what usually happens is that "your property" remains in a semi-complete state and any money paid thus far vanishes.

In fact, with failed off-plan developments, the situation is exponentially more complex; especially with inexperienced first-time developers where the legal situation is often so convoluted buyers have little hope of recovering their losses. In some cases, the developer is not the owner of the project land; this is typically still the Thai landowner with whom buyers have no contractual relations. Oftentimes, when the developer experiences cash flow problems and is unable to turn to commercial banks for assistance, private loans are taken against land plots, whereby the title to the land is transferred to the lender until the loan is repaid (i.e. the lender becomes the owner of the land when the developer is unable to repay the loan). The issue is further compounded because inexperienced developers tend to keep messy accounts and are often under investigation by the tax authorities (usually in relation to non-declaration of income).

The risk of non-completion is present to some degree with all off-plan investments, regardless of the size of the property developer or the size of the development.

Thailand's resort areas and islands are littered with half-complete villas and projects that were started by property developers both large and small: property investors have lost money buying off-plan properties ranging from town house apartments costing a few million Baht to super luxury villas costing millions of dollars.

Important tip: Don't be seduced by high profile developers or glossy brochures; by their very nature, all off-plan properties come with a measure of risk.

Summary

The main benefits and risks associated with buying off-plan properties are summarised below:

Benefits

- A new property is built for you with minimal involvement.
- Properties can be purchased at a discount to market value, which allows purchasers to lock in a future capital gain at the point of signing the contract.
- The purchase price is fixed.
- Buyers can take control of an asset with a small deposit or reservation fee.
- Payment can be made in stages during construction of the property.
- Higher rental yields upon completion.

Risks

- The finished property might differ from expectations.
- Market risk (property prices might fall during construction).
- Exchange rate risk (purchase currency might weaken during construction).
- Risk of non-completion.

63
Mitigating risks

There is a degree of risk associated with any off-plan property purchase. Thus, before moving onto a discussion of how to mitigate the risks, it should be noted that property buyers who are unwilling to assume the inherent risk of off-plan properties should buy a property that is already completed. When you buy completed property you can see exactly what you are getting and this is, in effect, the *ultimate* strategy for mitigating off-plan risk!

Alternatively, off-plan property can be purchased when construction is nearing completion, whereby non-completion risks are correspondingly diminished according to the stage of completion (but not altogether eliminated). The disadvantage of this strategy is that the choice of units is reduced and the most desirable units have usually been taken[122]. In addition, investment returns might not be as high because prices have a tendency to increase during construction to reflect the reduction in risk or the success of sales.

In general, it is unnecessary to assume the risks of buying property at the pre-construction stage purely for the purpose of buying below market value. It is often possible to buy an already completed property at a "distressed" or discounted price; indeed, plenty of opportunities exist for price negotiations in the secondary market, especially when a market is stagnant or in a downturn.

If you have the time and inclination, there is the alternative of purchasing land and building your own property, which has been covered in Steps 2 and 4 of this book. With this approach, you are able to assume a greater degree of control over issues of land title, access, ownership structures and construction finances. The other benefit is that you will be getting a property at land and construction cost, without the premium charged by a property developer.

For purchasers who are willing to assume the inherent risk of purchasing off-plan property, it should be recognised that risk is a normal component of any investment decision. The question is not whether risk exists; it is to ask, "What are the risks?" and through the process of identifying the risks, strategies can

---

[122] Although sometimes it is possible to negotiate a better price for the remaining units at the end of a project if the developer is having difficulty selling them; or in cases where a developer is eager to move onto the next project and assist marketing and public relations by promoting a current project as "Sold Out!"

be formulated to reduce and mitigate these risks.

The previous chapter highlighted the most obvious risks associated with buying properties off the plan. These were:

1. Finished property might differ from expectations
2. Market risk (property prices might fall during construction)
3. Exchange rate risk (purchase currency might weaken during construction)
4. Risk of non-completion

With the identification of the principal risks, strategies can now be formulated to minimise them. Each of these risks is examined separately in the following four chapters.

Summary

- If you want to completely avoid the risks associated with buying off-plan property, buy property that is already completed!
- Alternatively, buy off-plan property when construction is nearing completion.
- If you are considering off-plan property as a strategy to buy below market value, consider buying distressed property in the secondary market.
- When building your own property, you assume a greater degree of control over issues of land title, access, ownership structures and construction finances.
- If you are willing to assume the inherent risk of purchasing off-plan property, it is necessary to identify the risks and formulate strategies to mitigate them.

64
Mitigating risks (differing expectations)

As discussed in chapter 3, when buying condominium freehold property, developers have a statutory obligation to deliver on the promises made in marketing materials. However, for other types of property, a greater degree of caution must be exercised. The concern that a finished off-plan property might differ from expectations is fundamentally a matter of clarifying expectations at the outset and ensuring the developer remains consistent with them.

There are various ways to close the gap between what a finished property will look like and what you expect it to be like. To begin with, if there are doubts relating to any aspect of the property, it is your responsibility to clarify the details; if you have any questions about the design or you are unfamiliar with the material specifications, you need to make sure all questions are answered and make the effort to become familiar with the specified materials. In other words, it is necessary to find out exactly what you are buying (see also chapter 69 - "What else are you buying?").

If a property developer has built a show home (or a model), don't assume the actual finished property will be identical in all aspects. Sometimes one construction company is engaged to build a show house, with available materials, while the project is put out to tender and ultimately a different construction company is engaged for the construction of the remaining units in the development, using materials that accord with the final specifications. Bear in mind also that show homes are typically furnished by professional interior designers using top quality materials and the latest décor to create the most favourable first impression, instead of the "standard furniture package". For these reasons, finished properties often differ from the show home. It is therefore important to ensure a full set of dimensioned plans, elevations and three-dimensional perspectives are provided, together with the relevant material specifications, and where inconsistencies might exist between the plans and the show home, the details need to be highlighted and clarified.

It should be noted that if you engage a construction company to build a property, you would normally receive a bill of quantities (BOQ) as part of the quotation (see chapter 44), which is a full and detailed breakdown of the materials and labour required for the job. However, when buying off-plan property from a developer, this information is confidential between the developer and the construction company. Therefore, instead of a BOQ, the developer provides to potential purchasers a condensed, highlighted set of information, usually referred to simply as "material specifications". The level of detail included in the material specifications differs from developer to developer. In general, if material specifications and fittings and fixtures are high end, a developer usually makes a point to emphasise them; if they are not, details tend to be scarce and, in some cases, no detail is offered at all.

To minimise any divergence in expectations, a detailed list of material specifications should be requested from the developer. For example, for wall tiles, floor tiles, bathroom fittings and santitaryware, request sizes, specifications and manufacturers product codes; while for kitchen appliances, brands and model numbers should be specified (if only the brand is specified, enormous scope exists within a brand, ranging from basic models to top-end models). When you proceed to purchase the property, all these details should be incorporated into the contracts.

Important tip: Be wary of material specifications that state "Brand X *or similar*" and general clauses such as "the developer reserves the right to change specifications or substitute materials without prior notice." Developers use such wording to provide flexibility in cases where products or materials are out of stock or otherwise unavailable. However, when one brand or material is substituted for another, what passes for "similar" or "equivalent" is highly subjective. If possible, these words should be replaced with "any changes to the stated specifications must be authorised in writing by the purchaser prior to use or installation".

Material specifications should cover all aspects of the building, for instance:

- Substructure and superstructure (foundation type and specification, floor slab, suspended slabs, retaining walls and building walls)
- Roofing structure and materials
- Floor finishes
- Wall finishes
- Ceiling finishes
- Doors and windows
- Sanitaryware and bathroom fittings
- Swimming pool structure, tiles (or material finishes) and pump system specifications
- Type of handrails for balconies and terraces
- Plumbing pipework, water heaters, pumps and filters
- Electrical conduits, cables, switches, outlets and lighting systems
- Telephone, Internet, TV, acoustic and security systems
- Kitchen specifications and appliances

- Air-conditioners and fans
- Wastewater treatment
- Access roads and parking areas

If you are not familiar with the material specifications, ask to see samples of each material. Well-managed property developers should have samples available for all or most of the materials that will be used for construction. If they don't, it often means they are making thing up as they go along (sometimes according to changing budgetary and cash flow constraints!). In addition, purchasers must pay close attention to "dimensional tolerances", especially in relation to the overall size of a property. Naturally, developers seek as much tolerance as possible and will often insert contractual clauses that grant the developer, for instance, a dimensional tolerance of 5%. Purchasers need to pay attention to these clauses: by allowing such tolerance levels, purchasers might end up with something they didn't expect but will be unable to do anything about it.

With regard to build quality, the same advice applies for developers as for construction companies (see chapter 41): make sure to visit other projects completed by the same property developer. In addition, check whether the specifications for the other site (or property) you visit are of a similar standard to those specified for the off-plan property you are planning to buy. If you are visiting a high-end development, don't assume materials or standards will be the same for a property you are considering with a lower price per square metre; property developers market projects at different price ranges with correspondingly different material standards and specifications. In other words, don't take anything for granted.

For example, the sales manager for an off-plan developer took a potential purchaser to one of its recently completed developments. On site, the purchaser made a mental note of the top quality powder coated aluminium doors and windows that had been supplied by one of the top companies in the industry. He didn't mention it, the sales manager didn't refer to them, and the purchaser subsequently assumed the same standard of doors and windows would be installed in the property he was buying. Several months later, when the property had been completed, he arrived in Thailand to take possession and noticed the windows and doors were of a vastly inferior quality, whose lightweight frames and thin glass leaked in the rain. When he complained to the developer, he was shown a copy of the material specifications, which were consistent with the doors and windows fitted. In short, he had made an assumption and failed to confirm the details.

Doors and windows are a singularly important factor for tropical properties and there are significant variations in quality. It is therefore strongly advised to research the different specifications and to evaluate, preferably in situ, the type and quality of windows and doors that are specified for your property. Remember, in addition to construction quality and fitness for purpose, doors and windows are a security related issue.

In addition, when viewing a developer's other projects, check whether the same teams of workers (construction company workers, structural engineers, mechanical and electrical engineers, interior designers) are being used for the new off-plan development. If the same team is involved, you can expect a similar standard; if the developer is using a different team of contractors, standards might also differ.

Finally, with regard to making sure a property meets your expectations on finishing, it is worth mentioning the role of "snagging" (see chapter 58). It is important that the contract contains detailed procedures for submitting a snag list and for defects to be rectified before practical completion and handover of the property.

Summary

- When buying condominium freehold property the developer has a statutory obligation to deliver on the promises made in marketing materials; however, for other types of property, a greater degree of caution must be exercised.
- If a property developer has built a show home, don't assume the actual finished property will be identical in all aspects.
- Make sure a full set of dimensioned plans, elevations and three-dimensional perspectives are provided, together with the relevant material specifications.
- Be wary of material specifications that state "Brand X or similar" and general clauses such as "the developer reserves the right to change specifications or substitute materials without prior notice."
- If you are not familiar with the material specifications, ask to see samples of each material.
- When viewing a developer's other projects, check whether the same teams of workers are being used for the new off-plan development.

65
Mitigating risks (market risk)

Market risk refers to the risk that property prices might fall during construction with the consequence that upon completion you become the owner of a property worth less than the price you paid. The key to avoiding such a scenario is to ensure you are buying property at a discount to market value, or buying a property in a market at a time when property prices are expected to rise, ideally both.

Buying at a discount to market value

With regard to evaluating asking prices for off-plan property, it is necessary to research the prices of comparable properties, based on criteria such as price per square metre (PSM), yield, location, specifications, branding and aesthetics, which were discussed in detail in chapter 35. It should also be possible to engage a professional, independent company to appraise a property's value. Appraisals are generally conducted on behalf of banks and financial institutions prior to issuing a mortgage on a property, which assists the calculation of the correct loan-to-value (LTV) amount. While mortgages for foreign buyers are generally not available in Thailand, it should still be possible to get a property professionally appraised[123]. Provided there are sufficient comparables, an appraisal should be able to provide you with an estimated market value.

> **Important tip:** Once you have an estimated market value for an off-plan property (supposing it has already been completed), it is then necessary to compare this with the property's asking price to determine if the pre-construction price is suitably discounted to market value (to compensate for the inherent risk of purchasing off-plan property). *Remember, you are evaluating two different concepts: price and value. Price is a level at which you make an exchange; value is whether it is worth it.*

To lock in a potential capital gain, there are two conceptual possibilities. First, the asking price for an off-plan property must be below the "market price" so that upon completion you end up owning a property together with an automatic unrealised[124] capital gain. Generally, an off-plan "discount" should be at least 15% below market value to compensate for the risk of buying off-plan (and the fact that you are funding the developer). Second, the asking price can be equal

---

[123] Although it is important to specify the purpose of the valuation, and the method to be used.
[124] Capital gains only become *realized* upon sale.

to the estimated market price with the anticipation of property prices appreciating during construction. If the asking price of a property is above its current market value, it is not a property that could prudently be bought for the primary aim of investment (in such as case, it would be wiser to avoid the off-plan risks, wait for completion and buy a property in the development on the secondary market)[125].

Once you have an understanding of market values and pre-construction asking prices, the level of risk you are willing to assume or the return on investment you expect is entirely a personal matter. Some investors will only purchase off-plan properties if they are sufficiently discounted to market price *and* a reasonable appreciation of prices between commencement and completion is anticipated.

Conceptually, if you are expecting property prices to *fall,* an off-plan discount would need to be big enough to cover the anticipated fall in price *and* still provide a capital gain. However, in the real world this is highly unlikely because developers tend not to launch off-plan developments in an obviously falling market and you would be hard pressed to find a property developer that would admit prices were falling!

Another possibility is to negotiate a "buyback clause" in the contract. This is a provision in a sales contract whereby the seller (developer) agrees to repurchase the property at a stated price (for example, the purchase price) upon the occurrence of a specified event, within a certain period of time. For example, a buyback clause might require the developer to buy the property back upon completion if a (specified) independent property appraiser appraises the market value of the completed property at more than 5% below the purchase price. However, with regard to the practical utility of a buyback clause, while I have seen such clauses inserted into contracts, I have yet to see anyone successfully exercise one (such clauses also assume the developer will be in a financial position to be *able* to buy back the property).

Buying when property prices are expected to rise

While it is possible to ascertain the competitiveness of an off-plan property's asking price by researching comparable property prices, how can you be sure property prices will increase during the period of construction? The short answer is: you cant, not with a high degree of certainty. The only certainty is there is no certainty!

---

[125] It should be noted that some high-end or truly "unique" properties set their own prices by their very uniqueness. In this case, no comparables exist and it is a matter of pure niche market forces setting the price, i.e. the price is whatever someone is willing to come along and pay for it.

While it is not possible to make accurately predictions, it pays to keep three key concepts in mind:

First, the primary driving force behind property prices in Thailand's resort areas are foreigners, not Thais. This is particularly true for Phuket and Koh Samui and particularly true for the luxury end of the market.

Second, resort properties generally represent *discretionary* expenditure, which means people are buying properties as second homes, vacation properties or rental properties, rather than as primary residences.

Third, it is important to remember that mortgage financing for foreigners is generally unavailable. This means that Thailand resort property is not a place where the average investor can leverage their property investments, which in turn means that investment indicators such as affordability ratios, loan-to-value ratios and interest rates are largely redundant. Instead, tourist numbers and transaction data become more relevant: buyers tend to come to Thailand once or twice on holiday before taking the step to invest in property, so increasing tourist numbers presuppose an increase in property transactions[126].

While this is painting with a very broad brush, if the market mainly comprises of foreigners using discretionary cash, rising property prices depend on the improving health of the global economy. When people are secure in their jobs and are saving in excess of what they need for primary residences and family expenses, and when companies are performing well and paying bonuses, there is increased buying activity in resort markets. On the other hand, when economies around the world are in recession (or depression), and when people are in fear of losing their jobs, paying their mortgages or meeting their everyday expenses, they are not generally travelling on vacation to far away destinations or looking to invest money in vacation properties. *The relationship is therefore straightforward: the health of Thailand's resort markets depends to a large extent on the health of the global economy, rather than the local economy.*

Having said that, when property markets in Europe and America are stagnating or declining, some of the smarter investors are buying properties in Asia in search of higher returns or to preserve their wealth. At the same time, new classes of buyers – Russians, Indians and Chinese – are entering the market. However, their numbers are not yet sufficient to offset the decline of traditional buyers such as Europeans and European expats living in Asia. It should also be understood that each of the resort markets – Phuket, Koh Samui, Hua Hin, Pattaya and Krabi – have different supply and demand dynamics.

---

[126] Unless the increase is due largely to the "backpacker" segment.

Again, speaking in general terms, it is easy to see the signs of an improving property market: increasing tourist numbers, increasing property transactions, increasing property prices and increased activity by property developers. However, while spotting a rising market is easy, predicting when market activity and property prices will stagnate or fall is less so. There are innumerable factors influencing global markets, property demand and property prices at any point in time, together with countless unknowns that could present themselves at any time. Who can tell you with any degree of accuracy when the next Lehman Brothers will collapse or when will be the next military coup?

It is possible to read investment reports, listen to market commentators or take advice from so-called "professionals". However, no one can guarantee the future; in fact, markets have a tendency to correct well before any analyst or commentator predicts it. The best you can do is make informed decisions and use common sense (see also the discussion in chapter 9). With this in mind, it is essential to conduct your own extensive research before coming to any conclusions.

Summary

- Market risk refers to the risk that property prices might fall during construction with the consequence that upon completion you become the owner of a property worth less than the price you paid.
- To evaluate asking prices for off-plan property, it is necessary to research the prices of comparable properties, based on criteria such as price per square metre (PSM), yield, location, specifications, branding and aesthetics.
- Consider engaging a professional, independent company to appraise a property's value.
- To lock in a potential capital gain, there are two conceptual possibilities: either the asking price for an off-plan property must be below the "market price" so that upon completion you end up owning a property together with an automatic unrealised capital gain, or the asking price can be equal to the estimated market price with the anticipation of property prices appreciating during construction.
- The primary driving force behind property prices in Thailand's resort areas are foreigners making discretionary expenditures without the availability of mortgages, which means prices are to a large extent dependent on the health of the global economy.

66
Mitigating risks (exchange rate risk)

Exchange rate risk in the context of off-plan property arises when the purchase price is specified in one currency (usually Thai Baht), your money is kept in another currency, and payments are due later according to the stages of construction. Currencies fluctuate on a daily basis and, as a purchaser, the primary risk is that the currency in which you hold your money weakens in relation to the Thai Baht during the period of construction. Indeed, exchange rate movements have the ability to significantly impact the cost of an investment[127].

For example, suppose the price of an off-pan property is 20 million Thai Baht, the estimated construction period is 12 months and your money is kept in Euro. If, at the time of signing the contract, the Euro-Baht exchange rate is 50 (in other words, each Euro buys 50 Thai Baht), the purchase price is equivalent to 400,000 Euro. To provide a simple but graphic illustration to show the effect of exchange rate movements, lets suppose the payment terms agreed with the developer are a nominal deposit upon the signing of the contract and full payment on completion (instead of staged payments spread out over the construction period). Fast-forward 12 months, the property has been completed and payment is now due in full. The Euro-Baht exchange rate is now 40 (not 50), which means the effective *cost* of the property is now 500,000 Euro – a whopping increase of 100,000 Euro! While the *price* of the property remained the same in terms of Thai Baht (at 20 million Thai Baht), the *effective cost* of the property has increased by 25% or 100,000 Euro. In other words, the more the Euro weakens in relation to the Thai Baht, the higher the effective cost of a property.

To demonstrate that exchange rate movements like this are possible, the example above is precisely what would have occurred had a Euro-denominated purchaser signed contracts on a property in October 2009 and completed approximately twelve months later, as illustrated by the Euro-Baht exchange rate chart below[128].

---

[127] Currency volatility seems to have increased over the past few years, particularly due to market meltdowns, the risk of sovereign default and excessive printing of fiat money (Quantitative Easing) in the developed economies.
[128] Source: Pacific Exchange Rate Service http://fx.sauder.ubc.ca/

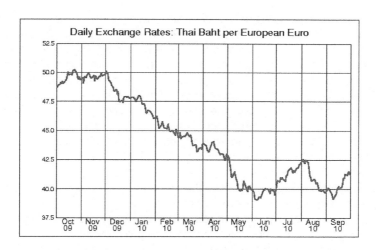

In the example above, if payments had been made according to a staged payment schedule over the course of a year, the effective price difference would not have been so acute, although it would still be significant. To illustrate the difference, imagine the payment terms required a 10% deposit upon the signing of the contract, followed by 3 subsequent payments of 30% at four-month intervals. Over the same time period, if Euros were exchanged into Thai Baht as each respective payment became due, the cost of the property would approximate the figures in the following chart:

	Month	%	Amount Baht	Exchange Rate €/THB	Amount € (EURO)
Payment 1	Oct 2009	10%	2M	50	40,000
Payment 2	Jan 2010	30%	6M	46	130,435
Payment 3	May 2010	30%	6M	40	150,000
Payment 4	Sept 2010	30%	6M	39	153,846
Total		100%	20M		474,281

While the purchase price of the property was equivalent to 400,000 Euro at the time of signing the contract, by the time of completion the actual cost became 474,281 Euro, which is an extra 74,281 Euro or a difference of 18.5%. As is evident from the chart, the reason is due to the fact that each 6 million Baht payment became progressively more expensive in Euro; the first 6 million Baht *cost* 130,435 Euro, while by the time the last payment of 6 million Baht became due, the *cost* became 153,846 Euro.

Without resorting to complex financial instruments, the best way to avoid exchange rate risk is simply to send the full amount of the purchase price to Thailand (exchanging foreign currency into Baht) upon signing contracts; to keep any portion of the purchase price in a foreign currency during the construction of an off-plan property is to be exposed to exchange rate risk. It is possible that the currency you are holding *appreciates* in value, which means each unit buys *more* Thai Baht, in which case the effective cost of the property is reduced; however, the currency you are holding can also *depreciate,* in which case the effective cost of the property *increases* because each Thai Baht costs more. This is the uncertainty you bear and the risk you take.

To successfully manage cash flow for the staged payments normally associated with off-plan properties, it is necessary to plan your finances with a mind toward exchange rate movements. If the off-plan property you are buying does not include a furniture package, the cost of furnishing the property must also be allowed for, together with transaction related costs such as legal fees and transfer taxes (see chapters 85 and 97).

For a more detailed discussion on exchange rates, see chapter 105, together with chapter 50 on "financial considerations" (in relation to building your own property).

Summary

- Exchange rate risk in the context of off-plan property arises when the purchase price is specified in one currency (usually Thai Baht), your money is kept in another currency, and payments are due later.
- Exchange rate movements have the ability to significantly impact the cost of an investment.
- Without resorting to complex financial instruments, the best way to avoid exchange rate risk is to send the full amount of the purchase price to Thailand (exchanging foreign currency into Baht) upon signing contracts.
- To successfully manage cash flow for the staged payments normally associated with off-plan properties, it is necessary to plan your finances with a mind toward exchange rate movements.

67
Mitigating risks (non-completion)
(Essential)

Of the four primary risks identified in relation to purchasing off-plan property, non-completion is the most significant risk, with the direst consequences. Ironically, it also tends to be the risk that is least considered at the time of purchase, due partly to the euphoria accompanying the purchase of a new property (where the very notion of non-completion is ignored) and partly because the consequences don't bear thinking about, so most people tend not to!

Before the risk of non-completion can be fully grasped, it is helpful to understand some of the reasons that might prevent a property developer from completing a project. In Thailand, projects are derailed for a multitude of reasons. For instance, property developers might go bankrupt through a combination of inadequate investment capital, poor financial planning and insufficient sales[129]. Inexperienced developers, especially, can become insolvent because they have no access to commercial bank loans[130] and their financial forecasts failed to take into account possible delays; if sales are slower than expected or there are construction delays, overheads (vehicle rentals, salaries, office running costs and rent) consume cash over time until there is none left to continue in business[131]. Other developers cease trading after directors or shareholders fall into conflict or disappear with investors' money. There are also cases where the principal construction contractors engaged by property developers have gone bankrupt at a time when work has fallen considerably behind the staged payments made by the developer, which in turn has caused the cessation of projects and, in the worst cases, the developer's bankruptcy.

Projects have also been cancelled or abandoned due to land ownership or title disputes, while other projects have come to a halt because subdivision, planning procedures or building regulations have been ignored and the necessary licences or building permits have not been granted.

---

[129] Often due to their absolute reliance on a few local (rather than international) property agents.

[130] Commercial banks in Thailand are reluctant to lend to resort developers managed by foreigners targeting foreign buyers, particularly first-time developers. If they will consider lending to a developer, the developer usually needs to prove 40% - 50% of the project has been "pre-sold".

[131] Overheads, together with payments to contractors and suppliers, overwhelm the money available and incoming scheduled payments from buyers. At some point bankruptcy becomes a self-fulfilling prophecy where *rumours* of bankruptcy cause contractors and suppliers to request immediate payment and buyers cease making staged payments.

For some problems – such as adverse weather, sudden changes in land-related laws or the odd military coup that brings the property market to a standstill – developers might be forgiven for not having anticipated events. However, as a purchaser you are generally relying on a developer to have the professionalism, expertise and resources to successfully deal with events and still manage a project through to completion. The fact is, not all property developers are equal; some developers are better managed and better equipped than others to deal with the challenges associated with developing property in Thailand.

> **Important tip:** A key point to remember when buying off-plan property is that you are trusting a developer with your money and trusting that the developer will do what has been promised; in effect, *you are entering into a partnership with a developer.*

At one end of the spectrum, there are large public listed, financially sound, cash rich property developers with strong management teams, directors with engineering backgrounds and years of construction experience in Thailand, together with a proven track record of high-quality, completed, sold-out projects. In the middle are developers whose principals have finance or sales backgrounds, some investment capital, little knowledge of construction but who have engaged experienced advisors and contractors.

At the other end of the spectrum are the so-called "property developers" who have just stepped off the proverbial banana boat and decided to set up as developers without sufficient funds or relevant construction experience, with no knowledge of local customs or procedures, who learn as they go, are quite content to cut corners, and who gradually discover the learning curve in Thailand is steeper than they ever could have imagined. These are typically the property developers led by charismatic individuals whose business plans consist of launching off-plan projects, taking deposits from purchasers, buying a range of luxury company cars and who are then left wondering why there is no money left for construction.

In most cases, however, it should be noted that inexperienced or first-time developers do not set out to cheat their customers. In fact, they start with good intentions and when they realise there is no financing available from commercial banks they do not hesitate to invest all their own savings because they believe in what they are doing. This means they also lose everything if they fail. Failure is therefore the result of inability matched with a challenging environment, rather than some grand design to redistribute wealth from the rich to the aspiring rich. Some first-time developers have finance backgrounds and others have construction backgrounds. Few have both. Indeed, even construction experience is not readily transferrable to Thailand without Asian management experience. In other words, with limited access to capital and inexperience, first-time developers are struggling against the odds from the outset.

The key point is to recognise the spectrum of risk, from experienced public listed property developers to inexperienced first-time developers. This does not mean that you should only buy off-plan properties from public listed companies. If this were the case, the choice of property developments would be limited, especially in some of the most highly sought after resort locations. It also does not mean avoiding all inexperienced developers; despite the odds, some of these developers succeed and prove everyone wrong, building beautiful properties and creating worthwhile profits for those who placed their trust in them. It simply means those considering the purchase of an off-plan property should do so with recognition of the risks; if risks are to be taken, it is better they are taken with all the facts in hand and with some degree of calculation.

There is a different level of risk associated with each developer and each development; however, when they all have glossy, full-colour brochures, how do you tell them apart? As with any commercial transaction, you need to have your wits about you, act with caution and make sure not to leave your common sense at home; instead, it is necessary to take a healthy level of suspicion with you, whether you are dealing with a professionally-managed organisation or a charismatic first-time developer who has generously invited you to his or her house for dinner[132]. Thus, the starting point for mitigating the risks of buying off-plan property is to conduct a thorough due diligence investigation of both the property developer and the development.

Financial

One of the most important parts of the due diligence process is determining the property developer's financial resources in relation to the development. For example, has the developer already paid for the land? Does the developer have sufficient funds to build the project without (off-plan) sales? More realistically, what percentage of overall construction costs does the developer already possess without depending on sales, and what sales projections form the basis for completion of the project? Must the developer rely on a handful of early investors (who pay in full for their properties) in order to secure enough money to start the project? In addition, how many *non-refundable* reservation deposits has the developer already taken and how many buyers have completed their

---

[132] It is a characteristic of the resort property market in Thailand (as opposed to the Bangkok market) that many off-plan developments are offered by inexperienced or first-time developers led by passionate, charismatic individuals. Don't feel guilty about investigating your friendly developer; it is a question of professionalism rather than distrust.

due diligence and confirmed the purchase by signing contracts and transferring the first payment?

> **Important tip:** The answers to such questions are important because they allow an insight into the developer's level of dependence on sales and the corresponding degree of risk being taken by purchasers. The best-case scenario is where a developer has sufficient financial resources to complete the project without off-plan sales and has *chosen* to start sales at the pre-construction stage[133]. The worst-case scenario is where a developer has no money and is therefore entirely dependent on sales to start *and complete* construction.

The usual scenario is somewhere in-between; developers have a *percentage* of total costs, enough to buy land and start construction, and then depend on sales to continue and complete the project. It is that "percentage", in concert with actual sales and cash flow management, which accounts for much of the risk you take when purchasing properties off-plan. The question is: How is it possible to obtain relevant financial information that will allow an assessment of a developer's financial position? If the developer is a publicly listed company, such as Raimon Land or Golden Land Property, a far greater level of information is available to potential investors. However, for privately owned developers, *reliable* information is difficult to obtain.

To form an accurate assessment of risk, nothing less than a complete financial audit and full disclosure by the developer is required, both in relation to the developer's company and the companies set up to "own" the project. This is all well and good in theory. However, in practice, few privately owned property developers willingly provide confidential financial information or are amenable to opening their books for inspection. It is possible to ask for sight of bank statements but even if you get to see them they are meaningless without a complete picture of the company's liabilities. Upon request, developers might be willing to provide financial references from their bankers although the dependability of such references is questionable. In short, unless a complete and up-to-date set of financial records is available, a developer's *true* financial position is unknown and, as a purchaser, you are taking a leap in the dark.

If you are able to successfully obtain reliable information, a good starting point is to work out the *approximate* costs involved in the off-plan development you are considering. One method is to separately estimate land and construction costs. For land, the site master plan (or marketing materials) should note the

---

[133] Although this is an unlikely scenario because the usual purpose of selling property at the pre-construction stage is to finance construction.

land size (in Rai) and local property agents can provide a guide price per Rai for land in the particular area with the same characteristics[134]. Construction costs can be *roughly* estimated by taking the overall square metre of floor area for the development (this should also be readily available from the developer or the marketing materials) and multiplying this by the construction cost per square metre, which can be estimated by a qualified architect or construction company (and will differ depending on location, the type of property development – villas, apartments, condominiums – and the material specification). An alternative method for estimating development costs is to work backwards from the total selling price: from the developer's price list, add the purchase prices for each property to calculate the total sales value of the development, and then remove the developer's profit, which is usually in the range of 35% to 50%.[135]

When total development costs have been estimated, it is then necessary to consider the developer's capital and funding structure. Has the land already been purchased by the developer? What percentage of development costs does the developer have in terms of personal equity? What percentage is being provided by equity investors or commercial loans? What percentage of the overall development costs depends on sales?

It should be recognised that a developer's payment schedule provides a unique insight into a developer's financial plans and resources. On one hand, if a developer requests only a small portion of the purchase price during the construction stage (such as 25% - 40%), while the bulk of the price (60% - 75%) is due upon completion and transfer, the developer is not wholly dependent upon sales and purchase money to finance the development. On the other hand, if 80% to 90% of the purchase price is required to be paid prior to completion, with only 10% - 20% on completion, it is evident the project is being financed through sales with clients money.

While reliable evidence is needed in order to evaluate the financial strength or weakness of a particular developer (in relation to a particular project), the mere exercise of going through this thought process puts the undertaking into some perspective. Success leaves clues; just as potential failure follows a pattern and hints at the future. In sum, if there is any doubt about a developer's solvency or ability to complete the project, it is generally wiser to run, not walk, to the nearest exit.

---

[134] If the land has been purchased several years prior to commencement of the project, a historical estimate is more relevant (indeed, some agents in the local resort area will be familiar with the precise sum paid by a developer for a particular plot of land).
[135] Without actual data, these figures can only be an educated estimate.

Sales

There is a greater chance of success in being provided with information related to reservations and sales. If sales expectations have been met or exceeded, developers are often pleased to show you the numbers. Indeed, sales statistics are often used for the purposes of marketing and public relations, with red circles or flags being pinned to site plans to proudly announce which units have been sold and to foster a sense of scarcity and urgency among potential buyers.

However, potential purchasers should not take these red flags or "sales statistics" at face value. It is prudent to read between the lines and to question whether the units marked "Reserved", "On-hold" or "Sold" represent *genuine* sales. Developers use all kinds of tactics to make a project appear more popular than it actually is; people want to buy into a successful development, not a struggling one, due partly to the herd mentality and partly because developments with high sales have a higher chance of success. In other words, if a developer can make a project appear successful by feigning higher sales, it can in some cases become a self-fulfilling prophecy.

I am familiar with cases where units set aside for the property developer's directors have been labelled "Reserved" or "Sold", while other units have been put aside for joint-venture partners (in case the developer fails to pay them) and labelled "On-hold" or "Sold". These labels help to make a project appear more successful but cannot be considered *real* sales in the sense that they will generate future cash flow and improve a developer's ability to finance construction.

In addition, there is a crucial distinction between reservations made with *refundable* deposits and those that have been made with *non-refundable* deposits. Refundable deposits or reservation fees are not purchases at all; they are more of an *intention* to purchase. In other words, buyers that have paid refundable deposits can usually pull out of the purchase with impunity. One property developer I know boasted that his development had been a huge success, that deposits had been taken on a high number of off-plan units and, consequently, the first phase of the development was virtually sold out. This boast also formed part of the sales pitch to prospective buyers. However, it later transpired that the majority of the deposits were *fully refundable* and the majority of these "purchasers" did indeed (shortly thereafter) exercise their right to pull out and ask for their money back, leaving the developer with hardly any sales at all, at least not enough to sustain the development[136].

---

[136] To my knowledge, several of the purchasers are still waiting for the return of their deposits.

As is evident, being provided with sales related information *by itself,* without understanding whether the underlying deposits are refundable or non-refundable, is of little practical use.

Determining the actual level of financial commitment from "purchasers" is crucial to understanding the true level of sales in a development. The more *genuine* sales a developer has made, the lower the risk to subsequent purchasers (all other things being equal) because sales have a direct impact on a developer's ability to complete a project. Without genuine and *accurate* sales information, it is impossible to assess the risk of non-completion; indeed, it is this financial opaqueness that adds to the risk of off-plan investments.

In the absence of unequivocal financial information and sales data, more informal methods must be used to provide clues in relation to a developer's solvency.

Site visits

If construction of a project is already underway, it is wise to visit the site on several different occasions in order to ascertain the following information: What is he number of workers on site? Does the site resemble an ant colony of workers, material deliveries and construction activity; or does it have the feel of an abandoned site with a few workers milling around or sweeping the floor and generally trying hard to look busy upon your arrival? A lack of activity on site is one of the classic signs of a developer's poor financial health. If there is little activity and only a few workers on site, it could mean the developer is depending on the proceeds of the next sale (yours) to continue!

Apart from the current project, it is also necessary to research a developer's track record of completed projects (in Thailand). A developer that has started and finished other developments is more likely to succeed again. In Thailand (where the learning curve is steep), a developer that has already managed projects to completion has experience in dealing with bureaucratic hurdles and obtaining the requisite licences and permits. Experienced developers also understand what is involved in the management of Thai construction companies, and have successfully managed project financing and the cash flow requirements integral to finishing a development. In short, they have been through the process of completing a project in Thailand, whereas a first-time developer is in uncharted territory and therefore represents a far greater risk. When purchasing off-plan property from a first-time developer, you are in effect financing their education.

Referrals

A key part of the informal due diligence process should be making contact with a property developer's previous clients. This is one of the best sources for "inside" information related to the integrity, reliability and level of service provided by a developer. How do you get hold of the names and contact details of a developer's previous clients? The answer is to simply ask the developer; indeed, the willingness of a developer to share information of this kind will be revealing in and of itself. If a developer's response is that its client details are confidential, this is fair comment. Nonetheless, ask if the developer would mind contacting the clients to ask their permission for being contacted directly by you. In some cases, if the suggestion is immediately dismissed without consideration, it might be that the developer has something to hide or has left a trail of dissatisfied clients in their wake! Some developers use client testimonials for their marketing materials; thus, asking for the contact details of advertised clients, subject to their permission, should be less of a challenge[137]. However, a developer would only use testimonials from *satisfied* customers and therefore such sources of information have an inherent bias.

Certainly, the more clients you are able to speak with, the more insights will be gleaned. This information should assist you with the decision as to whether you want to do business with the company.

Competitors

An often-overlooked source of information is a developer's competitors, i.e. other developers. The property development industry within Thailand's resort areas is compact; in other words, everyone seems to know everyone else's business (in fact, developers should make it their business to know their competition).

While accepted industry etiquette requires developers not to speak ill of other developers, it is surprising how often this rule is relaxed (especially when meeting developers during the process of comparing developments when you have yet to make a purchasing decision!). If one developer makes disparaging comments or supplies unfavourable information about another, such information might be designed to denigrate competing offers or it could be professional jealousy; however, it might also hint at the truth. For this reason, while such information cannot be treated as impartial, it might be worth corroborating or using as a basis for further enquiries. Sometimes, where there is smoke, there is fire.

---

[137] If they are *real* testimonials. i.e. they have not been fabricated by the marketing department!

Local lawyers are another good source of information. During the course of consulting with clients, lawyers gain a unique insight into the local property market and should be familiar with most of the local property developers, together with their sub-contractors and associated companies.

A further source of *informal* information is the local expat owners of bars, restaurants and businesses. Living in resort areas, locals get to know what is going on, together with the companies and characters involved. The same rules apply with this information as with information from other developers: it might not be impartial and needs to be verified.

It doesn't take a great deal of effort to build a body of "inside information" that will help you to form a judgement about which developers know their business and are reliable, and which ones are new to the game or are well-known for questionable ethics.

Developer's team

Another consideration is the experience of the property developer's management team. In Thailand, there is a wide chasm between plans on the drawing board and their successful implementation. The experience and ability of the management team is the crucial link between the two.

It is worth noting whether the management team entirely comprised of Thais, or whether it is a mixture of foreign and Thai managers. If management consists entirely of foreigners, what level of support do they have from Thais who better understand local business practices and can get things done on the ground? It is also important to note the credentials and experience of the developer's "team" of consultants, sub-contractors and advisors that have been brought together for a project. For instance, which legal, tax and accounting advisors has the developer engaged? Has the developer engaged an internationally renowned tax-consulting company with offices around the world and a head office in Bangkok, or a local accounting firm? Is the developer working with a well-known international law firm, a foreign lawyer with Thai partners, or a local law firm?

The quality of legal and tax advice received by the developer has a bearing on the quality of advice the developer has received, which in turn influences the manner in which due diligence has been carried out in relation to land titles, access and subdivision. The quality of legal and tax advice will also affect the manner in which corporate holding structures have been set up to develop the land and own (or control) properties. It also has a bearing on whether sales contracts have been properly drafted, whether they are in conformance with Thai law and adequately cover each contingency.

It is worth taking the time and effort to research the companies and consultants that a developer has appointed as architects, quantity surveyors, structural engineers, project managers, building contractors, interior designers, maintenance contractors and management companies. If a developer's team of contractors are not featured in marketing materials, request details from the developer. A simple check on the Internet should be able to provide details about their size, experience and the type of projects they are involved in.

However, a caveat: just because a developer has engaged the most expensive or high-profile advisors and contractors does not mean they are guaranteed to succeed; likewise, an inexperienced developer working with local companies and advisors is not guaranteed to fail. Some developers invest in the best advisors and contractors, and take time to make sure the fundamental issues have been properly taken care of, only to fail through insufficient sales. On the other hand, some of the best projects in Thailand have come to a halt despite high sales due to corners being cut in relation to land titles, or because they failed to get the necessary building permits or licences. This happened to a high-profile marina development on one of Thailand's most famous islands, which successfully sold out a quarter of the project, then closed its doors after failing to obtain the last and crucial permit from the Harbour Department.

In relation to the developer, it is certainly worth spending time on an informal basis with the managers and principals of the company (not the sales people) in order to get a feel for the way in which the company is managed. With smaller developers in particular, the principals should be only too pleased to spend time with potential clients to answer questions and fill in the gaps.

The development

As discussed in chapter 61, the developer assumes control and responsibility for most of the issues discussed in Steps 2 and 4 of this book. Notably, the developer must purchase land, subdivide the land if necessary, arrange access and utilities to the site, then supervise and manage construction. So far, the discussion has focussed on the evaluation of the property developer and its team of consultants and contractors. However, it is also crucial to perform due diligence on the *development*.

Land title, subdivision (land allotment) and access rights are facets that fundamentally underpin the value of completed properties. Properly checking the relevant legal documents in relation to these areas is therefore of paramount importance. In addition to an investigation of land title and access documents, a competent lawyer should also check that the developer has the necessary documentation for the project, such as a developer's licence, building permit and any relevant permission required by government departments, such as an Environmental Impact Assessment (EIA)[138]. Purchasers should exercise extreme caution if building permits and licences are not already in place[139].

Ownership structures

The holding structure and associated companies operated by the developer for the purposes of a project – i.e. Thai landowning companies, offshore companies, and management and maintenance companies – also need to be checked to ensure they are compliant with Thai law and appropriate to the type of legal ownership. The holding structure also needs to be evaluated in light of its tax efficiency for the purchaser (not just the developer). In addition, tax due diligence needs to be undertaken in order to uncover any potential tax exposure that might be inherited if the purchase of property entails taking over (all or part of) an existing corporate structure.

Further, it is important to find out if the developer actually owns the project land or has entered into a joint venture with a landowner, which is relevant in terms of the level of control the developer exercises over the land (it also reflects on the developer's financial strength).

In the case where off-plan properties are part of a "branded" development, which is managed by a professional, internationally recognised brand, it is crucial to check the terms of the agreement between the brand and the developer. The agreement needs to be evaluated in terms of the ease with which the contract can be terminated, together with the consequences of its termination, which would render the development "unbranded".

It is common for purchasers to assume that due diligence must automatically have been performed by a developer and therefore purchasers only need to perform cursory due diligence. It is equally common for purchasers to assume that if they are not the first to buy into a development, previous buyers must already have performed their own due diligence. Both of these assumptions would be erroneous, particularly with inexperienced or first-time developers.

During the initial consultation with a lawyer, legal costs are often quoted in segments where the perusal of sales contracts usually attracts a standard charge, while land title investigations or due diligence into the developer's company

---

[138] Developers generally need to wait until the EIA has been completed before commencing construction (for developments of more than 80 units).
[139] Unless it is condominium freehold title where building permits are issued near to the completion of a project.

structures are charged separately. For those trying to minimise legal costs, it is tempting to engage a lawyer for minimal or token due diligence so as not to increase legal fees by duplicating work that you assume has already been carried out by previous buyers. However, assumptions have no place in risk mitigation. Buyers need to take responsibility for the security of their own investments, which means that all possible checks should be made. Without a complete, detailed due diligence report conducted by an independent lawyer on behalf of another purchaser *who is buying an identical legal interest as yourself*[140], it is wise to engage your own lawyer to perform the necessary due diligence work.

> **Important tip:** It is important that legal due diligence is performed by a lawyer acting on your behalf and in your best interests, *as opposed to a lawyer appointed by the developer.* This sounds obvious; however, it is common practice for developers to offer purchasers a cost saving legal package, whereby the developer's lawyer acts for both buyer and seller (developer). These offers are often dressed up in the form of "special sale and purchase packages". In such cases, the lawyer is usually the same lawyer that has advised the developer, performed the legal work related to land titles, access and subdivision, in addition to preparing the sale and purchase contracts. The specially discounted legal package is possible because the "due diligence" has already been done. However, this is a perfect example of a professional conflict of interest; how is it possible for the same lawyer to act in the best interests of both buyer and seller, especially when performing due diligence, checking sale and purchase contracts or conducting any form of negotiations between the purchaser and developer (for a more detailed discussion see chapter 84).

If you are paying a deposit (or reservation fee) to secure an off-plan property, it is important that the deposit agreement allows sufficient time for your lawyer to conduct the necessary due diligence and that payments are refundable "subject to satisfactory due diligence findings" (see chapters 74 and 88).

Timing of legal ownership

Chapter 68, "What are actually buying?" discusses the type of legal ownership you are buying. For instance, upon completion of an off-plan development, do you receive a freehold interest in land through the operation of a Thai company, together with personal ownership of a villa; or a leasehold interest in an apartment, together with shared ownership of a Thai landowning company?

---

[140] For instance, an identical apartment in the same apartment complex sitting on the same land title owned by the same Thai landowning company.

With regard to the mitigation of off-plan risk, the crucial issue is not only the type of legal ownership you ultimately receive but also *when you receive it,* i.e. the timing or schedule for gaining control and ownership of an asset is equally important.

The vast majority of resort property purchasers get so wrapped up in the euphoria of buying their dream vacation home, and so focussed on the attributes of a property, that they fail to consider the potential risk of a developer's insolvency (or failure to complete the project). Indeed, developers pay similarly scant attention to the possibility of their own demise. As a result, there are usually no contingency plans in the event of non-completion, which includes the issue of the *timing* of the ownership transfer.

To illustrate the importance of both ownership and timing, it is worth comparing the purchase of off-plan property with the alternative of purchasing land and engaging a construction company to build your property. In the case where you have purchased land, engaged a construction company and the construction company becomes insolvent during construction, the usual consequence is financial loss, together with the complications associated with finding another construction company to continue the work[141]. *However, at least you maintain ownership or control of the land.* This is a critical distinction.

When buying off-plan property from a developer, the responsibility for purchasing land and building the property has been given to the developer. This generally means the developer maintains ownership and control of the land until completion. In other words, purchasers get *nothing until the property is completed* at which point legal ownership is transferred to the purchaser. Thus, in the event of the developer's insolvency during construction (or at any point before legal ownership is transferred), recovering the value of your investment can be extremely difficult because you have no *legal* ownership of property, only *contractual* rights to a completed property. In the worst-case scenario, this translates into a total loss of the money you have paid to the developer with nothing in return except an extraordinary legal and accounting mess where land plots has been mortgaged to lenders and title documents have been pledged for short-term *khaifak*[142] loans. It is as though a black hole has swallowed your investment.

---

[141] The section on "Financial Stability" in chapter 43 covers the consequences of a construction company's bankruptcy in detail.

[142] Landowners borrow money and transfer title of the land to the lender, where the lender is legally bound to transfer ownership of the land back if the borrower pays back the loan within a certain period.

What can be done to better protect your investment? In addition to performing thorough due diligence on the developer, it might be possible to bring forward the timing of legal ownership or control of the property (if the ownership structure allows such flexibility). For instance, if eventual ownership is a freehold interest in land plus the villa that sits on it, it might be possible to negotiate the transfer of land at an earlier stage, corresponding to payment of a certain proportion of the total purchase price (according to the payment schedule). For example, if you are paying a developer 10 million Baht (US$ 333,000) for land and villa with a payment schedule comprising a 1 million Baht (US$ 33,000) deposit followed by three staged payments of 3 million Baht (US$ 100,000), it might be possible for legal ownership of the land to be transferred upon payment of the second or third instalment, i.e. after payment of 4 or 7 million Baht. Thus, even in the case where a developer fails to complete construction, you remain the legal owner of the land.[143]

In the case of freehold land and a stand-alone villa, the opportunity to receive legal ownership at an earlier stage representing part of the value of your investment is more clear-cut. However, in the case of buying an apartment, the issue is more of a challenge. If the ultimate legal entitlement is a leasehold interest in one of a number of apartments in a development complex with shared common areas, sitting on land owned by one of the developer's landowning companies, there is generally little you can do but hope for completion when a lease can be registered in your name (or to a Thai company that you control).

Whether a contract can be negotiated and restructured in relation to the timing of ownership depends on how the legal ownership is structured and how flexible the developer is with regard to relinquishing control. For instance, consider the example where an off-plan development consists of half a dozen apartment units sitting on a piece of land (owned by a Thai company) and the developer intends to completely divest himself from the project upon completion (i.e. the developer has no plans to retain ownership of the land or common areas after completion). In addition to a leasehold interest in an apartment, purchasers receive shares in the Thai landowning company so the apartment owners collectively become owners of the land through the Thai company. In such cases, it might be possible for shares in the landowning company to be transferred to the purchasers prior to completion in accordance with pre-defined staged payments (provided the developer's ability to continue with construction is not affected).

In such cases, a *controlling* interest in the landowning company must be transferred to the purchasers in order to become a viable means of mitigating

---

[143] Even though building on the land or re-selling land in a failed development at a reasonable price might not be a simple matter.

non-completion risk; if only a tiny fraction of the company's shares are transferred to purchasers, with the developer retaining majority control of the company, the exercise is futile[144].

The ability to take earlier ownership or control of the underlying asset depends on the type of legal interest you are buying and the manner in which property ownership is structured. When considering the purchase of off-plan property, purchasers should therefore examine the ownership structure to see if it lends itself to earlier ownership or control of underlying assets since this is one way to moderate the risk of failure by the developer. In some cases it can be the difference between owning nothing and owning something, together with the possibility of completing your property.

Escrow

One of the most effective methods of protecting your money from the risk of non-completion is the use of escrow (see chapter 108). Escrow is a legal arrangement whereby an independent and trusted third party (the escrow agent) holds the purchaser's money for the transacting parties, which is dispersed upon the fulfilment of pre-defined obligations (such as completion of a property). If the developer accepts the use of escrow (in other words, if the developer does not need your money for construction) then the purchase money can be paid to an escrow agent instead of the developer and released only upon completion of the property. If the property is not completed – i.e. the developer has not fulfilled his obligations – the money is returned to you.

These arrangements do exist, although they tend not to be common because developers usually sell property off-plan in order to finance construction. However, in some cases, developers are able to borrow money backed by the funds held in escrow. If the opportunity does exist to avoid the risk of non-completion and protect your investment through the use of escrow, it usually comes with a higher price tag (or higher transaction fees).

---

[144] It also depends on sales; the developer cannot transfer the shares if the relevant apartments have not been sold.

Summary

- Of the four primary risks identified in relation to purchasing off-plan property, non-completion is the most significant risk, with the direst consequences.
- When buying off-plan property, you are trusting a developer with your money and trusting that the developer will do what has been promised; in effect, *you are entering into a partnership with a developer.*
- In Thailand, projects are derailed and property developers go bankrupt for a multitude of reasons.
- To mitigate the risks of buying off-plan property, it is necessary to conduct a thorough due diligence investigation of both the property developer and the development, which should include:
  - Determining the property developer's financial resources in relation to the development.
  - Determining the *genuine* level of sales and financial commitment from purchasers.
  - Researching a developer's track record of completed projects in Thailand and conducting site visits.
  - Communicating with a property developer's previous clients.
  - Speaking with a developer's competitors and seeking other sources of *informal* information.
  - Researching the credentials and experience of the developer's team of consultants, sub-contractors and advisors.
  - Conducting due diligence on the development, which includes checking and verifying documents related to land title, subdivision and access, together with build permits, developer's licence and any relevant permissions required by government departments.
  - Confirming that legal ownership structures are compliant with Thai law, appropriate to the type of property and tax efficient.
  - Checking the timing or schedule for receiving ownership or control of underlying assets.
  - The possibility of protecting your money from the risk of non-completion by using an escrow agent.

68
What are you actually buying?

When people speak about buying property, they generally refer to apartments, condominiums and private pool villas. However, these are just *physical* descriptions. With the distinct laws relating to foreign ownership of land and property in Thailand, together with the various property ownership structures, it is the type of *legal* ownership that becomes a more significance issue. Indeed, the type of *legal* ownership defines the security of an asset and this is where the true value of an investment lies.

For example, land and villas can be purchased on a leasehold or freehold[145] basis. An apartment can be purchased leasehold or with condominium freehold title, which is the closest from of complete ownership a foreigner can buy in Thailand. An apartment can also be purchased on a leasehold basis, together with some form of shared ownership of the land, through the ownership of shares in a landowning company (LOC).

The type of legal ownership in turn influences the choice of holding structure that is generally used for the property. For example, a lease (of an apartment or land) can be held directly in a person's name, or it can be registered to a Thai company (for reasons that are discussed in chapter 95). Freehold ownership of land by a foreigner is not possible, unless participation is through a Thai company.

The ownership structure, in turn, influences your legal expenses and ongoing holding costs associated with the property. For instance, if you set up a Thai company, there will be company set up costs, together with ongoing annual accounting fees. There might also be fees connected to company secretarial services, provision of the company's registered office address or fees related to the provision of company directors (see chapters 85 and 90).

The type of legal ownership and ownership structure also influence the procedure for on-selling a property. For example, a leasehold property held in a personal name requires the lease to be transferred and registered to the new owner; the sale of freehold property requires transfer of the property; while ownership of freehold or leasehold property held in a Thai company can be passed on by transferring shares of the Thai company[146]. In this way, the type of legal

---

[145] Through the utilization of a Thai company.
[146] If the new owner consents to buying the property by taking over a Thai company.

ownership and ownership structure determine the costs, transfer fees and taxes upon re-sale.

As is evident, buying off-plan property (or any property in Thailand) is not merely a question of buying a condominium, villa or apartment; the precise legal ownership and holding structure must also be considered (see chapter 95). The type of legal ownership, and the manner in which ownership is structured, differs from project to project and from developer to developer. For example, some developers offer the option of buying freehold or leasehold, while other developers build a project of private pool villas but only offer them for sale on a leasehold basis, intending to retain freehold ownership of the land (together with the common areas) for the purpose of securing on-going management and maintenance fees. Alternatively, a developer building apartment blocks might be selling leasehold ownership of apartments together with a share of the freehold land, with the intention of completely divesting his interest in the development to the owners upon completion.

When evaluating various off-plan properties, it is important that your focus extends beyond colour perspectives and floor layout plans. It is equally, if not more, important to understand *what you are buying* in terms of legal ownership and ownership structures, and to ensure that what you buy meets your requirements. For example, if you want to buy a freehold property, it is a waste of time looking at a development that offers for sale only leasehold properties. Although sometimes it might be necessary to compromise; for instance, if you had planned to buy freehold property but the most desirable property is offered only on a leasehold basis, getting the property you want might require the acceptance of leasehold ownership.

With reference to contractual documents, the type of legal ownership and the ownership structure subsequently determine the type of contracts that you will enter into in relation to the purchase, such as Construction Agreements, Land Lease Agreements (LLA), Apartment Lease Agreements (ALA), Sale and Purchase Agreements (SPA) or Share Sale and Purchase Agreements (SSPA). For example, if you are purchasing an apartment on a leasehold basis, you might enter into an ALA, while if you are taking ownership through an existing corporate structure it usually involves an SSPA.

Important tip: When buying off-plan properties, there are essentially two different ways for contracts can be drafted; either as a sale and purchase, or as a construction contract where a developer is engaged to provide the *service* of building the property. The two forms have significantly different

---

> tax consequences for purchasers since the former concerns the purchase of property, while the latter is concerned with paying for a service[147].

In addition to the primary legal agreements that deal with the transfer of property ownership, it is also necessary to consider any "secondary" agreements you might be required to enter into with the developer that bind you to certain services or place restrictions on the use of the property or common areas. Four common types of agreement you might encounter are as follows:

1. Management and Maintenance Agreements (or Service Contracts)
   This is an agreement between the purchaser and the developer whereby the developer (or an entity associated with the developer) is engaged to provide maintenance services for the common areas of the development in return for monthly or annual fees. Services covered by maintenance agreements generally include security, maintenance of access roads, electricity supply, water supply, drainage systems, waste disposal and telephone connections.

2. Rules and Regulations (or Owners Charter)
   These agreements contain rules for the use of the property and common areas. Depending on the development, such rules might cover the use of swimming pools, car parking areas, procedures for visitor access and whether pets are allowed into the development. In addition, there might be rules covering physical alterations that are permitted and restrictions with regard to painting the exterior of the property (in order to preserve the overall consistency or "look" of the project).

3. Rental Management Agreements
   These are agreements related to the rental management of your property. Some developers expect to be exclusively engaged to manage the rental of your property (when not in use by the owner). Such agreements usually specify the number of days that owners can use the property and the dates when owners are restricted from using the property; the rules and procedures related to booking the property for the owners use; and the fees charged by the rental management company for the services provided.

4. Leaseback Agreements
   With a leaseback agreement, the owner agrees to lease their property back to the developer in return for a monthly payment or specified annual

---

[147] The issue of obtaining a building permit must also be considered.

yield. Such agreements cover the terms and conditions of the leaseback, together with rules related to the owners use of the property.

When looking at off-plan developments, the main point to remember is to make sure you understand what you are *actually* buying into. In addition to the details and specifications of the property, this means you must become familiar with the type of legal ownership, the ownership structure, and any other contractual agreements you might be required to enter into with the developer. Furthermore, buying property in Thailand involves unique tax and legal considerations. It is therefore essential to take professional advice (see Step 6) before committing to a purchase. While the different types of legal ownership and the array of holding structures might appear complicated, they are straightforward issues for lawyers in Thailand to deal with since they are familiar with the issues and rules.

Summary

- To understand property in Thailand, it is necessary to look beyond *physical* property descriptions. It is the type of *legal* ownership that defines the security of an asset and is where the true value of an investment lies.
- The type of *legal* ownership, in turn, influences the choice of ownership structure that is generally used for the property.
- The ownership structure, in turn, influences your legal expenses and ongoing holding costs associated with the property.
- The type of legal ownership and ownership structure also influence the procedure for on-selling a property, which determines the costs, transfer fees and taxes upon re-sale.
- The type of legal ownership, and the manner in which ownership is structured, differs from project to project and from developer to developer; it is therefore important to understand what you are actually buying.

69
What else are you buying?

We are now familiar with the types of property (villas, apartments, condominiums), together with an understanding of the various forms of legal ownership offered by developers (freehold, leasehold or leasehold with a share of the freehold). It is now helpful to turn our attention to what else might be included with an off-plan property, i.e. in addition to the type of property ownership, what else are you buying?

Plans and material specifications

A good starting point is to make sure you receive a full set of plans, elevations and three-dimensional perspectives of the property, together with a detailed list of material specifications. Time needs to be spent familiarising yourself with the minute details and, as mentioned in chapter 64 (Mitigating risks, differing expectations), these details should form part of the sales contract. Material specifications should cover all aspects of construction, from wall and floor finishings to the specifications for windows and doors, and from bathroom fittings to light fittings. If you are not familiar with the materials or specifications, ask the developer for samples or ask to see the materials in situ at another property or development.

Fully furnished?

Furniture is an important consideration. Some developments are sold fully furnished, while others are sold unfurnished with various furniture packages being offered separately as optional extras (or sometimes as a mandatory requirement if the property is to become part of a rental programme).

When evaluating furniture packages, it is important to check precisely what is included. Some furniture packages offered by developers include only "large items of furniture", such as beds, settees, tables and chairs; while other furniture packages are "rent-ready" in that they include a full set of furniture, curtains, bed linen, towels, cushions, kitchen equipment and cutlery.

With regard to kitchens, the range of white goods and appliances needs to be considered. Depending on the developer and project, sometimes kitchens come with a fully installed range of kitchen appliances, including oven, hob, hood, microwave, dishwasher, fridge and washing machine. Sometimes only a few essential appliances are supplied as standard, usually oven, hob and hood, while the purchase of fridges, dishwashers, microwaves and washing machines are left to the purchaser. Brand names and specifications are also an important consideration. For instance, appliances could be Gaggenau, Smeg, Franke or Electrolux. Specifications within each brand can range from basic models to top end models. Another key factor is after sales service, which differs among brands depending upon which brands have local representation or service centres. Kitchen material specifications must also be noted, for instance, work surfaces can be granite or MDF-covered chipboard; kitchen cabinets can be MDF-covered chipboard or hardwearing high-gloss melamine.

Electrical appliances are a separate consideration. Some furniture packages include flat-screen TVs for the living room, kitchen and each bedroom; other packages include TVs in the living room and master bedroom, or for the master bedroom only; while some packages exclude electronics completely. As with kitchen appliances, brands and model numbers should be noted (such as B&O, LG or Samsung) and brands with local service and repair centres should be highlighted.

Fitted wardrobes, bathroom cabinets, curtains and blinds are additional considerations, which become additional costs if not included and fitted by the developer.

Car parking

Car parking is an often-overlooked issue. Does the property include sufficient parking spaces? If so, are car parking spaces "allocated" or "unallocated"?[148] For an off-plan apartment development, how is the each owner's car parking entitlement embodied in the contracts? Some first-time developers build properties and consider the issue of car parking at the end; from a purchaser's perspective, this issue should be settled at the contract stage.

Golf course, marina or hotel?

If you are buying an off-plan property with a distinguishing feature, such as a golf course, marina or hotel complex, there are other issues to consider.

In a development where a golf course, marina or hotel complex is the principal reason for investment, it is often the small print related to the unique feature that defines the value of the investment. For instance, with a golf-related development,

---

[148] Does each owner receive his or her own private, numbered car parking space?

do golf membership rights attach to the property or are they personal to the buyer? Is there a one-off lifetime membership fee or ongoing annual or monthly fees? Will membership fees remain fixed for a defined period or are they subject to change immediately after purchase? Are there reciprocal rights to other golf courses in Thailand or abroad?

If the property is attached to a hotel complex, it is necessary to determine the details regarding access to facilities such as restaurants, spas, business centres, swimming pools and gyms. Do owners get free access to facilities or are additional fees involved?

With regard to marina developments, is the property sold together with a berth? An experienced property lawyer needs to be engaged to identify the points of crucial interest to a property purchaser, such as mooring fees, defects liability, service and maintenance guarantees and, perhaps the most important issue, the company backing the guarantees. If the purchase of a property includes the use of a boat, it is necessary to check the terms related to booking the use of the boat; the number of hours use each month or year each owner is permitted free of charge; whether there are any additional costs involved for fuel or maintenance; and how these costs are apportioned.

Since the terms and conditions related to golf courses, hotels and marinas are assets in their own right, an extra degree of care needs to be taken when checking contractual documents. Sales contracts must be checked in relation to the property purchase but with a special focus on the element that distinguishes the property and for which a premium price is usually being asked. It is important to identify the value adding features, and to make sure you are satisfied with the way the details are reflected in the contract before proceeding with the purchase.

Finally, it is necessary to check the marketing materials and sales contracts to identify what is *not* included. It is important to read the small print contained in brochures, discuss any questionable issues with the developer's sales staff and cross-reference all the information with the sales contract to ensure consistency. Each oversight will either cost you money or decrease the investment value of the property. For instance, in relation to kitchens, if a salesperson has promised that a fridge is included with the property but the contract fails to mention it, such a small discrepancy could cost you an extra 30,000 - 80,000 Baht (US$ 1,000 – 2,650) to purchase a fridge. The process of double-checking details might be time consuming and tedious; however, it will save you money and help to avoid disappointment and disagreements.

Summary

- After a familiarity with the types of property and an understanding of the various forms of legal ownership, it is necessary to turn our attention to what else is included with an off-plan property.
- A full set of plans, elevations and three-dimensional property perspectives should be requested from the developer, together with a detailed list of material specifications.
- Is the property sold fully furnished, or unfurnished with various furniture packages available as optional extras? If furnished, what *precisely* is included with regard to furniture, appliances and electronics?
- Does the property include sufficient car parking spaces and are they "allocated" or "unallocated"?
- If a property has a distinguishing feature, such as a golf course, marina or hotel complex, it is necessary to carefully check the contracts with a special focus on the terms related to these features.

70
What to look (out) for?
(Essential)

The fact that a property is not yet built is a key factor distinguishing off-plan properties from other property investments. What this means in practice is that with *pure* off-plan investments, it is often difficult to visualise the finished product. The word "pure" is used here in the sense that the property exists *only* on paper, construction has yet to start and there is nothing to look at except a vacant plot of land (and if you purchase early enough, oftentimes the land is still covered by jungle!).

This contrasts with buying into an off-plan development *after* construction has started, in which case it is at least possible to walk through the construction site to get an idea of the size and layout of a property and its relationship to neighbouring properties. In other words, visualising a finished property gets easier the further construction progresses.

The fact there is little or nothing to look at when purchasing property off-plan or during the early stages of construction creates various hazards for purchasers. The purpose of this chapter is to identify the six key hazards buyers need to look out for to protect their investments. These are discussed under the following headings:

1. Density
2. Aspect
3. Phases
4. Orientation
5. Common areas
6. Access roads.

1. Density

When browsing off-plan property brochures, it is often the case that buyers focus almost exclusively on the attributes of the property of interest to the exclusion of other properties in the development and, in particular, how close to each other they will be built. What is being referred to here is the issue of land use or density.

While some developers plan projects where properties are generously spaced and each unit enjoys a reasonable level of privacy through the use of landscaping, lawns and terraces,[149] other developers try to cram as many units of property as they can onto a plot of land to maximise profits or lower unit prices[150]. For instance, with some luxury villa developments, construction might be limited to only one or two villas per Rai of land (see chapter 22), while developers seeking to maximise land use and minimise property prices might attempt to fit as many as six or eight villas per Rai of land. The result is a substantial difference in the feeling of space for occupants, which influences the overall property ownership experience.

Zoning and building regulations (chapter 21) might limit the percentage of land that can be used for construction, for instance, hotel complexes might be limited to using 45% of the overall land area for construction of buildings (leaving 55% for gardens, lawns and other communal facilities), while areas designated for residential use might limit the area of land to be used for buildings to 39%. However, within these guidelines developers and architects have significant scope in relation to the density of residential properties. As an off-plan property purchaser, density is something to pay attention to because it will not only affect your enjoyment of a property but also the value of your investment.

Therefore, in addition to the floor plans and perspectives for each individual property, it is also necessary to pay attention to site plans and project master plans. The distance between properties should be noted, together with the actual manner of their separation, for instance, are properties separated by trees, foliage and landscaping, or by two-metre high garden walls? In the case of apartments, are adjoining units separated by cavity walls or single-skin walls?

When buying a property as a residence, the desired level of privacy is purely a matter of personal choice. However, if you are planning to rent out a property to guests, the issue becomes a matter of making sure the density of a development and the level of privacy meets the requirements of the rental market. Small enclosed spaces might suit Asian honeymoon couples, although for Europeans venturing halfway around the world, sitting in a small courtyard surrounded by a high wall is not the ideal tropical vacation experience.

Rental property owners should also bear in mind that Thailand attracts a diversity of tourists from a wide spectrum of countries. A family with young children looking

---

[149] Lower density or land use for construction is generally offset by higher asking prices by the developer.
[150] Spreading the cost of land over a higher number of properties enables a developer to reduce asking prices.

forward to a quiet break might arrive at a rental property to find the adjacent property occupied by a rugby team on tour (not the prettiest of sights, or sounds) or a group of college students intent on partying. The proximity of a property to its neighbours (in combination with the type of guests) can make the difference between a quiet relaxing holiday and having to listen to the antics of neighbouring tourists for a week or more! While everyone has their own idea of an enjoyable holiday, there is a higher probability of guest complaints (and loss of business from returning customers) where properties are in a high-density development.

When evaluating off-plan developments, therefore, be sure to compare densities between developments (which should be reflected in published prices) and be sure to request information concerning land use and the number of villas being built per Rai of land.

2. Aspect

While focussing on the attributes of a property, it is easy to overlook not only what is happening around it *but also what might later be built around it!* The "aspect" or view from a property is an essential component of its value. This is especially the case with resort properties where sunset or sea views command a premium in terms of purchase prices and rental rates. An awareness of what is happening on the land around a property is therefore an essential part of the due diligence process *especially for off-plan developments* (refer to chapter 32 for a more detailed discussion of "Aspect and adjacent land").

Since off-plan property developments typically comprise multiple properties, it is first necessary to consider the view from each section of the development in order to choose the available property with the best views. The "orientation" of the property in relation to the sun (and particularly sunsets) should also be taken into account (see 4. below). It is then necessary to identity the risk of losing such views due to future construction on adjacent land. With off-plan property investments, the risks are greater than when purchasing secondary properties; with off-plan properties, views are at risk not only from the construction of properties on neighbouring land, they are similarly at risk from construction within the same development and from subsequent phases of the same development (see 3. below). For this reason, reviewing the site master plan is a key element of your due diligence.

Important tip: As part of the off-plan purchase process, it is highly advisable to visit the site, determine the exact location where your property will be built, and then identify and evaluate the risk of future development. Don't be an armchair investor that is content to invest solely based on descriptions and pictures in a brochure; neighbouring land plots are often airbrushed out for marketing perspectives or conveniently obscured by landscaping features to enhance the presentation. Provided the proper procedure is followed, it might be acceptable to reserve a property (with a *fully refundable* deposit) but buyers should not proceed with a purchase without visiting the site.

3. Phases

It is usually possible to identify the risk posed to a property's aspect by future development on surrounding land or by other buildings within a development. However, less obvious but equally important is the risk posed by subsequent phases *of the same development* ("multi-phase" developments). Indeed, if Phase I of a development is successful (and the land is available) many developers attempt to capitalise on their success by launching Phase II.

I have heard of developers buying large tracts of land with a view to building a large project in several phases. Phase I, comprising properties with beautiful sea views, is launched and is soon sold-out. Phase II is then launched and construction begins directly in front, permanently obscuring the sea views of Phase I properties and causing an immediate loss of the premium price paid for those views. While this is an extreme example, it illuminates the risk posed by subsequent phases of a development. If a property has a premium view, part of the due diligence process should include checking the ownership of surrounding land. If the land is already in the hands of the same developer (or indeed any developer), it is safe to assume the land will be developed in future. The only question relates to timing.

Important tip: Future construction not only has an impact in relation to the potential for losing premium views; it is also significant in relation to the impact of construction activity and noise on a property's ability to generate rental income.

Imagine you have taken possession of a property in Phase I of a development and future rental bookings have already been secured. Then the developer commences construction of Phase II. With construction of large-scale developments generally lasting at least one year, usually several years, the potential exists for serious loss of rental income during this time period[151]. For this reason, it is essential to be fully aware of a developer's plans. This is especially the case in Thailand where projects are rarely finished on schedule. In addition,

---

[151] The possibility sometimes exists to negotiate the use of an alternative unit on the other side of the same development until the completion of construction.

if a subsequent phase of a development introduces new common area features, such as water features, high maintenance lifts or landscaped areas, it might also result in higher management and maintenance costs for all owners, including property owners in previous phases.

4. Orientation

When visiting an off-plan development site or evaluating the master site plan, bear in mind that properties with sunset views often command higher prices and rental rates. Therefore, remember to plot properties in relation to their North-South-East-West orientation in order to determine where the sun rises and sets (bearing in mind sunsets vary according to the season).

In addition, if you plot the direction in which the sun travels during the day, it is also possible to identify properties with pool decks that receive sunlight in the morning and shade in the afternoon.

5. Common Areas

If a property is part of a project or gated community, another key factor is to determine which areas are *private* and which are *shared* (common areas). This is particularly important if you are buying an apartment. For instance, if you are considering an apartment with a communal swimming pool and the pool is directly in front of your living room, it might look convenient on a master plan; however, it also means other apartment owners (and their guests) will be splashing around just metres from your living room, removing any possibility of a peaceful residence. The location of adult swimming pools and children's pools should also have a bearing on the choice of apartment. The convenience of having your children playing nearby must be weighed against the tendency for children's pool areas to generate more noise!

A related issue is the purchase of pool deck furniture. If a terrace or pool deck is shared, it needs to be confirmed whether the relevant outdoor furniture is supplied and maintained by the developer (or management company), particularly in the case of small or first-time property developers. If the developer does not supply furniture, the issue arises whether individual owners need to purchase their own patio furniture or whether a common fund should be set up for the purpose. In the case where individual owners purchase furniture for common area use, bear in mind it is likely to be used by other visitors who will not distinguish private property from communally-owned property. While this appears to be a minor issue, details should be confirmed in advance to avoid additional costs, inconvenience and disagreements.

It is also necessary to consider the location of access roads, pathways and car-parking areas within a project. Having a path leading past your property, for instance, might increase a property's appeal on the plan but it often means neighbours will be walking past your property on the way to their units, which will affect the privacy and enjoyment of your property. For this reason, a villa or apartment at the end of a road or path is often more appealing. On the other hand, if the unit at the end of an internal project road faces an open expanse of land that could later become a construction site, buying a middle unit could be more prudent; the property might have less privacy but there is a certain peace of mind knowing the property will not be disturbed by future construction.

Communal areas, car parks, roads and paths are all issues that need to be considered during the selection of a property in an off-plan development. In some cases, after taking into consideration all the common area related issues, it might be preferable to increase your budget to purchase a private stand-alone villa!

6. Access Roads

The completion of the access road to a development is usually one of the last tasks to be scheduled by a developer, rationalised by the fact that if roads are concreted during the early stages of construction, delivery vehicles bringing heavy materials to the site will damage them. However, the possibility exists, as developers reach the end of a project, that they fail to put in the concrete road that has been promised (often due to tight cash flow) and instead leave a dirt track as the main access road (that could get washed away during the rainy season). Sometimes developers or their sales staff mention that the access road is owned by adjacent landowners who have all agreed to contribute funds to put in a concrete road at a later date; and all too often the landowners fail to contribute their share of the costs and the road never gets completed.

The quality of the access road to a development is crucial to the value of a property and for this reason a concrete access road of the prescribed width needs to become a condition of the contract, instead of a throwaway remark by a salesperson. Ideally, part of the purchase price (corresponding to the cost of the access road[152]) should be set aside and if the road is not completed by the date specified, that amount should become a penalty payment.

---

[152] The amount of the penalty payment should reflect the cost of putting in the prescribed road, although in practice this often proves to be difficult. Such clauses are generally easier to implement if the property is a villa with separate access, where a sum can be provisioned specifically to put in the access road for the individual property.

Summary

- The fact that a property is not yet built is a key factor distinguishing off-plan properties from other property investments, which means it is often difficult to visualise the finished product. This creates various hazards for purchasers.
- Off-plan purchasers need to evaluate the potential impact on their investments of the following issues:
  - Density or land use of the development
  - Aspect or view from a property and risk to that view
  - Phases of a multi-phase development
  - Orientation, particularly in relation to sunsets
  - Common areas, such as pools, car parking areas and roads
  - The access road to the development

71
Guarantees

If you are buying a property with "condominium freehold" title, the issue of construction guarantees is generally covered by statute: condominium units receive an automatic five-year structural guarantee and a two-year non-structural defects warranty, regardless of the terms included in the developer's contract.

For all other "non-regulated" developments, it is necessary to check the details related to the guarantees provided by the developer. The types of guarantees generally provided include Defects Warranties, Structural Guarantees, Return to site policies and procedures, and Manufacturers Guarantees. These construction-related guarantees were covered in more detail in chapter 48 although for quick reference they are summarised below:

- *Defects Warranties* cover any defects that are not of a structural nature discovered after completion and handover of the property.

- *Structural Guarantees* cover issues related to the structural integrity of the property, for example, foundation beams, columns, floor slabs, load bearing walls, roof structures and retaining walls.

- *Return to site policies and procedures* cover the details of how claims are submitted and evaluated, and how the defects are rectified.

- *Manufacturers Guarantees* are guarantees covering specialised equipment, such as air-conditioning units, pool systems, kitchen appliances, and windows and doors.

In addition, purchasers of off-plan properties should ensure there are detailed procedures covering the issue of "snagging", which is the process of identifying and rectifying defects *before* completion (see chapter 58).

In relation to off-plan property, the issue of guarantees is relevant not only to the type of guarantees provided, but *which company* is contractually responsible. For instance, if you have bought land and engaged a construction company to build a house, the defects warranty and structural guarantee (together with the return to site procedures), will be provided directly by the construction company and details should be set out in the Construction Agreement.

In the case of buying off-plan property where a developer is guaranteeing the work, details of the guarantees should be included in the agreement with the developer. In turn, a similar set of guarantees should be set out in the contract between the developer and the construction company. However, in cases where a separate Construction Agreement is signed, it is quite possible that the construction company (rather than the developer) is contractually responsible for providing construction-related guarantees.

In each case, it is important for professional legal advice to be taken to make sure any documentation or clauses related to guarantees, particularly *structural guarantees,* are clearly worded and enforceable. It is natural to think positively and to hope that no defects or structural issues will arise; indeed, no one really wants to discuss such issues when purchasing a new property. However, purchasers need to be properly prepared for such contingencies and if issues do arise, they need to be able to rely on the relevant contractual guarantee.

In the event that a defect or structural issue does arise, it is often easier to deal with a developer, with whom you already have a working relationship, rather than with a construction company with which you have had no direct dealings. The more important issue, however, is which company is more likely to be able to meet the financial obligations and practical responsibilities of a claim, particularly of a structural nature, bearing in mind that structural problems usually require significant remedial work. Remember, guarantees are only worth something if the entity standing behind them is still in business and has the resources (and commitment) to fix the problems. For this reason, and with the appropriate legal guidance, it might be possible to make both the developer and construction company "jointly and severally" responsible for the guarantees and subsequent rectification of work.

Finally, with regard to "manufacturers guarantees", it is important to make sure the developer provides the relevant documentation for pool pump systems, air-conditioning units, kitchen appliances, and windows and doors at the time of the handover of the property.

Summary

- If you are buying a property with "condominium freehold" title, the issue of construction guarantees is generally covered by statute.
- For all other "non-regulated" developments, it is necessary to check the details related to guarantees provided by the developer, particularly in relation to:
  - Defects Warranties
  - Structural Guarantees
  - Return to Site Policies and Procedures
- Ultimately, guarantees are only worth something if the entity standing behind them is still in business and has the resources to fix the problems. Thus, try to make both the developer and the construction company "jointly and severally" responsible for the provision of guarantees.

72
Customisation

Conceptually, buying off-plan property is a hybrid between buying a completed property in the secondary market, and buying land and engaging a construction company to build your house.

With off-plan property, a developer is building you a completed property although generally the design is determined by the developer. However, in most cases, the possibility exists to customise your property, particularly if you have purchased at the pre-construction or early construction stages.

The level of possible customisation possible depends on the developer and the project in question. Some developers, for example, will allow changes to floor layouts, while others might only allow changes to floor and wall finishings. There is typically more scope for the customisation of a stand-alone villa purchased off-plan, than an apartment in an apartment complex. However, changes are generally possible for all properties at the earlier stages; the determining factor being the developer's willingness to make them and whether building regulations permit them.

The overriding criteria for all developers is that modifications are subject to maintaining the consistency and overall design concept of the development; if complete flexibility is given to all purchasers, developments would resemble a hotchpotch of different colours and styles. For this reason, a degree of *inflexibility* in relation to design changes should be welcomed because it maintains the value of your investment. I recall, for instance, a sleek, minimalist, contemporary apartment building that looked stunning until residents erected bamboo structures on the rooftop, which was completely at odds with the visual appearance and overall design concept!

Therefore, within the constraints imposed by a developer, discussed below are some of the things that might lend themselves to customisation if a property does not fully meet your requirements.

Layout

The first thing a purchaser might wish to do is take a critical look at the floor layout of a property, together with the proportions and relationship between rooms. For instance, during the daytime, most of the activity in a tropical vacation home is focussed around the pool and the living areas leading from the pool. Therefore, check which rooms face the pool. Some purchasers prefer to have the pool terrace adjacent to the living room; others prefer bedrooms leading onto the pool terrace. For example, one European-expat couple were considering the purchase of a two-storey villa where the living room, dining room and kitchen were on the same level as the pool terrace, while the bedrooms were upstairs. They confirmed the purchase, subject to moving the bedrooms downstairs around the pool, and moving the living room, dining room and kitchen upstairs to take advantage of more expansive views.

In addition, if the property you are considering has a private pool, consider the proportions of the pool and pool terrace. Oftentimes, the size of the pool is reduced in order to create a larger pool terrace; other times a developer increases the size of the pool to the extent where there is no longer enough seating or dining space around it. Changes to proportions are easy to make, although remember that larger pools generally cost more, not only in terms of an increase in structural work and materials but also due to the capacity of the pool pump system.

Number of rooms

Unless internal walls are designed to be load bearing, changing the configuration of internal walls in order to create additional bedrooms or change the proportion of rooms is a relatively straightforward modification. For example, a two-bedroom apartment can be made into a three-bedroom apartment just by adding a wall, without any change to the total floor area. Naturally, bedroom sizes will be reduced, although a three-bedroom apartment might better match your family size or the demands of the rental market.

In the case of an off-plan villa, extra bedrooms can be created either by changing the configuration of internal walls or by adding to the floor area, i.e. by extending the villa (provided such changes fall within the building regulations).

Windows and doors

Subject to building regulations, you might decide to remove walls and replace them with floor to ceiling windows to increase the amount of light. Alternatively, sliding doors can be changed to concertinered doors in order to turn indoor rooms into "outdoor living areas". Alternatively, you might want to remove a window and make it a wall due to issues of privacy or, for instance, if the room lacks space for mounting a flat-screen TV.

Shade

Once the North-South-East-West orientation has been established, it should be easy to determine which parts of a property will be in shade and which areas will be in bright sunlight during the day. If the property does not provide adequate shade, you might wish to add more shaded areas through the use of additional roof structures, sail-type structures or canopies. I recently met a middle-aged couple that cut short a one-month rental agreement for a beautiful three-storey property and moved out because "it was too hot and there was nowhere to sit in the shade!" Remember, roof structures can sometimes serve the dual purpose of providing shade to lower areas, while providing roof terraces for the floor above.

Kitchen layout

The kitchen area might lend itself to being expanded, or you might simply want to reorganise the ergonomic layout of the three key kitchen appliances: sink, hob and fridge. Alternatively, a breakfast bar could be added to separate the kitchen and living room, or a breakfast bar can be removed to increase the open-plan feel of a small apartment. Some property owners like to add a second kitchen or a kitchenette for the use of staff or guests.

Material Specifications

While many property brochures for off-plan property developments focus on the emotional aspects of the property – breathtaking sunsets, panoramic views, luxury furnishings – it is important to become familiar with the less emotional and more mundane issues, such as the materials being used for construction. There is always scope for changing material specifications or substituting materials. For example, you might wish to change polished concrete floors for tiles or marble imported from Italy; ceramic bathtubs could become Terrazzo baths; bathroom fittings can be upgraded from generic Chinese imports to European brands; balcony railings can be changed from brushed steel to toughened glass; pool terraces can be changed from sandwash to sandstone.

Lighting

As noted in chapter 54, it is wise to get involved with the lighting design plan to ensure it reflects your personal requirements, such as adding feature lighting in the garden; adding (or deleting) lights in the swimming pool or Jacuzzi; changing halogen lights to LED lighting in the kitchen or living areas; adding dimmer switches; or simply changing the configuration in which certain switches turn on certain lights.

> **Important tip:** If you want to make design changes to an off-plan property, it is highly recommended that changes are agreed *before* the purchase is confirmed and contracts are signed. There are three reasons for this: firstly, once contracts have been signed, you might find the developer is less flexible or accommodating to the desired changes; secondly, all details and specifications related to the changes should be included in the contracts; and thirdly, if there are additional costs involved, these can best be negotiated at the time of purchase, rather than separately.

Never allow a salesperson to talk you into signing agreements with the comment that "any alterations or customisation can be discussed later". This is a sure-fire means to reduce your bargaining power in relation to any proposed customisation. If necessary, agreements should be signed "subject to acceptance by the developer of the following modifications…"

Finally, if you are planning to rent out or re-sell the property, take care that any changes or "improvements" are not too personal. For example, one investor I know took the developer's original architectural plans and modified the entire layout and configuration; he moved bedrooms around, changed the shape of the living room, reduced the size of the pool deck, removed windows in the hallway and bathrooms, and made one of the bedrooms into an office. When he decided to sell two years later, he couldn't find a buyer, despite a steady stream of interested parties and despite significantly dropping the price. The property agent involved said the principal comment from each potential buyer was, "what a strange layout!"

The fact is there are certain materials, configurations and layouts that meet the accommodation needs of most residents, tourists and tenants; and there are those that don't! In other words, if you customise excessively to your personal taste or depart too radically from accepted principles, you might find the property is no longer marketable. While it is great to have the flexibility of customising certain aspects of a property, unless you are planning to keep the property for your own use forever, be careful that you don't change too much so that the property becomes undesirable for everyone else!

Summary

- When buying off-plan property, in most cases the possibility exists to customise your property, particularly if you have purchased at the pre-construction or early construction stages.
- There is typically more scope for the customisation of a stand-alone villa than an apartment in an apartment complex.
- These are some of the things that might lend themselves to customisation:
  - Layout
  - Number of rooms
  - Windows and doors
  - Shade
  - Kitchen layout
  - Material specifications
  - Lighting

73
Payment schedules

Off-plan properties are generally paid for over the course of construction according to a pre-defined payment schedule, although payment schedules differ from developer to developer and from project to project. For instance, some developers ask for a small initial deposit followed by progressively larger payments as construction nears completion, while other developers request a large initial payment, followed by a number of equal payments spread over the duration of construction. There are rare instances in Thailand where developers ask for a nominal initial payment and no further payment until the end of the project, usually in conjunction with some form of bank guarantee or escrow[153] arrangement (and usually in conjunction with higher prices). It should be noted that many developers, especially smaller developments, are willing to negotiate the payment schedule to ensure it fits your personal financial circumstances.

Chapter 47 provided two staged payment examples in the context of engaging a construction company to build your property. A variation is shown here in order to provide an example of an off-plan payment schedule:

10%	• within 7 working days of signing the sales and purchase agreement
20%	• upon completion of the foundation and ground floor structure
25%	• upon completion of the first floor and roof structure
35%	• upon completion of roof tiling and masonry works, plastering of interior and exterior walls, installation of the ceilings, windows and doors
10%	• upon completion of the property

---

[153] See chapter 108.

With off-plan property developments, developers typically require an initial deposit or reservation fee (see chapter 74) to demonstrate good faith and an intention to purchase. This is then followed by a payment schedule that generally corresponds to the cash required by the developer to build the property[154]. If a developer is willing to negotiate the payment schedule, the purchaser's objective should be to agree smaller payments at the initial stages, with the bulk of the investment payable toward the final stages of construction. For example, one developer was requesting five payments of varying amounts over the course of construction; after negotiation he agreed to accept a buyer's proposal to make an initial payment of 20% with payment of the remaining 80% due upon completion.

Each developer's willingness to negotiate typically depends on their eagerness to make a sale, in combination with the developer's financial circumstances. Developers with sufficient capital to start construction might accept modified payment terms from initial buyers to kick-start sales, while other developers might be more amenable to negotiating payment terms towards the later stages of a project when sufficient sales have already been made to fund construction.

> **Important tip:** A common strategy employed by off-plan property developers is to offer a price discount (for example 3 – 5%) if a purchaser pays in full at the time of signing the contract. However, with inexperienced or first-time developers in Thailand's resort areas, it is not recommended to take advantage of such discounts; the risks are too high. In effect, you are being asked to become an equity investor in the development without the corresponding reward.

The two key principles in regard to staged payments for off-plan property are, first, not to pay more than one instalment before construction commences and, second, ensure payments do not get ahead of actual construction; for example, if you are paying up to 75% of the purchase price when construction is only 50% complete, this is one sure way to increase risk.

One common issue that arises with staged payments is determining whether a developer has reached the stage where the next payment becomes due. There are several things you can do to protect yourself:

- First, make sure the sales contract gives you a "right of access" to the site so you can check the progress of construction for yourself.[155]

---

[154] Remember, payment schedules provide an insight into a developer's financial resources and level of dependence on sales to finance construction (see chapter 67).

[155] Usually accompanied by the developer or under the supervision of a project manager.

- Second, make staged payments only upon receipt of a formal payment request from the developer, together with a certificate from the supervising architect or project manager attesting that the appropriate stage has been reached.

- Third, if necessary, hire a surveyor or engineer to independently certify that each stage has been reached.

- Fourth, make sure that payments to a developer are made through your lawyer (or under the supervision of your lawyer) who will ensure that the correct documentation and invoices have been prepared, and that payments are being made in accordance with the terms of the contract.

In relation to the wording used to describe the point when a staged payment becomes due, it is important that the relevant contractual clause identifies each stage *in precise construction terms.* If a stage payment is not accompanied by a clear description, it leaves space for interpretation, and argument. For instance, if a payment is due "upon completion of 50% of the property", who decides when 50% of the property has been completed? For this reason, staged payments are less susceptible to misinterpretation when linked to specific construction steps, for example, "upon completion of roof tiling and masonry works, plastering of interior and exterior walls, installation of the ceilings, windows and doors".

In addition, the advice of an architect, project manager or construction professional should be sought to ensure payment schedules are closely aligned with construction progress. Beware of payment schedules that specify staged payments on certain dates or within a certain number of days following the signing of the contract, *without any reference to actual construction,* for instance, "the Third payment is due 120 days following the date of this agreement". In such cases, the purchaser is contractually required to make the next payment even when there has been no progress on site since the previous payment.

Any contractual term referring to the consequences of late payment must also be carefully examined. For instance, a developer's standard contract will sometimes specify the payment of interest for each day or month a staged payment is late, while other contracts have more severe consequences for the purchaser, such as if a payment is late (by a specified period of time) "the developer has the right to terminate the contract and retain all payments made thus far". Due to these issues, professional legal advice should be sought before signing a contract with a developer. A competent lawyer should bring these clauses to your attention and any overtly unfair or punitive terms should be negotiated[156]. In the case of off-plan Condominium Freehold purchases, the standard contract form stipulates that the interest rate may not exceed 15% per year and the total paid to the developer may not exceed 10% of the purchase price. There are also specific terms restricting a developer's ability to terminate contracts with a buyer.

In the event that you are buying an off-plan property *after* construction has commenced, some developers might exaggerate progress on site in order to secure a larger initial payment upon the signing of contracts. It is therefore necessary to ascertain the precise stage of construction that has been reached, prior to confirming the staged payment schedule in the sales contract. In such cases, it is advisable to engage an engineer or surveyor to independently verify the work.

Summary

The key advice in relation to staged payment schedule for off-plan property is as follows:

- The purchaser's objective should be to agree smaller payments at the initial stages, with the bulk of the investment payable toward the final stages of construction.
- Don't pay the purchase price in full in exchange for a small discount, especially with inexperienced or first-time developers.
- Take professional advice to ensure payment stages are closely aligned with construction progress and that the relevant contractual clauses clearly identify each stage *in precise construction terms.*
- Don't accept a payment schedule that specifies staged payments on certain dates or within a certain number of days following the signing of the contract, *without any reference to actual construction.*
- Don't pay more than one instalment before construction commences and never allow payments to get ahead of construction.
- Make staged payments only upon receipt of a formal payment request from the developer; if necessary, hire a surveyor or engineer to independently certify that each stage has been reached.
- Pay careful attention to unfair or punitive terms relating to late payment.

---

[156] Penalty clauses relating to late payments should also motivate purchasers to carefully plan their cash flow requirements (see chapter 50).

74
Reservation agreements and deposits

Entering into contracts for the purchase of an off-plan property is generally a two-stage process. The signing of a reservation agreement or "preliminary contract" is generally the first step, while signing a more comprehensive sale and purchase contract is generally the second step. Strictly speaking, there is no obligation to sign a reservation agreement before signing the sale and purchase contracts. Indeed, if you have doubts about signing a preliminary agreement that lacks sufficient detail, you can proceed directly to the final contracts *after* due diligence has been conducted, at the risk of losing the particular property should another buyer step forward during the due diligence process.

> **Important tip:** Many reservation agreements are just one or two page documents that are designed for simplicity in order to get customers "signed up" without scaring them with too much contractual detail. In such cases, it is necessary to add detail to them to better protect yourself.

To understand the *purpose* of a reservation agreement, it is helpful to look at things from the perspective of both the developer and purchaser. From a developer's perspective, buyers ask endless questions and often procrastinate for weeks or months deciding whether or not to commit to a purchase. The signing of a formal reservation agreement demonstrates the conclusion of the decision-making process and signals the buyer's intent to proceed. However, signing a piece of paper doesn't mean very much without also "putting your money where your mouth is"; thus reservation agreements generally come with a requirement to pay a deposit or "reservation fee" to demonstrate good faith and to secure the buyer's commitment. Reservation fees are usually required at the time of signing the reservation agreement, or within a specified number of days thereafter.

From the perspective of a purchaser, signing a reservation agreement and paying a reservation fee secures the chosen property and (in theory) prevents the developer from selling it to someone else. The terms and conditions of the reservation agreement should then provide the purchaser with sufficient time to conduct the necessary due diligence before signing the more comprehensive Sale and Purchase Agreement (SPA).

One of the key issues in relation to the payment of reservation deposits is whether they are refundable or non-refundable. Again, from the perspective of a developer, it is obviously preferable if payments are *non-refundable,* to prevent the purchaser from changing his mind, pulling out of the deal and wasting the developer's time. It also covers the legal fees involved in the drafting of the reservation agreement. In fact, developers prefer reservation fees to be non-refundable *under any circumstances* because when a deposit is refundable, it cannot really be considered a sale at all until the buyer has unequivocally parted with his money. In addition, sales managers working for the developer are typically paid commissions either upon the signing of the Sales and Purchase Agreement or upon receipt of the first significant (staged) payment. However, in the case where a purchaser decides not to proceed and they lose their (non-refundable) deposit, under some circumstances the sales person gets to keep a portion of it. Therefore, both company policy and salespersons incentives are often aligned in preference of non-refundable deposits.

Purchasers, on the other hand, prefer reservation payments to be completely refundable *without conditions,* which gives purchasers the best of both worlds: it reserves the property, and at the same time allows them to change their mind, for any reason whether or not there are adverse due diligence findings.

Due to the different perspectives of the developer and purchaser, what usually happens in practice is that deposits become refundable, subject to certain conditions. These conditions need to be carefully scrutinised and the onus is on the purchaser to negotiate the most favourable conditions. When contemplating the payment of a reservation deposit, the following 11 considerations are relevant:

1. Amount

The standard amount for a reservation deposit on resort properties generally ranges from 100,000 Baht to 300,000 Baht (US$ 3,300 – 10,000); alternatively, it is expressed as a percentage of the purchase price (for example 1% or 2% of the purchase price). As a purchaser, the strategy should be to *control* the property with the smallest possible refundable deposit.

2. Refundable or non-refundable

A purchaser's objective should be to make any reservation deposit paid to a developer "fully refundable, without conditions" or "refundable for any reason whatsoever". If this is not possible, at the very least purchasers should give themselves a way out of the purchase in the case of adverse due diligence findings that cannot be easily or satisfactorily resolved. A common method is to use words such as "the purchaser may terminate the Reservation Agreement based on due diligence findings".

3. Refundable "less costs"

Even when reservation deposits are refundable, some developers still attempt to retain some of your money to cover costs and inconvenience. These are formally referred to as "administrative charges", "office costs", "cancellation fees" or "processing fees". To avoid these charges, ensure the reservation agreement states that deposits are refundable *in full.*

4. Timing of refund

If you decide not to proceed with a purchase, it is sensible to state a time limit for the repayment of deposits; for instance, "the deposit will be returned to the purchaser within 7 days of such request".

5. Part of purchase price

The reservation agreement should clearly state that if you proceed with a purchase, the deposit will be applied as part of the purchase price. If it is not mentioned, the possibility exists for the reservation deposit to become an additional stealth payment (or commission for the salesperson), which has no relation to the purchase price of the property. The contract should then clarify *how* the deposit is to be applied, i.e. will it be deducted from the first payment, or from the last. From the purchaser's point of view, it is better for the amount of the reservation deposit to be deducted from the first payment in line with the objective of keeping payments smaller at the beginning and larger towards the end.

6. Deposit not to be used for construction

In some European countries, consumer protection legislation exists to prohibit developers of off-plan properties from using reservation fees for construction. The aim is to prevent reservation deposits from going into the "general financial melting pot" where the money is used by the developer for any purpose; in other words, the objective is to ensure funds are available for refunding deposits should purchasers decide not to proceed. In Thailand, with the general absence of consumer protection for property buyers (of unregulated developments), it is still worthwhile specifying that deposits should not be used for construction, although the practical effect is diminished when not supported by legislation (to better protect your deposit, it is preferable for deposits to be paid to a lawyer and held in escrow, see chapter 108).

7. Sufficient time for due diligence

Reservation agreements are entered into for three main purposes. First, to reserve a property while due diligence is carried out; second, for the details of the sale and purchase contract to be clarified and negotiated; and third, for the sale and purchase contracts to be prepared. It is therefore important that reservation agreements allow sufficient time for these things to be done. The lawyer conducting due diligence on your behalf should advise you how much time is needed, although generally 28 days is adequate for a standard transaction.

8. Subject to site visit

Purchasers signing reservation agreements for off-plan property usually fall into two categories: those who have visited the site, and those who haven't. The latter category generally comprises people who have signed up for a property at an international property exhibition or who have otherwise communicated with the developer without an opportunity to view the site. In such cases, developers are usually flexible in allowing purchasers time to travel to view the site before proceeding with due diligence. This should be reflected in the reservation agreement and any deposit should be paid "subject to satisfactory site visit".

9. "Free" flights

A common marketing tactic used by developers is to offer so-called free flights (or hotel accommodation) to encourage potential purchasers to visit the site of an off-plan development. These flights are not "free", for two main reasons. Firstly, the costs involved are normally allocated as marketing costs and have already been factored into the pricing structure for the development. However, if flights and hotels are offered only to the first three or five purchasers, you might as well take advantage of them since the associated costs have usually been amortised over the total number of units (rather than built into the price of your property). Secondly, "free" flights (or hotel accommodation) are often only free if you proceed with a purchase. In other words, the costs are either refunded to you after you have confirmed to proceed or, if paid initially by the developer and you decide *not* to proceed, they might be deducted from the reservation deposit prior to being refunded. Any conditions attached to such offers should be studied carefully and incorporated into the reservation agreement.

10. Assignment

If possible, a reservation agreement should provide you (as the purchaser) with the flexibility to assign the rights set out in the contract (and the deposit) in the event that (a) you decide to purchase the property through a different person, entity or company, or (b) you decide to transfer (sell) the rights and obligations to another person, entity or company. In addition, the contract should provide flexibility in the event you wish to transfer the reservation deposit to a different property within the same development.

11. Identification of the property

The reservation agreement should identify the specific property you are reserving by the full address of the development; its unit number corresponding to the master plan; the size of the property; together with the purchase price, title deed number and build permit number.

It should be noted that there is no standard reservation contract or format used by all off-plan developers in Thailand and terms and conditions differ from developer to developer. It is therefore essential to fully understand what you are agreeing to before you sign a reservation agreement or pay a reservation deposit.

> **Important tip:** It should be remembered that reservation agreements are contractual documents and, as with most contracts, you can add any terms or conditions that you want, *so long as it is consistent with Thai law and the other party agrees!* Therefore, if you are paying a reservation deposit, make sure it is being paid on based on terms you are comfortable with.

75
Negotiating with developers
(Essential)

Whenever a company offers something for sale, especially something of high value, there is generally a willingness to be flexible (on certain issues) in order to secure a deal. The extent to which issues can be negotiated with a developer depends largely on three things: the nature of the developer, the stage of completion of the project and market conditions.

For instance, large, publicly listed property developers often set prices and stick to them. In contrast, small, privately owned developers are usually willing to compromise on virtually any issue in order to make a sale. For a financially strong property developer, the odd deal might not be important in the grand scheme, while for a small developer the next sale could effectively make or break a project.

With regard to the stage of completion of a project, developers tend to be more flexible when a project is first launched to sell the first few units and get the ball rolling; indeed, special incentives are often used to encourage initial purchasers. Alternatively, a developer might be flexible towards the end of a project when the remaining units tend not to have the best view or location. Sometimes developers seek to unload the remaining units so that a "Sold Out" sign can be turned into a public relations event or press release.

Market conditions obviously influence a developer's willingness to negotiate; while poor market conditions and periods of slow sales have a tendency to encourage promotions, special payment terms and price reductions, a hot property market or a successful project launch often leads to reduced flexibility and increasing prices.

When approaching negotiations for the purchase of an off-plan property, purchasers should bear in mind that published prices, terms and conditions are not always set in stone, despite initial appearances. Many issues are open to negotiation if approached in the right manner, under the right circumstances.

This chapter discusses some of the potential topics for negotiation with off-plan developers and should be used as a checklist for negotiations. However, before approaching negotiations with a developer, since negotiations take place against the backdrop of changing market conditions and a project's stage of completion, it is important to do your homework. The more information you have to start with, the better you will be able to assess your position in potential negotiations. Therefore, at a minimum, it is helpful to find out the following information:

- How many units (or what percentage of units) have already been sold?
- When was the project launched (and therefore how long has the development been selling)?
- What is the *feel* of the sales office? Is it a hive of activity or is it empty except for one bored salesperson reading a newspaper in the corner?
- Are the developer's sales targets and expectations being met?
- Ask local lawyers if the project is selling well?
- Ask property agents if the developer is generally flexible on terms?

With regards to the *approach* to negotiations, instead of asking a developer what they are able to offer, it is often more effective to "suggest" in plain terms what it is that you want. In this way, the salesperson has an objective to meet, rather than having to conjure up an offer that may or may not meet your expectations.[157] Whenever possible, use the "if … then…" negotiation technique. For example, "*if* you can give me a certain discount, *then* I will pay a deposit today". Instead of the one-way street of asking for a concession, this gives the salesperson something in return; something they can go back to their boss with.

Some investors believe you should either negotiate price or terms, not both. For example, they believe the best way to get what they want is use the formula, "*if* you agree to upgrade the kitchen work surfaces to granite and adjust the payment schedule, *then* I will pay the full purchase price". However, if price is considered as just another term of the contract, it is perfectly feasible to put together a "packaged" offer that expects flexibility on price and other issues. If you are flexible and your interest is sincere, such an approach will often be reciprocated. The key is to recognize the inherent flexibility in a sales situation and not to be easily cajoled into signing standard contracts or lazily accepting what is initially presented.

Finally, before commencing a discussion of specific topics for negotiation, mention should be made of "entire agreement" clauses, which are commonly found in sales contracts (either under their own heading or in the "miscellaneous provisions" section). Entire agreement clauses state that a contract contains all the details agreed by the parties and therefore *any other verbal statements or previous understandings do not form part of the contractual agreement.* In other words, if something has been negotiated and agreed but is not mentioned in the contract, technically it is not part of the agreement. Thus, it is imperative to

---

[157] Once approach is to ask first about which issues the developer is able to be flexible on and to frame your offer accordingly.

check the sales contract to make sure everything that is subject to negotiation is clearly detailed in the contract.

The potential topics for negotiation with off-plan developers discussed in this chapter are as follows:

1. Price
2. Furniture packages
3. Upgrades
4. Payment terms
5. Rental guarantees
6. Own use of property
7. Customisation or extras
8. Penalty clauses
9. Developer finance

1. Price

To successfully negotiate with developers, it should be understood that the issue of pricing from a developer's perspective is usually an issue of maintaining *consistency*. For instance, if a developer separately negotiates the purchase price with each customer, customers will be angry if they discover a neighbouring owner bought their property at a lower price. Therefore, by engaging in direct negotiations on purchase price, a developer opens himself to potential conflict and jeopardises his reputation for fairness and professionalism; haggling over price with each customer is more reminiscent of a Middle Eastern bazaar. Lack of price consistency also tends to encourage further negotiations.

Thus, in order to successfully negotiate on price, it is necessary to give the developer a legitimate reason (or *rational excuse*), which can be used in good faith to justify a price difference. One valid method is the purchase of more than one property (referred to by investors as the purchase of *multiple units*). Developers are habitually open to price negotiations if they can sell more than one unit at a time. While this strategy is generally not viable for most property purchasers, if you know a friend or relative who is also looking to buy property it is often possible to negotiate a discount together.

Another way to provide a developer with a legitimate reason for discounting the price is to modify the payment terms in a way that is beneficial to the developer. For instance, "if you discount the price by 5%, then I will increase the first payment from 15% to 45%"[158]. At the early stages of a project, smaller, less well-funded developers that are keen to kick-start a project will obviously be more receptive to this approach than larger, well-funded companies; a busy construction site tends to encourage sales more than a vacant field.

If you are not an investor seeking to purchase multiple properties and you are unwilling to pay more of the purchase price in advance, it might still be possible to negotiate the purchase price with a developer if the market is flat, sales are slow or if you are among the first or last buyers. This is where an understanding of market conditions and research on the developer are invaluable. It might also be possible to compare the attributes of properties within the same development and to make a lower offer for a property with less spectacular views or that is further away from amenities (or closer to busy or noisy communal areas)[159].

Saving the developer money is another option; if a lower price is offered in combination with a reduction in property size or specifications, it gives the developer a valid justification for discounting the purchase price, sometimes disproportionately to the changes. A developer's objective is to make profit. If the purchase price is above the combined cost of land and construction costs, a developer makes a profit (notwithstanding marketing costs and overheads). It is the amount of profit that is usually being negotiated; and a developer might be more willing to accept a sale with a small profit margin if design or cost modifications allow a price reduction to be justified.

Another method is to perform market research and present the findings in such a way that it can reasonably and logically justify the developer's acceptance of a lower price. For instance, after researching *comparable* developments you might identify that other developments are asking 80,000 Baht (US$ 2,650) per square metre, while the project of interest is priced above 100,000 Baht (US$ 3,300) per square metre for no reason that you are able to discern. If a competitor is carrying out a special promotion or offering a special discount on another project, this might be another basis for negotiating a discount. A developer will often attempt to justify the higher price by drawing your attention to different features, material specifications or a superior location; however, approaching a price negotiation backed by sound research and actual price comparables is hard to refute (if it doesn't result in a price reduction, it might be used to upgrade material specifications).

---

[158] Although note the comment in chapter 73 that it is not recommended to pay the purchase price in full in order to achieve a small discount. To reduce off-plan risk, it is better to weight payments so they are smaller at the beginning and larger towards the end of construction.

[159] This is assuming that current prices do not fairly or accurately take into account each unit's individual attributes and location.

However, as already noted, due to the developer's desire to maintain price consistency and reluctance to engage in direct price negotiations, it is often better to obtain "discounts" surreptitiously or indirectly via other means, such as free furniture packages, upgrades, higher rental returns, or by having the developer cover travel or accommodation related costs.

2. Furniture packages

Furniture packages are an obvious topic for negotiations with a developer. In fact, property developers often put together furniture packages for the specific purpose of using them as marketing tools (or concessions for use in negotiations).

Furniture packages are often used by developers in combination with a time limit; for instance, "free furniture packages for purchasers paying reservation deposits before the end of the month". Alternatively, furniture packages are used to facilitate initial sales, for example, "the first five buyers receive free furniture packages". However, such sales tools can easily be hijacked and used with equal effectiveness by purchasers. For example, "we will pay a deposit today *if* you include a free furniture package" or perhaps more effective, "we have narrowed our choice to two developments; if you include a furniture package, we will choose this development and pay a deposit today".

Bear in mind that there are often different furniture packages with various material specifications at different price levels. This lends itself to the negotiation of specific items within a furniture package, such as outdoor furniture for the pool deck or sala, kitchen equipment and appliances, fitted wardrobes or a rent-ready furniture package that includes towels, linen and cutlery.

3. Upgrades

Developers are usually open to negotiation on material specifications, for two reasons: first, it has an *invisible* impact, i.e. the purchase price is not visually affected, which maintains pricing consistency; secondly, since the developer is the "builder" and is able to perform the work at cost, the cost of changing specifications to the developer is less than the perceived value to the purchaser.

In addition, the scope for negotiating upgrades is virtually limitless: laminate kitchen work surfaces can be upgraded to granite; fans can be changed to air-conditioning; bathroom fittings can be upgraded from Chinese imports to local brands such as Cotto or European imported brands such as Gröhe; lightweight aluminium windows and doors can be upgraded to high-quality powder-coated windows and doors with double-glazed, Argon gas-filled, UV filtering glass!

4. Payment terms

Payment terms (discussed separately in chapter 73) offer good potential for negotiation. Modifying payment terms is also a method that can be used to reduce off-plan risk. For instance, a published payment schedule of five equal payments could be negotiated to an initial deposit of 30% and the remaining 70% due upon completion. The developer receives the same amount of money for the property; only it is received on a different schedule with the developer having to fund a chunk of construction, while the purchaser significantly reduces his exposure to off-plan risk.

5. Rental guarantees

Developers try to make their properties more appealing as an investment by offering guaranteed rental returns for certain periods of time after completion (see next chapter). Terms and conditions related to rental returns are often negotiable, particularly if the source of rental revenue has already been secured. It also has no visible effect on the advertised price of the property. For example, a developer might offer a guaranteed rental return of 6% for the two years immediately following completion. To secure a deal, the developer might be willing to extend the guarantee to three or four years. In addition, it is often possible to negotiate the manner in which the rental return is received; for instance, annual or bi-annual payments could become monthly or quarterly payments.

> **Important tip:** The *ultimate* negotiation objective in relation to rental guarantees is to receive the full rental income in advance in the form of a discount off the purchase price. If a developer proudly and confidently asserts his ability to achieve a certain rental yield, this is in essence calling the developer's bluff (and would only affect the developer's cash flow!).

6. Own use of property

If you agree to your property entering a "rental programme", as the property owner you are generally permitted to use the property for a certain number of days each year. The annual number of days use is often negotiable, together with the restrictions on dates or the procedures that owners must follow to book the use of their own property (sometimes a certain number of days advance notice needs to be given). It might also be possible to negotiate the use of another property if your property is occupied when you want to use it.

7. Customisation or extras

Property purchasers might wish to change or modify certain aspects of a property, such as those mentioned in chapter 72 on customisation. This might include changing the layout or proportions of rooms; adding extra rooms; changing material specifications; or negotiating extras, such as mosquito screens on doors and windows. If changes are discussed and agreed before the sales contract is signed, any additional costs can also be negotiated at the same time as the purchase price. If a developer is keen to secure a sale, it is often the case that (some of) the desired modifications can be included without charge.

8. Penalty clauses

Contracts for off-plan properties should contain a clause covering late completion penalties (just as there are penalties for late payment). This is another issue that lends itself to negotiation. In some cases, if the property is completed late, the penalty payments effectively become a price discount.

If you are planning to rent out the property upon completion, late completion usually translates into loss of rental income. Alternatively, if you plan to move into the property or spend a vacation at the property upon completion, there are alternative accommodation costs or cancellation fees to consider. These might also be discussed and any relevant terms incorporated into the contract.

9. Developer finance

Mortgage financing is generally not available to foreigners buying property in Thailand (see chapter 107). However, some developers offer "developer finance", which effectively means that the developer accepts payment of a proportion of the purchase price by instalment after completion of the property, usually over several years. If developer finance is being offered, the relevant terms and conditions are a valid topic for negotiation.

Summary

- The extent to which issues can be negotiated with a developer depends largely on three things: the nature of the developer, the stage of completion of the project, and market conditions.
- Before approaching negotiations with a developer it is important to do your homework. The more information you have to start with, the better you will be able to assess your position in potential negotiations.
- Potential topics for negotiation with developers include:
  - Price
  - Furniture packages
  - Upgrades
  - Payment terms
  - Rental guarantees
  - Own use of property
  - Customisation or extras
  - Penalty clauses
  - Developer finance

76
Guaranteed rental returns

Off-plan property developers offer guaranteed rental yields for three main reasons:

- First, offering a guaranteed rental return makes a property appear to stack up better as an *investment* (rather than just a property purchase).
- Second, it removes the anxiety investors might have about renting out a newly completed property, which is unfamiliar to the market and has no rental history[160].
- Third, if the developer can take over the management of property rentals, the properties become an ongoing source of revenue for the developer after a project is finished.

If a developer is offering a guaranteed rental return, it is safe to assume that upon completion the property must in some manner be passed back to the developer (or an affiliate company) for rental management. The method of "passing back" is typically through a contractual rental programme, which involves either a rental management agreement or some form of leaseback agreement. These agreements define the terms and conditions with regard to the use of your property.

The purpose of this chapter is to take a look at the issues purchasers need to consider in relation to the rental programmes offered by off-plan developers. It is important to see through the sales hype surrounding "guaranteed returns" and to carefully check the details. Only when you are familiar with the small print is it possible to make an informed decision as to whether a rental programme is suitable for you.

1. Who is behind the rental guarantee?

The key question with regard to any guaranteed yield is, *how is the developer able to guarantee the yield?* On what basis are they able to make these promises? Does the developer have experience in generating revenue for completed developments, or are you dealing with a first-time developer that has little or no

---

[160] It generally takes at least a year to establish a new rental property or to build a client base of returning customers.

idea how to implement a rental management programme? Is the guaranteed return backed by a bank guarantee?

Fulfilling the promise of a rental guarantee is a professional business that requires professional management; in other words, it is a business that requires a completely different set of marketing and management skills to those required for the business of property development. An insurmountable difference therefore exists between a rental guarantee offered by an international five star hotel group and a guarantee offered by an inexperienced developer. International five star hotel groups have the global network and expertise to support a rental guarantee; first-time developers don't, although they offer it anyway because it helps to sell properties![161]

With regard to the source of the rental income, it is important to confirm with the developer whether an agreement has already been signed with a hotel group or an international tour operator to generate rental income for the development; or is the developer planning to set up its own rental management and marketing company to attract rental guests? In other words, is a future rental income stream already in place or must it be created? If the developer must start marketing the development from scratch, do they have the in-house expertise and resources bearing in mind the specialist nature of the task?

When comparing off-plan developments, it is sometimes more prudent to accept a 5% yield offered by a developer with an established source of future rental income (or one that is in partnership with an international hotel group), than a 7% yield with a developer that is new to the rental business or that must create rental revenue from scratch.

> **Important tip:** Do not buy off-plan property purely based on the promise of a rental guarantee, particularly from a first-time developer. Thoroughly research the entity that is supporting the rental guarantee and whether it has the expertise to deliver the promised yield.

2. Which company will manage the development upon completion?

Is the developer planning to set up its own property management company to manage and operate the developer upon completion or has an experienced five star property management company been contracted? It is all well and good generating rental bookings and achieving high occupancy rates but it will be a

---

[161] Professional developers sometimes do not offer a rental guarantee to sell properties because they don't need to.

disaster if the development is not properly managed. The property management company should ideally have a track record of professional, five-star property management.

3. Is the developer offering a *guaranteed* rental return or a *projected* rental return?

Projected rental yields are just estimates, often exaggerated estimates that the developer is not obligated to pay you. *Guaranteed* rental yields, on the other hand, are usually contractual promises, whereby the stated amounts should be paid to you according to the terms agreed. The key point to consider in relation to guaranteed returns is whether the "guarantee" is *legally* valid. In other words, it is necessary to ask your lawyer to check the form and wording of the guarantee to ensure they are sufficient to create a legally binding contractual obligation.

4. What yield is being offered and for what time period?

Rental yields differ from developer to developer, depending on the source of rental income and their marketing expertise (or desperation to sell properties!). For instance, some developers might offer a 6% guaranteed annual yield for the first 2 years after completion, while others might offer 5% or 8.88% for 3 years. It is necessary to evaluate how the rental yield and duration compare with average market yields and offers from other off-plan developers?[162]

It is also necessary to look at the assumptions behind the figures. For example, if the purchase price is 10 million Baht (US$ 330,000) with a rental guarantee of 6%, the gross annual return is 600,000 Baht (US$ 20,000). If (after performing market research on comparable properties), the daily rental rate is estimated at 4,500 Baht (US$ 150), taking into account high and low seasons, the property would need to be rented out for 133 days to generate this return[163]. Is this *realistic?*

Taking a close look at the figures is a worthwhile exercise for two reasons: first, to evaluate whether the purchase price is realistic based on anticipated rental income, and second, to decide whether you might be better off renting out the property yourself, rather than entering the property into a rental programme with a fixed yield. In addition, if the period of the rental guarantee is two years, with an option to extend for a longer period, it might help you to decide whether or not an extension makes sense.

---

[162] Although, as discussed in points 1 and 2, the source of rental income (and the professionalism of the rental management team) should be considered a higher priority than the actual sums guaranteed. Sometimes lower yields are more realistic, and sometimes higher yields are an overly optimistic marketing ploy.

[163] Refer to chapter 10 for the calculation of rental yields.

5. Is the rental yield based on the full purchase price of the property?

If the rental yield is 6% and you are paying 10 million Baht (US$ 330,000) for the property, the gross annual yield is 600,000 Baht (US$ 20,000). If you are purchasing a fully furnished property or buying a furniture package, it is necessary to ascertain whether the rental yield is based on the full value of the investment (property + furniture) or the value of the furnished property *less* furnishing costs[164].

6. Is the rental programme compulsory?

Is entering the property into a rental programme conditional upon purchasing the property or is it possible to opt out? If you agree to enter the rental programme, is it possible to change your mind and withdraw later? Is it possible to opt out at the beginning and enter the rental programme at a later date?

If entering the rental programme is not a compulsory element accompanying the purchase of an off-plan property, can you do significantly better on your own? Can you achieve a higher yield through better marketing, higher rental rates or higher occupancy levels than the developer is able to guarantee via the rental programme? Would you prefer to take responsibility for the rental of your own property or take a hands-off approach by leaving the details to the developer?

7. Is the rental return *genuine* or has it just been built into the price?

If a developer does not have a legitimate source of rental income in place upon completion, it sometimes means the so-called "guaranteed rental return" has already been built into the price (a rental *gimmick* instead of a rental guarantee!). By extension, it also means that you are overpaying for the property; if a developer has no idea how to operate a rental programme or generate consistent rental revenue, the simplest solution is to calculate the cost of the rental guarantee and increase the purchase price to fund it![165] To guard against such practices, it is necessary to determine who is behind the rental guarantee (see point 1 above) and to perform market research in order to establish comparable market prices (see chapter 35).

---

[164] In such cases, it is important to make sure furniture costs are not overstated.

[165] Even this doesn't mean you are guaranteed to receive the promised return; the developer, having received enough money in the purchase price to cover a rental guarantee, might have spent it by the time rental returns need to be paid back to owners.

8. Is the guaranteed rental yield quoted on a gross or net basis?

Developers might advertise a guaranteed return of 7% but how much do you actually get to keep after the rental management company has taken out its fees? If the rental yield is given on a *net* basis, this is what you should receive[166]. If the guaranteed rental yield is stated on the basis of *gross* income, it is necessary to work out precisely how much will be taken out and how much you will be left with (see also chapter 115).

9. How is the rental guarantee paid?

Does the developer (or management company) make a monthly, quarterly or annual payment? Must it be paid into a bank account in Thailand or can it be paid to an offshore account? If different currencies are involved, what mechanism is used for establishing the exchange rate?

10. Can the guaranteed rental return be received in advance?

If the rental return is *guaranteed,* and if the developer is confident in his ability to achieve the particular rental yield, ask if it is possible to receive the full rental amount in advance *in the form of a discount off the purchase price?* For example, if the purchase price is 10 million Baht (US$ 330,000) and the guaranteed rental return is 6% for 2 years, gross rental income over 2 years is 1.2 million Baht (US$ 40,000):

$$10,000,000 \times 6\% \times 2 = 1,200,000$$

On the basis of the guaranteed rental income, a discount of 1.2 million Baht (US$ 40,000) could be requested off the purchase price, which, if accepted, would mean paying 8.8 million Baht (US$ 290,000) for the property instead of 10 million Baht (US$ 330,000); however, *the property still enters the rental programme for 2 years with the developer keeping the rental income.* The principal benefit is therefore risk mitigation in relation to the rental income. As mentioned in the previous chapter, this is the ultimate negotiation strategy in relation to the payment of a rental guarantee.

---

[166] There may be tax implications depending on your individual circumstances and professional tax advice should be sought. Most developers, especially inexperienced or first-time developers, have no idea about taxes on rental income.

11. Furniture packages

If your property enters the rental pool, does a furniture or interior design package from the developer become a compulsory requirement? If the developer is operating a rental programme, it is important that the resort is consistent in relation to furnishings and décor; if each owner were allowed complete freedom to furnish their own property, the resort would lack consistency and would be furnished with an array of different designs and colours. In addition, furniture purchased by individual owners might not be suitable for the purpose of rental in terms of durability or taste; indeed, when owners furnish with a rental programme in mind, it is common for the cheapest furniture to be purchased. For these reasons, buying a full "rent-ready" furniture or interior design package is often compulsory when a property enters a rental programme. In such cases, make sure you are getting value for money and the developer is not using this as an opportunity to overcharge.

12. Own use of property

If your property enters a rental programme, what are the terms and conditions relating to your own use of the property? For example, terms generally apply to (a) the number of days you are able to use the property each year, (b) the procedures and the advance notice required to book the use of your own property, (c) restrictions on dates or seasons, for example, Christmas, New Year and Chinese New Year are often restricted, (d) the cost for additional days use of the property, (e) whether another property can be used in case your property is occupied when you want to use it, and (f) the rules and regulations related to the use of common areas and facilities (see chapter 79), and whether additional fees are payable.

13. Insurance

It is important to check which party is responsible for the cost of insuring the property and its contents for the duration of the rental programme? In addition, public liability and indemnity insurance are required if the property is occupied by rental guests.

Summary

Many off-plan property developers offer guaranteed rental returns; however, it is important to see through the sales hype and to carefully check the details in relation to the following:

- Who is behind the rental guarantee?
- Which company will manage the development upon completion?
- Is the developer offering a *guaranteed* rental return or a *projected* rental return?
- What yield is being offered and for what time period?
- Is the rental yield based on the full purchase price of the property including furniture?
- Is the rental programme compulsory?
- Is the rental return genuine or have the returns simply been built into the price?
- Is the guaranteed rental yield quoted on a gross or net basis?
- How is the rental guarantee paid?
- Can the guaranteed rental return be received in advance in the form of a discount off the purchase price?
- Are furniture packages a compulsory requirement?
- What are the terms and conditions relating to your own use of the property?
- Who is responsible for the cost of insurance for the duration of the rental programme?

77
Management and maintenance

Off-plan property developers generally build a number of properties that share common areas or facilities. After a project is complete, these common areas and facilities need to be managed and maintained on an ongoing basis and this is generally arranged by a company associated with, or separately engaged by, the developer.

The costs involved are typically charged to property owners through "management and maintenance fees" and the associated terms and conditions are contained in Management and Maintenance Agreements, which are contractual documents integral to the purchase of a property[167]. Management and maintenance of the common areas should not be confused with rental management (which is the management of your property for rental guests, see chapter 115).

When referring to common areas or facilities, this might refer to any of the following:

- Access roads and paths within the development
- Car parking areas
- Swimming pools and pool terraces located within common areas
- Gardens and landscaping
- Drainage systems
- Lifts
- Reception areas and facilities such as gyms, tennis courts, club houses, restaurant areas, pool bars, playground areas, saunas and gyms
- Security infrastructure such as CCTV systems and security safes
- Infrastructure and supply of utilities, including water storage facilities, electricity pylons, transformers, generators and cables, telephone, Internet, satellite and cable TV equipment

If you are buying an off-plan property where entering a management and maintenance agreement is a mandatory part of the purchase, the associated fees, terms and conditions generally last for the entire duration of ownership. In

---

[167] Integral in this sense means the amount of management and maintenance fees payable, together with the associated terms and conditions, bears on the desirability of ownership and on the property as a potential investment.

other words, they are not something you can opt out of later if they don't suit you. The general issue concerning management and maintenance is straightforward: it is a matter of finding out the costs and precisely what you are getting in return for your money.

This chapter covers the key issues to consider in relation to common area management and is divided into three sections. The first section addresses the issue of costs, while the second section discusses services. There are several other issues that appear to be details, yet they are nonetheless significant and these are discussed in the third section: "other key issues".

> **Important tip:** Condominium owners benefit from specific legislation governing the management of condominium buildings, and the Condominium Juristic Person is the legal entity established to own, manage and maintain the common property. For non-regulated developments, the relevant provisions can vary considerably and for this reason, the fine print needs to be checked carefully.

1. Fees

With regard to the issue of management and maintenance fees, it is not only necessary to check the level of fees but also the *basis* upon which they are charged. Some developers charge a set fee each month, while others charge based on the floor area of your property on a per-square-metre basis. In addition, rates usually differ according to the type of property; for instance, within a development there is typically one per-square-metre rate for villas and another for apartments. For instance, owners of one apartment complex in Koh Samui are charged 35 Baht (US$ 1.15) per built up square metre per month, while a newly completed condominium project nearby charges 95 Baht (US$ 3.15) per square metre per month for condominiums and 50 Baht (US$ 1.65) per square metre for villas. Naturally, such rates must be considered in the context of the size and complexity of the development, together with the quality and scope of services provided.

To provide examples of total monthly costs, the owner of an apartment with a floor area of 180 square metres when paying management and maintenance fees at the rate of 35 Baht per square metre must pay 180 x 35 = 6,300 Baht (US$ 210) per month, while the owner of a similar sized condominium unit in the development referred to above pays 180 x 95 = 17,100 Baht (US$ 570) per month. If the owner of a 300 square metre villa is charged according to the example above at 50 Baht per square metre, the monthly fee would be 300 x 50 = 15,000 Baht (US$ 500). Per square metre rates for villas tend to be lower because floor areas are larger.

However, there is more to management and maintenance fees than per-square-metre rates. Perhaps equally important is the basis on which floor areas are calculated and it is at this point where the distinction between private areas and common areas becomes significant. For instance, is the size of the property, for the purpose of management and maintenance fees, based on "net floor area", which is the *real* size of your private apartment (excluding common areas) or is it based on "ground floor area", where a proportion of common areas can be included, such as lift areas, landings, balconies and terraces. If a proportion of the common areas are included in the calculation for the "chargeable" size of a property, it swells monthly management and maintenance fees (and revenue for the management company).

For instance, if the net floor area of your apartment is 150 square metres and fees are 50 Baht (US$ 1.65) per square metre, the monthly fee is 7,500 Baht (US$ 250). If an extra 25 metres of technically "common areas" are included, monthly fees become 8,750 Baht (US$ 290). The difference might not appear significant on a monthly basis, although it becomes substantial over several years. In the case of a rental property, such fees reduce profit margins; if you are not renting out a property and the property is a place of residence, these monthly fees can become a financial burden. For this reason, the precise basis for calculating management and maintenance fees needs to be scrutinised to ensure you are not paying more than necessary. Generally speaking, the chargeable area of a property should be the floor area of which you have exclusive and private use.

Roof areas are another issue. I recall the case of an owner of a 175 square metre penthouse apartment who was charged management and maintenance fees on double this area because he had access rights to a footprint of the roof equal in size to the floor area of the apartment. Instead of paying 7,000 Baht (US$ 230) per month, he was being invoiced in excess of 13,000 Baht (US$ 430) each month.

Sometimes, the method of calculation can be used to your advantage. Occasionally there are common areas of the development adjoining your property that could potentially be re-defined as private areas for your exclusive use. Naturally, this increases the calculable area for management and maintenance fees (and potentially the purchase price). However, you end up with a larger private area, while the management company gains by receiving additional fees.

The next important consideration is whether management and maintenance fees are "fixed" according to a square metre calculation, or whether they are based on the *actual* costs incurred by the management company. In the latter case, the management company adds up the total costs and expenses incurred and, in the event of a shortfall, property owners receive a bill for the difference[168]. I am familiar with this practice at some developments and in such cases purchasers must read the small print and be fully aware of the implications. It is also necessary to check for the existence of a "management charge" for the management company itself (for instance, 20% of the management fees are sometimes taken by the management company before they are applied to actual management and maintenance expenses). In addition, it is necessary to note any provision for "salaries", together with any omissions; any issue that is not properly detailed in the management contract has the potential to be abused, which results in higher costs for each owner.

Property purchasers must exercise caution, especially with smaller, unregulated, private property developers. When you have no control over the budget or expenses of a management company, and no control over the transparency or auditing of the accounts, then you also have no control over management and maintenance fees. In cases where the management company charges a fixed fee, it is necessary to evaluate the scope and level of services provided. However, when management fees are based on *actual* expenses, owners should be able to exercise some degree of collective control or decision making over the budget and expenses, and the management company should be under the obligation of full disclosure. After all, common areas are maintained for the benefit of the owners, not the management company. A few management companies tend to overlook this concept and view it instead as a personal profit centre.

A developer's ability to increase management and maintenance fees is another consideration. It is necessary to check the contracts to ensure there are restrictions on a management company's ability to increase fees. If the contracts fail to address the issue, technically the developer can increase fees without restraint; indeed, if management and maintenance fees constitute a source of revenue for the developer, or if the developer is unable to keep costs within reasonable budgetary constraints, property owners could find themselves open to substantial and unreasonable fee increases.

For example, some agreements contain wording such as *"management and maintenance fees can be increased according to the annual rate of inflation (CPI) published by the Bank of Thailand and not exceeding 5% per annum"*, while others mention that *"management and maintenance fees can be increased in accordance with the consumer price index and market conditions"*. The latter gives a developer carte blanche to increase fees.

---

[168] There are cases where inexperienced developers have significantly underestimated the management costs for a project and fees have almost doubled in the first year after completion to cover the expenses.

The next thing to check is when fees are payable. Management and maintenance fees are typically paid in advance, although some developers invoice on a monthly basis, while others request payment on a quarterly or annual basis. One high profile developer in Pattaya expects purchasers to pay 2 years of management and maintenance fees in advance upon purchase.

It is also necessary to confirm the start date for management fees. *Conceptually,* fees should commence when a project is complete and ready for owners to move in; in other words, at the transition point when a project moves from the construction stage to the stage where the completed development needs to be managed and maintained. In practice, however, most contracts are vague on the precise point that fees commence. For instance, do management fees start from the date that keys are collected; upon acceptance of practical completion; on registration of the lease or transfer of the legal property ownership; or upon delivery of vacant possession together with a certificate signed by an architect certifying completion? Or do management fees start from the date that all communal areas and facilities become fully operational, i.e. when gyms are properly equipped and swimming pools are full of (clean) water?

Property purchasers should recognise that, on one hand, it is in the developer's interests to start receiving management fees as early as possible so that the management costs can be covered by owners; while, on the other hand, it is in the interests of owners to start paying management fees only when the development is fully operational. Until all common areas and facilities are functional, while it might be possible to move into your property, it cannot be fully enjoyed or rented out. Some developers attempt to shortcut the procedure by issuing management and maintenance invoices and expecting fees to be paid once keys have been collected, even when the common areas are unfinished. Thus, to avoid being charged fees prematurely, it is wise to add the following wording to the sale and purchase contract: "management and maintenance fees commence from the date of delivery of vacant possession, *provided all common areas and facilities are fully operational".*

2. Services

In combination with management and maintenance fees, off-plan property purchasers also need to understand the scope and level of services being provided for their money. Depending on the development, management and maintenance fees might cover any of the following:

- Costs related to the repair and upkeep of roads, paths, car parking areas and drainage systems
- Maintenance and painting of building and property exteriors

- Cleaning and maintenance services for pools and water features, including pool chemicals and repairs to pump systems
- Cleaning services for all common areas and facilities
- Landscape gardening services
- Garbage disposal
- Waste water disposal
- Maintenance and repair of common area furniture
- Lift maintenance services
- Technical and engineering services
- Maintenance and repairs to the utilities infrastructure (water, electricity, telephone, Internet, satellite and cable TV)
- Payment of utility bills and services on behalf of owners
- Security services
- Pest control services
- Vehicle or transportation services (courtesy cars or cars used for transportation to the beach; and sometimes boats)
- Office and administrative salaries and expenses
- Insurance for the development

Important tip: The key issue is often not the services that are provided; rather, it is the services and costs that a developer fails to include. *Professional* developers generally account for all the services required for the management and upkeep of a development's common areas. However, *unprofessional* or *inexperienced* developers will cobble together a list of basic services and anything not expressly included is then billed separately and additionally to owners.

Management and maintenance agreements therefore need to be read carefully to ensure everything is covered and that there are no significant exclusions. The key is not to assume anything. I am familiar with instances where management and maintenance fees failed to include (and were therefore charged separately to owners on top of the monthly fee) security, swimming pool management, pool chemicals, accounting fees, and even tools for the gardener!

With regard to swimming pools, it is standard for the cleaning and maintenance of *common area* swimming pools to be included in management fees; however, it should be confirmed whether fees include the cleaning and maintenance of *private* pools, i.e. those within your privately owned space. In some developments, common pools are managed while private pools are left to the devices of owners, which means owners need to engage a pool cleaning company at their own expense.

In relation to security, an issue worth checking is the liability of the security company, especially for theft. It is commonplace for security companies to be engaged for the provision of security for developments and for both the security company and the management company to disclaim responsibility and liability in the event of loss or damage. In other words, many security companies take no responsibility for the services they provide. Perhaps that's why sleeping security guards are a common sight in Thailand!

With regard to insurance, it should be ascertained whether the management fees include adequate third party and public liability insurance for the development (this does not include home and contents insurance, which owners must arrange separately for their individual properties).

3. Other key issues

In addition to the issue of management fees and the scope of services provided, there are other key considerations that have a significant bearing on the attractiveness of a development:

Ownership and control of the management company

The first issue to note is which company will assume responsibility for the management and maintenance of the development upon completion and what degree of control, if any, are owners be able to exercise over the budgets and decisions of the management company?

In addition to selling leasehold or freehold property interests, some developers also transfer a share of the ownership of the management company to property owners, and sometimes owners are also able to appoint directors to the management company[169]. While this sounds like an additional layer of security for purchasers, the relevant issues are what percentage of ownership is transferred and what *level* of control (over the management company) is exercisable by the owners? In other words, if the percentage shareholding given to owners is negligible, the exercise is largely pointless. In addition, if the developer retains ownership of the shares until properties are sold, and if a certain percentage of the development must be sold in order for the owners to exercise any meaningful degree of collective control, then until such point where a sufficient number of properties have been sold owners remain unable to exercise any meaningful control.

---

[169] In the case of condominium buildings, the Condominium Juristic Person is the legal entity established to own, manage and maintain the common property and owners also have the option (if elected) to become *active* members of the juristic person committee, which oversees the work of the property manager.

Whatever the situation, off-plan purchasers should at least be aware of what they are actually getting before contracts are signed. Some developers give each owner shares in the management company only to give them the *sense* of ownership and control, although in relation to the total shareholding the number of shares is such that no effective control can be exercised at all. In a limited number of cases, developers do in fact give a controlling interest in the management company to the owners in accordance with their desire to pass full ownership and responsibility for the management company to the owners upon completion.

Do procedures exist for the removal of the management company?

A related issue is whether property owners are tied into using the services of the developer's appointed management company or whether they possess the collective authority to change the management company.

It is true that some property management companies provide an exceptional level of service: common areas are maintained to the luxury standards; landscaping is always immaculate; swimming pools are crystal clear; if anything needs to be repaired, it is done immediately; and whenever you have questions, it is possible to pick up the phone and get answers. Everything works like a well-oiled machine. However, other management companies are poorly organised, unprofessional, and the inferior standard of management is plainly visible: badly maintained common areas; unkempt gardens; murky swimming pools; dark common areas at night because light bulbs have not been replaced; facilities and equipment not working; and there is no-one to answer the phone if you have a question.

> **Important tip:** Badly maintained buildings and poorly managed common areas cause developments to prematurely show their age and can significantly depreciate the value of the properties. For this reason, contractual provisions that provide for the removal and replacement of a management company are *crucial.*

The problem is that most contracts do not contain provisions that are in the long-term best interests of the owners; few developers consider the possibility that they will fail to meet the required standard of property management expected by owners. More to the point, if the fees generated by the management company provide a revenue stream for the developer, the developer will certainly not want to make it easy for owners to remove the management company. In the event where there is no procedure for the owners to remove a poorly performing management company, the task is onerous. Owners must first get into contact with each other, and then organise themselves to take appropriate collective legal action[170]. Who will lead and organise such an endeavour? The developer has an advantage because it is notoriously difficult to get a quorum of owners that are usually scattered around the world to agree on anything!

If procedures for the removal of a management company do exist, their effectiveness depends upon the clarity of the procedures and the particular majority required for owners to take collective action. If you are unhappy with the procedures, due to the nature of off-plan sales it is improbable that you will be able to modify any contractual clauses related to control over the management company (at least in a way that would meaningfully and collectively bind the developer); as there are multiple properties, a strong likelihood exists that numerous contracts have already been signed and the requirement for consistency means a developer cannot negotiate issues separately with one purchaser and is understandably reluctant to make amendments to contracts that have already been signed. The contractual clauses relating to the ability of property owners to change a management company therefore become a factor influencing whether or not a particular development makes for a suitable investment.

Are owners liable for the management fees of unsold units?

Suppose a property development has a total of thirty apartments and, by the time the development has been completed, only five units have been sold. If management and maintenance fees are paid by the five owners according to the prescribed per-square-metre rate, it is unlikely to be enough to cover the actual cost of managing and maintaining the development. Therefore, who makes up the shortfall? In particular, does a provision in the contract allow the management company to increase the contributions of the five owners to make up for the shortfall?

In a buoyant property market, such a scenario is unlikely. However, in a flat market it is a distinct possibility (assuming the developer has enough funds to complete the project with the revenue from only five sales) and purchasers in unregulated developments need to be on their guard to ensure they are protected from such an eventuality. For condominium developments, this is an issue specifically addressed by the Condominium Act to protect property owners.

---

[170] While corporate law *and* legislation cover the co-owner governance of condominiums; issues related to unregulated developments are enforced only by private legal action under civil law.

Utility Bills

As mentioned in chapter 19, if the developer or a private company owns the utility infrastructure (water storage facilities, electricity pylons, transformers, generators, cables) it generally means water and electricity usage is invoiced with a profit margin, in some cases a large margin. For instance, owners can be invoiced at a unit rate that is 30%, 50% or 100% more than the government rate; while the government electricity rate might be 4 Baht per kW, developers regularly invoice owners at 6 or 8 Baht per kW. In the long-term, such rate differences make quite an impact to utility bills, especially for rental properties where electricity use is higher due to the (unrestricted) use of air-conditioning. In the management contract, therefore, be sure to check the unit rates for utilities.

Late payment of management fees

The consequences in relation to late payment of management and maintenance fees are an issue of considerable importance. The procedure stipulated by some developers requires a reminder to be issued after 30 days and a second reminder after 60 days before late payment surcharges are levied, or before access to common areas is restricted and utility services are suspended. However, other developers have no properly defined procedures (or fail to follow the ones they have) and act as a law unto themselves, for instance, levying 12% per month penalties on late payments and cutting off electricity and water supplies without notice, which causes havoc with rental guests. It is therefore important that the procedures and penalties related to late payment are checked by your lawyer.

Emergency Remedial Action

Management companies do not normally have access to your private property unless you have signed up to rental management services or your property has entered a rental programme. An exception is where emergency remedial action is required, for instance, where a plumbing leak inside your unit has the potential to cause damage to other properties or to common areas. It is therefore worthwhile noting the procedure covering such events. If the management company has to break into your property to deal with a problem, there may or may not be the requirement to inform you in advance and in all likelihood you will be liable for the costs, including the cost and replacement of doors! Owners should weigh the issue of privacy and security with the potential benefit (and risk) of leaving a key with the management company.

Summary: Management and maintenance checklist

Fees

- Are management and maintenance fees fixed or calculated on a square metre basis?
- Is the calculation based on net floor area or ground floor area, i.e. does it include a proportion of the common areas?
- Are fees fixed or based on *actual* expenses?
- Are there restrictions on the developer's ability to increase fees?
- When are fees payable (monthly, quarterly, annually) in advance?

Services

- Do management and maintenance fees cover all relevant services for the development?
- Are there any notable exclusions?

Other key issues

- Do owners receive a share of ownership in the management company?
- Are owners able to exercise any meaningful control over decision-making?
- Do the owners have the (collective) ability to remove and replace the management company?
- Are owners liable to make up any shortfall in management and maintenance costs due to unsold units?
- Does the developer supply water and electricity and, if so, how do the rates compare with local government rates?
- What are the penalties and consequences for late payment of management and maintenance fees?
- Do procedures exist in relation to entering private property due to emergency remedial action?

78
Sinking funds

When buying property in a development with common areas that need to be managed and maintained, the issue of a "sinking fund" usually arises.[171] A sinking fund is a sum of money that is set apart[172] by the developer (or management company) to meet the cost of major replacements or repair work to the development's common areas. As a development ages, parts need to be replaced and sometimes major renovation work needs to be undertaken, without which the development deteriorates. The sinking fund is therefore an important reserve of funds designed to maintain the standards of a development over the long-term (sinking funds should not be confused with management and maintenance fees, which are meant for the general management and maintenance of the common areas).

Each developer has a slightly different policy and approach to the sinking fund, particularly unregulated developers[173]. Some developers request a one-time payment from owners upon the transfer of the property and thereafter the sinking fund is topped up with a percentage of the monthly management and maintenance fees; while other developers start the sinking fund with their own money and then invoice owners each year to maintain the sinking fund at a pre-defined level. Then there are the developers that make no provision for a sinking fund and request payment from owners each time renovation work is to be undertaken. Finally, there is always a class of developer that don't even understand what a sinking fund is and wait for a major catastrophe to happen before they contact owners and request money to fix it!

Sinking fund payments can be substantial so it is important to know in advance what a developer's policy is, together with the sums that need to be budgeted. Sinking fund payments usually vary according to the size and type of property, for example, sinking fund fees for one apartment development in Koh Samui ranged between 100,000 - 200,000 Baht (US\$ 3,300 - 6,600) per owner depending on the unit size, while sinking fund fees at another development were 950 Baht (US\$ 31) per square metre for a condominium and 500 Baht (US\$ 16.50) per square metre for a villa. In the latter development, the sinking fund payment for a 140 square metre condominium would work out to 133,000 Baht (US\$ 4,430), and

---

[171] Sometimes referred to as a "Reserve" or "Special Fund".
[172] Preferably in a separate bank account or "sinking fund account".
[173] As opposed to developers regulated by the Condominium Act.

the payment for a 400 square metre villa would be 200,000 Baht (US$ 6,600).

It should be noted that once sinking fund payments have been made to the management company they are generally non-refundable and upon re-sale accrue to the new owner's account, together with the property. This means it might be necessary to recoup sinking fund payments upon resale from the new buyer (on a pro rata basis).

> **Important tip:** *In essence,* money paid into a sinking fund is held in trust by the management company on behalf of owners, to be used for the long-term upkeep of the development. As the management company is responsible for the upkeep of a development, and the owners are collectively responsible for sinking fund costs, it is important that owners exercise some level of control over decisions related to sinking fund expenditures.

In the absence of legislation covering the collection and use of money held in sinking funds, combined with a lack of transparency on behalf of most developers, sinking fund fees are a source of potential disagreement. Thus, it is essential for owners to become familiar with the rules and operation of the sinking fund. In some cases it might be necessary to form a resident's association to prevent misappropriation or to enforce transparency and accountability in relation to sinking fund expenditure. Owners need to take responsibility for ensuring funds are being used in the best interests of the development, rather than misallocated or misspent by the management company.

The goal of the management company should be the long-term maintenance of a development, which requires spending money on replacements, repairs or renovations *in order to prevent more expensive remedial work later.* It is in the owners' interests for there to be a sufficient amount set aside for future works, although the fact is that most sinking funds are undercapitalised, meaning that when funds are needed for significant repairs, owners have to be tapped again for additional contributions. If these are not forthcoming, developments quickly fall into a state of disrepair, which adversely affects rental potential and property values.

Owners should keep in mind that the long-term capital appreciation of their properties is related less to property type and architectural design, and more to a combination of location, build quality and, especially, the quality of the ongoing management and maintenance of the development within which the property is located.

If the sinking fund is to be maintained at a pre-determined level, and payments to the sinking fund are requested annually, the amount requested should be the result of a well thought out sinking fund plan that identifies the work to be undertaken and budgets for that work. This generally involves estimating the life of each asset, together with the timing and cost for replacement. For instance, are common area fixtures and fittings and the wooden pool deck scheduled for replacement after five years or ten years? Such studies need to be reviewed and regularly updated. Owners making contributions to the sinking fund should receive a full set of accounts detailing the budget allocations and expenses. However, there are few resort developers that take such a thorough approach to the planning of sinking fund expenditures.

This leads to the next issue: how is a major repair or replacement (funded through the sinking fund) to be distinguished from work covered by the monthly management and maintenance fees? Does the developer provide a detailed schedule? For instance, does re-painting of the common area fall within the remit of management and maintenance fees or does it fall within the type of work for which expenses are drawn from the sinking fund? Are any surplus monies from the management and maintenance fees transferred to the sinking fund? If questions arise in relation to the scope of work or the manner in which owners cover costs, are they decided at the sole discretion of the management company or subject to the majority approval of the owners? In addition, if substantial repair work is required, who ensures that the work is competitively and transparently quoted?

It is evident that there is a number of issues related to the sinking fund that off-plan property properties owners need to be aware of before committing to a purchase. If these issues are not properly understood, they have the potential to turn into sources of disagreement, or nasty surprises when unexpected payment requests are received in connection with the sinking fund.

Summary

- A sinking fund is a sum of money that is set apart by the developer (or management company) to meet the cost of major replacements or repair work to the development's common areas.
- It is therefore an important reserve of funds designed to maintain the standards of a development over the long-term.
- As the owners are collectively responsible for sinking fund costs, it is important that owners exercise some level of control over decisions related to sinking fund expenditures.

79
Rules and regulations

Whenever a property development has common areas and facilities, there are usually rules covering their use and enjoyment by owners, tenants and guests. While these rules place restrictions on you as an owner, don't forget they are also designed to protect your investment and enjoyment of the property by restricting the antisocial, hedonistic behaviour of others. Given the extreme differences in the behaviour standards of international visitors, a set of rules covering what is considered to be socially acceptable behaviour is a necessity!

Depending on the development (and facilities), rules and regulations generally cover the following:

- The use of access roads and car parks.
- The use of communal facilities such as swimming pools and fitness gyms, including the hours that they may be used.
- Prohibition on any construction or modifications to your property that are not in keeping with the style of the development (this might include the colour that you are able to paint the exterior of the property).
- Noise.
- Pets.
- Prohibition of hanging laundry on balconies or terraces.
- Dress code.
- Damage caused to common areas.
- Admission procedures for visitors.
- Health and safety issues.
- The disposal of rubbish.
- Storage of certain substances or products within the development.
- Prohibition on commercial use (i.e. residential use only).
- Liability of owners for their guests and tenants.

With regard to the rules and regulations that govern the use of common areas, there are three main issues to consider. First, as a potential off-plan purchaser it is necessary to check that the rules meet your personal requirements. For example, if apartment rules and regulations specifically prohibit pets and you can't go anywhere without your poodle or pet snake, the development might not be suitable. Similarly, if your penchant is for wild all-night parties and the rules specify no visitors after 10pm, you might need to look elsewhere (or for a stand-alone property).

Second, bearing in mind that rules and regulations are designed to create a pleasant, social environment, who is responsible for their enforcement? For example, imagine you are sleeping soundly after a long day on the beach when all of a sudden the neighbours return home drunk at 3am and start frolicking loudly in the pool. Shouting obscenities from the balcony might make you feel better but it is not the ideal solution. Who can you call? Is there an on-site management office? Does the management company operate a 24-hour hotline? Is a security company engaged for the development and, if so, are personnel authorised to enforce the rules and regulations? Checking these details prior to purchase is important because if rules are not clearly defined or consistently enforced it can not only ruin your holiday but also affect the rental potential of your property.

Third, does a procedure exist for modifying the rules? Once a development is operational, it might be necessary to modify the rules from time-to-time to better reflect the requirements of owners and guests. Is there a procedure for changing or adding new rules? Does it require the consent of a specific majority of the owners?

Summary

- Whenever a property development has common areas and facilities, there are usually rules covering their use and enjoyment by owners, tenants and guests.
- While these rules place restrictions on you as an owner, they are also designed to protect your investment and enjoyment of the property by restricting the antisocial behaviour of others.
- Check that the rules for a development meet your personal requirements?
- Who is responsible for the enforcement of rules and regulations?
- Does a procedure exist for modifying the rules to better reflect the requirements of owners and guests?

80
"Flipping"

When buying an off-plan property, as the property is not yet built, you are in effect buying the *rights* to a property. Once the price has been confirmed and contracts have been signed, this "right" to a property becomes an asset that can be bought and sold during construction, prior to the completion of the property.

For example, suppose a purchase price of 10 million Baht (US$ 330,000) has been agreed for an off-plan property, contracts have been signed, and the initial staged payment has been made. During construction the market price of the property increases and you are offered 12 million Baht (US$ 400,000) for the property. It is possible to "on-sell" the contract and make a 2 million Baht (US$ 66,500) profit[174] even though the property has yet to be finished. The new purchaser then takes over the remaining staged payments to the developer.

On-selling an off-plan property prior to its completion is generally referred to as "flipping". Flipping properties is a strategy commonly used by property investors in developed property markets. If a property investor is able to secure a property with a small deposit, with the balance of the purchase price due on completion (or in stages according to construction), the possibility exists to make significant profits in an upwardly moving market if the right to the property can be sold[175].

However, a property can only be flipped if it is permitted by the contract (or provided the contract does not *prevent* it). Therefore, if you intend to profit by flipping a property prior to completion (or if you wish to retain the option), it is important that the sale and purchase contract allows for the contract to be *assigned*[176]. An example assignment clause would be:

"The buyer shall have the right to assign the rights and obligations set forth in this agreement to another party, at any time".

This means the contract containing the rights and obligations in relation to the property can be sold to a third party *without requiring the permission or authority*

---

[174] In the case, for instance, where you have so far paid only 2 million Baht to the developer, you have effectively made 100% cash on cash return.

[175] If the investor is unable to "flip" the property prior to completion, he must have the financial resources available to meet the remaining payments or be willing to forfeit the deposit.

[176] It is generally a condition that the rights and obligations of Management and Maintenance Agreements, and agreements concerned with Rules and Regulations, must also be assigned.

of the developer, which is the ideal situation. However, due to the desire of some developers to control or profit from an assignment, developers' standard contracts sometimes state that an assignment requires the authorization or permission of the developer, and in some cases it will specify a cost in relation to an assignment[177]. Here is a typical example:

"The buyer may assign all of its rights and obligations hereunder to another party only with the prior written consent of the developer. The buyer shall pay the developer the administrative fee of 40,000 Baht for each assignment made".

In such cases, terms should be negotiated or, if possible, removed. If a developer insists on retaining consent to an assignment, at the very least the contract should state: *"consent shall not be unreasonably withheld".*

Finally, the tax consequences of selling the rights to a property prior to completion and prior to taking title should be checked. It would be wise to seek advice that is appropriate to the individual circumstances. In addition, it is especially important to compare the taxes payable upon sale before and after taking title, particularly if the property is nearing completion.

Summary

- Once the price has been confirmed and contracts have been signed, the "right" to a property becomes an asset that can be bought and sold during construction, prior to the completion of the property.
- On-selling an off-plan property prior to completion is generally referred to as "flipping", which is a strategy commonly used by property investors in developed property markets.
- Properties can only be flipped if it is permitted by the contract. If you intend to profit by flipping a property prior to completion, it is important that the sale and purchase contract allows for the contract to be *assigned.*
- It is wise to compare the taxes payable upon sale before and after taking title, particularly if the property is nearing completion.

---

[177] Condominium developers are no longer able to charge buyers "administrative fees" when agreements are transferred to third-parties prior to transfer of the condominium unit at the Land Department.

81
Snagging

With any newly built property, there will inevitably be faults, defects or things that have been left unfinished by the construction company. "Snagging" is your opportunity to go through the property, identify the defects and then arrange for them to be rectified by the developer before you take possession. It is also an important step because it is linked to the formal acceptance and practical completion of the property.

Chapter 58 has already discussed the importance of snagging and the key issues to look for in relation to a newly built property. Since snagging is a relevant consideration for off-plan property, off-plan purchasers would be advised to refer to this chapter.

In the context of off-plan properties, it is important to recognise that many (inexperienced) developers will try to transfer ownership of the property prior to the repair of defects; however, transfer should not take place if there are defects that prevent the property from being properly used or that cannot be repaired without prejudicing its convenient use.

STEP 6
Legal and tax considerations

82
A practical approach

The purpose of a legal contract is to clearly define in writing what has been agreed between the parties. Instead of relying on verbal assurances and promises, legal contracts formally set out the respective responsibilities and obligations of each party. In this way, contracts prevent disagreements because if there is any doubt, the parties can refer back to the contracts and are legally bound by their contents. In the event of a serious disagreement, contracts form the basis for arbitration or legal action.

Taking legal action in Thailand, however, is generally a slow, cumbersome process, which involves costly on-going legal representation, while outcomes remain uncertain[179]. Legal action should therefore be considered a last resort and should be avoided if at all possible. Purchasers need to bear in mind that legal contracts are no substitute for common sense, which is your most valuable asset, especially in Thailand where flexibility and compromise are often better suited to achieving objectives.

The best way to avoid legal action is to take more care about what you are getting into in the first place. Time should be taken to conduct background research, to properly investigate unknowns instead of hoping for the best, and to follow procedures, without taking shortcuts. In other words, it is necessary to do your homework before going to contract. With off-plan properties, for instance, having a lawyer check the wording of a sales and purchase contract will not protect you a poorly funded developer's bankruptcy. Performing informal research, a healthy level of suspicion and following your intuition will often serve you better as tools of financial self-defence.

Due to the nature of the resort property market, purchasers are often tempted to rush into things due to the constraints of a limited vacation. However, *Thailand is no place for impulse purchases of property*. In Thailand, things cannot be rushed. When acting on impulse, property transactions can become minefields.

Not rushing into things does not mean you can't act quickly to take advantage of an opportunity; it means acting with a level of caution befitting the nature of

---

[179] Unless the aggrieved party is able to seek redress from the Administrative Court, or file a "consumer case" under the Consumer Case Procedure Act, which considers cases on an expedited basis (and in certain cases covers claims filed against property developers by their customers).

the situation. For example, if you come upon an opportunity, a property can be secured with a fully refundable deposit paid to a lawyer, subject to satisfactory due diligence. Following proper procedure means buying off-plan properties, but only after you have had the chance to thoroughly investigate the developer and conduct due diligence on the development.

Property buyers would also do well to keep their investment objective in mind, such as buying a beautiful residence, a vacation home or investing in a rental property. The excitement of the property viewing process causes many purchasers to forget their investment objective. For instance, they will come to Thailand with the intention to invest in a rental property and end up buying a "bargain" that has little rental appeal.

Common sense in Thailand often dictates that property buyers should not be in a rush to take legal action when things don't turn out precisely as they expect. For instance, construction is not a precise science in Thailand, which is a difficult operational environment where issues sometimes need to be solved on a personal basis. To successfully resolve issues often requires you to keep your cool; to step back and calmly consider your options. Decisions and responses cannot be based on emotions or frustration, especially when dealing with Thais who don't take too kindly to ranting, raving or emotional outbursts. There will certainly be frustrations and challenges; the key is to stay calm and not to take actions where consequences cannot be undone.

This does not mean forgiving builders or developers that are late in completing your property; it simply means that results tend to be better if you work with them instead of against them. In other words, a degree of *flexibility* might be called for to better achieve your goals. For example, when a construction company is behind schedule building your house, re-negotiating payment terms is often wiser than suing the developer. *Prematurely* suing a developer or construction company might be the worst way to deal with a problem. It is generally better to try to resolve problems and maintain relationships; whereas taking an inflexible stance or legal action usually signals the end of both personal and professional relationships, and with it the possibility of more practical solutions. Westerners should stop thinking in terms of litigation or zero-sum negotiations; in Thailand it is *compromise* that often leads to superior solutions.

Undoubtedly, there are circumstances where legal action is the only appropriate action to take. Just make sure it is taken after other avenues have been exhausted, based on a careful consideration of all the facts and sound legal advice.

Summary

- The purpose of a legal contract is to clearly define in writing what has been agreed between the parties.
- In the event of a serious disagreement, contracts form the basis for arbitration or legal action, although legal action should be considered a last resort and should be avoided if at all possible.
- Legal contracts are no substitute for common sense, which is your most valuable asset, especially in Thailand where flexibility and compromise are often better suited to achieving objectives.

83
Invest in a lawyer

It is surprising how many people view legal advice as a cost rather than an *investment*. As a consequence, they attempt to buy property without the assistance of a lawyer or try to save legal fees by opting for the most "economical" legal advice instead of the most "competent".

However, legal due diligence in Thailand is not a mere formality. Thailand's property related laws and land registration procedures are not the worlds most straightforward or transparent. As a result, lawyers must earn their fees, performing numerous checks to ensure your property investment is protected. In such an environment, common sense suggests that instead of trying to *save* on legal costs, purchasers should be engaging the best legal advice from the most reputable, competent and professional law firm that they can afford; if they cant afford legal advice, they shouldn't be buying property.

In addition, it is not enough to assume – due to the honourable nature of the legal profession – that all lawyers act honestly and in the best interests of their clients. Quite simply, it is not true. Some lawyers and law firms operating in Thailand's tourist areas – where property transactions generate the vast majority of legal fees – are unreliable *due to their dependency on the local property market*. For instance, tight relationships between lawyers, property developers and real estate agents often preclude due diligence being conducted to the proper extent and in such cases, legal opinions might not reflect the true risks involved.

Other lawyers are unreliable because of their personal commercial interests in the property market, whereby legal opinions might contradict what would otherwise be considered sound advice in situations where vested interests are not present. I heard of a case where a lawyer, instead of acting in the best interests of the purchaser, acted instead as a de-facto broker in a land deal. The lawyer had taken an option on the seller's land and proceeded to negotiate a price with the purchaser (his client), in which case the lawyer planned to keep the difference in price between the purchase price and the price already agreed with the seller, *in addition to receiving legal fees on behalf of the law firm*.

I have also heard of instances where lawyers have been complicit in the removal and substitution of shareholders of Thai companies without consulting the shareholders, and situations where principal shareholders have been removed as signatories and directors without their knowledge. There are also examples where lawyers have colluded with land officials to upgrade land titles to sell land at higher prices, and cases where building permits have been arranged for land that under normal approval procedures would be eligible for construction. I have even heard of a case where a so-called lawyer received the purchase money from his client and then promptly disappeared with it! Another case in point relates to the fact that foreigners cannot (directly) own land in Thailand, yet there are law firms that are still content to assist their clients in setting up Thai companies with obvious nominee shareholders (see chapter 91).

Purchasers of property in Thailand would do well to understand that lawyers and law firms are far from equal in terms of ethics, professionalism and the quality of their advice. For this reason, buyers should seek legal advice only from the most reputable and professional law firms, instead of viewing legal fees like a painful but necessary surgical operation and engaging the lowest cost lawyer to perform the minimal possible amount of legal work! Remember, there is no professional indemnity in the event of due diligence failure.

In addition to costs and ethics, there is another dimension to consider when buying properties in Thailand's resort areas: - whether to engage a local law firm or a Bangkok-based law firm with an international reputation. Each approach has its pros and cons. The quality and expertise of lawyers working for prestigious Bangkok law firms are generally of a different level than those working at small law firms in resort areas (legal fees also tend to reflect the difference!). In addition, law firms that are part of an internationally renowned network clearly have a reputation to uphold.

However, when trying to get things done at the local level, whereas Bangkok law firms might send to resort areas inexperienced trainee lawyers with no local connections for checking documents and dealing with local government departments and officials, local law firms tend to have better local connections and relationships that make it easier to find out information and resolve complicated disputes. For instance, if land disputes exist between neighbouring landowners, local law firms might know the landowning families involved and be able to mediate solutions. We are not speaking of corrupt practices here (although corrupt practices are not unheard of!); we are speaking of local knowledge and relationships that help to get things done.

Summary

- It is surprising how many people view legal advice as a cost rather than an investment and try to save legal fees by opting for the most "economical" legal advice instead of the most "competent".
- Lawyers must perform numerous checks to ensure your property investment is protected.
- Lawyers and law firms in Thailand are far from equal in terms of ethics, professionalism and the quality of their advice.
- Purchasers should be engaging the best legal advice from the most reputable, competent and professional law firm that they can afford.

84
Appoint your own lawyer
(Essential)

One of the basic rules when buying property is to appoint a lawyer to act in *your* best interests.

Unfortunately, it is a common practice for property sellers to offer buyers the use of the seller's lawyer to "save time and legal costs". If buyers have any questions, sellers are all too accommodating when they point you in the direction of their own lawyers "who will be happy to answer any questions". However, buyers would do well to bear four things in mind about lawyers that are engaged by the seller:

1. The lawyer is being paid by the seller
2. The lawyer is acting on behalf of the seller
3. Contracts will be drafted to reflect the best interests of the seller
4. The lawyer owes no duty to the buyer.

A variation on this theme is where both the seller and the buyer agree to save costs by *sharing* a lawyer, which is equally unacceptable. It is also common practice for property developers to offer purchasers specially discounted legal fees through using the developer's "appointed" or "recommended" law firm. Further, property developers often give potential purchasers their standard sale and purchase contract and expect purchasers to sign it *without appointing a lawyer at all*. Their justification is usually that "*our* lawyer has already performed the necessary due diligence so you don't need to duplicate work by paying someone to do it again".

> **Important tip:** The practice of sharing a lawyer might be tempting, as it appears to save time and legal fees. However, such convenience and simplicity disguises the fact that buyers would be making a fundamental mistake; property buyers should never fall into the trap of using the same lawyer as the seller due to the inherent conflict of interest.

It is *impossible* for one lawyer to simultaneously act in the best interests of both buyer and seller. For instance, in the case where there are adverse due diligence findings, how is it possible for a lawyer to act in the best interests of both clients? It is only possible to mediate; to act as a go-between.

This issue also has a cultural aspect. While all lawyers understand the inherent conflict of interest, some Thai lawyers are happy to "represent" both buyer and seller. These lawyers can be appointed to oversee a sale and purchase transaction and will *in good faith* represent both sides, seeing it as a case of bringing both parties together to facilitate a deal. If a conflict arises, the lawyer will explain the situation to both parties and help to find a mutually agreeable solution. This is a *practical* approach to transactions, which is in contrast to Western culture where lawyers tend to be adversarial, acting to protect and secure the best deal for their clients.

Summary

To properly protect yourself as a purchaser, it is wise to follow these golden rules:

- Never accept an invitation by the seller to use the seller's lawyer or to "share" a lawyer.
- Always appoint your own lawyer to act in your best interests (one that is not connected with the seller or property developer).
- Never be tempted to cut corners for the sake of expediency or to save legal costs.
- Never sign a developer's standard sale and purchase contract before a lawyer representing your best interests has had the opportunity to review it.

85
Legal fees

Legal fees for property transactions vary, sometimes significantly, depending on the particular law firm engaged, the complexity of legal work involved, and the scope of services required (such as land title investigations or the incorporation of a Thai company). The purpose of this chapter is to provide an indication of the legal fees a property purchaser might expect to pay in Thailand for an average property purchase.

Legal fees vary from law firm to law firm. A local one-man law practice might be less expensive, while a large international law firm is usually more expensive. As mentioned in chapter 83, it is important to engage the services of a competent law firm instead of trying to save costs either by purchasing a property without being advised by your own lawyer or by obtaining the cheapest legal advice.

It is a good idea to meet with more than one lawyer, engaging the law firm you consider to be most competent and the one you feel most comfortable working with. Most law firms provide free initial consultations during which your individual requirements can be discussed. During this meeting, it should be possible to determine the nature and scope of legal work required and to get an estimate of legal fees, based on the time and resources involved. Since the vast majority of property transactions involve work of a similar nature and lawyers are performing the same type of work on a regular basis, they should quickly be able to advise what your needs are and estimate the legal fees involved. A detailed fee proposal is sometimes provided during the meeting; other times it is emailed to you separately after the meeting.

To provide an example, below are the legal fees quoted by a well-known law firm:

Property Acquisition Package

Property purchases under 15M Thai Baht = <u>100,000 THB plus VAT and disbursements</u>

Property purchases in excess of 15M Thai Baht = <u>120,000 THB plus VAT and disbursements</u>

The property acquisition package includes the following:

    a) Due Diligence investigation and searches (checking land title; land size; whether the land is encumbered in any way; history of the purchased

land including sub-divisions; legal right of access to the land from the public road; location of the land in respect of the Zoning Regulations and what uses are permitted; if there is a building erected on the land, the address of the building and whether it has been built legally and with a valid building permit.
b) Contracts (drafting of a Sale and Purchase Agreement)
c) Attendance at the Land Office

Incorporation of Thai limited company

The cost for setting up a Thai company with a share capital of 2M Thai Baht is 50,000 THB plus VAT[180] plus disbursements payable to the government of 15,000 THB

The cost for setting up a Thai company with a share capital of 4M Thai Baht is 70,000 THB plus VAT plus disbursements payable to the government of 25,000 THB

> **Important tip:** Once the nature and scope of the required legal work have been estimated, it is good practice to request that legal fees be fixed or "capped" to avoid legal fees ticking away by the hour (or minute) and getting out of hand. When legal fees are capped, you know precisely what your legal bill will be, which allows you to set aside an appropriate amount in your budget and cash flow forecasts[181].

To provide an idea of legal costs when charged at an hourly rate (i.e. when legal fees are not capped), below are the hourly rates for lawyers at the Bangkok office of a leading international law firm:

Position	Hourly Rate (Baht)
Partners	18,000 – 20,000
Senior Consultants	16,000 – 17,000
Senior Associates	10,000 – 12,000
Associates	5,000 – 9,000
Junior Associates	3,800

In addition to hourly rates, the issue of "disbursements" must also be considered. These are the additional costs charged for expenses such as copying, printing, travelling expenses and courier charges.

---

[180] VAT is charged on legal services at the current rate of 7%.
[181] If later the amount of work varies significantly or falls outside the scope of the agreed services then fees will be increased correspondingly, with your authorization.

Due to the nature of due diligence and property transactions, not intended purchases proceed to completion. It is therefore useful to check the lawyer's policy and fees in relation to "failed" transactions. This is important because if a property transaction fails to proceed for any reason, you do not want to be liable to the full legal fees for the transaction; alternatively, if you move on to buying another property, legal fees can quickly accumulate. In the case where you have attempted and failed to complete on two or three properties, legal fees as a percentage of the eventual purchase price can be unreasonably high.

> **Important tip:** It is important to confirm what the legal fees will be in the event that you decide *not* to proceed with a purchase upon receipt of the due diligence report or for any other reason, such as the seller pulling out of the deal. Lawyers often have an alternative basis for the calculation of legal fees for occasions where work on a sale and purchase transaction commences but is not completed.

Don't forget that legal fees do not include property transaction taxes, which are separate and must also be taken into consideration (see chapter 97). It is a good idea to request a detailed breakdown (or estimate of total transaction costs) in advance to avoid any nasty surprises later.

It is also a useful exercise to consider legal fees and transaction taxes in relation to the purchase price, i.e. as a percentage of the purchase price. Suppose legal fees for a sale and purchase transaction are fixed, this means the higher the purchase price, the lower legal fees become as a percentage of the purchase price; conversely, the lower the purchase price, the higher legal fees become as a percentage of the purchase price. It should be noted that due to the added complexity of legal work and the less developed property registration system, legal fees and taxes as a percentage of property prices tend to be higher in Thailand than in countries with more transparent property registration systems.

In addition to obtaining quotations for legal work, it is also important to understand how legal fees are invoiced. Some lawyers ask for an initial sum or "retainer" upon engagement, which is common for international clients, while others perform the necessary legal work and invoice the client later.

> **Important tip:** It is good practice to engage a lawyer *before* you start viewing properties or making offers. Once engaged, your lawyer will then be available to offer advise during the entire viewing, negotiating and purchasing process. In addition, if you have already engaged a lawyer, you will be able to move quickly once a property has been identified.

86
Power of Attorney

Power of attorney (POA) is an authorisation that allows someone else to act on your behalf in legal and business matters. With regard to terminology, the person authorizing the other to act is the *principal* or *granter* (of the power) and the person that is granted the authorization to act is the *agent* or *attorney-in-fact*.

Foreign purchasers of property living outside Thailand often use a power of attorney for convenience; allowing a friend or lawyer in Thailand to act on their behalf in a property transaction avoids the need for original documents to be sent backwards and forwards by international courier to be signed[182].

However, despite the fact that a power of attorney helps to streamline property transactions and make them more convenient for foreign buyers, granting power of attorney should not be treated as giving a blank canvas to anyone to carry out your business affairs, however well intentioned they might be.

Property buyers should be aware that there are different types of power of attorney, such as *general, specific* and *enduring*. A *general* power of attorney authorises the agent to act on your behalf in any way that you would be able to act in a whole variety of situations, whereas a *specific* or *limited* power of attorney only allows an agent to act on your behalf in specific situations or those relating to a specific aspect of your affairs, such as buying a property or signing a reservation agreement. A power of attorney may also be limited as to time. Usually, a power of attorney becomes ineffective if the grantor dies or becomes "incapacitated"[183]. An *enduring* or *durable* power of attorney allows the grantor to specify that the power of attorney will continue to be effective even if the grantor becomes incapacitated (although ends when the grantor dies).

As an agent acting on your behalf, the person to whom you have granted power of attorney is acting in a fiduciary capacity and must therefore act in your best interests. However, it should always be born in mind that when a person signs a document on your behalf with power of attorney, it means that you are bound by the contents of the document as if you had signed the document yourself (provided the agent signs within the powers granted)[184].

---

[182] Bearing in mind that unnecessary delays sometimes result in a deal falling through; in other words, delays give the seller (or purchaser) more time to change their mind.

[183] Meaning that they are unable to grant such a power because of mental illness.

[184] An agent might be liable for *unauthorized* acts.

If you are not resident in Thailand and have granted power of attorney to a friend to sign documents on your behalf, it is crucial that you have the opportunity to read the documents and agree to the contents before the document is signed. If you have granted power of attorney to a Thai lawyer, you should also make sure you have read through the documents before the lawyer signs them on your behalf. It should be standard practice for lawyers to forward copies of contracts by email and to receive your acceptance before original documents are signed.

> **Important tip:** Since power of attorneys are granted to facilitate property transactions and to save the time and costs associated with sending original documents by international courier, property buyers need to weigh up, on one hand, the cost savings and convenience with, on the other hand, the inherent risk of giving the power to someone else to sign documents on your behalf and legally bind you to their contents.

If you are buying property while on holiday in Thailand, lawyers often recommend that you should give them a *general* power of attorney to deal with a transaction after you return home. If you are uncomfortable with this, just say no. Instead, request draft documents to be emailed to you so that you can check and confirm the contents and, when both parties have agreed the details, an original set of documents can be couriered to you. If you are signing on behalf of a Thai company, this means you should also keep the company stamp in your possession.

Caution should be exercised when considering the grant of a *general* power of attorney. The golden rule should be to maintain as much control as you feel comfortable with over the transaction. Remember, if you don't want to grant a *general* power of attorney, a power of attorney can be limited to specific durations or for specific tasks, or it can be granted for a fixed period of time, such as three or six months, after which the power to act on your behalf automatically expires.[185] Alternatively, you could grant power of attorney to your lawyer to sign only a Reservation Agreement, or a Sale and Purchase Agreement, or agreements related to a particular property.

The issue of revoking a Power of Attorney must also be considered. If power of attorney has been granted without an expiration date, cancelling the power requires a specific procedure to be followed. If third parties are not properly informed and it is reasonable for the third parties to rely upon the power of attorney being in force, as a principal you might still be bound by the acts of the agent unless the power is properly revoked.

---

[185] If you want the agent to act for you after the expiration, a new power of attorney must be created.

Summary

- Power of attorney (POA) is an authorisation that allows someone else to act on your behalf in legal and business matters.
- Property buyers should be aware that there are different types of power of attorney, such as *general, specific* and *enduring*.
- Caution should be exercised when considering the grant of a *general* power of attorney. The golden rule should be to maintain as much control as you feel comfortable with over the transaction.
- Power of attorneys are granted to facilitate property transactions by saving the time and costs associated with sending original documents by international courier to be signed.

87
Arbitration and mediation

When signing a construction agreement with a builder for your dream home or a sales contract for an off-plan property in tropical paradise, the last thing on most peoples minds is that something could go wrong. However, while it is natural to think positively, disputes and disagreements do happen. Parties find themselves in breach of contract and relationships, when given enough distress, do invariably break down and this happens more frequently with property related transactions in Thailand than most purchasers suspect. What happens then?

In the absence of an arbitration clause in the contract, the default mechanism for resolving a dispute is litigation, i.e. taking legal action and settling the dispute in court. Litigation must, however, be considered the recourse of last resort since it is a slow, cumbersome process[186] with an uncertain outcome. It is also generally the most expensive way for a party to enforce contractual rights and recover damages. In addition, court proceedings in Thailand are conducted in Thai, which means a Thai lawyer must be engaged to represent you[187].

Arbitration is an alternative method for resolving disputes, one that seeks to *avoid* formal legal action. In essence, it requires the inclusion of an "arbitration clause" in contracts in order to prevent either party from litigation ensuring that disputes are referred instead to an independent party for arbitration. Technically, no party should be allowed to commence legal action upon any matter until it has been submitted and determined by arbitration. Arbitration is therefore the resolution of a dispute outside of the court system, wherein the parties refer a dispute to one or more impartial referees (the "arbitrators", "arbiters" or "arbitral tribunal") appointed by mutual consent and by whose decision (the "award") parties agree to be bound. In this sense, arbitration could be considered a more practical method for the resolution of disputes.

Arbitration has three key features: Firstly, arbitration is a consensual process, in that the sides must agree (contractually) to submit to arbitration. Secondly, the parties must also formally agree to accept the ruling of the arbitrator. Thirdly, and perhaps the key consideration, lengthy and costly legal proceedings should be

---

[186] Unless, as mentioned previously, a "consumer case" can be filed under the Consumer Case Procedure Act.

[187] Law is a protected profession in Thailand, which means foreign lawyers are not allowed to practice law in Thailand and are only able to provide limited assistance in court.

avoided. Therefore, while it is natural not to think about future disputes when you are buying a new property, it is only sensible to include a contractual provision to cover the eventuality of a dispute, especially one that provides an alternative to legal action.

If an arbitration clause is included in a contract, the following six issues should be covered:

1. Arbitrators. The contract should specify the arbitrators or arbitration company, together with the number of arbitrators (usually one or three) to whom a dispute will be referred. It is also possible to specify the qualifications, nationality and experience of the arbitrators, for instance: *arbitrators should possess ten years structural engineering or construction experience in Thailand.*

2. Rules. The arbitration rules to be used for the conduct of the arbitration need to be stated, such as the rules of the Thai Arbitration Institute (TAI), Singapore International Arbitration Centre (SIAC)[188] or UNCITRAL[189] rules.

3. Venue. The contract should specify a convenient location or venue where the arbitration hearing should take place[190]. For example, a hotel in Bangkok or Phuket could be specified.

4. Language. Parties can agree, for example, that arbitration proceedings shall be in the English language and any documents shall be translated into English (unless otherwise required to be in Thai under the Rules).

5. Law. Just because the arbitration is in Thailand does not mean that it has to be governed by Thai law; it is possible to use English law or any other law to govern the proceedings.

6. Procedures. The procedures for initiating arbitration need to be outlined; for example, "any dispute that cannot be settled amicably within sixty days of the first written notification to the other party shall be referred to binding arbitration".

---

[188] www.siac.org.sg/cms/
[189] United Nations Commission on International Trade Law, see www.uncitral.org/uncitral/en/about_us.html
[190] Bearing in mind that a convenient location for the parties might involve travel expenses for the arbitrators, which must be covered by the parties.

Many property-related contracts fail to include arbitration clauses either because the person drafting the contracts is unfamiliar with alternative forms of dispute resolution or because the parties simply cannot foresee any difficulties arising in future. For contracts that do cover the issue of arbitration, the relevant clauses often tend to be insufficiently detailed to be used effectively.

> **Important tip:** If an arbitration clause is inserted in a contract, it is crucial that it is sufficiently detailed for the purposes of preventing litigation and successfully referring a dispute to arbitration. The law firm advising you in relation to the purchase of property will usually have a standard arbitration clause handy, although these are often insufficiently detailed. If you wish to seek specialist arbitration advice, you might consider contacting a professional arbitration firm[191].

Arbitration has its advantages and disadvantages. The main advantage is that the process tends to be swifter than litigation in courts, and therefore less expensive. Another advantage is that arbitration tends to be more flexible in that dates, venues and formalities can be adjusted to suit the circumstances (rather than waiting for court availability and dates being fixed by the court).

There is also the matter of expertise. With arbitration, technical matters can be referred to a person with expert knowledge so that a matter can be quickly understood, whereas court judges are rarely industry specialists. Other advantages include that arbitration proceedings are private[192] and decisions are more easily enforced than a court award in a foreign jurisdiction.

The main disadvantage is the requirement for consent: there are no means to bring the parties together to arbitrate *unless* the parties consent because it is a dispute resolution mechanism that requires mutual consent. Another disadvantage is that while judges might not be industry specialists, they are more familiar with the ins and outs of the law than most arbitrators. In addition, with binding arbitration, the right to appeal tends to be limited (although some consider this to be an advantage).

In relation to costs, taking legal action involves hiring lawyers to represent you on an ongoing basis, although the costs involved in utilising the court system are minimal, (although the fact that court decisions can be more easily appealed adds to litigation costs). Arbitration, on the other hand, involves the cost of the arbitrators; travel and accommodation related costs; and the expenses involved in providing a venue for the hearing.

---

[191] Such as Charndell Associates Company. Ltd, www.charndell.com
[192] As opposed to civil court proceedings that are generally a matter of public record.

As has been noted, arbitration is a form of *binding* dispute resolution because the parties agree to refer disputes to arbitration and to be bound by the arbitrator's decision. For this reason, it could be considered equivalent to litigation in courts. If a party fails to comply with the decision or arbitration award, the other party can normally enforce the award through the courts by either a summary judgement or an "action on the award".

In addition to arbitration, there are other forms of *non-binding* dispute resolution procedures, such as negotiation and mediation, which are forms of dispute settlement facilitated by a neutral third party. These are referred to as "pre-arbitral" forms of dispute resolution; in other words, it is hoped that disputes can be settled quickly and easily through a mediator without the need for parties to go to arbitration, although if mediation fails, arbitration is the next stop for settling the dispute.

Thus, as well as a contractual clause that refers disputes to arbitration, it is recommended that a contract includes provisions for disputes to be settled by negotiation or mediation, prior to being referred to arbitration. Including negotiation or mediation procedures in a contract give the parties an opportunity to resolve their differences in a less formal manner before the dispute is referred to arbitration. This, in turn, often proves to be a less expensive and quicker way to settle an issue than both arbitration and litigation. To be effective, the contract should *require* the parties to negotiate before a dispute can be referred to arbitration (although it is essential that a time limit be placed on such negotiations).

A contract containing a proactive two-tier approach to resolving disputes must be superior to having a contract that is without any provision for dispute resolution, whereby cumbersome and expensive litigation remains the only course of action.

Summary

- In the absence of an arbitration clause in the contract, the default mechanism for resolving a dispute is litigation, i.e. taking legal action and settling the dispute in court.
- Arbitration is an alternative method for resolving disputes, wherein the parties refer a dispute to one or more impartial referees appointed by mutual consent and by whose decision parties agree to be bound.
- If an arbitration clause is inserted into a contract, it is crucial that it is sufficiently detailed for the purposes of preventing litigation and successfully referring a dispute to arbitration.
- There are other forms of non-binding dispute resolution procedures, such as negotiation and mediation, where disputes can be settled quickly and easily through a mediator without the need for parties to go to arbitration.

88
Paying deposits

The key issues concerning the payment of deposits have been covered in detail in chapter 74 – "Reservation agreements and deposits" – in the context of purchasing off-plan properties. As the issues are of considerable importance, much of the chapter is reproduced here with appropriate additions and modifications for the legal section. If you have read chapter 74, you might consider skipping this one.

Entering into contracts to buy a property is generally a two-stage process. The first stage is usually signing a Reservation Agreement (or preliminary contract), together with payment of a deposit to "reserve" the property; the second stage is signing a more comprehensive Sale and Purchase Agreement (SPA), upon which the purchase price is usually payable (less the deposit).

Signing a Reservation Agreement and paying a deposit secures the chosen property and (in theory) prevents the seller from selling it to someone else. The terms and conditions of the Reservation Agreement should then provide the purchaser with sufficient time to conduct the necessary due diligence before signing the more comprehensive Sale and Purchase Agreement.

> **Important tip:** Strictly speaking, there is no obligation to pay a deposit or sign a reservation agreement before signing the Sale and Purchase Agreement. Indeed, if you have doubts about signing a preliminary agreement that lacks sufficient detail, you can proceed directly to the final contracts *after* due diligence has been conducted, at the risk of losing the particular property should another buyer step forward during the due diligence process.

To understand the role of deposits and reservation agreements, it is helpful to look at things from the perspective of both the seller and buyer. From a seller's perspective, buyers ask endless questions and often procrastinate for weeks or months deciding whether or not to commit to a purchase. The signing of a formal reservation agreement demonstrates the conclusion of the decision-making process and signals the buyer's intent to proceed. However, signing a piece of paper doesn't mean very much without also "putting your money where your mouth is"; thus reservation agreements generally come with a requirement to pay a deposit or "reservation fee" to demonstrate good faith and to secure the buyer's commitment. Deposits or reservation fees are usually required at the time of signing the reservation agreement, or within a specified number of days thereafter.

From the perspective of a buyer, signing a reservation agreement and paying a reservation fee secures the chosen property and (in theory) prevents the seller from selling it to someone else. The terms and conditions of the reservation agreement should then provide the buyer with sufficient time to conduct the necessary due diligence before signing the more comprehensive Sale and Purchase Agreement (SPA).

One of the key issues in relation to the payment of reservation deposits is whether they are refundable or non-refundable. Again, from the perspective of the seller, it is obviously preferable if payments are *non-refundable,* to prevent the buyer from changing his mind, pulling out of the deal and wasting the seller's time. It also covers the legal fees involved in the drafting of the reservation agreement. In fact, sellers prefer reservation fees to be non-refundable *under any circumstances* because when a deposit is refundable, it cannot really be considered a sale at all until the buyer has unequivocally parted with his money.

Buyers, on the other hand, prefer reservation payments to be completely refundable *without conditions,* which gives buyers the best of both worlds: it reserves the property and prevents it from being sold to another party, and at the same time allows them to change their mind for any reason whether or not there are adverse due diligence findings, or if contract negotiations cannot be satisfactorily resolved.

Due to the different perspectives of the seller and buyer, what usually happens in practice (especially when lawyers are involved) is that deposits become refundable, subject to certain conditions. These conditions need to be carefully scrutinised and the onus is on the buyer to negotiate the most favourable conditions. In practice, many buyers are so caught up in the excitement of reserving a property by paying a deposit that they fail to pay attention to the small print, particularly with regard to whether deposits are refundable or non-refundable. However, such distinctions are crucially important and any conditions related to the payment of a deposit need to be carefully checked. If the conditions are not acceptable, they should be negotiated.

A buyer's objective should be to make any deposit paid to a seller "fully refundable, without conditions" or "refundable for any reason whatsoever". If this is not possible, at the very least buyers should give themselves a way out of the purchase in the case of adverse due diligence findings (that cannot be easily or satisfactorily resolved). A common method is to use words such as "the purchaser may terminate the Reservation Agreement based on due diligence findings". In addition, it is wise for a buyer to have alternative ways to walk away from a deal (together with the deposit) by making the contract subject to certain other considerations. With commercial contracts, it is possible to include any terms, providing the seller agrees. For example, agreements can be made "subject to the agreement of terms", "subject to a satisfactory structural survey or home inspection", "subject to site visit" (if you are not resident in Thailand and have yet to visit the site or property) or even "subject to business partner's approval".

An issue related to whether deposits are refundable or non-refundable is the matter of costs. Even when reservation deposits are refundable, some sellers (usually developers) still attempt to retain some of your money to cover costs and inconvenience. These are formally referred to as "administrative charges", "cancellation fees", "office costs" or "processing fees". To avoid these charges, reservation agreements should state that deposits are *"refundable in full"*. The timing of refunds is another issue. It is sensible that a time limit is stated for the repayment of a deposit, in case the buyer decides not to proceed with the purchase, for instance, "the deposit will be returned to the purchaser within 7 days of such request".

The next consideration is the size of the deposit required to secure a property. Deposits vary from negligible amounts to amounts that represent a significant percentage of a property's price. On the lower end of the scale, amounts could be 100,000 Baht or 200,000 Baht (US$ 3,300 or 6,600) or the amount could be expressed as a percentage of the purchase price, such as 1% - 2% of the purchase price; just enough to demonstrate that the buyer's interest is serious. On the upper end of the scale, sometimes as much as 10% or 20% of the purchase price can be requested as a deposit[193].

> **Important tip:** Buyers should bear in mind that the objective of paying a reservation deposit should be to *control* the property with the smallest possible *refundable* down payment.

When a deposit is paid, the contract should clearly state that if you decide to proceed with the purchase the *reservation deposit will be applied as part of the purchase price*. If it is not mentioned, the possibility exists for the reservation deposit to become an additional stealth payment (or commission for a salesperson), which has no relation to the purchase price of the property. The contract should then clarify *how* the deposit is to be applied, for instance, in relation to an off-plan property purchase with staged payments, will the deposit be deducted from the first payment, or from the last. From a purchaser's point of view, it is better for the amount of the reservation deposit to be deducted from

---

[193] If you are buying off-plan property after construction has commenced, deposit payments should not be confused with the initial staged payments that might be requested pursuant to construction progress.

the first payment in line with the objective of keeping payments smaller at the beginning and larger towards the end.

Purchasers should avoid oversimplified reservation agreements designed "to keep things simple" or rough and ready agreements scribbled on a scrap of paper "to save legal fees". If you are paying a deposit on a property, do it properly; deposit agreements need to be sufficiently detailed to protect you. If you decide not to proceed with a purchase, without a sufficiently detailed agreement you could find yourself in disagreement over the refund, or the timing or amount of the refund. It is important to resist sales pressure and not to be rushed into "reserving the property before someone else does".

Another crucial matter which company or entity should the deposit be paid to? This might at first appear to be a strange question but sellers are often looking for evidence of good faith and the intent to purchase: in other words, they want to see you *part* with your money; they don't necessarily want to get their hands on it immediately. This means it is sometimes possible to pay the deposit to your lawyer (or the seller's lawyer), rather than directly to the seller. In this way, good faith can be demonstrated while at the same time a higher degree of protection is retained over your money, which a lawyer should ensure is paid strictly subject to the agreed terms.[194] If a deposit is paid directly to the seller and you later decide not to proceed with the purchase, it is often more difficult to enforce its return. Further, as deposits are small relative to the purchase price, the legal costs involved in recovering a deposit often make the exercise pointless. Remember, *control* over money is "nine tenths of the law", particularly in Thailand!

In a conceptual sense, when a deposit is paid directly to the seller, they *effectively* hold it "in escrow" subject to the agreed terms. However, in private sales, especially off-plan property sales, the seller often holds your money in the hope or on the *assumption* of a deal being done and is often reluctant to return it. This reluctance can translate into deposits being held for unreasonable periods of time[195] or subjected to unreasonable "administration fees". An unscrupulous developer has little to lose (except their reputation) by holding on to your deposit once you have decided to pull out of a deal. Indeed, deposits are often spent (on construction-related expenses or overheads) before a final decision as to the purchase has been made, which makes it even more of a challenge to obtain a refund.

---

[194] Paying a deposit to a lawyer or any trustworthy independent third party is *in effect* putting the money in escrow where professional ethics should ensure the deposit is subject to the terms of the contract (see chapter 108).

[195] With underfunded developers or developers with cash flow problems, the refund of a deposit will enter the accounting system as just another bill to pay, and it will certainly not be a priority.

> **Important tip:** If an "escrow" arrangement is not acceptable to the seller, you have a choice between two opposing risks: paying a deposit directly to the seller with the attendant risk of non-return; or proceeding as quickly as possible with due diligence and conducting the purchase without securing the property with a deposit, at the risk of losing the particular property to a buyer acting with less caution.

The purpose of paying a deposit is to reserve a property (and thereby prevent it from being sold to another party) while several things take place: due diligence must be carried out (see next chapter); the details of the Sale and Purchase Agreement must be clarified and negotiated; and the sale and purchase contracts must be prepared. It is therefore important that Reservation Agreements allow sufficient time for these things to be done. The lawyer conducting due diligence on your behalf should advise you how much time is needed, although generally 28 days is adequate for a standard property transaction.

Finally, the Reservation Agreement should provide you (as the purchaser) with the flexibility to assign the rights set out in the contract (and the deposit) in the event that (a) you decide to purchase the property through a different person, entity or company according to the most appropriate ownership structure for the asset, or (b) in the case of off-plan properties, you decide to transfer (sell) the rights and obligations to another person, entity or company or transfer the reservation deposit to a different property within the same development.

Summary

The following is a checklist of items to consider when paying deposits:

- Is the deposit refundable or non-refundable?
- Make the deposit refundable *subject to...*
- Is the deposit refundable *in full?*
- Is a time limit specified for the refund?
- What is the deposit amount?
- Will the deposit be applied as part of the purchase price?
- Is the Reservation Agreement sufficiently detailed?
- Is the deposit paid directly to the seller or to a lawyer (escrow)?
- Does the Reservation Agreement allow sufficient time for due diligence?
- Is there an assignment clause?

89
Due diligence?
(Essential)

In the context of property transactions, due diligence is the name given to the process of investigating the details of an investment and verifying the material facts before a buyer makes the final decision about whether or not to complete a transaction. In other words, it is an audit for the purposes of preventing foreseeable risks and the process of making sure you get what you are paying for.

If your goal is a secure and trouble-free property investment, it is absolutely essential to conduct proper due diligence *before* committing to a purchase. Signing contracts first and asking questions later is not a suitable approach in Thailand, where *Caveat Emptor* or "buyer beware" is the prevailing paradigm. Indeed, just because Thai people approach land and property issues in an informal manner doesn't mean you can afford to as a foreign purchaser. When no consumer protection exists,[196] property buyers need to take additional precautions *before* the purchase to save tears later on.

To an objective observer, buying a property in Thailand *without* performing due diligence is hard to imagine. At best it would be considered imprudent; at worst, it would be foolhardy and reckless. But it happens. People buy land and properties without checking title documents or access rights; buyers believe the reassuring words of a friendly seller instead of engaging a lawyer to check the facts. I have heard of cases where buyers have met sellers in hairdressing salons or cafes and money has been transferred to complete strangers to buy land these "sellers" don't own.

Some readers might gasp at the ludicrousness of such reckless action but holidaymakers abandoning common sense when buying tropical resort properties is not an unusual occurrence. Indeed, it is an anomaly that in the more challenging environment of a South East Asian property market, foreign buyers often exercise a lower standard of care than they would when purchasing property in their home country (even though they are exponentially more familiar with the property market and purchasing process in their home country). One of the justifications given is the haste of making decisions while on holiday; but this is no excuse in the context of a large investment.

---

[196] Except, most notably, in the case of condominium freehold property, which is covered by the Condominium Act.

> **Important tip:** It should be understood that while conducting due diligence on a property does not guarantee there will be no problems, *not* engaging a competent lawyer to verify the elements of a transaction *significantly* increases risks.

Due diligence needs to be considered from several perspectives, not just the narrow perspective of paying a lawyer to look over the relevant contractual documents, which by itself gives buyers a false sense of security[197]. When people refer to due diligence, they commonly think of *legal* due diligence, which is the process of checking land titles, access documents, legal contracts and ownership structures. However, there is also *financial* due diligence, which is checking financial records and documents and is particularly relevant when buying a property through the purchase of shares in a company. There is also *tax* due diligence, which attempts to uncover the potential tax exposure that would accompany the purchase of a property where the official price has been understated or the potential liabilities that would be inherited by purchasing a company. In the case of off-plan properties, the due diligence process should also include an investigation of the developer. Then there is *structural* due diligence, which involves engaging structural engineers or surveyors to verify that a property is structurally sound and to identify problems that might need to be fixed in the coming years.

Perhaps the most overlooked form of due diligence is *informal* due diligence. This involves making informal enquiries about a property, which includes speaking with neighbours and local business owners. Informal research can prove to be an invaluable source of information about a property or an area and can alert you to potential risks. For investors, due diligence also includes research on foreign exchange rates, political risk, macro-economic trends and forecasts.

To better protect your investment, a more holistic approach needs to be taken in relation to the due diligence process. Looking purely at the financial details of a property purchase does not provide an insight into the authenticity of land titles; investigating only land documents will not, for instance, reveal the existence of family graves on the land or whether it is prone to flooding during the wet season, which falls under the scope of *physical* due diligence. Physical due diligence also requires purchasers to walk on the land to ensure it is vacant of any occupation. Due diligence must be approached from several angles; the more information that can be discovered about a property through both formal and informal sources, the higher the probability of preventing foreseeable risks.

---

[197] Receiving a quotation for the full scope of legal due diligence work is enough to dissuade the average purchaser from proceeding with all but the most elemental legal checks, i.e. looking over the contractual documents.

As a buyer, the key is never to let emotions, holiday deadlines or sellers rush you into a purchase without engaging a lawyer to perform due diligence on an investment prior to purchase. If a deposit or reservation contract is signed, it must allow sufficient time for due diligence to be performed.

In relation to legal due diligence, a reputable law firm should check the following:

- Land title documents (have title documents been lawfully issued, who is the current owner and is the land is encumbered in any way by endorsements, liens, mortgages, easements or any evidence of a dispute).
- History of the purchased land (i.e. subdivisions and upgrades).
- Land size, shape and orientation of the property and its border to public property, such as a road, stream or beach (to ensure the title accurately represents the offered property).
- Legal right of access to the land from a public road.
- Location of the land with respect to zoning regulations and permitted uses within the area.
- If there is a building erected on the land, the address of the building and whether it has been built legally and with a valid building permit.
- The drafting of the Sale and Purchase Agreement.

While most law firms automatically perform these checks, it is wise to double-check. Sometimes, items are excluded or charged for separately. For instance, purchasers of leasehold apartments in an apartment complex might engage a lawyer to check the Sale and Purchase Agreement but would usually be charged separately for a title investigation on the project development land.

With regard to due diligence on companies, in the case where a company is purchased as a means to purchase a property, tax due diligence needs to be conducted to uncover tax liabilities that might be inherited. For example, Thai companies must in many cases self assess their liability to taxation, which means if a company has underpaid its taxes and tax returns have not been audited by the tax authorities prior to purchase, the purchaser could assume a tax liability that (in the absence of a proper audit) might only be discovered if the company is subsequently audited by the authorities.

No discussion on due diligence would be complete without mentioning that due diligence has its limitations. For example, off-balance sheet or undocumented liabilities, debts or obligations of the Thai company you might be taking over (to own a property) are unlikely to be picked up. Another example is fraudulently issued land titles or title upgrades (see chapter 17 on land title insurance).

Summary

- If your goal is a secure and trouble-free property investment, it is absolutely essential to conduct proper due diligence *before* committing to a purchase.
- Never let emotions, holiday deadlines or sellers rush you into a purchase without engaging a lawyer to perform due diligence on a property.
- Reservation Agreements must allow sufficient time for due diligence to be performed.
- Due diligence should be considered from several perspectives, including:
  - Legal due diligence
  - Financial due diligence
  - Tax due diligence
  - Structural due diligence
  - Informal due diligence
  - Physical due diligence

90
Thai companies

As discussed in chapter 4 on "Freehold", Thai law does not allow foreigners to own a direct freehold interest in land. Due to this restriction, using a Thai private limited company (as an investment vehicle) has become an "accepted" method[198] for buying and holding freehold property (including land and villas)[199].

The reason this works is that a Thai-majority company has the right to purchase and own land and properties because a Thai company or "juristic person"[200] commands the same rights as a Thai citizen. It is therefore equivalent to the land or property being owned by a Thai person.

Shareholders and Directors

In order to be considered a Thai company, at least 51% of the company's shares must be Thai owned. In other words, if more than 49% of the registered capital of a Thai limited company is held by foreigners (or foreigners constitute more than half of its shareholders) the company will be subject to the same property ownership restrictions as a foreign investor.

Therefore, Thai companies (for purposes of property transactions) are set up so that at least 51% of the registered share capital is in the name of Thai shareholders, with the remaining shares being owned by the foreign property buyer (or a company controlled by the foreigner). One of the most common share structures is 51% Thai and 49% foreign shareholding (foreign individual or foreign company), although other variations are possible, such as 61% Thai and 39% foreign shareholding, which in some cases is considered more prudent.

In relation to the number of shareholders, at least three shareholders are required to register a Thai company[201] and there must be more Thai shareholders than

---

[198] Where there is a law, there is a loophole and using a Thai company is the loophole. Indeed, lawyers in Thailand have become expert at setting up companies to facilitate real estate transactions.

[199] The use of Thai companies to own land should not be mistaken for secure freehold ownership. The Thai company owns the land and the foreigner *controls* the Thai company. The foreigner does not directly own the land, and shares are not a valid title establishing rights to land ownership.

[200] An entity, other than a natural person, that is created by law and recognized as having a distinct legal identity, together with duties and rights, that can enter into contracts and own property as though it were a person. Otherwise referred to as an "artificial person", "juridical entity", "juridical person", "legal person", "body corporate" or "vehicle".

[201] This is a recent change. Seven shareholders were required up until mid-2008.

foreign shareholders. For instance, if there are two foreign shareholders, there must be three Thai shareholders. A Thai company also needs at least one person to act as director, which is the most important role in the company.

Ownership and Control

Those unfamiliar with Thai law and company structures often wonder how it is possible to safely purchase and own a property through a company that is at least 51% Thai-owned and the foreign purchaser has a minority ownership? To explain this apparent anomaly, it is important to appreciate the crucial difference between *ownership* and *control*. Thai shareholders might *own* more of a company than the foreigner by having a majority of the registered share capital, but the foreigner *controls* the company through voting rights (even though the foreigner owns less than half the shares). In other words, foreigners have a *controlling* interest, albeit with a minority shareholding. This is achieved by dividing the company's share capital into different classes of shares, which each have different voting rights. For example, the 51% Thai-owned shares might be "common" or "ordinary" shares, while the 49% of shares under foreign ownership are "preference" shares, whereby (in relation to decision-making and control of the company) the Articles of Association specify that "common" shareholders have one vote for each share, while "preference" shareholders have the equivalent of ten ordinary votes[202].

This is the manner in which foreigners employ Thai companies to purchase and hold land and other property rights in Thailand, circumventing the restrictions in regard to *direct* foreign ownership[203]. In accordance with the law, a Thai entity is the registered owner of the property, although a foreigner (or foreign company) retains effective *control* over the Thai company. By any means it is not the same as direct ownership of land; it is indirect control of it. Having said that, ownership is continuous as long as the company stays in existence and does not sell or transfer the land.

Setup Costs

The setup costs for a Thai company depends on the level of share capital (and the particular law firm engaged). As a reference point, below are the fees charged for the incorporation of a Thai company by one law firm in Thailand.

---

[202] The controlling or preference class of shares also has superior rights in relation to dividends and distribution upon liquidation.
[203] However, the "evidence of funds" requirements (see next chapter) should dissuade foreign buyers from purchasing land using a Thai company.

Incorporation of a Thai limited company
The cost for setting up a Thai company with a share capital of 2M Thai Baht is 50,000 THB plus VAT[204] plus disbursements payable to the government of 15,000 THB
The cost for setting up a Thai company with a share capital of 4M Thai Baht is 70,000 THB plus VAT plus disbursements payable to the government of 25,000 THB

Setup Procedure

There is a five-step procedure for setting up a Thai company. For those unfamiliar with the process, these procedures might seem complicated but in practice the law firm engaged for the company set up generally takes care of the details.

Important tip: Most property buyers focus almost exclusively on their investment in property and consider the setting up of a Thai company as a mere formality; however, it is important to get involved with the company formation and to understand the obligations and formalities that the company, together with its shareholders and directors, must comply with.

The Five Steps to Registering a Thai Company		
Step		**Remarks**
1	Register the name of the company	The name is reserved for 30 days so registration needs to be completed within this time.
2	File the Memorandum of Association	This document includes the company's name, objectives, location, the amount of registered share capital, share distribution, together with the names and addresses of shareholders.

---

[204] VAT is charged on legal services at the current rate of 7%.

The Five Steps to Registering a Thai Company		
Step		**Remarks**
3	Convene a Statutory Meeting	At this stage, the Articles of Association are adopted and various decisions are made regarding the share capital of the company. While this is an important part of the process, it rarely involves an actual meeting, usually a "documentary meeting".
4	File the Company Registration Documents	This is where the establishment of the company occurs. It is also the point where Thai shareholders might be required to disclose the source of their investment (see chapter 91, "Nominee shareholders?")
5	Register with the Revenue Department	This entails obtaining a tax number and corporate tax identity card.

Ongoing Fees

Don't be among the majority of property buyers who, after paying the set up costs for establishing a Thai company, are then shocked to receive subsequent invoices for services, fees and taxes related to the operation of the company. Many property buyers believe a Thai company can be set up to purchase property and the company can then be treated as a dormant company, which is not true[205].

There is a reasonable level of ongoing administrative fees involved with the operation and maintenance of a Thai company. A qualified accounting or legal firm must be engaged to prepare the accounts, file corporate tax returns with the relevant authorities and maintain regulatory compliance of the company[206]. This might include fees for corporate secretarial services; preparing and submitting annual accounts; providing a registered office address for the company; and the provision of company directors and shareholders. On an annual basis, these fees can be substantial; depending on the services required, annual company

---

[205] The Revenue Department treats companies according to their purpose of making profit. Technically, companies that are not earning income are subject to de-listing.

[206] Thai companies must amend their basic corporate documents to comply with changing legislation and new court rulings. Failure to maintain compliance could result in the company being subject to investigation by the Ministry of Commerce, Ministry of Interior or the Revenue Office.

related fees could be in excess of 100,000 Baht (US$ 3,300). For this reason, the fees related to the operation of a Thai company must be a consideration when determining the optimal ownership structure for a property (see chapter 102, "Corporate structure or personal name?").

Taking over a Thai Company

If you are buying property through the taking over of a Thai company, it is essential to perform thorough legal and tax due diligence to uncover any potential risks and liabilities that might be assumed. In fact, due to the possibility of undisclosed liabilities, many lawyers advise against taking over a Thai company for the purpose of purchasing real estate. However, after weighing the various advantages and disadvantages, for foreigners it remains in many cases the most viable method for purchasing and holding property.

Perhaps the greatest concerns in relation to the use of Thai companies is the increased scrutiny of companies with foreign shareholders and the issue of "nominee" shareholders, which is discussed in the next chapter. In any event, if any of the Thai shareholders have been "supplied" by the law firm acting for the seller, it is likely that these shareholders will need to be "replaced" upon purchase, and this is a matter that needs to be discussed your lawyer.

Summary

- Thai law does not allow foreigners to own a direct freehold interest in land; using a Thai private limited company has therefore become an "accepted" method for buying and holding freehold property.
- A Thai-majority company has the right to purchase and own land and properties because a Thai company commands the same rights as a Thai citizen.
- In order to be considered a Thai company, at least 51% of the company's shares must be Thai owned, although variations such as a 61% Thai and 39% foreign shareholding are also common.
- Thai shareholders might *own* more of a company than the foreigner by having a majority of the registered share capital, but the foreigner *controls* the company through voting rights according to different classes of shares.

91
Nominee shareholders?

If you are considering the use of a Thai company for purchasing property, it is important to understand the issue of nominee shareholders or "nominees". While Thai law does not clearly or precisely define what a "nominee" is, the general idea is that nominee shareholders are shareholders that lack a real financial stake or interest in a company and are shareholders only "to make up the numbers". In other words, a nominee is not a genuine investor but a pseudo-stakeholder whose name is used to hold shares in a company under the control of foreign shareholders.

The distinction between ownership and control was discussed in the previous chapter. This distinction allows foreigners to purchase land using a Thai company, which they are able to *control* through special voting rights even though foreigners are minority shareholders. Since the investment into the company (to buy property) is foreign, and the foreigner (or foreigners) exercises effective control over the company, the Thai shareholders are deemed "nominees" acting under foreign instruction and, as such, are being used as a front by foreigners to secure effective ownership of land. The use of nominees is therefore at the very heart of the mechanism used by foreigners to get around the laws forbidding direct foreign ownership of land. For this reason, the practice of using nominee shareholders is illegal under the Foreign Business Act, the Land Act and other laws.

The fundamental objective for allowing foreigners to own up to 49% of the shareholding of a Thai company is to encourage Thai investors to form legitimate, strategic joint ventures with foreigners. However, for many years law firms and accounting firms in Thailand have been using this as an opportunity to set up nominee company structures so that foreigners can circumvent the law and buy land. During this time, the definition of "shareholder" has been somewhat stretched and the invisible line blatantly crossed in cases where gardeners, maids and drivers have been used as shareholders for Thai companies. In some cases, secretaries and clerks of law firms engaged to set up Thai companies for their clients became shareholders for hundreds of companies!

For many years, a blind eye has been turned to this practice. What a "nominee" is has never been clearly defined and it can only be illegal if the law is clear enough to determine illegality! However, the issues of nominee shareholders and Thai companies with foreign shareholders have come under increasingly greater scrutiny[207]. Laws already in existence relating to the use of nominees are now being more strictly enforced and a series of guidelines and Ministry of Interior Circular Letters[208] have outlined and standardized procedures for Land Department officials to follow when dealing with land acquisitions by companies with foreign directors or shareholders.[209]

These procedures establish disclosure requirements or "evidence of funds" rules for Thais[210] holding shares in companies (purchasing land) with foreign shareholders or directors in an effort to ensure Thai shareholders are genuine investors instead of "nominees" – in other words, the aim is to prevent Thai companies being established to acquire land for the benefit of foreigners. Thai shareholders[211] must disclose their source of investment and Land Department officials are required to examine the occupation and income history[212] of Thai shareholders to prove their ability to co-invest with foreign shareholders. These rules have certainly influenced the manner and procedure by which Thai companies are set up in relation to real estate transactions[213], if indeed a law firm is willing to set up a new company to assist foreigners to purchase land under such circumstances.

In addition to the "evidence of funds" rules, foreign property buyers should also be aware of the Foreign Business Act (FBA) or, more pertinently, the proposed amendments to the Foreign Business Act (see next chapter).

---

[207] It is interesting to note the recent increase in scrutiny can be traced back to Prime Minister Thaksin's overthrow by military coup in September 2006. The military coup followed shortly after the sale of the Thaksin family's 49.6% stake in Shin Corp Telecommunications to the Singapore government's investment arm, Temesek. The Shin Corp-Temesek deal drew massive attention because Thaksin's family pocketed $US1.9 billion without paying any taxes (due to favorable changes to tax regulations that had been rushed through Parliament shortly before the sale). This perceived abuse of power caused senior politicians to turn on Thaksin, resulting in the military coup, the dissolution of Thaksin's government and suspension of the operation of the Thai constitution. Whether in an attempt to legally justify the military coup or in the genuine interests of Thai nationalism, the issue of nominee shareholders became politically significant. Aside from Thaksin's alleged undermining of democracy, Shin Corp Telecommunications controlled Thailand's satellites (a matter of national interest) and after its sale to Temesek, these technically came under the control of a Singaporean company through its preferential voting rights. Shortly after, an 800-page report by the Minister of Commerce condemned the use of "nominee companies" as undesirable.

[208] Starting in May 2006 with the most recent issued in July 2008.

[209] Or Thai shareholders and directors only but there are reasonable grounds to suspect that Thai shareholders are nominees holding shares for foreigners.

[210] Either Thais holding shares as individuals or the Thai director of a corporate shareholder of a Thai company.

[211] Foreign investors are not required to disclose the source of their investment.

[212] Such as savings accounts, income received from land sales, inheritance and loans (together with documentary evidence of the loans). Thai shareholders must also sign a declaration that they are not holding the shares as a nominee for a foreigner or foreign company.

[213] It also influences the manner in which money is transferred into Thailand for the company setup and property purchase.

Summary

- Thai companies are used by foreigners as a means to circumvent the restrictions in regard to direct foreign ownership, whereby Thai companies own land and foreigners *control* the companies through preferential voting rights.
- A nominee shareholder is a shareholder that lacks a real financial stake or interest in a company and is a shareholder only to "make up the numbers".
- The issue of nominee shareholders has come under increasingly greater scrutiny and "evidence of funds" rules are in force aimed at preventing their use.

92
The Foreign Business Act

The Foreign Business Act (FBA) is the main legislation regulating the scope of foreign business activities in Thailand. Through a simple 3-step procedure, the act defines what "foreigners" are, lists the categories of businesses that foreigners cannot engage in without permission, and sets out procedures for foreigners to obtain such permission.

The FBA is not a new law. It is the successor of the "Alien Business Law" (ABL) of 1972 that aimed to limit foreign participation in some business activities, either because they were sensitive sectors for Thailand (such as national security or resources) or because the Thai people were not competitive in those sectors. Of relevance to property investors, there have been several recently *proposed* amendments to the FBA aimed at addressing the two major loopholes of (1) the use of "nominee" shareholders, i.e. shareholders that are not genuine investors but instead hold shares in a company that is under the control of foreign shareholders, and (2) foreigners using preferential voting rights to effectively control a Thai company even though they are minority shareholders. It is important to note that the proposed amendments have not become law; such amendments have been under discussion for years and still have not become law. Indeed, they might never become law.

There are three (different) *proposed draft* amendments for the FBA. The Ministry of Commerce submitted a draft bill to the cabinet to amend the Foreign Business Act on 9 January 2007. On March 14, certain members of the National Legislative Assembly (NLA) drafted an entirely different proposed bill, which conflicted significantly with the earlier bill. Then the Council of State, which is in charge of re-drafting all proposed legislation, suggested a third approach. In order for any proposed amendments to become effective, the cabinet must approve the bill, the Council of State must give it legal clearance, any changes must be resubmitted again to the cabinet, followed by three readings by the National Legislative Assembly, before being endorsed by His Majesty the King and published in the Royal Gazette. In other words, there is still uncertainty in relation to the scope and nature of the amendments, and any amendments are some time away from being passed into law. For foreign investors considering the purchase of land through a Thai company, these proposed amendments to the FBA have cast a cloud of uncertainty over the property market.

So what are the details of the proposed amendments? The draft bill from the Ministry of Commerce, for instance, proposed that a company where foreigners have more than 50% of the voting rights should be considered a foreign company, even if foreign shareholders own less than 50% of the shares. In other words, Thai shareholders should have 51% of the shares *and* 51% of the voting rights in Thai companies (which would remove foreign ownership *and control* of Thai companies). With reference to "nominees", there are no changes that might elaborate further on what a "nominee" is (apparently because the nominee issue is already deemed illegal under the current Foreign Business Act).

This failure to precisely define what a nominee is has created a great deal of uncertainty for property investors, developers and buyers. Draconian measures restricting foreign ownership *could* be implemented at some point in the future or a diluted version of the amendments might become law[214]. Or nothing might happen, which means the status quo prevails. For foreign investors with existing Thai companies (holding their property assets), the main point is that it would be premature to restructure a company without a clear legislative framework.

If the amendments do become law, the government recognises that companies that were not in violation of the FBA before will almost certainly have a period of time to restructure to comply with any new law. Indeed, if the Thai government is able to clarify the issue of voting rights and make a precise determination about what is, and what is not, a nominee, Thai companies can hopefully be restructured accordingly and the property market can proceed with certainty (for better or worse). In the meantime, with potential amendments to the FBA on the drawing board, foreigners planning to purchase land might consider structuring purchases on a leasehold basis (or leasehold with an option to purchase the freehold), while company structures that include nominees should be avoided. Completely risk-averse buyers wishing to purchase freehold land might wish to wait until the relevant laws are clarified[215].

Summary

- The Foreign Business Act (FBA) is the main legislation regulating the scope of foreign business activities in Thailand.
- There have been proposed amendments to the FBA aimed at addressing the use of "nominee" shareholders and foreigners using preferential voting rights to control Thai companies.
- It is important to note that the proposed amendments have not become law.

---

[214] There has also been discussion of increasing the legal maximum period of time for leasehold property ownership, which is currently 30 years.
[215] Although they could be in for a long wait!

93
Thai companies and corporate income tax

Thai limited companies are subject to corporate income tax (CIT). Net profit for tax purposes is calculated by taking all revenue arising from business carried out in the tax year and deducting all allowable expenses.

This means that if you own land (or other types of property) in a Thai company, *and you sell assets out of the company*[216] any capital gain is considered normal income and subject to CIT just like any other form of income.

However, if you sell the Thai company (which owns the property) instead of selling the property, this is a transfer of shares and not a transfer of property, in which case the issue of corporate income tax[217] is avoided[218], together with the fees associated with the transfer of property (see chapter 97).

For reference, the current corporate income tax rates for a Thai company with paid up share capital not exceeding 5 million Baht are as follows[219]:

Net Profit (Baht)	Tax Rate
0 to 150,000	Exempt
150,001 to 1,000,000	15%
1,000,001 to 3,000,000	25%
3,000,001 and over	30%

---

[216] As opposed to selling the property by selling the company.
[217] Although *personal* income taxes might be applicable to the shareholder.
[218] Unless the property is later sold "out of the company".
[219] Source: BDO Advisory Limited, www.bdo-thaitax.com

94
Personal income tax

Foreign individuals earning income from property situated in Thailand have a duty to file a personal income tax return. For individuals, personal income tax is calculated on a person's net income *after* deductions for expenses and allowances.

Filing a personal income tax return allows a number of deductions to be claimed, which have the effect of reducing the overall income that is subject to taxation. For instance, the first 150,000 Baht of an individual's net income is exempt from personal income tax. In the case of rental income, property owners are allowed a standard 30% deduction (for expenses) against rental income, no questions asked[220].

Personal income tax is calculated according to progressive tax rates ranging from 10 - 37%, as shown in the chart below[221]:

Net taxable income (Baht)	Marginal tax rate 1[222]
1 – 150,000	0%
150,001 – 500,000	10%
500,001 – 1,000,000	20%
1,000,001 – 4,000,000	30%
More than 4,000,000	37%

---

[220] There is also the option of claiming *actual* expenses incurred, although supporting documentary evidence is required (corporate tax provisions governing the deduction of expenses will apply).
[221] Source: BDO Tax & Legal Property News, www.bdo.co.th
[222] In Thailand, the tax scales for non-residents and residents are the same.

95
Ownership structures
(Essential)

As discussed in chapter 2, to understand property ownership in Thailand we need to move beyond the physical description or attributes of property (land, villas, apartments) and think instead in terms of *legal* ownership. Property ownership is ultimately defined in terms of legal concepts, which grant owners legal rights corresponding to the particular ownership type. Thus, it is necessary to think in terms of "leasehold", "freehold", "condominium freehold" and variations based on these legal forms of ownership. Each type of legal ownership, in turn, lends itself to various choices in regard to how assets can be owned, influenced by Thai laws relating to foreign ownership. We are referring here to "ownership structures".

The purpose of this chapter is to explain the various possible ownership structures a foreigner can potentially use for each type of legal ownership. Once the various possibilities have been outlined, it is then a matter of selecting the most suitable ownership structure in accordance with your objective and circumstances.

Leasehold

A lease is a *personal* interest in property.[223] As noted in chapter 5, a leaseholder does not actually own land or property but is instead granted the right to exclusive possession and use of land or property for a specific period of time. The maximum lease period currently permitted under Thai law is 30 years.

With leasehold, as no freehold ownership of land involved, there is no prohibition on foreign participation. It is therefore possible for foreigners to lease all types of property – land, villas or apartments[224] – and to register leasehold interests in their personal name. Alternatively, a lease can be registered to an offshore company or a Thai company[225]. In other words, just because a lease can be owned directly in a personal name, does not mean it is always the most favourable

---

[223] As opposed to *real* property. Real property is land and ordinarily anything erected on or affixed to it, whereas *personal* property is anything other than land that can be the subject of ownership, including stocks, bonds, money and patents.

[224] With regard to renting a building or apartment, technically the "contract is terminated if the whole of the property is lost" unless contractually provided for otherwise.

[225] Establishing a Thai company to enter into a lease is often not the most attractive option from a tax-planning viewpoint. If company ownership of a lease is preferable, a foreign company is usually chosen; however, Land Department officials might examine the transaction purpose before accepting a long-term lease registration by a foreign company to ensure it is not being registered for the purpose of carrying out a business.

structure. Indeed, there are three reasons why a company might be chosen to own a lease instead of registering a lease in a personal name.

First, there is the issue of inheritance. As a lease is a "personal" interest in property, it terminates upon the death of the lessee[226] if the lessee is a person unless a succession clause is inserted into the lease agreement,[227] whereas a company doesn't "die".[228] Company structures are therefore used to avoid leases becoming the subject of probate procedures and having to be registered again to a new owner upon the death of a personal individual. If a lease is registered in the name of a company, shareholders can change but both company and lease continue without the need for the lease to be registered to a new owner.

The second reason has to do with privity of contract[229]. If the leasehold interest is the standard 30 + 30 + 30-year leasehold structure (an initial lease term of 30 years with two *contractual* 30 year options to renew), the second and third options to renew depend to some degree on privity of contract between the original lessor (freehold owner) and original lessee (leasehold owner). If the lease is transferred, there is no longer privity of contract between the new lessee and original lessor, i.e. the new lessee cannot automatically enforce the contractual obligations of the original lessor unless the original lessor agrees to be subject to the same terms[230]. This is usually solved with a "succession" clause that extends the terms of the lease to *heirs* and *successors*. However, despite this, some buyers are still more comfortable owning a lease through a company. In the case where the lessee is a company, shareholders (ownership) might change but the original lessee (company) remains the same, subject to the terms of the original contract.

The third reason is related to structuring ownership to facilitate re-sale, and the mitigation of tax liabilities arising on capital gains. For instance, the sale (transfer) of a lease registered in a personal name requires the lease to be registered by the new owner, together with the payment of registration fees, and the seller has a liability to personal income tax on "capital" gains; whereas, the "sale" of a lease registered, for instance, to a foreign company can be performed offshore

---

[226] A "lessee" is the owner of the lease with the right to possession and use for a specified period of time, while the freehold owner is termed the "lessor".

[227] The succession clause stipulates that the rights and obligations of the lease agreement will be transferred to the lessee's heirs; alternatively, the heirs of both lessee and lessor can be included as parties to the agreement if they have reached the age of legal maturity, whereby the lease continues between the surviving parties. Consider also the use of the right of superficies, which is legally transmissible by inheritance.

[228] They continue unless bankrupted, closed, abandoned or "struck off".

[229] The doctrine of privity of contract provides that a contract cannot confer rights or impose obligations arising under it on any person or agent except the parties to the contract.

[230] The more significant risk is generally the sale or transfer of the freehold land, whereby there is a change of lessor, not lessee.

via the sale of the company, without incurring a liability to Thai taxation (see chapter 99, "Taxes upon sale, leasehold").

Condominium Freehold

Condominium freehold (discussed in chapter 3) is a special type of freehold that foreigners can directly and legally own in Thailand.[231] As such, condominium freehold titles, like leases, can be registered directly to a personal name, or to an offshore company or Thai company.

Freehold

The most common form of freehold (see chapter 4) relates to the purchase of land.[232] With the exception condominium freehold (which is a special case), Thai law contains no provision for foreigners to own a direct interest in land.

Foreigners are therefore left with the option of *leasing* land (see above under the heading "leasehold") or, if a *freehold* interest is desired, the most common method is to establish a Thai company (whereby the company owns the land and the foreigner *controls* the company, see chapter 90).[233]

In the case where you buy a property (usually a villa) together with the freehold land on which it is built, there are two primary options: both the land and villa can be owned by a Thai company; alternatively, the freehold land can be owned through a Thai company, while the structure (villa) can be owned separately[234], either in a personal name or by an (offshore) company.

The question is: what is the best ownership structure for a particular property? Unfortunately, the answer is not straightforward: the best ownership structure is the one that is most suitable to a purchaser's individual circumstances, bearing in mind the options provided by the current (existing) ownership structure. A decision as to the optimal ownership structure should take into account the following criteria:

1. The purchaser's nationality and country of residence
2. The current ownership structure
3. Tax planning, particularly the mitigation of taxes upon sale
4. Facilitating an efficient exit strategy

---

[231] Provided the condominium property is within the "foreign quota" of units. If it is within the "Thai quota", a condominium can only be owned leasehold or through a Thai company.

[232] Foreigners can also own "structures" (usually villas) sitting on the land, which could, in some respects, be considered a form of freehold ownership.

[233] The foreigner can either own shares in the Thai company, or own an offshore company that, in turn, owns the controlling shares in the Thai company.

[234] Land title documents serve only to evidence rights to land and contain no mention of structures built on the land. Buildings are a form of immovable property that can be owned separately from the land.

The current ownership structure is discussed in the next chapter, "Who is the seller?" while tax planning and facilitating an efficient exit strategy are covered in chapters 98 - 101.

> **Important tip:** The particular ownership structure established to hold an asset is, *in effect,* an asset in its own right. Some purchasers will only buy property of a certain legal type that is held in a certain ownership structure, and will avoid property held in other structures. In this way, a particular ownership structure can deduct or add to the perceived value of a property.

It is essential to take professional tax and legal advice to ensure an ownership structure is both tax-efficient and compliant with Thai law. It is equally important that legal and tax advice is taken *prior* to acquisition so that a structure can be established to meet your objectives, rather than trying later to make the best of a structure that is already in place and which can only be changed by incurring unnecessary additional costs.

Summary

- Property ownership is ultimately defined in terms of legal concepts, which grant owners legal rights corresponding to the particular ownership type.
- Each type of legal ownership, in turn, lends itself to various choices in regard to how assets can be owned, influenced by Thai laws relating to foreign ownership.
- The basic ownership options are summarised in the chart below:

Legal ownership	Possible ownership structures
Leasehold	i) Personal name ii) Company (offshore company or Thai company)
Condominium freehold	i) Personal name ii) Company (offshore company or Thai company)
Freehold	Land only – Thai company Land and villa 　i) Land and villa in Thai company 　ii) Land in Thai company, villa in personal name 　III) Land in Thai company, villa in offshore company

96

Who is the seller?

While the majority of residential properties in western property markets are registered in the name of individuals, in Thailand's resort markets, due to the restrictions on foreign ownership, properties tend to be owned in the name of individuals, companies, or a combination of both. If the different types of legal ownership – leasehold, freehold and condominium freehold – are thrown in on top, the result is a wide array of possible ownership structures.

As will be discussed in the following chapters, the particular ownership structure of a property influences the manner in which it is transferred upon sale, together with the taxes that must be paid in relation to the transaction. For these reasons, the question "who is the seller?" of a property becomes significant. We are not speaking here about whether the seller is Mr. Jones from London or Miss. Wu from Hong Kong (although this might determine who we are negotiating with and how payment is made for the property); instead, we are speaking of the specific legal ownership structure or entity in which the property is currently being held and from which it must be transferred.

The current ownership structure employed for a property could therefore be considered the starting point for our own choice of ownership structure because the current ownership structure might present us with options that are otherwise unavailable. For instance, if the property we are interested in is currently owned by a Thai company, there is often the option of taking over the Thai company through the purchase of shares[235], rather than transferring the property at the land department, thus avoiding the scrutiny of the authorities and the taxes and fees associated with the *transfer* of real estate. Similarly, if a property is currently owned by an offshore company, the option usually exists to purchase the company offshore instead of transferring property within Thailand.

In the case of properties being owned by individuals, if the seller is a Thai person there is unlikely to be a Thai company involved, thus a transfer of the property from the Thai individual to the new owner (or entity) will be necessary. Likewise, if a foreign owner has registered a property in their personal name (for example, a lease, condominium freehold or a structure), a *transfer* of the property will also be required.

---

[235] Provided the property is the sole asset owned by the company, i.e. the company does not own multiple properties.

With regard to transaction fees, the current ownership structure and the manner of transfer influences the type of taxes that are paid and therefore the transaction costs associated with the deal[236]. For example, if a foreigner is buying *freehold* land currently owned by a Thai person, unless he or she is willing to consider a leasehold interest there is no option other than to transfer the land (to a Thai company). This entails payment of the relevant fees and taxes for land transfers. If, on the other hand, the land is registered to a Thai company, and the buyer is content to "buy" the land by taking over a Thai company, transaction costs consist only of stamp duty in connection with the sale of shares.

As is evident, the current legal ownership structure – and hence the question "who is the seller?" – is significant in that it influences the manner in which property is transferred, the type of transaction fees and taxes that are payable upon purchase, and whether there is an option to buy a property by taking over the current ownership structure. The different forms of "seller" also come with different types of risk. For instance, buying land by taking over an existing company (whether a Thai or offshore company) comes with the risk of undisclosed liabilities and, with Thai companies, the possible existence of nominee shareholders (see chapter 91).

However, when a property is currently held in a Thai company, it does not necessarily mean that a buyer *must* take over the Thai company in order to buy the property. It is also possible to transfer property assets "out of a company" and, depending on the type of asset, into your personal name or into another company (however, some sellers insist on a takeover of their company for reasons of tax liability).

In the case of buying off-plan property from a developer, property ownership structures are often unduly influenced by tax considerations favouring the developer. In other words, the lawyer engaged to set up the company structures and draft sales contracts for the developer is typically acting to minimise taxes upon sale *for the developer,* which could potentially create an undue tax burden for buyers. In addition, some lawyers set up ownership structures to guarantee future revenue in the form of company setup fees, ongoing company maintenance fees, secretarial services and accounting fees, instead of designing the most simple or suitable structure.

With regard to condominiums, if the unit is one of the 49% of the condominium that can be owned by foreigners, purchasers can normally choose between buying the unit in their own name or that of an offshore company. However, the

---

[236] Some of these are payable by the seller and some will be shared between buyer and seller, unless otherwise agreed.

51% under the Thai quota (if marketed to foreigners) can only be purchased leasehold (in a personal name or through a company) or freehold through a Thai company. When looking at condominiums, it is therefore important to check the availability of properties under the foreign quota to make sure you are getting the desired legal title and security of ownership.

Paying attention to a property's current ownership structure is therefore an important element of the viewing process. If you have a preference for a particular ownership type, it also helps in the short-listing of properties.

Summary

- The particular ownership structure of a property influences the manner in which it is transferred upon sale.
- With regard to transaction fees, the current ownership structure and the manner of transfer influences the type of taxes that are payable upon purchase and therefore the transaction costs associated with the deal.
- The question "who is the seller?" is therefore significant, i.e. what is the specific legal ownership structure in which the property is currently being held.
- The current ownership structure might present the option of buying a property by taking over an existing company.

97
Transaction costs on purchase
(Essential)

In addition to legal fees, property buyers need to be aware of the transaction costs involved in buying and transferring a property. Transaction costs in Thailand can be significant (in some cases as much as 6% of a property's price) so they must also be budgeted for.

> **Important note:** This chapter is concerned with transaction costs upon the *transfer* of property, i.e. the transfer of a leasehold or freehold interest from one owner to another, or the sale of a property "out of a company". In other words, if a property is purchased by taking over a company (whether a Thai company or an offshore company) this is a sale of shares and *not the transfer of property;* you are buying a company not a property and for this reason, the transaction is not a transaction that involves the land office or the fees and taxes associated with real estate transfers.

This is indeed one of the main advantages of holding a property in a company structure (see chapter 102, "Corporate structure or personal name?"). In such circumstances, unless property assets are transferred "out of the company", transactions costs are often limited to stamp duty payable on the sale of shares,[237] which in the context of a multi-million Baht transaction is negligible.

Therefore, with regard to *transfers of property,* various taxes and fees are payable, depending whether legal ownership is leasehold or freehold.

Leasehold

If you are buying a long-term lease, it is necessary to pay stamp duty and a lease registration fee. A lease of land or buildings is subject to stamp duty under the Revenue Code at the rate of one Baht for every 1,000 Baht of rent for the entire lease period; in other words, stamp duty is 0.1% of the lease value. The lease registration fee is 1% of the rent for the entire lease period, which is payable upon registration of the lease at the Land Department. Transaction costs for a lease of property are therefore 1.1%.[238]

---

[237] Personal income tax might also be applicable on gains. Or if assets are transferred "out of the company", Corporate Income Tax (CIT) might be payable on gains (see chapters 93 - 94).

[238] Leases of land or buildings do not attract VAT. However, VAT might come into play if the lease covers fixtures and fittings.

As an example, if the lease value or "rent" is 6 million Baht (US$ 200,000), transaction costs will be 66,000 Baht (US$ 2,200):

$$6,000,000 \times 1.1\% = 66,000$$

Who is liable under the law for these fees? Technically, the lessor (owner of the freehold) is liable for the stamp duty, whereas the registration fee should be borne equally between buyer and seller (although the parties can contractually agree to apportion fees in another manner).

Here is a summary for leasehold transfers:

Tax or fee	Rate	Who is liable?
Stamp duty	0.1%	Lessor
Registration fee	1%	Shared equally between lessor and lessee

Freehold

If you are buying freehold property (such as land, or property with condominium freehold title), there are several taxes to consider: transfer registration fees (government fee), withholding tax, and either stamp duty or specific business tax (SBT).

The transfer registration fee is currently 2% of the Land Office *appraised value*[239] of the property. This is a government fee for the registration of the transfer. Note that the Land Office appraised value or "official appraised" value is the Land Office's own assessment of a property's value, which is often much lower than the actual purchase price or market value of the property.[240]

Withholding tax is charged at the rate of 1% of the Land Office appraised value or the actual transaction value of the property, whichever is higher, *if the seller is a company.*[241]

---

[239] In Thailand, three values are commonly referred to: *appraised* or *assessed* value, which is the value of a property as determined by the Land Department; *registered* or *declared* value is the transaction price that is actually declared by the parties; and *market* value, which is the true "value" of the property determined by market forces.

[240] The actual contract value, sale price or market value is not relevant.

[241] If the seller is an individual, the withholding tax payable is calculated using a complex formula based on the assessed value of the property, the length of time owned and the applicable (progressive) personal tax rate.

Stamp duty is charged at the rate of 0.5% of the Land Office appraised value or the actual transaction value of the property, whichever is higher. Stamp duty is only due if SBT is not payable (see below).

Specific business tax (SBT) is charged at the rate of 3.3% of the Land Office appraised value or the actual transaction value of the property, whichever is higher[242]. However, SBT is only payable if the property has been transferred within the last five years; in other words, if the property has been held for more than five years, it is not considered to be sold in a commercial manner and SBT is not payable. Therefore, if the property has been transferred within five years, SBT is payable, not stamp duty. If the property has not been transferred for five years, stamp duty is payable instead of SBT.

For example, suppose a condominium is being purchased, which has been owned by the previous individual for 2 years, the purchase price is 12 million Baht (US$ 400,000) and the Land Department has *appraised* or *assessed* the value at 8 million Baht (US$ 265,000). Transaction costs (excluding personal or withholding taxes, see chapter 94) are as follows:

2% transfer registration fee based on the "appraised value":
2% x 8,000,000 = 160,000

3.3% specific business tax based on the purchase price:
3.3% x 12,000,000 = 396,000

Stamp duty (not applicable)

TOTAL = 556,000

Who is liable for the payment of these fees? By law, the transfer registration fee should be shared equally between buyer and seller, while the seller is liable to pay withholding tax and stamp duty or specific business tax.

Important tip: While under law the seller is liable to pay withholding tax and stamp duty or specific business tax for freehold transactions (or stamp duty for leasehold), there are numerous instances where sales contracts shift the seller's share of taxes and fees to the buyer (in addition to the agreed purchase price). Alternatively, contracts specify that *all* fees will be shared equally between buyer and seller. An awareness of the law should help buyers to negotiate these fees to reduce acquisition costs.

---

[242] Parties might be tempted to under declare the actual sales price at the Land Office to reduce taxes, although if there is a later tax audit that discovers the actual sales price is higher, the Revenue Department has the power to collect the tax shortfall plus penalties and surcharges.

Here is a summary for freehold transfers:

Tax or fee	Rate	Who is liable?
Transfer registration fee	2%	Shared equally between buyer and seller
Withholding tax	1%	Seller
Stamp duty; or	0.5%	Seller
Specific business tax	3.3%	Seller

At first glance, transfer fees and taxes appear to add up to more than 6% of the value of the property[243]. However, the burden is generally lower in practice because some fees are not based on the actual transaction value but on *Land Office appraised values,* which tend to be lower.

---

[243] To stimulate the property market, the Thai government significantly cut property transaction taxes in 2008. Transfer registration fees were cut from 2% to 0.01% and SBT was cut from 3.3% to 0.11% - an effective 5% reduction in transaction costs. These special rates ended in March 2010 and taxes are currently back to normal levels.

98
Minimizing taxes upon sale

Before proceeding, it should be noted that Thai tax law is a complex area and relevant laws and provisions are prone to change. It is therefore essential to seek professional tax and legal advice in relation to any property investment to ensure the advice you receive and the decisions you make are based on current, up-to-date information. In addition, the optimal ownership structure for buying and holding a property depends upon an investor's individual circumstances; therefore, what follows should be treated only as a simplified introduction or general summary and does not constitute advice.

While the previous chapters discussed possible ownership structures for the different types of legal title, and transaction costs *upon purchase,* this chapter focuses on structuring ownership of property for *sale.* In particular, how can property ownership be structured to minimise taxes on gains upon exit?

It is crucial to understand that the various different ownership structures have significantly different tax consequences upon the re-sale of a property. In other words, some ownership structures are more "tax efficient" than others upon exit *and without proper advice you could find yourself giving up a significant part of any capital gain in taxes.* Most purchasers fail to realise the importance of professional tax advice in relation to property investments. If they seek tax advise at all, they usually do so once a purchaser has expressed an interest to purchase or just prior to sale. However, at this stage it is too late to structure ownership to reap maximum tax saving benefits.

Important tip: The ownership structure that best fits your objectives and individual circumstances must be determined at the *acquisition stage,* not when you are thinking of selling. Tax planning to maximise capital gains (and minimise taxes) upon exit therefore requires professional tax advice to be taken during the initial stages of your property search.

One of the guiding principles behind tax planning is that everyone has the right to organise their business and personal affairs so as not to pay more tax than the law requires. In relation to Thai property, this means you are able to structure property ownership in compliance with the law to minimise (mitigate) taxes[244]. While Thailand doesn't technically have "capital gains" tax, capital gains are certainly taxed, just like any other form of investment income, albeit through personal or corporate income taxes. For this reason, the manner in which a property is held (ownership structure) and the manner in which it is sold (transferred) affects whether or not you pay tax in Thailand on a capital gain and the amount of tax due.

When structuring ownership for re-sale, we are speaking of making an optimal decision based on the interplay between legal ownership (leasehold, freehold, condominium freehold) and ownership structure (personal name, Thai company, offshore company) bearing in mind the tax consequences upon sale for each possible combination. The question of minimising taxes is therefore about understanding the taxes payable upon sale for each ownership structure and method of transfer, then selecting the optimal ownership structure for buying and holding your property.

The following three chapters discuss various possible ownership options for leasehold, condominium freehold and freehold property and summarise the respective tax consequences for each upon sale.

Important note: When speaking about property ownership through a company (Thai company or offshore company) and the transfer of property ownership through the sale of a company (by way of share transfer), it is assumed (unless otherwise stated) that the principle "one-asset-one-company" applies. In other words, the company does not own more than one property and selling the company therefore transfers ownership of a single property asset.

When a company is involved in property ownership, there are usually two options upon sale: either selling the company (by way of share transfer) or selling the property asset "out of the company". In the case where a property is sold out of a company, it should be noted that the company originally owning the property remains in existence and the previous "owner" remains a shareholder of the company.[245]

---

[244] As opposed to *evading* taxes, which is the avoidance of taxes by illegal means.
[245] This entails ongoing company administration costs or fees involved in the dissolution of the company, which are in the region of 30,000 Baht (US$ 1,000).

Summary

- One of the guiding principles behind tax planning is that everyone has the right to organise their business and personal affairs so as not to pay more tax than the law requires.
- While Thailand doesn't technically have "capital gains" tax, capital gains are certainly taxed, just like any other form of investment income, either through personal or corporate income taxes.
- Structuring ownership of property for *sale* means structuring ownership of property to minimise taxes on gains upon exit.
- It is crucial to understand that different ownership structures have significantly different tax consequences upon the re-sale of a property, and some ownership structures are more "tax efficient" than others upon exit.

99
Taxes upon sale (leasehold)

As there are no restrictions on the foreign ownership of a lease, it is possible for foreigners to buy leasehold interests in property and register the lease directly in a personal name, or in the name of a Thai or foreign company.

The transfer procedure and tax consequences upon sale for each of the three primary forms of leasehold ownership – personal name, Thai company and foreign company – are discussed below.

Personal name

If you are selling a lease that is registered in your personal name, upon sale the lease must be transferred ("assigned") and registered in the name of the new owner. This means the taxes discussed in chapter 97 will apply, i.e. 0.1% stamp duty and 1% registration fee.

In addition to these transaction fees, and because the lease was owned personally (registered in a personal name), any "capital" gain on the sale of the lease is subject to *personal* income tax at the marginal tax rates ranging from 10% - 37% (see chapter 94), depending on net taxable income. It is the responsibility of the seller to file a personal income tax return based on the declared purchase price.

Thai company

If you have chosen to purchase and hold a lease through of a Thai company, there are two options when it comes to "selling" the lease: either selling the company or transferring the lease "out of the company".

If the change of ownership is performed by the sale of a Thai company, the transaction is conducted by share transfer, i.e. via the transfer of the controlling shares in the Thai company to the new owner. In this case, transaction fees are limited to payment of 0.1% stamp duty on the paid up shares. However, as the seller of the shares, you are subject to *personal* income tax on any gain at the marginal tax rates ranging from 10% - 37% (see chapter 94).

If a purchaser is not willing to take ownership of the lease through the purchase of a Thai company, then it is necessary to transfer the lease "out of the company". In other words, the lease is "sold" by the company to the new owner and registered in the name of the new owner (or to an entity chosen by the new owner, such as another Thai company or an off-shore company).

In cases where a lease is transferred "out of a company", the transaction fees applicable to the *transfer* of a lease will apply, i.e. 0.1% stamp duty and 1% registration fee. Since the selling entity is a Thai company, any gain will be subject to *corporate* income tax at the rate of 15 – 30% (see chapter 93).

Foreign company

In the case where a foreign (offshore) company is the vehicle used for the original purchase of the lease, there are again two options upon sale: either selling the company, or transferring the lease "out of the company" to the new owner.

Selling a foreign company is performed by share transfer, i.e. through selling the shares of the foreign company. In such cases, no taxable event in Thailand takes place (although there might be taxes to pay in the other jurisdiction or in the seller's home country). In other words, selling shares in a foreign company has nothing to do with the Thai taxation system and this is precisely the reason (or one of the primary reasons) why foreign companies are used as vehicles for property ownership in Thailand.[246]

In the alternative case, where the lease is transferred out of the foreign company, this becomes a *transfer* of the lease, whereby the transaction fees are 0.1% stamp duty and 1% registration fee. In addition, the foreign company is subject to 15% withholding tax.[247]

The chart on the following page summarizes the transaction fees and taxes in relation to the sale of leasehold property interests.

---

[246] Either directly, as in the case where property is registered in the name of the foreign company, or indirectly, where the foreign company owns the controlling interest of a Thai company.

[247] While Thai companies are subject to Corporate Income Tax (CIT) on their worldwide income, foreign companies carrying on business in Thailand are subject to CIT only on net profits arising from their business activities in Thailand.

Legal type	Ownership	Form of transfer	Transaction costs / fees	Taxes on gains upon sale or transfer
	Personal name	Assign lease	0.1% Stamp duty 1% Lease registration fee	10 - 37% Personal income tax
	Thai company	Sell company (share transfer)	0.1% Stamp duty	10 - 37% Personal income tax
		Transfer lease out of company	0.1% Stamp duty 1% Lease registration fee	15 - 30% Corporate income tax
Leasehold	Foreign company	Sell company (share transfer)		No taxable event in Thailand
		Transfer lease out of company	0.1% Stamp duty 1% Lease registration fee	15% Withholding tax

100
Taxes upon sale (condominium freehold)

As already mentioned, "condominium freehold" is a special type of legal ownership that foreigners can own outright. In a similar manner to leasehold property, therefore, it is possible for foreigners to buy condominium freehold property and register the title in their personal name, or to a Thai company or foreign company. This chapter discusses the transfer procedure and tax consequences for each of these types of ownership (for a more detailed explanation of the transaction fees in relation to the sale of freehold property, refer to chapter 97).

Personal name

If ownership of a condominium freehold property is registered to a personal name, ownership must be *transferred* upon sale. This entails a 2% transfer registration fee and either 3.3% Specific Business Tax (SBT) *or* 0.5% stamp duty, depending whether the property has been transferred within the last five years.[248]

In addition, by reference to the *official appraised price* of the condominium, a withholding tax of 10 - 37% is payable at the Land Office at the time of transfer, based on the sliding scale of *personal* income tax (see chapter 94).

Thai company

If the chosen ownership structure for a condominium freehold title was a Thai company, it is possible to transfer ownership of the property either by selling the controlling shares of the Thai company (share transfer), or by transferring (selling) the property asset "out of the company".

If a buyer is willing to "purchase" the property by purchasing the (controlling) shares of the Thai company, transactions costs are limited to 0.1% stamp duty payable on the sale of shares, although the seller has a *personal* income tax liability of between 10 - 37% on gains (see chapter 94). Depending on the circumstances, this often translates into a substantial tax saving on exit through the avoidance of transfer taxes, registration fees and corporate income tax on capital gains that would arise if the *property* were transferred "out of the company".

---

[248] If the property has been transferred within five years, SBT is payable, not stamp duty. If the property has not been transferred for five years, stamp duty is payable instead of SBT.

In the case where a purchaser is unwilling to assume property ownership through a Thai company, the condominium freehold title must be transferred "out of the company". A transfer of freehold property attracts a 2% transfer registration fee, 1% withholding tax (as the seller is a company), and 3.3% Specific Business Tax. In addition, the Thai company (of which the seller remains a shareholder) is liable to 15 - 30% *corporate* income tax on any "capital" gain.

Foreign company

In the case where a foreign company is the registered owner of a freehold condominium property, the same two options are available: selling the company by way of share transfer, or transferring the freehold property asset "out of the company" to the new owner or entity.

As mentioned previously, selling the shares of a foreign company is not a taxable event in Thailand, although the foreign shareholder needs to consider the tax consequences in the other jurisdiction or his or her home country.

In the case where the condominium freehold title is transferred out of the foreign company, this becomes a transfer of property where freehold transfer fees and taxes are applicable; i.e. 2% transfer registration fee, 1% withholding tax and 3.3% Specific Business Tax. The foreign company is also subject to 15% withholding tax.

The chart on the following page summarizes the transaction fees and taxes in relation to the sale of condominium freehold property.

Legal type	Ownership	Form of transfer	Transaction costs / fees	Taxes on gains upon sale or transfer
Condominium Freehold	Personal name	Transfer freehold	2% Transfer registration fee 3.3% Specific Business Tax or 0.5% Stamp duty	Withholding tax of 10 - 37% based on sliding scale of personal income tax
	Thai company	Sell company (share transfer)	0.1% Stamp duty	10 - 37% Personal income tax
		Transfer freehold out of company	2% Transfer registration fee 1% Withholding tax 3.3% Specific Business Tax	15 - 30% Corporate income tax
	Foreign company	Sell company (share transfer)		No taxable event in Thailand
		Transfer freehold out of company	2% Transfer registration fee 1% Withholding tax 3.3% Specific Business Tax	15% Withholding tax

101
Taxes upon sale (freehold)

With the exception of "condominium freehold", discussed in the previous chapter, the most common forms of freehold relate to land or structures built on land (usually villas). Since land and structures are treated differently by Thai law with regard to foreign ownership, each will be discussed separately.

Land

As outlined in chapter 2, Thai law contains no provision for foreign individuals or foreign-owned companies to own a *direct* interest in land (in other words, foreigners cannot own land in Thailand). This means that the only way for foreigners to participate in *freehold* land ownership is through a Thai company.[249]

Thai company

When land is owned by a Thai company, there are two ways for "ownership" of the land to be passed to a new owner: either to sell the company (share transfer) or transfer the land "out of the company".

Once again, if a purchaser is willing to "purchase" land by purchasing the shares of a Thai company, the transaction is a sale of shares, not a sale of property, and transactions costs are therefore limited to 0.1% stamp duty payable on the share sale, although the seller has a *personal* income tax liability of between 10 - 37% on gains.

In the case where land is transferred "out of the company", this constitutes a transfer of property, and a transfer of freehold land attracts a 2% transfer registration fee, 1% withholding tax (as the seller is a company), and 3.3% Specific Business Tax. In addition, the Thai company (of which the seller remains a shareholder) is liable to 15 - 30% *corporate* income tax on any "capital" gain.

Structure or building

Structures or buildings are different to land in that they can be owned directly by foreigners. Therefore, ownership of a structure or building can be registered in a personal name, or to a Thai company or a foreign company.[250]

---

[249] If a leasehold interest in land is taken, refer to chapter 99, "Taxes upon sale, (leasehold)."

[250] When transferring ownership of a building separately from the ownership of land, the transaction

Personal name

If an individual is the current owner of a building or structure, the only option upon sale is to transfer ownership of the building, i.e. a *transfer* of freehold property, which means a 2% transfer registration fee and *either* 3.3% Specific Business Tax (SBT) *or* 0.5% stamp duty, depending whether the property has been transferred within the last five years[251].

In addition, a withholding tax of 10 - 37% is payable at the Land Office at the time of transfer, based on the sliding scale of *personal* income tax (see chapter 94).

Thai company

If the chosen entity for ownership of a building is a Thai company, it is possible for the building to pass to the new owner either by selling the (controlling) shares of the Thai company (share transfer), or by transferring (selling) the building "out of the company" to the new owner.

If the purchaser is willing to take ownership by purchasing the shares of a Thai company, transaction costs are 0.1% stamp duty payable on the sale of shares, although the seller has a *personal* income tax liability of between 10 - 37% on gains.

Where a purchaser is unwilling to assume ownership of a structure or building through a Thai company, the structure or building must be transferred "out of the company", attracting the standard fees and taxes associated with the transfer of freehold property: 2% transfer registration fee, 1% withholding tax (as the seller is a company), and 3.3% Specific Business Tax. In addition, the Thai company (of which the seller remains a shareholder) is liable to 15 - 30% *corporate* income tax on any "capital" gain.

A special note should be made concerning the case where one Thai company owns both the land and building. In such cases, the land and building can be "sold" together to the new owner by way of share transfer, i.e. by transferring the (relevant) shares in the Thai company.

---

must be published at the Land Department for a 30-day period.
[251] If the property has been transferred within five years, SBT is payable, not stamp duty. If the property has not been transferred for five years, stamp duty is payable instead of SBT.

Foreign company

In the case where a foreign company is the owner of a building, the two options available are either selling the company by way of share transfer, or transferring the building "out of the company" to the new owner or entity.

Selling the shares of a foreign company is not a taxable event in Thailand, although the foreign shareholder needs to consider the tax consequences in the other jurisdiction or his or her home country.

In the case where a building is transferred out of the foreign company, this becomes a transfer of property where freehold transfer fees and taxes are applicable; in other words, 2% transfer registration fee, 1% withholding tax and 3.3% Specific Business Tax. The foreign company is additionally subject to a 15% withholding tax.

The chart on the following page summarizes the transaction fees and taxes in relation to the sale of freehold land and buildings.

Legal type	Ownership	Form of transfer	Transaction costs / fees	Taxes on gains upon sale or transfer
Freehold (land)	Thai company	Sell company (share transfer)	0.1% Stamp duty	10 - 37% Personal income tax
		Transfer freehold out of company	2% Transfer registration fee 1% Withholding tax 3.3% Specific Business Tax	15 - 30% Corporate income tax
	Personal name	Transfer structure	2% Transfer registration fee 3.3% Specific Business Tax or 0.5% Stamp duty	Withholding tax of 10 - 37% based on sliding scale of personal income tax
(Structure or building)	Thai company	Sell company (share transfer)	0.1% Stamp duty	10 - 37% Personal income tax
		Transfer structure out of company	2% Transfer registration fee 1% Withholding tax 3.3% Specific Business Tax	15 - 30% Corporate income tax
	Foreign company	Sell company (share transfer)		No taxable event in Thailand
		Transfer structure out of company	2% Transfer registration fee 1% Withholding tax 3.3% Specific Business Tax	15% withholding tax

102
Corporate structure or personal name?

There are many considerations to take into account before the most suitable property ownership structure can be determined. However, at the heart of the matter is usually the decision between holding an asset in a corporate (company) structure or a personal name.

Corporate structures play a central role in the legal and tax planning for Thai real estate and the choice between holding an asset in a personal name or a corporate structure is therefore a key decision to make when planning a tax-efficient ownership structure. This chapter discusses some of the advantages and disadvantages of using a corporate structure, and then considers various other issues relevant to the structuring of ownership for eventual exit.

Advantages

The principle advantage of a company structure is that (in certain circumstances) it allows you to take freehold property ownership where otherwise only leasehold is available. The prime example is using a Thai company (which enjoys the same legal rights as a Thai citizen) to own freehold land, where otherwise only a leasehold interest would be possible when purchasing as a foreign individual or foreign company. The fact is, no matter how well a lease agreement is drafted, it is still a lease (of limited duration with only *contractual* options to renew) as opposed to freehold ownership[252]. As a foreigner, being a shareholder of a Thai company is the *only* way to "own" freehold land. As discussed in chapter 2, while this arrangement might not be consistent with the *spirit* of the law, as long as the company is set up in compliance with the law it is legal.[253]

Another advantage of using a company to own property is that it provides the potential exit strategy of selling the company rather than selling the property[254]. This has two main benefits: first, transferring ownership can be performed by share transfer, thus avoiding the scrutiny of the land department; second, since the transaction is a sale of shares, not a sale of property, transaction fees are related to the share transfer (i.e. stamp duty) and the transaction does not attract

---

[252] Leasehold is a poor alternative to freehold due to the maximum leasehold period of 30 years in Thailand and the problems associated with lease renewals and succession.

[253] Unless the law is changed or clarified to make it *illegal*. See also chapter 91 on "Nominee shareholders".

[254] In other words, selling *movable* property instead of *immovable* property.

taxes and fees related to the transfer of real estate; thirdly, and consequently, using a corporate structure lends itself to a cleaner and quicker exit strategy.

Owning a property through a company also allows the flexibility of selling assets "out of the company" in cases where a purchaser is not willing to take over the existing corporate structure. In other words, it provides the option to sell the company *or* the asset (although transaction fees and taxes will correspond to the type of transaction).

Another advantage of using a company to own an asset is that a company provides a greater degree of protection from liability than when an asset is owned in a personal name (the liability of a company is technically limited, while for an individual it is technically unlimited); dividing a company's capital into shares and keeping personal funds separate from company funds is a means of protection from private liability and bankruptcy. For owners of rental properties, a company also presents a more professional image to tenants who often feel safer transacting with a company than with an individual.

Using a corporate structure for owning assets that could be held personally is also useful when making *off-plan* investments. For example, in the case where a leasehold property interest is purchased from a developer at the pre-construction stage, and the purchaser plans to on-sell the leasehold interest prior to completion of the property (see chapter 80 on "flipping"), the sale often requires the consent of the developer (and usually a payment). In the case where the contracts are entered into in a personal name, it is almost certain that some form of consent will be required. However, if contracts are signed in the name of a company (and you have full control over the company), it is often possible to transfer the rights (to the leasehold interest) without such consent, since it involves a transfer of shares in the company rather than a change of lessee.

Using a corporate structure also allows the employment of two-tier ownership structures. An example of a two-tier system is where an offshore company (such as a Hong Kong or BVI company) owns the controlling or "preference" shares of a Thai company, which in turn owns the property. Depending on the circumstances, this can prove to be a tax-efficient structure upon eventual sale. It also allows a property asset, such as freehold land, to be owned by a Thai company but "sold" through the sale of the offshore company, without any tax consequences in Thailand[255]. However, due to the costs involved in setting up and administering two companies, this is generally only cost-efficient for high-end real estate.

---

[255] So long as the funds are not paid from Thailand or into Thailand.

Corporate structures could also prove to be beneficial in relation to probate. If a real estate asset is owned personally, death of the owner requires the asset to enter the probate process and for ownership of the asset to be transferred. In the case of a lease, in the event of the lessee's death *in principle* the contract ends. However, if a company owns property, companies don't die; instead, upon the death of a shareholder the company remains the owner of the asset; ownership of the shares will change, but there is no actual transfer of property. Further, in the case of an offshore company, it is possible to will the offshore company's shares, whereby there is no need to probate the estate in a Thai court. When a shareholder dies, however, there is often inheritance tax to pay on the value of the shareholder's share of a company's assets, even if there is no change of ownership of the company's underlying assets. In such cases, corporate structures can also be used as the basis for a trust structure or foundation, which are used by the wealthy as tax shelters or for multi-generational tax planning.

In sum, depending how ownership is structured, and depending on the value placed on the different types of property ownership by potential purchasers, corporate structures can be a selling point and an asset in their own right.

Disadvantages

One possible disadvantage of a corporate structure is the additional cost of setting up a company. Company set up costs differ from law firm to law firm and according to jurisdiction; for instance, there is a difference in cost between setting up a Thai company and setting up (and administering) an offshore company, such as a British Virgin Islands (BVI), Seychelles or Hong Kong company. There are also ongoing administration and auditing costs to consider, which in the case of Thai companies are increasing due to the requirement to comply with ever-changing laws, rules and regulations.

When property assets can be registered in a personal name, company setup costs can be avoided; however, setup costs and running costs should be evaluated in relation to the advantages that companies provide, such as facilitating an efficient exit strategy by enabling the "sale" of a property through the sale of shares, or avoiding the transaction costs involved with the transfer of property. Company setup costs must also be considered in relation to both the value of the property and complexity of the investment. From a purely financial point of view, there is no point setting up a company if the costs exceed the potential tax-savings. To be viable, tax savings need to be sufficient to warrant incurring the upfront costs of setting up a company. For this reason, corporate structures and especially trust structures, are more commonly used by wealthy owners of high-end luxury properties.

Another perceived disadvantage is the issue of nominee shareholders (discussed in chapter 91) and the creative company structures that are necessary to comply with Thai law. In cases where companies are *legally* compliant, yet at the same time are contrary to the *spirit* of Thai law – such as when they are used by foreigners to buy freehold land – the arrangements depend on the ongoing complicity of the Thai authorities. In other words, such practices are perfectly within the law until they are unequivocally made illegal!

Perhaps the greatest potential disadvantage of using a company to own property in Thailand is the hope that, upon sale, a purchaser will take over the existing corporate structure. If they don't, the property must be "transferred out" of the company, which often defeats the purpose of setting up the company in the first place. The fact is, most legal advisors worth their fees usually advise clients *against* the takeover of an existing company (for the purpose of buying property) because of the risk of undisclosed liabilities and potential tax exposure[256] the buyer assumes. It is impossible, even for the most thorough due diligence, to discover all potential liabilities, particularly off balance sheet liabilities. The best that can be done is to include a detailed indemnity clause in the sales contract[257] or for the purchase price to be sufficiently reduced to insure against potential liabilities. However, with the cost of setting up a new company, together with the increased scrutiny of Thai companies with foreign shareholders, the takeover of existing Thai companies has become accepted practice, often born of necessity; in other words, after weighing the potential risks, a takeover appears the lesser of two evils.

When buying a property through the take over of a Thai company, there is also the issue of the recorded value of the property in the company's accounts. If a company is taken over, the value of the property is still recorded in the books at the property's original cost price and not the purchase price paid by the new owner[258]. Consequently, when the new owner comes to sell the property in the future, it is likely that he or she will also prefer to sell the company rather than the property because selling the property "out of the company" means not only the payment of property transfer taxes but also a taxable gain equal to the real gain made by the new owner *plus the gain made by the previous owner.* In the case where a property is held over time and its value has increased dramatically, the tax on unrealised gains can become considerable for each subsequent buyer.

---

[256] Simply checking that tax returns have been filed can give a misleading level of comfort. If companies submit their accounts based on a self-determination of tax liability, and then the company is audited by tax authorities in future and found to have underpaid its taxes, penalties can be severe.

[257] Although this is of little use if the seller has absconded or has become insolvent.

[258] It is possible to record a revaluation of the property in the accounts, although this has no effect on the cost base for tax purposes.

This is not a problem if the sale of the property continues to be concluded through a sale of the company; however, like a game of musical chairs, when the music stops it becomes a problem if and when the property needs to be transferred "out of the company". A properly advised buyer might request a discount on the purchase price to cover the potential tax liability.

Marketability

If the objective of using a company for property ownership is to assist a clean and efficient exit upon sale, the key consideration is that of *marketability*. In other words, a decision as to the optimum ownership structure should be taken in relation to what is most "attractive" to potential purchasers. Attractive in this sense means a structure that a purchaser is *willing* to take over to purchase a property. If the ownership structure is such that a purchaser is unwilling to purchase a company's shares in order to purchase a property, it cannot be considered "efficient", since the alternative requires a transfer of the property out of the company.

Choosing an attractive ownership structure therefore requires an understanding of the marketplace; it requires putting yourself in the shoes of potential buyers, recognising their preferences and putting the property into a structure that will appeal to (the majority of) potential buyers. For instance, while European property buyers are receptive to leasehold ownership, Russian buyers usually prefer freehold ownership, which often means taking over a Thai company to own freehold land is more attractive than purchasing leasehold (or registering a property in a personal name). On the other hand, there are always cautious buyers that will never take over an existing company under any circumstances.

It should be noted that companies set up in different jurisdictions have different characteristics and not all companies are perceived equally. Thai companies are used because they are the perennially "accepted" mode of ownership and Thailand is the jurisdiction of the property (notwithstanding concerns related to foreign shareholders and Thai nominees). Both Thai companies and Hong Kong companies, due to their annual reporting requirements, have a higher perceived degree of transparency than, for instance, a BVI company. One of the attractions of a BVI company is the relaxed reporting requirements[259]. However, this directly conflicts with the professional responsibility of any lawyer conducting due diligence on behalf of a client to investigate a company's accounts and financial history. Therefore, while the sale of a property can be quickly and easily conducted offshore through the sale of a BVI company (with no tax implications

---

[259] For instance, there is no accounting, organizational or shareholder meeting requirements.

in Thailand), buyers are more hesitant to purchase BVI companies because of the lack of transparency and non-compulsory reporting (for this reason, owners of BVI companies might wish to voluntarily file accounts).

Therefore, while structuring ownership to assist an efficient sale often points towards the use of a corporate structure, it is also necessary to ensure the company is the type of company a purchaser is comfortable taking over, i.e. a company with transparent accounting in a desirable jurisdiction.

Another aspect of facilitating an efficient exit strategy is being prepared for a sale. There are ways of holding ownership that lend themselves to a quick and easy transfer, and others that do not. For example, one foreign property owner who was trying to sell his villa had, for reasons of "convenience", registered the freehold land in the name of the Thai wife of his builder (who was frequently travelling to other provinces), while the villa (structure) was in the name of his sister who lives in Australia. In the absence of any power of attorney (that would allow a lawyer or agent to sign documents on behalf of either of the "sellers"), endless delays ensued as documents were couriered back and forth to be signed.

I recall another example where one buyer bought a villa from a friend by signing a "memorandum of understanding" and paying cash, but without actually transferring the *legal title* of the property (his idea was quickly re-sell the property and to register the property directly into the name of the new buyer). The property was put up for sale and a buyer was found almost immediately. However, significant delays ensued while contracts were drafted and re-drafted by the law firms involved, due to the fact that the seller did not have legal title to the property and was technically only a "beneficial" owner. After several months, the new buyer lost patience and pulled out of the deal.

The simple lesson is this: if you are selling a property, make sure the ownership structure allows for a simple, straightforward transfer and that, whatever the ownership structure, all documents are in a state of readiness, including any necessary power of attorney. If the property is owned by a company, this includes making sure the company's bookkeeping and tax returns are up-to-date.

Double Taxation Agreements

Another factor that buyers should be aware of is Double Taxation Agreements (DTA). A DTA is an agreement signed between two countries for the purpose of avoiding double taxation of their residents. Thailand has a comprehensive record of DTAs with more than fifty countries, which work by allowing one country only to tax income.[260] However, the terms of each DTA varies from country to country and therefore need to be checked on a case-by-case basis according to the seller's country of residence.

DTAs are interesting not only because of their possible effect on Thai taxes, but also because of the investor-friendly tax rules that prevail in other countries, such as Hong Kong and the Seychelles, which, with their capital gains tax laws, make them favourable for the inclusion of companies in these jurisdictions into offshore ownership structures. While DTAs might be of less use in relation to reducing taxes on income derived from real estate, they might have a substantial effect if a deal involves leasehold property or the sale of a corporate vehicle where a gain is made through the sale of shares.

"One-asset-one-company"

When using corporate structures for property ownership, it is important to follow the principle of "one-asset-one-company", mentioned in chapter 98. If a company holds only one property, it is possible to transfer ownership of the property through the sale of the company. However, if more than one property is held in the same company, this is not possible[261] because selling a company transfers all of the company's underlying assets. Individual property assets cannot be separated by the sale of certain shares, and selling a proportion of a company's shares only transfers ownership of a proportion of the sum total of the assets owned by the company[262]. Thus, if a single company holds multiple properties, the only way to sell an individual property is to transfer it "out of the company", which attracts property transfer fees and taxes.

Allocation of the sale price

A further consideration is the "allocation" of the purchase price between the constituent parts that comprise a "property". In the case of leasehold property, for instance, the investment value might contain elements of rent and contents (furniture and fittings), while in the case of land and villas, purchase prices often need to be apportioned between land, building and contents. The manner in which the sale price is divided can have a significant impact on liability to tax upon transfer.

---

[260] DTAs generally deal only with income taxes, i.e. personal tax, corporate tax and withholding tax (not transfer fees and taxes such as registration fees, stamp duty or Specific Business Tax). In addition, DTAs generally cannot be used to reduce Thai taxes on rental income.

[261] This does not mean that land and a structure built on the land should not be held in one company because for all intents and purposes it could be considered one property.

[262] Assuming all shares are of the same class.

Tax on rental income

The question of taxation on rental income (see chapter 123) should also play a part in a determination of the optimal ownership structure. All rental income derived from a property situated in Thailand is taxable, although the rate of tax depends on whether a property is held personally or by a company (Thai or offshore). Up to a certain level of rental income, it is often beneficial when a property is purchased in a personal name, due to the "no questions asked" 30% expenses deduction against rental income and a tax-free allowance of 150,000 Baht.

In addition, some lawyers advise against owning a holiday home in a corporate structure because when the property owner – who is usually a director of the company – stays at the property, the company is deemed to be providing accommodation for its director. In practice, few "directors" consider they are staying at the company's property. In such cases, the Revenue Department has the power to assess the monetary value of these "rent free" stays as taxable personal income.[263]

Thailand's House and Land Tax is another relevant issue. For instance, if a villa or condominium is purchased in Thailand using a company (whether a Thai company or an offshore company), the owner has a potential liability to 12.5% house and land tax on the "rental value" of the property (see also chapter 123). An exemption exists for property owners that use the property as their own residence, although this exemption is not available when the property is owned by a company, even if the "owner" is a director of the company and resides at the property. Owning a property in a personal name, therefore, allows the owner in some circumstances to use the property as his or her own residence, thus avoiding House and Land Tax.

Evading taxes

Finally, no discussion about ownership structures would be complete without mentioning the issue of tax evasion[264]. Qualified tax and legal advisors can clarify the rules concerning foreign ownership, transaction fees and income taxes for anyone who wishes to pay taxes in accordance with the law. However, what *actually* happens in the reality of the marketplace can be completely different.

---

[263] The company is also required to deduct withholding tax on assessable income even though the amount was not actually paid.

[264] Tax *evasion* should be clearly distinguished from tax *avoidance*. Tax evasion is the effort not to pay taxes by *illegal* means, while tax avoidance (or tax mitigation) is the *legal* utilization of prevailing tax rules to reduce the amount of tax payable.

Numerous ways exist for taxes to be evaded, such as failing to submit personal tax returns when the onus is on the individual to *voluntarily* file an income tax return; understating the purchase price upon the sale of property[265]; or failing to declare income, particularly when being paid offshore. This is all well and good … until the Revenue Department decides to conduct an investigation, which could result in heavy penalties.

Summary

When deciding the optimal ownership structure for holding Thai property, the following factors should be included:

- Designing an efficient and flexible exit strategy through the sale of a company instead of the transfer of property.
- Transaction costs and fees in relation to the transfer of different types of property.
- Personal or corporate income tax on gains (taking into account the particular circumstances of the owner).
- Protection from personal liability provided by a corporate structure.
- Whether consent is required by a developer to "flip" off-plan property.
- Two-tier structures, trust structures and foundations.
- Inheritance and probate.
- Set-up costs and ongoing administration costs for a company.
- Marketability or "attractiveness" to potential purchasers.
- Double Taxation Agreements (DTA).
- The principle of one-asset-one-company.
- Allocation of the purchase price between rent and contents; or land, house and contents.
- Taxes on rental income.
- Land and House Tax.

---

[265] Why would a buyer agree to an understatement of the purchase price? Sometimes the seller makes it an "informal" condition of the sales price; or in the case where buyer and seller share transaction costs, both benefit in the short-term. Where the asset is held in a company, the buyer normally plans to pass on the potential tax liability to the next buyer.

103
Inheritance

Any discussion of the legal and tax issues pertaining to Thai property would not be complete without mentioning the issue of inheritance. Property buyers tend to assume that a will executed in their home country covers their assets in other countries; however, this is not always the case. With "immovable" property in particular (i.e. land and houses, not the shares of a company that owns land or houses) the distribution of assets is often governed by the laws of the country in which the property is located.[266]

Therefore, if you own assets in Thailand, it is strongly recommended that you have a correctly executed will to cover those assets (to be valid a Thai will must be in writing, signed, dated, witnessed by at least two other people and executed within Thailand). Without a correctly authorised will, the Civil and Commercial Code (CCC) determines what happens to your assets in Thailand when you die. The Civil and Commercial Code lists the classes of statutory heir that inherit more or less according to a predetermined formula: legal spouse, descendants (children), parents, brothers and sisters of full blood, brothers and sisters of half blood, grandparents, uncles and aunts.

This clearly defined order of beneficiaries typically means that heirs in the lower classes receive nothing if heirs exist higher up in the hierarchy. It also means that if you are unmarried but living with a partner, your partner may not be entitled to anything and thus will be totally disinherited. Similarly, if you are in a second marriage and you have children from the first marriage, the children may not be entitled to anything if the entire estate passes to the new spouse.

> **Important tip:** Unless the trouble is taken to execute a valid will, it might mean property and assets are distributed according to Thai law rather than in accordance with the wishes of the deceased. In other words, only a correctly authorised will ensures assets pass to the chosen beneficiaries.

For assets in Thailand, foreign wills are acceptable in Thai courts if they have been translated and authorised at the Ministry of Foreign Affairs. However, preparing a will in Thailand is perhaps the easiest and most straightforward method (if you are drafting a will in Thailand, it should include a limited jurisdiction clause, which limits the disposal of assets to those that are related to Thailand).

---

[266] As opposed to the laws of the country where the deceased was domiciled at the time of death.

The law firm engaged for the purchase of property will usually be able to assist you with the drafting of a will[267], although it is essential that property owners seek the advise of competent professionals because inheritance is a complex area of law that requires specific wording to be used in the drafting of wills. The cost for drafting a will (relative to the property assets covered) is usually minimal. For instance, many law firms quote in the region of 10,000 Baht (US$ 330) for the preparation of a standard will.

In relation to off-plan investments, the issue of preparing a will should be addressed at the time of purchase, not upon completion. While there is no finished property at the time of purchase, it is still necessary to have a will to specify the beneficiaries who will inherit the rights created by the contractual documents. This is also the case where a lease has yet to be formally registered.

In the case where you are a director and shareholder of a Thai limited company, matters become more complicated. The control of the company shares, and thus the assets, do not automatically transfer to heirs. It is necessary for a general meeting to be called where a new director is appointed by shareholder decision, and the shares transferred at the Ministry of Commerce. This can become complicated without the director being able to sign.

If an offshore company is involved – such as where Thai property (leasehold or condominium freehold) is directly owned by an offshore company or an offshore company owns the controlling shares in a Thai company – the issue of inheritance does not arise in Thailand. The owner of the assets in Thailand remains the same (the offshore company) and the death of a shareholder of an offshore company is a matter to be addressed in the jurisdiction where the company is set up.

In addition to addressing the distribution of assets through the drafting of a will, consideration must also be given to selecting an "executor". Due to the nature of the work, simply naming a trusted friend or family member is often not the most prudent course of action: the executor of a will must travel to Thailand to liaise with lawyers and Thai officials and also has the onerous task of signing numerous official documents that are usually in the Thai language. For this reason, it is often wiser to name a law firm or an independent company as the executor.

---

[267] Although a lawyer should also be consulted in your home country to address the issue of "moveable" property.

Summary

- If you own assets in Thailand, it is strongly recommended that you have a correctly executed will to cover those assets.
- Without a correctly authorised will, the Civil and Commercial Code (CCC) determines what happens to your assets in Thailand when you die.
- For assets in Thailand, foreign wills are acceptable in Thai courts if they have been translated and authorised at the Ministry of Foreign Affairs. However, preparing a will in Thailand is perhaps the easiest and most straightforward method.
- Consideration must also be given to the choice of "executor".

STEP 7

Financial considerations

104
Paying for your property

Paying for a property in Thailand is not just a matter of handing money to a seller and getting the keys in return. Due to currency exchange controls in Thailand and requirements related to the purchase of property by foreigners, there are specific procedures for remitting money to pay for property, which depend on the type of legal ownership and the ownership structure employed to hold the property.

In addition, it should be understood that whether the correct procedures have been followed in regard to sending purchase funds influences the ability of owners to take funds out of Thailand upon re-sale.

> **Important note:** There are specific rules and requirements in relation to remitting money to pay for property in Thailand. These rules change from time to time so it is important not to send purchase money until appropriate, up-to-date legal advice has been taken. The following information should therefore be considered as a general discussion of the subject, rather than specific advice.

The purpose of this chapter is not to concern investors with the details of international money transfers; it is primarily to make investors aware that restrictions and procedures exist.

When planning the transfer of funds, it is necessary to consider the following five issues:

1. Where to transfer funds
2. The specific wording used on transfer documents
3. The currency of the transfer
4. The amount to be transferred
5. Documentation related to taking money out of Thailand

1. Where to transfer funds

The law firm handling the purchase of property on your behalf should provide detailed information concerning how the purchase price should be transferred. For example, purchase money is sometimes required to be transferred to a client account at the law firm from which the funds are transferred to the seller (or seller's lawyer) once the sale and purchase document has been signed. Alternatively, the sale and purchase contract might specify that funds are to be transferred to an escrow account or directly to the bank account of the seller (in Thailand or offshore)[268]. In cases where a Thai company has been set up to purchase property, parts of the purchase price are sometimes required to be transferred separately, in different ways, to different accounts.

2. Wording used on transfer documents

When transferring money to Thailand (for the purchase of property), an integral part of the procedure (at the time of remittance) is the specific remarks used to describe the purpose of the transfer. Due to foreign currency controls instigated by The Bank of Thailand, every Thai Baht must have a source and a reason, and Land Departments must perform due diligence in accordance with this regulation. *Generally speaking,* when transferring sums into Thailand, the stated purpose of the remittance is usually "FOR INVESTMENT IN THAILAND" or "TO PURCHASE PROPERTY IN THAILAND". When sending money to purchase condominium freehold property, it is also recommended to state the number of the unit and name of the development, for instance, "FOR THE PURCHASE OF UNIT 19 OF SEAVIEW CONDOMINIUMS".[269]

As mentioned in point 1 above, in the case of a Thai company is being used as a vehicle to own property, parts of the purchase price might need to be remitted in different ways. For instance, part of the purchase price corresponding to the foreign shareholding might need to be transferred to a lawyers client account as a "LOAN TO THE COMPANY", while part of the purchase price corresponding to the Thai shareholding might need to be sent to another account "FOR INVESTMENT IN THAILAND".[270]

The correct wording used on documents related to the transfer of money depends on the type of property and the manner in which the asset is transferred. It must therefore be dealt with on a case-by-case basis with the supervision of your lawyer.

---

[268] Caution should be exercised when funds are transferred directly to the seller's account to ensure that ownership of the asset is already transferred, or the seller has signed the documents required to irrevocably relinquish control of the asset, which allows the asset to be transferred.

[269] If sending money directly to a developer, make sure to send *from* an account that is in your own name. If you are married, your married status must be declared at the time of the purchase. If purchasing jointly with a foreign spouse and the money is not sent from a joint account, it is also recommended to state the transfer is also made on behalf of the (name of the) spouse. If you are not buying together with your spouse, the spouse must authorize the purchase of the condominium solely in your name.

[270] In addition, the part of the purchase price corresponding to the Thai shareholding must be transferred *from* an account that is not in the name of the foreign shareholder.

3. The currency of the transfer

When transferring funds to Thailand for property investment, money must usually be sent in foreign currency, which means the actual currency exchange takes place in Thailand (in other words, you should not exchange foreign currency for Thai Baht abroad and send Thai Baht). In relation to condominium freehold purchases, section 19(5) of the Condominium Act specifically requires foreigners to bring foreign currency into Thailand (or withdraw purchase money from a foreign currency deposit account or non-resident Baht account in Thailand).

In addition to being a requirement, sending foreign currency (where the currency exchange takes place in Thailand) is advantageous in that the rate of exchange in Thailand tends to be more favourable than the exchange rate you get when buying Thai Baht in another country. This is because the Baht is not a widely used or freely convertible currency in other countries; in other words, it is not a global reserve currency like the US dollar or Euro. If the US dollar is the remittance currency, the exchange to Thai Baht takes place at the receiving bank in Thailand at the "bank-buying rate". However, when Thai Baht is the currency of remittance and US dollars are exchanged to Thai Baht at the overseas bank, the rate used is an "offshore rate". If investors are not careful, it is possible to lose three or four percent of the investment through a poor exchange rate, which is a significant amount on large transactions.

In some cases, the sale and purchase contract specifies all or part of the purchase price to be paid to an offshore account in a different currency. For instance, this might occur when a property transaction involves the sale of shares in a foreign company.

4. The amount to be transferred

When purchasing condominium freehold property, the Condominium Act requires foreigners to present evidence of bringing foreign exchange into Thailand[271] to an amount not less than the purchase price of the condominium unit[272]. Indeed, in any case where foreign currency is sent to pay a Thai Baht denominated purchase price, the issue of exchange rates arises.

---

[271] Or the evidence of withdrawing money from a non-resident Baht account or withdrawing from the foreign currency deposit account in Thailand.

[272] There is no restriction on the amount of Thai Baht transferred or brought into Thailand.

A useful resource for current exchange rates are the websites of Thailand's major commercial banks, such as Bangkok Bank[273] or Siam Commercial Bank[274] where exchange rates for buying and selling Thai Baht are updated on a daily basis. If you are sending foreign currency to Thailand, the relevant rate is the "TT Bank Buying Rate", which can be used to convert a purchase price in Thai Baht to its equivalent in foreign currency.

In relation to the transfer amount, purchasers should always remember to send extra to cover bank charges, which are usually levied by both the sending bank and the receiving bank. The purchase amount usually needs to be paid to the seller net of bank charges.[275]

When the purchase price of a property is specified in Thai Baht and payment is to be made offshore *in a foreign currency at a future date,* the sales contract needs to be sufficiently detailed to cover the question of exchange rates; if the contract fails to provide sufficient detail, the buyer and seller often pick different exchange rates or end up arguing over shortfalls. If the contract does not specify the exact foreign currency amount, four points need to be covered. First, the currency of the remittance must be specified. Second, rate details must be noted, for instance, the USD bank buying, selling or mid-rate (between the buying and selling rate). Third, an independent source of exchange rate information should be specified, such as the Foreign Exchange Rate webpage at one of Thailand's commercial banks or a website dedicated to the provision of daily exchange rate information, such as www.x-rates.com. Fourth, a date must be specified for the establishment of the effective exchange rate, for instance, a fixed date in future or the prevailing rate on the date of transfer.

5. Documentation related to taking money out of Thailand

When you wish to take money out of Thailand or "repatriate funds" upon eventual re-sale of a property, it is necessary to provide documentary evidence to demonstrate funds were originally remitted into Thailand. Documents evidencing the remittance of original sums might also affect taxation of the proceeds.

When foreign currency is remitted to Thailand for the purchase of property, the primary evidential document is the "Tor Tor 3" or "Foreign Exchange Transaction Certificate" (FETC or FEC), which is issued by the receiving bank for transfers exceeding a predetermined amount. The threshold amount to qualify for an

---

[273] www.bangkokbank.com (Personal Banking > Currency Exchange > Exchange Rates)
[274] www.scb.co.th or www.scb.co.th/scb_api/index.jsp
[275] Some law firms also charge for incoming and outgoing payments.

FEC has recently been increased from US$20,000 to US$50,000.[276] Foreign Exchange Transaction Certificates contain information such as the amount transferred in foreign currency, the corresponding amount in Thai Baht, the name of the sender and the purpose of the transfer. In the case of condominium freehold units, these certificates must be shown to the Land department in order to register the condominium.

In cases where Thai Baht is the remittance currency, the bank issues a credit advice instead of an FEC, which also serves as proof of the original payment for the purpose of taking money out of Thailand. Depending on the particular ownership structure, supporting documentation might also be required. For instance, in the case where money is remitted to Thailand as a "loan to a company", supporting documentation of the loan is often necessary.

When funds are transferred, it is important to follow up to ensure the correct documents have been issued and that they are kept in a safe place.

Summary

- Due to currency exchange controls in Thailand and requirements related to the purchase of property by foreigners, there are specific procedures for remitting money to pay for property.
- The specific procedure depends on the type of legal ownership and the ownership structure employed to hold the property.
- When planning the transfer of funds, it is necessary to consider five issues:
  - Where to transfer funds
  - The specific wording used on transfer documents
  - The currency of the transfer
  - The amount to be transferred
  - Documentation related to taking money out of Thailand

---

[276] The Central Bank of Thailand announced the change on 12th October 2010.

105

Currencies and exchange rates
(Essential)

An exchange rate[277] is the number of units of one currency that are needed to buy another currency, i.e. it is what one currency is worth in terms of another. In other words, each currency has a market price or value at which it can be exchanged for another currency, which is influenced by a wide variety of factors such as interest rates, inflation, trade balances, political stability and the general state of the economy.

Due to the numerous factors impacting exchange rates at any given time, comparative movements in exchange rates are difficult to predict. Indeed, currencies and exchange rates are recently making the headlines due to increased volatility and questions about the continued viability of the world's major fiat[278] currencies, which is an issue of concern for the global financial system (and national security). While currencies should not be the overriding concern when considering international property investments, they need to be understood and taken into account because of their direct effect on the "cost" of an investment. Investors therefore need to keep a close eye on exchange rates and to manage finances with a mind toward exchange rate movements.

Changes in exchange rates have potentially the greatest impact on the purchase of property when payment is due at some point in the future, or when payments are made in stages over the course of construction, such as with off-plan property investments (mitigating exchange rate risk has already been discussed in chapter 66 in relation to off-plan property). The biggest risk is that the currency in which you hold your money weakens in relation to the Thai Baht (or the Thai Baht strengthens in relation to the currency in which your investment funds are denominated), which effectively means the property becomes more expensive.

If you already own a property in Thailand, the issue is the reverse. The property is an asset denominated in Thai Baht and the risk is therefore that the Baht might weaken in relation to the currency into which you plan to repatriate your money upon sale. The best way to demonstrate these risks is by way of example:

---

[277] Also referred to as foreign exchange rate, currency exchange rate, or rate of exchange.

[278] A fiat currency is a currency created by government decree to become legal tender; it has no intrinsic value in itself and is not backed by anything other than trust, i.e. it is not backed, for instance, by gold or silver. Today, most national currencies issued by central banks such as the USD and Euro are fiat currencies (the US dollar became a fiat currency when Nixon abandoned the gold standard in 1971).

Suppose you were on holiday in Thailand in August 2009 and signed contracts on an off-plan property priced at 10 million Thai Baht (THB). Your savings are denominated in US dollars (USD) and at the prevailing USD/THB exchange rate (see chart below)[279] one US dollar was worth 34 Thai Baht, which means that in August 2009 the "cost" of the property in USD terms was approximately US$ 294,000.

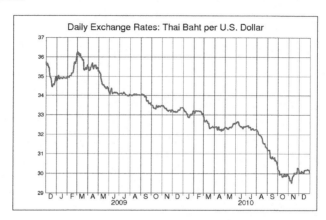

As the property is an off-plan purchase, for the purposes of illustration, suppose that completion was scheduled for October 2010 and payment was due in full upon completion. Referring to the chart, the exchange rate in October 2010 was 30 Thai Baht for each US dollar. In other words, the US dollar weakened during this period of time (relative to the Thai Baht) and in October 2010 each US dollar bought only 30 Thai Baht instead of 34. The consequence, in terms of the 10 million Thai Baht purchase price, is that by the time payment became due, the purchase price (in US dollar terms) has become US$ 333,000, which represents an increase of US$ 39,000. While the "price" of the property remained exactly the same at 10 million Thai Baht, the "cost" of the property has effectively increased by 13%, from US$ 294,000 to US$ 333,000. In other words, the purchaser must now find an extra US$ 39,000 to cover the original purchase price of the property.

Looking at the same situation from another perspective, imagine you owned a property in Thailand, which you bought in August 2009 for *10 million Baht,* spending US$ 294,000. If you sold the property in October 2010 *at the same price of 10 million Baht,* when the purchase price is converted back to US dollars you have made a *gain* of US$ 39,000 dollars[280] through the change in exchange rate without any increase in the "price" of the property.

---

[279] Source: Pacific Exchange Rate Service http://fx.sauder.ubc.ca
[280] Without taking into consideration the issue of taxes.

Over the past few years, the Thai Baht has strengthened against most major currencies; or stated more accurately, most major currencies have weakened against the Thai Baht. For instance, the chart below compares the Thai Baht with the Euro, which shows the Euro has weakened over the past three years from a high of 53 to a low of 39 Thai Baht. This is a 26% decline from the strongest point to the weakest point.

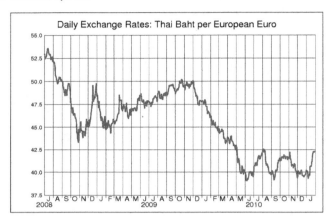

The chart below plots the exchange rate movements of the British Pound in relation to the Thai Baht and a similar pattern can be observed over the same time period, although with an even greater percentage weakness of the British Pound. At its strongest point, the British Pound bought 67 Thai Baht; while at its lowest point, it bought only 47 Thai Baht. This is a massive decline of almost 30% in the value of the British Pound when measured against the Thai currency.

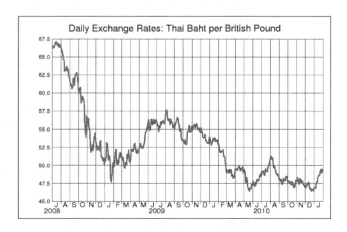

The point of this chapter is not to get into a complicated analysis of exchange rates. It is merely to demonstrate that currencies are in a constant state of change and that exchange rate fluctuations can significantly affect property investments involving currency transactions. In relation to the purchase of property in Thailand, the key is to keep an eye on the movements and trends of the Thai Baht relative to the currency you will either be using to purchase property or into which you plan to repatriate the proceeds of a sale. The bottom line is this: sometimes currencies move in your favour; other times they move against you. If you are planning to buy a property and the Thai Baht is getting weaker relative to your currency (i.e. each unit of your currency buys more units of Thai Baht), the effective cost of the property is falling. On the other hand, if the Thai Baht is getting stronger relative to your investment currency (i.e. it takes more of your currency to buy a given amount of Thai Baht), the cost of the property is effectively increasing.

If you already own a property in Thailand and the Thai Baht is getting stronger (against your home currency), the longer you hold it, all other things remaining constant, the more profit you are effectively making. Bear in mind that if the Baht has strengthened during the time you have held the property, it is often possible to sell at the same Thai Baht buying price and still make a profit when measured in the repatriation currency. Conversely, if the Thai Baht is weakening against your home currency, the longer you take to sell a property, the less you will receive in your home currency. In other words, it is possible to sell your property at the same price (or higher than the price you paid for it) and still make a currency related loss.

Due to these considerations, property investors would do well to bear in mind the following 4 points:

1. While currency exchange rate valuations should not be the prime concern when considering an investment, it is wise to keep an eye on exchange rate trends.
2. Exchange rates might influence your decision as to the timing of entry and exit of an investment; i.e. when to buy, hold and sell.
3. If you are purchasing an off-plan property with staged payments over the duration of construction, the risk of currency fluctuations must be taken into consideration and should influence the timing of the transfer of foreign currency to Thailand. The only way to completely avoid exchange rate risk is to send the purchase price in full to Thailand (exchanging foreign currency into Baht) upon the signing of contracts.
4. If you are planning to sell a property that you already own in Thailand, the asking price should be determined bearing in mind both the value of the property in Thai Baht *and* the currency into which you plan to repatriate the proceeds.

106
Using finance to increase gains?

Property purchasers have two primary motivations for using mortgages or financing when purchasing property: either because they have insufficient funds to cover the purchase price in full, or because financing allows a property to be purchased with less capital, which means financial leverage can be employed on the investment.

The purpose of this chapter is not to discuss the types of financing available in Thailand (see next chapter). Instead, it is to discuss the concept of leverage and how investors can use it to increase profit (while the discussion is geared toward investors, the principles are equally relevant to purchasers with insufficient funds). The best way to illustrate the use of financial leverage is to use examples, which compare the profit potential of a property purchased with cash and a property purchased using finance. For instance, suppose you have purchased a villa for US$ 500,000 (approximately 15 million Baht at the current exchange rate) and payment was made *in full with cash.* Lets assume that general property demand increases, which results in capital growth of 15% each year for 5 years. The following chart illustrates the gains if you sell the property after 5 years:

Cash Purchase (no financing)

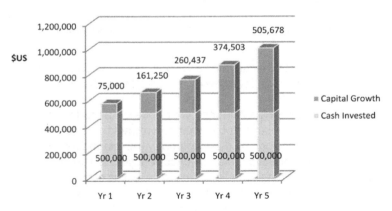

The lighter colour shows the initial cash investment of US$ 500,000, while the darker colour illustrates 15% compounded growth over five years. At the end of the first year, the property has increased in value by US$ 75,000 and is now worth US$ 575,000. After the second year the property has increased in value by $161,250 and is worth US$ 661,250, and so on.

After five years, assuming consistent 15% growth each year, the property has increased in value by US$ 505,678 and is now valued at US$ 1,005,678. If the property is then sold, this represents a (pre tax) return on investment (ROI) of 101% based on the initial cash investment of US$ 500,000. In other words, after five years, you have doubled your money.

Now lets look at the potential impact of financing. Again, suppose you have purchased a villa for US$ 500,000. However, instead of paying cash, you managed to secure financing for 65% of the value of the property[281]. This means the initial capital required is reduced to US$ 175,000, while the balance of US$ 325,000 is provided by mortgage or finance. Again, lets assume general property demand increases, which results in capital growth of 15% each year for 5 years. The following chart illustrates the gains if the property is sold after 5 years:

Purchase with 65% Financing

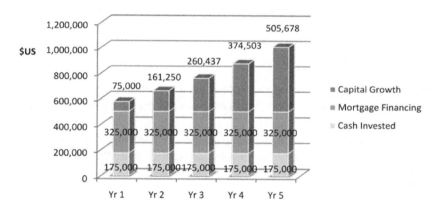

This time the lighter colour shows the initial cash investment of US$ 175,000; the medium colour shade shows the US$ 325,000 financing; and the darker colour illustrates 15% compounded growth over five years. Again, at the end of the first year, the property has increased in value by US$ 75,000 and is now worth US$ 575,000. After the second year the property has increased in value by $161,250 and is worth US$ 661,250, and so on.

After five years, assuming consistent 15% growth each year, the property has increased in value by US$ 505,678 and is now valued at US$ 1,005,678. The property is then sold and the company providing the mortgage or finance is repaid. The same gain of US$ 505,678, when compared to the lower initial

---

[281] A Loan to Value (LTV) ratio of 65%.

cash investment of US$ 175,000, now represents a return on investment (ROI) of 288% (as opposed to 101% when payment for the property was made in full with cash). In other words, after five years you have almost *trebled* your money using financial leverage (or as investors say, by using "other peoples money")[282].

As is evident, if financial leverage is used correctly, it can significantly enhance gains for investors. However, it is important to recognise that the example above that illustrates the successful use of leverage does not take into account monthly finance payments. In other words, the *cost of capital* is not taken into account or *it assumes monthly payments are covered by rental income.* This is a key point in relation to the use of financing. If you do not have sufficient funds to meet the full purchase price of a property in cash and you manage to secure some form of financing, it is crucial that you are able to meet mortgage repayments (including interest) for the duration of the loan. Indeed, many investors will not use financing unless they are certain monthly payments can be covered by rental income. Put another way, they will only buy properties that generate *positive cash flow,* i.e. properties that generate enough rental income to cover finance payments and provide additional monthly income on top (these investors define an asset as something that puts money in your pocket each month; not something that costs you money each month!).

Property investors usually seek to profit in two ways: through capital appreciation of the property and positive monthly cash flow generated by rental income.

Important note: When considering the use of financing, it is important to keep in mind the *purpose* of your investment (see chapter 8). Most foreigners that buy property in Thailand are buying properties as a source of enjoyment, not hardship. In such cases, it is important not to take on financial obligations that you might find hard to meet; when you are struggling to meet monthly finance payments your enjoyment of the property will certainly be effected!

It should also be noted that financial leverage is a double-edged sword. It works wonderfully as a tool to maximise gains when a market is booming, property prices are rising and you are able to generate consistent rental income from the property. However, in a declining market, characterised by falling prices and intermittent rental income, the use of financial leverage can exacerbate losses and monthly payments can become a burden. In other words, leverage can magnify gains and it can also magnify losses.

---

[282] Note that this example is based on a Loan to Value (LTV) ratio of 65%, i.e. the loan amount is 65% of the value of the property. If the LTV is higher, the leverage is higher, and vice versa.

Remember also that the successful utilization of financial leverage depends on managing cash flows and accurately forecasting rental income,[283] which tends to be easier in principal cities. In cities, a large proportion of property buyers and tenants are using properties as primary residences, where they live in proximity to their place of work, and where supply and demand information is more transparent and easier to measure. In contrast, accurate supply and demand figures for tropical resort destinations can be harder to obtain and the ability to generate consistent rental income is more fickle since it depends on the influx of tourists, which in turn depends on factors such as tourist destination trends, the weather, outbreaks of influenza and volcanic dust clouds!

Summary

- If financial leverage is used correctly, it can significantly enhance gains for investors.
- Many investors will not use financing unless they are certain monthly payments can be covered by rental income. Put another way, they will only buy properties that generate *positive cash flow*.
- Financial leverage is a double-edged sword: it works wonderfully as a tool to maximise gains when a market is booming; however, in a declining market, the use of financial leverage can exacerbate losses and monthly payments can become a burden.

---

[283] Unless you buy property, hold it, then sell later into a rising market, making enough profit to cover finance costs without renting out the property.

107
Mortgage financing for Thai property?

Mortgages and financing are not widely available for foreign buyers of Thai property. The purpose of this chapter is to discuss what limited offers there might be, and to provide a list of key points that should be considered in relation to any offers of financing.

Mortgages from Thai banks or financial institutions[284]

Standard mortgages in western, developed countries tend to be where a bank or financial institution provides part of the purchase price (based on a valuation) and registers a legal mortgage on the property (on the property registration system) where the property acts as collateral for the loan until it is repaid in full, with interest. In Thailand, due to the restrictions on foreign ownership, the absence of a reliable central property registration system and the lack of a transparent legal system that allows the proper enforcement of property rights, the number of banks and financial institutions willing to lend to foreigners buying Thai properties is, to put it mildly, *limited*. The notable exception tends to be in the case of condominium freehold properties where banks are more willing to lend because, being a special type of freehold property that foreigners are permitted to own outright, they satisfy the requirements for the asset to act as collateral.

However, from time-to-time a bank or financial institution will come out with a lending package designed for foreigners, which proceeds to make front page news (at least in property magazines) but, upon inspection of the small print, the offers are invariably limited in scope and generally come with prohibitively high interest rates and high set up costs. In other words, despite all the hoo-ha, the offerings are never the mortgage panacea that foreign buyers have been waiting for.

One example is the offering by United Overseas bank in Singapore, which provides financing to foreigners for freehold condominiums for up to 70% of the purchase price or valuation price (whichever is lower) at an interest rate of 5.25%[285] per annum (for a USD loan) with a processing fee of US$ 2,000. Taking

---

[284] www.bankthailand.info
[285] At the USD Prime Lending Rate (which at the time of writing is 3.25%) + 2.00% = 5.25% per annum.

a recent look at their website[286] the "UOB International Home Loan Thailand" is currently only open to citizens or permanent residents of Singapore and foreigners aged 21 and above with a minimum income of $US 65,000 per annum.

The latest offer of note is from MBK PLC through its subsidiary MBK Guarantee Ltd, which according to marketing materials (at the time of writing) is offering two types of property finance[287]. One type is "Home Loan Financing" for foreigners purchasing *"freehold condominiums in prime areas"* with an interest rate of MLR[288] plus 2% (roughly 8.375%), an LTV[289] of up to 50% of the appraised price (minimum 2 million Baht), a loan tenor of 2 - 10 years, and monthly instalments. Fees include "front-end fees" of 1.25%, a "commitment fee" of 2%,[290] a "mortgage fee" of 1%, plus an "appraisal fee" and other "out-of-pocket expenses" for property inspection, registration and fire insurance premium. The other type is for "Property Refinancing or Bridging Loans" for *"freehold or leasehold properties in Bangkok, Phuket, Hua Hin, Cha Am, Samui and Pattaya"* with an interest rate of MLR (currently 6.375%) plus a whopping 5.625% (which means an interest rate of approximately 12%!), an LTV of up to 50% of the appraised price (minimum 5 million Baht), a loan tenor of 1 - 3 years and quarterly interest payments. Fees include an upfront "processing fee" of 1.5%, a "mortgage fee" of 1%, plus an appraisal fee and fire insurance premium.

This is an example of a financial institution foraying into the market of financing for foreigners. As is evident, the interest rates and fees charged reflect the lack of competition in the marketplace for loans to foreigners. The range of properties against which the company lends is also restrictive. Whether it offers a viable long-term solution for a sufficiently wide range of properties or whether other major banks and institutions will follow suit remains to be seen.

Another company with a history of arranging mortgage loans to foreigners for Thai properties is MBMG.[291] To keep abreast of any new mortgage offers, it is also useful to pick up copies of local property magazines or to check the property-related Internet forums[292] (although details should be sought directly from the companies and not from comments posted by members).

---

[286] www.uob.com.sg

[287] Contact details: Khun Sakchai Suthipipat (sakchais@mbk-center.co.th) or Khun Natacha Preeprem (natacha@mbk-center.co.th)

[288] MLR = Minimum Lending Rate, which at the time of writing is 6.375%.

[289] LTV = Loan To Value (the amount of the loan expressed as a percentage of the property value)

[290] Charged only when the borrower signs the agreement and does not draw down the loan amount.

[291] www.mbmg-international.com

[292] For instance: www.thaivisa.com

> **Important note:** it is strongly advised not to seek private loan financing secured against an original Chanote or other land document[293]. If you are that desperate to secure financing, it is wiser to buy a less expensive property or delay purchasing until you have adequate funds.

Developer Financing

In the absence of traditional mortgages or widespread finance packages for foreign property buyers, property developers are forced to rely on their own initiative to assist buyers to purchase their properties; in other words, some are offering "developer finance".

When buying property (usually off-plan property from a developer or construction company), developer finance packages require purchasers to cover the initial staged payments up to a certain percentage of the purchase price, while the outstanding amount is either deferred into a monthly payment plan lasting several years, or a formal loan agreement is entered into with the developer (or a related company) that might spread monthly payments over as much as ten or fifteen years. An example of developer finance would be where 50% of the purchase price is paid in two or three staged payments following the signing of contracts, with the balance payable in 24 monthly instalments that start upon completion of the property.

The main advantage of developer finance is that there is no need to look around for an alternative lender. The developer is basically providing a "one-stop-shop" service. It also means you can negotiate as one package the purchase price, any extras or customisation *and* the financial arrangements. Interest rates are usually at or slightly above prevailing market rates because the developer's main objective is to make a sale of property. In addition, the developer has an added incentive to provide a good quality product because payment is not received in full upon completion and the property acts as collateral.

There are two primary disadvantages. First, since a developer provides the finance, it is typically available only for a specific development or project phase; in other words, it is not blanket market financing.[294]

---

[293] Bear in mind the maximum *legal* interest rate in Thailand is 15%.
[294] There might be more flexibility where financing is offered by a construction company.

> **Important note:** Second, and most significantly, the developer usually retains title and ownership of the property until the purchase price and interest component have been paid in full, which means security of ownership of the property depends to a large extent upon the continued financial solvency of the developer.

For this reason, obtaining financing through an independent third party financial institution might be preferable to developer finance, where security of ownership is subject to the vagaries of the developer's ongoing operations.

It should be noted that, in some cases, developer finance packages are genuine attempts to provide financial assistance to purchasers, offered by developers that are either sufficiently cash rich or that have access to the resources of financial partners, whereby financing is offered to purchasers meeting strict loan criteria. However, in other cases, the so-called "developer finance packages" offered by smaller or first-time developers are no more than a desperate ploy to sell properties, rather than genuine financial assistance. These developers do not have sufficient funds to complete the project without sales, let alone extra cash to lend to buyers, so property prices are increased to a point where the cash portion paid by the buyer covers construction costs, while the "financial assistance" is merely the acceptance of profit over a longer period of time. In such cases, purchasers should not only be aware of inflated property prices but also the contractual terms that are used to define default, which are often narrowly drafted to allow properties to be quickly re-sold if repayments are late. Thus, when evaluating off-plan property developments where financing is available, it is important to read the small print and, perhaps more importantly, to perform thorough due diligence on the developer (see chapters 67 and 89).

Foreign banks or loans

If you are unable to secure appropriate property financing within Thailand, the remaining option is to obtain financing in your home country. However, it is rare for a bank or financial institution abroad to accept a Thai property as collateral for a loan for the same reasons that Thai banks do not generally lend to foreigners: restrictions on foreign ownership, the absence of a reliable central property registration system and the lack of a transparent legal system to properly enforce property rights. Therefore, securing financing for a Thai property in your home country usually depends on your credit standing, together with your ability to provide alternative collateral for the loan.

Key points to check in relation to property financing

The terms and conditions in relation to each offer of financing differ from institution to institution and also on the type of property you are purchasing. Following are some of the key points to consider:

1. Type of property: banks and financial institutions, especially in Thailand, have strict criteria for the type of property against which they will consider lending. For instance, most offers of financial assistance for foreigners buying Thai property are for condominium freehold properties only, while some lenders will only consider condominium properties in Bangkok and Phuket. In the case of developer finance, financial assistance is usually limited to a particular development, or specific units within a development. Therefore, before too much time is spent on the details of a finance package, first check that a lender will consider lending on the type of property in the location you plan to purchase.

2. Set up costs: Purchasers tend to focus on interest rates, loan tenors and loan-to-value ratios, and often fail to pay sufficient attention to "set up costs", "front-end fees", "administration fees" or "commitment fees", which can be significant to the point where they render the offer unattractive. Indeed, lenders often use "set up costs" to enable them to advertise lower interest rates; in other words, these additional costs *disguise* the true cost of capital.

3. Loan-to-value (LTV): The LTV ratio is the amount of money the lender is prepared to lend you, expressed as a percentage of the property's value. Two points need to be checked in relation to LTV ratios. First, what is the percentage? For instance, banks and financial institutions might lend 60-70% of a property's value, whereas developer finance tends to be in the range of 40-60%. Second, it is necessary to confirm the "Value" component of LTV. For instance, for a bank or financial institution, LTV is usually be based on a valuation of the property; while for a developer it is normally based on purchase price (it is unlikely that a developer will sell you a property then value it at less than the purchase price!)

4. Does the loan cover extras? If you are making improvements to a property or buying a furniture package from the developer, will the loan amount cover these extras?

5. Interest rate: Interest rates are usually expressed as a percentage above the minimum lending rate (MLR),[295] which at the time of writing is currently 6.875%. For instance, the offers by MBK Guarantee referred to above mention MLR + 2% and MLR + 5.625%.

6. Fixed or floating? Is the interest rate fixed (the same interest rate for the duration of the loan) or floating[296] (variable and liable to change). If you believe interest rates are going to increase over the term of the loan, a fixed interest rate is preferable; if you believe rates will fall, a variable rate is preferable. Some loan packages offer a fixed interest rate for the first few years, then the interest rate switches to a variable rate. This might be suitable if you plan to repay the loan in full within the initial fixed rate period (subject to an early repayment penalty, see point 15 below); however, care must be taken because monthly repayments can significantly increase upon expiration of the fixed rate.

7. Type of loan: The two basic loan types are *interest-only* loans, and *capital and interest repayment loans.* With interest-only loans, monthly repayment amounts are considerably lower because you are only paying the interest element of the loan; the original capital amount borrowed must be repaid as a lump sum at the end of the term, which means the borrower must carefully plan finances to repay the capital. Capital and interest repayment loans are the most common type of loan, whereby the loan is paid off by regular payments that comprise part of the capital and a bit of interest. In the initial years, payments mostly consist of interest and then gradually more of the capital debt is paid off. There are also "balloon loans", which are a hybrid of the two loan types. Typically, balloon loans have a fixed interest rate for a set number of years, at the end of which the outstanding sum of the balloon loan must be repaid in full. For instance, using again the example of MBK Guarantee (due to the lack of other examples), with "Home Loan Financing" there is an option for a balloon payment of 50% at the end of the term.

8. Term: Loan terms for property finance in Thailand tend to be shorter, usually 10 years or less[297]. Developer finance or extended payment terms offered by developers tend to be even shorter, such as 2-3 years. Generally, the longer the term, the lower the monthly payment, which

---

[295] Otherwise referred to as the Bank Base Rate; the rate of interest charged by the Central Bank of a Country when lending to Financial Institutions in the money market.

[296] Sometimes referred to as variable or adjustable rate mortgages.

[297] With "Home Loan Financing" MBK Guarantee is offering monthly payments from 2-10 years. Occasionally longer terms are offered, such as 15 years, see for example www.palmgroupasia. com

means the optimum strategy is generally to secure the longest possible term together with the option for early repayment (subject to an early repayment penalty).

9. Monthly payment: The most crucial issue is how much must be paid each month and whether the amount is affordable. In the case of rental properties, rental income should ideally exceed the monthly repayment amount.

10. Payment procedure: This concerns the physical payment procedure, i.e. *how* is the money to be paid? For instance, is there need for a Thai bank account and can payments be made by direct debit?

11. Drawdown date: This is a crucial consideration, especially when buying off-plan property. When you buy a completed property, it is possible to rent out the property and cover monthly finance payments with rental income. However, when buying off-plan property, the developer or construction company usually receives funds gradually over the course of construction; therefore, if accepting finance from a developer to meet staged payments, it is important to confirm the drawdown dates and when monthly repayments commence. If monthly repayments commence *prior* to completion of a property, there is no opportunity to cover monthly repayments with rental income; money must therefore be budgeted to carry these payments until the property is able to generate rental income.

12. How is ownership of the property held until the loan is paid off? This is a crucial consideration. In the case of major banks or financial institutions in developed countries, the property purchaser is usually the registered owner of the property and a legal mortgage is registered against the property in the property registration system. In Thailand, with the restrictions on foreign ownership, together with the various ownership structures employed to hold property, who will be the legal owner of the property until the loan is fully paid? What will be the ownership structure for the duration of the loan and where will original title documents be kept? This is particularly relevant in the case of developer finance where the issue of a developer's solvency is critical. What are the consequences upon bankruptcy of the lender?

13. Fees and taxes in relation to ownership transfer: If a property is legally registered to the lender or held in a particular ownership structure for the term of the loan, there are usually fees and taxes involved to transfer ownership of the property to the borrower upon full repayment of the loan. Which party is responsible for paying these fees and taxes?

14. Currency of loan: This is another key issue to consider. If you are borrowing from a bank or financial institution abroad, sometimes a choice of currency is offered for the loan.[298] Borrowing money in a different currency might appear attractive due to a lower interest rate; however, in any case where different currencies are involved, there is currency-related risk in relation to the loan amount (see chapter 105, which discusses currency-related risk). If you are securing Thai Baht denominated financing and rental income (in Thai Baht) is not expected to cover monthly payments, then the repayment amount needs to covered from another source, which might also involve currency related risk.

15. Early repayment penalty: It is necessary to ensure, firstly, that you have the flexibility to repay a loan before the end of the loan term and, secondly, what is the penalty fee for early repayment? (A standard penalty amount is usually 1% of the outstanding balance)[299].

16. Supporting documents: What documentary evidence is required for the loan application? Standard requirements often include employment contracts, evidence of salary, bank statements, sale and purchase agreements, and land documents.

17. Collateral: What collateral or personal guarantees are required as security for the loan? Traditional mortgages are usually secured by the property on which the mortgage is registered. In Thailand, due to restrictions on foreign ownership, an opaque legal environment and the various ownership structures used to hold property, additional collateral or personal guarantees are sometimes required for Thai property related loans. For instance, if you secure a loan in your home country, the lender might require additional collateral in your home country.

18. Assignment: Does the loan contract allow the borrower to assign the loan? If so, what are the conditions?

19. Late payment fees: What is the "default interest" rate charged on late payments? Are there any other late payment fees or penalties?

20. Grounds for default: What are the *specific* grounds that give rise to termination or default of the loan agreement? This is a crucial consideration because you could potentially lose your right to the property if you are in default, or if you do something (or fail to do something) that

---

[298] "International currency mortgages".
[299] Although note the offer from MBK where the early repayment penalty is 2%.

> gives the lender the right to terminate the contract. The terms related to default must be carefully checked; the more strict the terms of default, the greater the risk.

21. Insurance: Which party is responsible for insuring the property for the duration of the loan? What type of insurance is required and what is the premium?

22. Approved lender: Does the lender belong to any professional industry organisations or is it approved or licensed by a regulatory authority, such as the Bank of Thailand or the Ministry of Finance?

23. Alterations to the property: If a property is legally registered to a lender until the loan is repaid, restrictions often exist relating to the ability of the borrower to make structural alterations or changes to the property. In other words, the consent of the lender is usually required.

> **Important tip:** If you are relying on finance to purchase property, it is wise not to commit any money to a deal until you are certain financing has been secured. If you do commit money, for example by making a reservation deposit, make sure it is fully refundable "subject to mortgage or finance approval" or "subject to securing finance on satisfactory terms".

Summary

- Mortgages and financing are not widely available for foreign buyers of Thai property.
- This is due to the restrictions on foreign ownership, the absence of a reliable central property registration system and the lack of a transparent legal system that allows the proper enforcement of property rights.
- The notable exception tends to be in the case of condominium freehold properties where banks are more willing to lend because foreigners are permitted to own such properties outright.
- From time-to-time a banks, financial institutions or developers offer lending packages to foreigners; it is important to check the small print, particularly in relation to:
  - Type (and location) of property.
  - Set up costs, "commitment fees" and "processing fees".
  - Loan to value ratios.
  - Interest rates.
  - What is the monthly payment and is it *affordable?*
  - How is ownership of the property held while the loan is paid off?
  - What are the specific grounds that give rise to termination or default of the loan agreement?

108
What is escrow?

It's a dark night. Two black limousines, with lights off, approach an abandoned warehouse and pull up within thirty metres of each other. Two groups of muscle-clad occupants emerge from the cars. The leader of one group carries a briefcase full of money; the leader of the other has "the merchandise". They slowly walk towards each other and stop a few metres apart. There is a standoff. The person carrying the briefcase is reluctant to hand it over until he gets the merchandise; the person with the merchandise is reluctant to part with it until he gets the money.

Such a scenario should help us to appreciate the role of "escrow" in property transactions. Escrow is where a neutral trusted third party plays the role of a middle entity, making sure documents or money are released only when both parties have fulfilled the conditions of the contract. In other words, an "escrow account" is usually established where one party transfers funds, which are then held until the appropriate written instruction is received notifying the escrow agent that the other party's contractual obligations have been fulfilled. Thus, in the event where a seller is unable to perform the property transfer, or is in breach of contract, the funds held in escrow are not distributed to the seller but are instead returned to the buyer (this effectively provides a non-judicial recourse in the event of default).

Escrow accounts prove useful in property transactions in circumstances where a buyer is reluctant to hand over money to the seller until he is certain the asset will be transferred; and where the seller is reluctant to transfer legal ownership of an asset until he is sure he will receive payment. Put succinctly, there is risk and distrust associated with property transactions and escrow offers a tri-party solution.

> **Important tip:** It should be understood that it is the *terms and conditions* attached to the escrow arrangement that define it. In other words, it is the terms defining how the transaction is to be conducted and when money is to be released to the seller that determine the level of security of the escrow. For this reason, property buyers should be involved in process of drafting the escrow contracts.

In practice, it is necessary to recognise the distinction between a *formal* escrow agent and a party *acting* as escrow. A formal escrow agent is an escrow agent *authorised* to provide escrow services, whereas lawyers or trusted third parties that hold funds on your behalf until a seller performs his contractual obligations might not be authorised but are nonetheless *acting* in the capacity of an escrow agent and providing a similar service.

In Thailand, an escrow business law was enacted by Parliament in 2007 and the Escrow Act came into force on 21 May 2008. It is designed to offer buyers and sellers of property a greater level of protection from fraud and deceit through the services of a neutral third party who is responsible for the safekeeping of any money, assets or documents deposited by the parties, and for overseeing both the transfer of ownership and the transfer funds when required. The Act specifies that the escrow service provider must be a financial institution, commercial bank or finance company that has received authorisation to provide escrow services from the Ministry of Finance. In turn, the Escrow Business Operation Supervision Committee ("Escrow Committee") monitor the service providers authorised to provide escrow services to ensure they perform their duties in accordance with the Act. Criminal penalties are prescribed for escrow agents committing fraud.

With regard to the mechanics of the escrow, in addition to the sale and purchase contract, buyer, seller and escrow agent must also enter into an escrow contract. The escrow agent must then open a bank account with a financial institution for the parties to the contract, and inform the appropriate land office that the property in question comes under an escrow agreement. The transfer of ownership is not permitted *until* the escrow agent provides the Land Department with a written notice authorising the transfer. In the event of disagreement between the buyer and seller, the escrow agent must not transfer funds until the parties have come to an agreement. In addition, if an escrow agent becomes bankrupt, the funds in the escrow account are protected.

If you are considering the purchase of property in Thailand, it is useful to be aware of the existence of escrow and how it can be used to provide an additional level of security to a transaction. The use of an escrow arrangement in property transactions is not compulsory; it is voluntarily entered into by the contracting parties[300]. In addition, depending on the manner in which the transaction is to be performed, it might be possible to use an international escrow agent in another jurisdiction.

Naturally, using an escrow agent adds to transaction costs. Fees could be a set amount or a percentage of the escrow sum. If you prefer not to use an *authorised* escrow agent, in many cases your lawyer can act in the capacity of

---

[300] In the case of purchasing property in off-plan developments, many developers will not agree to an escrow arrangement because they need buyers' funds to construct the project; only developers that have pre-financed a project might consider the use of escrow.

an unofficial escrow agent by holding funds in a client account until satisfied with the performance of the seller's contractual obligations. However, while a lawyer is under a professional duty to act in your best interests, in Thailand authorised escrow agents are safer because the Escrow Act governs their actions.[301]

Summary

- Escrow is where a neutral trusted third party plays the role of a middle entity, making sure money is released only when both parties have fulfilled the conditions of the contract.
- It is necessary to recognise the distinction between a *formal* escrow agent and a party *acting* as escrow.
- The Escrow Act is designed to offer buyers and sellers of property a greater level of protection from fraud and deceit through the services of a neutral third party. Escrow service providers are monitored to ensure they perform their duties in accordance with the Act.
- If you are considering the purchase of property in Thailand, it is useful to be aware of the existence of escrow and how it can be used to provide an additional level of security to a transaction.

---

[301] And your lawyer is unlikely to have indemnity insurance.

STEP 8
Renting out your property

109
Renting your property?

In general, there are only two ways to generate profit from your property: either through capital appreciation (where a property increases in value and the gains are released upon sale)[302] or rental income[303]. In most cases, it is the revenue generated by an asset or business that determines its value, which is evident from Wall Street's preoccupation with "earnings" that are used to derive the market value of stocks. Thus, in a fluid and transparent property market, the rental income generated by a property should provide an indication of the property's value (see chapter 10, "Investing for rental income"). For instance, if a property generates 840,000 Baht (US$ 28,000) of annual rental income and the expected yield is 7%, the property's value (in pure financial terms) would be 12 million Baht (US$ 400,000).[304]

However, the relationship between yield and price is less clear in resort property markets due to the lack of transparency in transactional information and less reliable supply and demand data[305]. In addition, rental income is less reliable, while emotions play a greater part in purchasing decisions (with the consequence that property values sometimes bear little relation to their income earning capacity). Nonetheless, a property with a *proven* track record of rental income is often able to justify a higher asking price upon re-sale. It also makes it easier for a buyer to justify an emotion driven purchasing decision if the numbers stack up; in such cases, the buyer is purchasing both a property and a viable business.

Thus, if you are planning to rent out your property and successfully generate rental income, it pays to think about it as a business with the objective of profit maximisation. Whether the property is rented out year-round or if part of the rental calendar is blocked out for your own use, the principles are similar.

> **Important note:** If you rent out a new property, it immediately affects your ability to sell the property "as new", which might affect its re-sale value. Using the property for a week might not make a great difference but renting a property consistently for a year will almost certainly cause signs of wear and tear, which puts the property in a different category. For this reason, the decision to rent out a property is not one that should be taken lightly; it needs to be taken consciously.

---

[302] Or the property is refinanced.
[303] In some other jurisdictions such as the US, there are four ways to profit if tax advantages and depreciation are included.
[304] (840,000/7)*100
[305] As many properties are "sold" through the sale of companies, and due to the practice of understating transaction amounts, it is difficult to compile accurate information on property transactions.

It should be noted that, depending on the type of property and the manner in which it has been purchased, your ability to rent out a property could be limited by the terms of the sales contract[306], particularly if you purchased from a developer; i.e. you might be tied into using a particular rental management company or into a rental programme (see chapter 76). The relevant contracts must therefore be checked before embarking on a plan of action for renting out a property.

Property owners should also bear in mind that managing a rental property is an entirely different proposition from owning a residence or vacation home. Consideration must be given to a whole host of issues, ranging from property design and furnishings to the taxation of rental income.

The objective of Step 8 is to discuss the principal considerations related to renting out a property. There are 101 ways to approach the rental market and after a discussion of the pertinent issues, you should be in a position to make choices better suited to your circumstances.

Summary

- The revenue generated by an asset or business generally determines its value.
- A property with a *proven* track record of rental income is often able to justify a higher asking price upon re-sale.
- If you are planning to rent out your property, it pays to think about it as a business with the objective of profit maximisation.
- Your ability to rent out a property could be limited by the terms of the sales contract, particularly if you purchased from a developer.
- If you rent out a new property, it immediately affects your ability to sell the property "as new".

---

[306] It might also be limited by law; for instance, if you have purchased several condominium units, renting out immovable property is a service business (property owner or landlord service) that requires a Foreign Business License under the Foreign Business Act.

110
Understanding rental demand
(Essential)

If you want to successfully rent out a property, preparing for rentals does not merely consist of cleaning the property and putting up a sign. Maximising rental income requires careful planning and some fundamental decisions to be made. Ideally, the requisite planning and decision-making should commence at an early stage, prior to the viewing of properties and certainly prior to the purchase of a property.

Location, location, location

At the beginning of this book, chapter 8 discussed a fundamental question; namely, what is the purpose of investment? The decision as to whether a property is to be used for rental purposes needs to be made at the outset because it influences key choices such as the location and type of property you purchase (or build).

The owner of a villa holiday company catering to the Russian market once told me that 80% of initial enquiries are for beachfront properties, while the remaining 20% are for "properties with sea views" and "properties within walking distance to the beach". The term *"initial enquiries"* is used instead of *"actual bookings"* because, after learning of the high rental rates for beachfront properties, many beachfront enquiries are modified to "properties within walking distance to the beach" or "properties with sea views!"

This is mentioned because it provides an insight into rental demand and "consumer" behaviour. Beachfront properties are the most sought after rental properties and therefore command the highest rental rates (rental rates for properties with direct beach access reflect the scarcity value of beach land). In recognition of this fact, the property portfolios of some property rental companies are comprised solely of beachfront properties. However, not all beachfront properties are equal. Different "segments" of beachfront property exist; for instance, there are beachfront properties on *swimmable* beaches and there are beachfront properties with sunset views, both of which are more highly sought after within the general category of beachfront properties.

Properties within walking distance to a beach and properties with sea views might therefore be considered "second-tier" market segments. They are also in high demand and command high rental rates, although the rates are generally not as high as beachfront properties. Different segments also exist within each of these categories. For example, properties that are two minutes walk to the beach are, all things being equal, more sought after than properties that are ten or fifteen minutes walk to the beach. In addition, it should be understood that "walking distance to the beach" and "near to the beach" are separate market segments; one requires the added expense of car rental (or taxi fares) on top of property rental costs, the other doesn't.

In a similar manner, segments exist within the general category of "sea view properties". Properties with "panoramic sea views" are generally more sought after and outperform properties with "partial sea views" (or "sea glimpses!"). For instance, one luxury branded villa development used the slogan, "Sunrise. Sunset. Which do you prefer? Now, imagine you didn't have to choose".[307] One thing is certain: the average person's dream holiday is not flying halfway around the world to stare at a garden wall; they want to know and feel they are on a tropical island and a sea view is perhaps the most effective way to achieve it.

Location is perhaps the key factor determining the success or failure of a rental property. A small fortune can be spent building a beautiful property but if it is located in the middle of nowhere it will not consistently generate rental income. Similarly, a luxury property built in a non-prime area, surrounded by corrugated tin huts or an abandoned semi-finished building site will struggle as a rental property due to its surroundings. Surroundings make a difference: a five minute walk to the beach along an avenue lined with swaying palm trees is not the same as a five minute walk to the beach through a construction site or shantytown!

When evaluating potential rental properties, each property must be considered in terms of its "package" of distinguishing features. The most successful rental properties usually have several distinguishing features or attributes that are valued by the rental market; for instance, "stunning panoramic sea views and sunset views ... five minutes walk to the beach ... private location ... ten minutes drive to restaurants, bars and nightlife".

Beachfront properties, properties within walking distance to a beach and properties with sea views or sunset views are each examples of properties with distinguishing features. Alternatively, properties can be distinguished by architectural design, facilities, and proximity to entertainment areas or restaurants. A rental property needs to distinguish itself in some way that is valued by the rental market, which is the only way to maintain high occupancy levels and achieve

---

[307] W Retreat Koh Samui.

superior rental earnings. In the absence of a valued distinguishing feature, a rental property is competing for rental revenue with the hundreds of other rental properties in the "nondescript category", which generally means the only way to compete is on *price*. In such cases, competition naturally forces rental rates and occupancy levels lower.

Matching your property to market demand

To earn rental income, a property must meet the requirements of the rental market or a segment of the rental market. Visitors to Thailand come from all over the world and different types of traveller demand different types of property. When this demand is aggregated, different segments of demand are created and your property must meet one or more of them. For instance, there is a market for honeymoon couples, who generally require one-bedroom properties, ideally with a private pool; there is a market for young families, with a general preference for two-bedroom properties that are child-safe; there is a market for families where the preference is for three, four or five bedroom villas plus a maid's room; and there is a market for couples or groups of people travelling together, where properties with three, four or five equally-sized bedrooms are preferred, together with a large pool and private seating areas.

There are also specific market "niches". For instance, there is a niche market for conferences or corporate meetings for which large, eight or nine bedroom villas with meeting rooms and spacious dining facilities are preferred. There is a market for vacation weddings, which generally requires large, beachfront properties with reception areas and spacious lawns. There is also a market niche for one-bedroom Jacuzzi apartments for single travellers, in close proximity to nightlife and entertainment areas.[308]

If you want to successfully position your property to meet rental demand, it is essential to understand the requirements of the various market segments. Speaking with local property rental agents is one way to get a quick education on the different market segments existing in a particular area. Agents should also be able to tell you which types of properties are in highest demand and achieve the highest occupancy rates. For instance, in one area demand might consist entirely of three-bedroom pool villas, while rental demand in another area might be for one-bedroom apartments or studio units.

An alternative approach is to research the number of tourist arrivals to a particular resort area by nationality and then find out the general requirements and

---

[308] One company that has successfully exploited this niche in Phuket is Absolute Bangla Suites with its "Jacuzzi Condominiums".

preferences of each nationality. For example, visitors that make up the highest proportion of arrivals to Koh Samui are from the UK and Germany, followed by Australia, Sweden and Russia. In addition, different nationalities tend to have different "high seasons" that are influenced by vacation dates in their home countries and this should influence your marketing strategy. A useful place to start is the Department of Tourism website[309] or contact the Tourism Authority of Thailand (TAT)[310].

Obviously it is not possible to perfectly match all requirements of every market segment; further, market demand evolves over time. The key point, however, is to understand the dynamics of a rental market, to recognise the requirements of the various segments, and buy a property or position your property to meet the needs of the market.

Standard of property

It is also necessary to consider the price range of the target market, i.e. whether a property is positioned to meet the needs and expectations of the budget, mid-range, luxury or super-luxury markets. Once the price range has been identified, it is then necessary to position your offer to meet the requirements of the particular price segment. *Most importantly, there must be total consistency throughout all elements of the property and rental management services.* In other words, there must be consistency in terms of the materials used for construction; the brand names selected for appliances and accessories; the quality of furniture, interior décor, bed linen and cutlery; the type of vehicle used for airport transfers; and the standard of housekeeping and cleaning services. One of the noteworthy inconsistencies in the rental market is luxury property in prime locations whose owners have failed to invest in luxurious interiors.

In its *Phuket Property Market Buyers Guide,* CBRE[311] identified 5 segments from "Local Market", which comprises townhouses and villas under 4 million Baht ($US 133,000), to "Luxury" with villas over 40 million Baht (US$ 1.33 million) and condominiums over 30 million Baht (US$ 1 million), as shown below.[312]

---

[309] www.tourism.go.th/2010/th/statistic/tourism.php
[310] 1600 New Phetchaburi Road, Makkasan, Ratchathevi, Bangkok 10400. Tel: +662 250 5500, TAT Call Center: 1672
[311] CB Richard Ellis www.cbre.co.th
[312] Bearing in mind these "characteristics" were noted in 2006, prior to the global financial crisis.

Price Range	Characteristics
Local Market	Villas and townhouses under 4 million Baht (US$ 133,000). Properties in large Thai projects, located in areas with lesser land value. Very few facilities provided.
Low-End Market	Villas under 15 million Baht (US$ 500,000), condominiums under 10 million Baht (US$ 333,000). Properties generally enjoying mountain/lake views. Set in more affordable areas, yet offering facilities to western standards.
Middle Market	Villas over 15 million Baht (US$ 500,000), condominiums over 10 million Baht (US$ 333,000). Good quality homes in gated communities, offering a range of facilities.
High-End	Villas over 30 million Baht (US$ 1 million), condominiums over 20 million Baht (US$ 665,000). Properties in sought after locations, generally close to the sea, with high quality materials used throughout. High-end villas have private pools.
Luxury	Villas over 40 million Baht (US$ 1.33 million), condominiums over 30 million Baht (US$ 1 million). Stunning properties with very high construction and equipment specifications. Units enjoy great sea views and are usually part of a small-scale prestigious development.

In Koh Samui, CBRE identified 3 segments[313]:

Price Range	Characteristics
Middle to Low-End Market	Villas priced between US$ 750,000 and $US 1 million and condominiums under US$ 250,000. Good quality homes, individual properties or part of a gated development. Properties in this category are located further inland but still offer panoramic sea views. Many developments are high density with smaller land plots.
High-End	Villas priced between US$ 1 and 2 million, condominiums priced between US$ 250,000 and 500,000. High quality materials used throughout; most villas have private pools. Properties in sought after locations on hillsides or headlands; only some have direct beach access. All properties offer panoramic sea views.
Luxury	Villas over US$ 2 million, condominiums over US$ 500,000. Stunning properties with very high construction and equipment specifications. Most villas are located in beachfront locations with sea views and with low density to offer privacy and seclusion. Most developments offer professional property management with optional concierge services.

While the characteristics of the different price segments change and evolve over time – influenced by design, construction standards and the health of the global economy – the characteristics noted above demonstrate the existence of different price categories.

---

[313] Bearing in mind these "characteristics" were noted in 2007, just prior to the global financial crisis.

In terms of rental rates, nightly rates can range from 2,000 Baht to 10,000 dollars and it is important to understand the expectations of guests and the commensurate level of services required at each level.

> **Important tip:** The problem for many property owners is that they think their properties are in the "luxury" segment but they are unaware of the levels of luxury that exist. In other words, most rental property owners are unfamiliar with the property market and the range of price segments. As a potential rental property owner, it is strongly advised to spend more time researching a market and viewing as many different types of property as possible, before identifying which price range they wish to target.

In general, when guests are paying 3,000 Baht (US$ 100) per night, they usually forgive mistakes and inconsistencies. However, when rental guests are paying 30,000 Baht (US$ 1,000) per night, they are much less forgiving; such guests rightly expect a product and service corresponding to the rates they are paying and will not be shy to complain if anything falls short of expectations.

Summary

- Maximising rental income requires some fundamental decisions to be made at an early stage, such as the location and type of property you purchase.
- Location is perhaps the key factor determining the success or failure of a rental property.
- A rental property needs to distinguish itself in some way that is valued by the rental market.
- It is necessary to become familiar with the various price ranges and to position your offer to meet the requirements of a particular price segment.
- There must be total consistency throughout *all* elements of the property and rental management services.

111
Short-term or long-term rental?

One fundamental decision property owners must make in relation to property rental is the decision between short-term and long-term rentals. Short-term rental typically refers to vacation rental to tourists lasting from a few days to a few weeks and charged at daily (nightly) or weekly rates; while long-term rental generally refers to rentals to long-stay tourists or residents for several months or more, usually charged at a monthly (or sometimes annual) rate.

The obvious advantage of short-term rentals is higher pro-rata rental income; rental rates tend to be higher when charged at a nightly rate, while monthly rates tend to be significantly lower. For instance, an apartment might be rented out at a nightly rate of 9,000 Baht (US$ 300), while the market rate for the same apartment on a monthly basis might be 90,000 Baht (US$ 3,000) per month, which is a *pro-rata* equivalent of only 3,000 Baht (US$ 100) per night.

There are four general reasons for the rate difference. First, it is generally accepted that the longer the rental period, the lower the pro-rata rate, which is consistent with the principle of *economies of scale.* Second, with short-term rentals, the property owner generally assumes the utility costs (electricity, water, etc), while for long-term rentals, guests usually pay the utility bills according to metered use. Third, higher rates are required to cover the additional marketing, management and administration costs associated with short-term rentals. Fourth, it is difficult to ensure continuity of short-term rentals; in other words, as guest schedules do not generally coincide[314], calendar gaps are common between departing guests and arriving guests and higher rates compensate for these gaps.

However, higher rates must be *earned.* Short-term vacation rentals involve the full gamut of property rental management services including meet and greet at the airport, transfer to the property, property orientation upon arrival, housekeeping and cleaning services, and changing of linen and towels. Depending on the requirements of guests, it might also be necessary to arrange car rental, concierge service or the services of a chef. This is in addition to property management services, which includes garden management, swimming pool management and general property maintenance. Guests must also be checked-out, the property must be inspected and deposits need to be refunded. Long-term tenants, on the other hand, are often left to their own devices once they are at the property.

---

[314] Unlike European ski holidays where bookings are normally from Saturday to Saturday.

Generally, only maintenance services are required (including a contact person to call in case of emergency), unless the rental agreement includes other services, such as cleaning and changing of linen and towels.

In addition, shorter average rental periods involve more marketing, management and administration. The confirmation of each rental booking often involves communicating with the guest (or agent) to answer questions about the property and location, the exchange of contracts, and bookkeeping related to the receipt of security deposits and rental payments. This is not to mention the time involved to answer enquiries in relation to potential customers that fails to result in a confirmed booking. With long-term tenants, however, once they have checked in, there is no further management or administration required, apart from meter readings in connection with the payment of utility bills.

With regard to rental contracts, bear in mind that short-term and long-term rentals generally require different rental agreements (together with a different commission structure for rental agents).

For property owners that are deciding between short-term and long-term rentals, it is useful to consider the respective advantages and disadvantages. If you prefer to take a hands-off approach to renting out your property, you might consider long-term tenants instead of short-term vacation rentals, or short-term rentals in combination with the engagement of a full-service professional rental management company.

For investors seeking to maximise rental income from their properties, the general focus is on short-term rentals with the objective of maximising occupancy at higher nightly rates. However, those investing for capital appreciation will often consider a long-term tenant in order to cover costs and reduce management and administration, with the expectation of property values increasing during the holding period.

Summary

The characteristics of short-term and long-term rentals are summarised below:

Short-term	*Long-term*
Higher pro-rata nightly rates	Lower pro-rata monthly rates
Property owner generally assumes utility bills (electricity, water, etc.)	Tenant usually pays bills according to usage (meter readings required)
Full rental management services, including meet-and-greet, airport transfer, property orientation, regular cleaning and changing of towels and linen.	No service or minimal service, such as maintenance and possibly cleaning services and the changing of towels and linen.
Increased level of marketing, communication, management and administration.	Minimal management and administration.
Investors maximising rental income	Investing for capital appreciation

112
Being prepared for property rentals

Prior to renting out a property, there are a number of issues to consider and numerous preparations to make. While some of these issues might be considered "tactical" in nature, others are of more fundamental importance. This chapter discusses the issues and preparations that are of fundamental importance, namely ownership structures, liability, taxes on rental income and property insurance. In addition, it discusses the issue of "snagging" in the context of a rental property. The issues of a more tactical nature are discussed in subsequent chapters.

Ownership structures and taxes on rental income

Chapters 98 - 101 discussed the various ownership structures that are used for buying and holding property in Thailand in relation to taxes upon re-sale. In the case of rental properties, the choice of ownership structure should also take into account the issue of taxes on rental income.

Rental income derived from property in Thailand is subject to taxation. However, the manner in which a property is owned dictates the manner in which taxes are assessed and collected. In other words, taxes depend on whether property is owned in a personal name, or by a Thai or foreign company. For instance, if a property is registered in a personal name, every person deriving rental income from a property situated in Thailand (whether the income is paid within or outside Thailand) is liable to pay personal income tax (see chapter 94), although a standard deduction of 30% is allowed.

If a Thai company owns the property, net profits, including those derived from rental income, are taxable according to the sliding scale of corporate income tax rates (see chapter 93). However, the Revenue Department has the power to assess rents at *market value,* as opposed to *actual* rental income.

If the property is owned by a foreign company, the tax rate on rental income depends on whether the rental income is paid from or within Thailand and whether the company is "carrying on business in Thailand" for the purposes of taxation. For instance, if rental income is paid from or within Thailand to a foreign company not carrying on business in Thailand, tax is 15% on gross income, while rental income received by a foreign company carrying on business in Thailand is assessed at corporate income tax rates with a maximum rate of 30%. If rental income is paid from a foreign tenant to a foreign company (i.e. not paid from or within Thailand) there may be significant tax savings.

The following chart summarises the taxes on rental income, although as with other tax-related issues, professional advice should be sought to ensure any decisions taken are based on up-to-date advice that is appropriate to individual circumstances.

Property ownership	Tax on rental income
Personal name	10 - 37% personal income tax on rental income (whether paid within or outside Thailand), with an allowed standard deduction of 30%.[315]
Thai company	15 - 30% corporate income tax, although the Revenue Department has the power to assess rents at "market value".
Foreign company	15% of gross income if rental income is paid from or within Thailand to a foreign company not carrying on business in Thailand. 15 - 30% corporate tax rates apply if income received by a foreign company carrying on business in Thailand. Significant tax savings if rental income is paid from a foreign tenant to a foreign company.

In addition, it is necessary to consider the issue of land and house tax (see chapter 123).

---

[315] There is an option to claim *actual* expenses incurred in deriving rental income, which are necessary and reasonable, whereby corporate tax provisions governing the deduction of expenses will apply.

Liability

If a property is rented out, the owner or "landlord" automatically assumes some degree of "occupiers liability". Landlords generally owe a "duty of care" to ensure that visitors[316] are reasonably safe in the property, and could find themselves liable for injury caused to others (or their property) by defective or dangerous conditions of the property. In other words, if someone gets hurt or injured while staying at or visiting your property, you could find yourself at the receiving end of a legal claim. It is therefore necessary to take proactive steps to protect tenants and visitors from injury, and yourself from liability. There are three main issues to consider:

First, it is your responsibility to ensure the property, together with any equipment and appliances, is safe before guests are accepted. This is an issue that concerns architectural design, the choice of materials, construction quality, and ongoing management and maintenance of the property.

Second, the issue of liability should be taken into account when deciding the most suitable property ownership structure, i.e. whether to buy and hold the property in a personal name or a corporate structure. In the case of a limited company, liability is generally considered to be limited, while personal liability is technically *unlimited*.

Third, it is important to protect yourself by properly and adequately insuring the property for rental use.

Insurance

Insurance policies that cover properties for fire, theft and contents do not always include liability coverage for rental guests. It is often necessary to notify an insurance company if a property is to be rented out and insurance premiums tend to be higher, corresponding to the wider coverage and increased risk.

To provide adequate protection, a property insurance policy should include liability coverage, workmen's compensation and employer's liability, especially if there are permanent staff (domestic servants, drivers, gardeners, etc). Such insurance coverage should help to pay legal defence fees and any legal claims you might be obligated to pay (up to the policy limit).

---

[316] This generally includes guests who are occupying the property pursuant to rental agreements, and visitors, whether invited or not.

Taking time to look at the details of the insurance coverage is essential. It is also important to note the exclusions, category limits, per item limits, excesses and deductibles. Remember, the level of protection provided by an insurance policy is often determined by the small print. Don't make the mistake of checking the details of an insurance policy only when there is a claim.

> **Important tip:** In order to be prepared for any future claims, it is recommended to take an inventory of furniture and personal belongings and to photograph (or video) each room of the property. In addition, it is wise to keep receipts for all major purchases at an offsite location.

Snagging

Snagging is the process of identifying and rectifying defects when taking possession of a newly built property (either by a construction company or developer). The issue of snagging has already been covered in depth in chapter 58; however, in the context of rental properties, the snagging process becomes particularly significant. In other words, it is essential that snagging is performed *before guests move into a property.*

If guests move into a property before the snagging process has been completed, any defects or improperly functioning equipment can potentially cause inconvenience to guests; and any defect or repair work requiring builders or technicians to enter the property tends to cause even greater inconvenience. Such disturbances usually result in claims for compensation and certainly reduce the likelihood of repeat bookings. In addition, it can result in negative comments being posted on rental websites with the consequence of reduced *future* bookings. More importantly, particularly in cases of electrical problems, defects can pose a danger to guests; and electrocutions really don't look good on tripadvisor.com!

All too often, owners take possession of properties and immediately accept rental guests in an attempt to earn a return on their investment as quickly as possible. However, the fact is if snagging has not been properly performed prior to the acceptance of guests, guests are effectively snagging for you, which is not ideal. An example that comes to mind is the case of a young couple with a baby that moved into a recently completed villa for a one-week vacation and were continually disturbed by technicians arriving at the property to fix things, including toilets that wouldn't flush, water not coming out of taps, an oven that didn't heat up due to incorrect wiring, and a Jacuzzi that didn't work due to an incorrectly installed piping system (the Jacuzzi happened to be the key feature in the marketing materials). In the grand scheme of things, each of these issues was relatively minor; however, they combined to cause significant inconvenience to the guests, which ruined their privacy and severely affected their enjoyment of the property. The most disappointing aspect is that all of these issues could have been identified during the most perfunctory snagging inspection of the property.

In sum, not only should the snagging process be properly completed before accepting tenants but ideally owners should live in the property for at least a week, during which the operation of the entire property can be checked before putting it on the rental market.

Summary

- Prior to renting out a property, there are a number of fundamental issues to consider.
- The choice of ownership structure should take into consideration the issue of taxes on rental income.
- Landlords generally owe a "duty of care" to visitors, which means property owners should ensure their properties are safe before guests are accepted.
- It is important to protect yourself by properly and adequately insuring properties for rental use.
- It is essential to perform snagging before guests move into a property.

113
Design tips for rental properties

If you are building your own property with the intention of renting it out in future or if you have the ability to influence the design of an off-plan rental property, this chapter provides some useful tips for aligning a property with the requirements of the rental market. It also contains useful tips for property owners in relation to furnishing and preparing properties for rental. It should be noted that many of these tips for designing a rental property serve equally well as a checklist for buying a completed property that is to serve as a rental property.

Property design and layout

When designing and building a rental property, a fundamental understanding of how a tropical rental property is used is essential. While guests at winter ski resorts want to return to a warm cosy room and sit in front of a log fire, holidaymakers travelling to tropical resort destinations want to spend their time *outside*[317]. This propensity for "outdoor living" should therefore be one of the key driving forces behind tropical property design. On a practical level, this translates into the incorporation of swimming pools, Jacuzzis, pool decks, outdoor dining areas, balconies, rooftop terraces, outdoor bathtubs and showers.

The *interface* between interior and outdoor living areas is also of prime importance; indoor spaces should open seamlessly onto outdoor areas such as pool decks and terraces through the use of sliding or folding doors. Swimming pools should be the focal point of a tropical property. Indeed, rental guests – particularly those on short vacations – will spend the vast majority of their time around the pool and in the living areas leading from the pool deck.

When given a choice, rental guests prefer spacious properties; however, the way in which space is used is vitally important. Rather than one large outdoor area, rental guests (particularly when a property is designed for several couples or a group of people travelling together) often prefer various separate seating areas where they can read, entertain or simply enjoy their privacy.

Shade must also be a consideration. When the sun is at its strongest, rental guests should not be expected to retreat into air-conditioned rooms. Thought must be

---

[317] With the exception of many Asian guests who tend to stay inside with the air-conditioning on full power!

given to creating areas that provide adequate shade at various times of the day. As mentioned in chapter 28, once the North-South-East-West orientation of a property has been established, it is easy to design roof structures or canopies for providing shade; alternatively, when inspecting completed properties, it is quick work to identify which areas of the property receive shade and which ones will be in bright sunlight during the day. A talented architect can design roof structures that serve the dual purpose of providing shade to lower floors while serving as terraces for upper floors.

Bedroom configuration

Chapter 110 discussed the importance of matching rental properties to market demand, which includes determining the optimum number of bedrooms to meet the requirements of defined market segments. However, it is not only the *number* of bedrooms that is significant. It is equally important to consider bedroom size and, in particular, the size of the beds. There is a commonly accepted notion that properties need a master bedroom (which is generally larger and has a king-sized bed), while other rooms are generally smaller with queen-sized or single beds. While this configuration might meet the expectations of some families, where parents take the master bedroom and children choose among the other rooms, it certainly does not meet the expectations of all market segments. For instance, imagine the case where several couples are travelling together on holiday and each couple has contributed equally to the cost of the rental property. Upon arrival, arguments generally ensue about which couple gets to sleep in the master bedroom with its panoramic sea views, en-suite bathroom and Jacuzzi on the balcony, and which couples take the other rooms, which are smaller, less well-equipped and have no views.

In order to satisfy the requirements of a broader range of rental guests, it is often more desirable for a property to have two or three equally sized "master bedrooms" with king-sized beds. Indeed, there is a vast difference between a three-bedroom rental property with one master bedroom with a king-sized bed and two guest rooms with single or queen-sized beds, and a three-bedroom rental property with three master bedrooms and three king-sized beds. Both properties are technically "three-bedroom properties"; however, the properties or "product" in terms of marketing appeal are qualitatively different.

Alternatively, it is possible for each bedroom to be differentiated by different facilities. For instance, the "master bedroom" might have an en-suite bathroom and a private pool; the "second" bedroom might feature an outdoor Jacuzzi bathtub; while the "third" bedroom might have a large wrap-around terrace. In this way, while one bedroom might technically be larger or superior, the other bedrooms at least have compensating features.

Privacy

Privacy is a key issue for rental guests. In relation to the configuration of bedrooms, guests prefer to rent a property that is unlike a hotel (where guest bedrooms are immediately adjacent to each other); for reasons of privacy, rental guests generally prefer floor layouts where bedrooms are separated or dispersed throughout the property, i.e. on different floors or on different sides of the property. It is also sensible to design separate areas where guests can enjoy their privacy; for example, where couples can seek privacy when staying at a property with friends, or where parents can escape the kids! Private areas can be created in many ways, either through architectural design layout or by separating areas with landscaping features.

With rental properties, the activities of staff also need to be considered. Properties should be designed so that the movement of pool cleaners, gardeners and housekeepers causes minimal disturbance to guests, which usually means providing separate entrances, together with storage rooms that do not require access to main living areas. To give an example of how highly some rental guests value their privacy, one young couple staying at a private villa asked the villa manager if they could water the lawn themselves each day to avoid being disturbed by gardeners!

Privacy must especially be considered in relation to bathrooms. Whenever possible, each bedroom should have its own bathroom, preferably en-suite. The idea of two bedrooms sharing one bathroom significantly lowers the perceived appeal of such bedrooms. To further improve utility, there should be an extra bathroom for visitors to avoid visitors having to use en-suite or private bathrooms. Extra bathrooms are especially important for properties with swimming pools where bathrooms should ideally be located to prevent pool users having to walk through the house.

With regard to bathrooms, I am amazed at some of the modern, minimalistic bathroom designs that have no doors, no locks or glass walls[318]. These might work well if the property is for the exclusive personal use of the owner. However, it is not ideal for (most) rental guests; while a small minority might find glass walls or the absence of bathroom doors agreeable (such as honeymoon couples where the bodily functions of spouses are still a novelty, or the infirm who prefer to be observed in case they fall off the toilet and injure themselves), the majority of rental guests value their privacy and the thought of performing their business in view of others is horrific! In other words, if a property is to receive rental guests, make sure guests have the option of bathroom privacy.

---

[318] Unless they are fitted with blinds or are the kind that can be darkened at the flick of a switch.

Storage

Ensuring a property has sufficient storage space is an issue that is frequently overlooked. During the property design phase, attention tends to be focussed on bedrooms, kitchens, dining areas, living rooms and swimming pools; in sum, everywhere except storage. Unsurprisingly, when properties are completed, whether they are rented out or used as residences, one of the most commonly heard complaints is the shortage of storage space!

Adequate storage space is essential for rental properties. Rental property owners must plan for guests arriving with large suitcases; if adequate space is not provided, these will be lying around and taking up space in guest bedrooms. An essential requirement for rental properties is a separate storage room with sufficient storage space for rental management and cleaning-related items, such as spare beds, mattresses, linen, towels, amenities, mops, brushes and other cleaning equipment. Ideally, these storage rooms should be able to be separately locked for exclusive access by rental management staff; if a management company is engaged, the cleaners can be provided with a key (storage rooms for linen should be properly ventilated).

A storage room is also required for garden and pool related items. This includes gardening tools, pool cleaning equipment and pool chemicals (unless space has been allocated in the pump room). In addition, it is wise to design a separate storage room for outdoor furniture and cushions, particularly for the storage of furniture during the monsoon season or during gaps between rental bookings.

Additional storage space might also be considered for personal belongings. This is particularly useful for property owners that are renting out their properties for part of the year and using them as a vacation homes for the other part. Personal storage space allows belongings to be left at the property and saves property owners having to bring items back and forth for vacation use.[319]

Furniture and decor

While rental properties need to look visually stunning, the key point to remember when furnishing a rental property is to use furniture, materials and fabrics that are *durable and hardwearing.*

When furnishing for your personal residential use, a property can be adorned with the most expensive and exquisite furniture *because you will take care of*

---

[319] It also allows owners to travel with hand luggage only.

it. However, the fact is, the average rental guest will treat a rental property as though the owner is anonymous, much like a hotel room. For instance, rental guests will not look around for a coaster before setting down a hot coffee cup on a high gloss table and children will jump up and down on your furniture. For these reasons, furniture and materials for rental properties need to be hardwearing and able to withstand a high level of wear and tear: non-scratch and non-stain surfaces should be selected throughout; hardwearing granite should be used for kitchen worktops and bathroom counters instead of MDF-covered chipboard (which is less durable, prone to chipping and will expand if water penetrates the surface); cupboard doors should hardwearing, high-gloss melamine instead of MDF-covered chipboard; felt patches or sliders should be added to the bottom of table and chair legs to prevent them scratching wooden or tiled floors.

In relation to sofas and chairs, fabrics should not only be durable but easy to clean. Naturally, darker colours do not show stains as easily as lighter colours and, while it might look stylish, white should be avoided for rental properties, unless spare covers are available and they are easily changeable. Indeed, regardless of colour, all sofas and chairs should allow covers to be changed and a replacement set needs to be kept in reserve.

With regard to seating, remember to provide adequate seating for the maximum number of guests, plus visitors. For instance, if there are three bedrooms, there should be minimum seating for six, both indoor and outdoor. There should also be a minimum of six loungers by the pool.

With regard to interior décor and art objects, rental properties are no place for Swarovski Crystal ornaments and (real) Ming vases; instead, consider objects with large, stable bases that are less prone to shatter upon impact! These should be positioned in protected locations where they are less likely to be casually knocked over.

Consideration must also be given to achieving a balance between "over-decoration" and "excessive-minimalism". Some rental properties are so full of artwork and decorative pieces that arriving guests need to move things out of the way in order to clear space for their personal items; while other rental properties are so sparsely furnished they promote the feeling of an army barracks or a museum. Furnishings for rental properties should give a property a "soul", without overdoing things. Properties should be comfortably furnished, ideally equivalent to a five-star hotel, and provide a cosy, home away from home feeling. A balance therefore needs to be struck between tastefully chosen sculptures and ornaments, yet at the same time providing a sufficient sense of personal space for guests to move into. Bear in mind also that professional photography is a crucial element in attracting rental guests (as discussed in chapter 120) and interior décor plays a key role in the presentation of a property.

Finally, a word of warning on the subject of interior décor: owners should be careful not to furnish a rental property with too many personal items, or accessories that excessively reflect personal "taste". In other words, avoid lava lamps, favourite Botero paintings and Austin Power colour schemes. Instead, rental properties should be stylish but neutral; subtly designed to appeal to a broad cross-section of the rental market.

Child safety

Many luxury resort properties are architectural wonders, featuring stepping-stones through ponds, open staircases and infinity pools cascading down rock walls. They are also a danger to children. In other words, some luxury properties don't make for child-safe rental properties; indeed, some design features actually preclude properties from being safely rented to guests with young children.

If you plan to include guests with young children in your target rental market, there are a number of things that need to be taken into account to make a property more "child-friendly"[320]. A good place to start is swimming pools. I am reminded of the property owner who determined the depth of his pool by thinking only in terms of his own height and whose pool was subsequently built to a uniform depth of 1.7 metres. He realised only later – when attempting to rent out the property – that it prevented the property from being rented to non-swimmers and guests with young children!

If children are part of your property rental programme, pools need to be designed to ensure they are safe for children to use. For example, depths of 50 - 60 centimetres should be considered for younger children and up to 90 centimetres for older children (for adult pools, a depth of 1.5 metres is usually considered the starting point). The ideal case is a separate children's pool.

Pool outlet drains also need to be considered. European safety standards require swimming pools to have an outlet drain measuring at least 50 centimetres square to prevent small children being pinned by suction to the bottom of the pool. In Thailand, where there is no such legislation, drain sizes tend to be significantly smaller, which is potentially dangerous for children.

Safety at pool edges is another consideration. Children love to climb, which means steep drops over infinity edges are potentially dangerous (safety netting is one solution that does not require a design change). Another essential safety feature (for both adults and children) is the use of non-slip surfaces or tiles

---

[320] This is not just an issue of making a property safe for children; it also brings into question the issue of your liability as a landlord (see chapter 112).

around the pool; tiles with smooth surfaces are an accident waiting to happen the moment they get wet.

Railings around balconies and stairs also need to be carefully thought out. Open staircases are particularly dangerous for young children; so too are balcony railings with widely spaced wire rope, where gaps are often wide enough for children to fall through. Low walls should be avoided for the same reason.

If you are designing a property from the outset, other features that help to make a property child-friendly (and therefore more attractive to family rentals) include gardens areas where children can play in the shade (many rental enquires request properties with walled gardens where children do not need to be constantly supervised) and "media rooms" where children can play games or watch TV without disturbing parents. Families renting holiday properties also expect or request baby chairs and cribs so it is useful to have these on hand.

Flexibility

Maximising rental opportunities and boosting occupancy rates requires flexibility in several areas. For example, with regard to the number of bedrooms, connecting rooms (where a common door allows access between adjacent rooms) sometimes help to meet the demands of guests and are especially useful when parents need to keep an eye on children.

Another way to meet the requirements of a wide range of rental guests is to provide a flexible configuration of beds. For instance, a room with two single beds is ideal for children and also enables the beds to be put together to make a king sized bed.[321]

The option of allowing two beds in one room is the ideal solution for two children; it is also useful when a rental group comprises single men or women who don't mind sharing a room but prefer not to share beds! An alternative method is to have extra beds available upon request or sofas that can be turned into beds[322]. In this way, it is possible to accept rental bookings that would otherwise be declined due to insufficient occupancy.

Flexibility must also be considered in relation to workspace. Many people travelling on holiday bring laptops[323] and need desk space to work at. Rather than setting aside a room to act as an office, which reduces the sleeping capacity

---

[321] To resolve the issue of the "gap" between beds, keep a spare king-sized mattress.
[322] It is also a means to increase rental revenue by charging for additional guests.
[323] Some luxury hotels provide iPads for guest use.

of the property, an alternative is to provide desk space within each bedroom. In addition, wireless Internet, which is a standard expectation, should allow guests to work anywhere in the property, for instance, at the breakfast bar, indoor and outdoor dining areas, living areas, and on balconies, terraces and pool decks. Providing the flexibility to work anywhere in a property requires the location of power outlets to be carefully considered at the planning stage of construction. This includes waterproof power outlets for the pool area, sala and terraces, and flip-up floor outlets in living areas. Another useful idea is the provision of multi-function or "international" plug sockets in each bedroom so unprepared guests do not need to go shopping for adaptors. With rental properties, these details make a difference and are appreciated by guests.

Flexibility must also take account of TVs and TV channels. Some property owners go to the trouble of installing TVs in each bedroom but do not subscribe to the correct Satellite "package", which allows different channels to be simultaneously viewed in different rooms. If you are making the effort of installing TVs in each bedroom, they should be supported with the right equipment to provide independent content. Furthermore, with the ever-decreasing cost of electronic items, equipping each bedroom with a DVD-player is an insignificant expense.

With regard to security safes, a guest's perspective should be taken. Most rental property owners install one safe in the master bedroom; few recognise the convenience to guests of installing one in each bedroom. The fact is that friends or couples travelling together generally don't want each other to have access to their money, valuables and personal items or to disturb other each time they need to access the safe. For this reason, safes in each room are appreciated; in addition, the risk of theft is reduced.

Cost saving tips

When rental rates include utility bills, which is usually the case for short-term vacation rentals, guests often treat this as a licence to leave air-conditioners running continually, day and night, even when patio doors are wide open (despite what is said at the guest orientation or what is written in the guest information book). Many guests also leave air-conditioning units running all day while they go out to the beach or join full-day excursions. Irrespective of environmental considerations, such behaviour significantly increases electricity bills and therefore eats into rental profits.

A useful idea to address such practices and reduce electricity bills is to use auto-cut off sensors on main doors and windows. These are small devices that attach to the closing edges of doors and windows; when they are opened, and left open for a predetermined length of time, the sensors trigger air-conditioning units to cut out. While the initial cost of sensors is several thousand Baht, the investment usually pays off over a short period of time through lower electricity bills.

Preventing air-conditioners from being left on while guests are out all day is more difficult to resolve. In hotels, door keys are generally inserted into a slot to turn on the electric supply, which shuts off when the guest removes the key to go out. A similar system can be installed in private rental properties; however, this only works when one key is provided and the reality of most rental situations is that several guests or couples each require their own key, which allows one key to be left in the property to power the air-conditioning while others are carried with the guests. There are high-tech solutions, such as motion-sensors, although the cost of equipment and installation is often disproportionate to cost savings. In such cases, the low-tech solution is the most effective: asking the cleaners to turn off air-conditioning if guests are out!

Providing fans in each room in addition to air-conditioning is another way to reduce electricity bills. By providing guests with a choice, some will opt for fans, particularly at night if they prefer not to sleep in an air-conditioned environment. This is potentially a win-win situation in that guests are more comfortable and electricity bills are reduced. The fitting of mosquito screens operates on a similar principle: if there is a breeze, many guests prefer natural cooling than the use of air-conditioning. Roof insulation is another tried-and-tested way to reduce energy costs; again, there are upfront installation costs, yet these are made back over time through lower electricity bills.

From a design perspective, full-frontal windows are highly suited to tropical properties, allowing inside areas to open onto outdoor terraces. However, when large windows are in the sun, rooms become like greenhouses, which generally means higher electricity bills unless efforts are made to reduce the heating effect. At the architectural stage, therefore, consideration should be given to structures, canopies and awnings, and even the strategic use of landscaping and tall canopy trees to mitigate the effect of direct sunlight. Selecting the right specification of glass for windows and doors, together with the installation of curtains or blinds on windows and doors in full sunlight is essential.

A final mentioned should be made about pool lights and Jacuzzis. When rental guests use the pool at night, pool lights tend to get left on after use; indeed, guests often go to bed and leave pool lights on during the night. The same is true of Jacuzzis: guests rarely remember to turn off a Jacuzzi after use, which means the system is left running for hours after use. It is therefore good practice to install automatic time delayed cut-off switches for both pool lights and Jacuzzi systems to save running costs.

Summary

When designing a rental property, consideration should be given to:

- Property design and layout, with a particular focus on "outdoor living" based on a fundamental understanding of how a resort property is used.
- Bedroom configuration and the importance of matching rental properties to market demand.
- The issue of privacy, particularly in relation to the configuration of bedrooms and bathroom design.
- Ensuring there is adequate storage space for rental management related equipment, outdoor furniture and personal belongings.
- Interior décor, particularly with a view to using durable, hardwearing furniture, materials and fabrics.
- The issue of child safety and designing properties that can be safely rented to guests with young children.
- The importance of *flexibility* to maximise rental opportunities.
- Cost savings, especially in relation to reducing utility bills.

114
Property management

Planning the management of a rental property could be considered a process with five distinct steps:

- Property management
- Rental management
- Additional services
- Marketing, bookings and administration
- Deciding who is responsible for each task

Breaking the task of rental management into five steps helps us to appreciate its scope and to divide the decision making process into manageable parts. For convenience, each of the five steps is discussed in a separate chapter, commencing with this chapter, which discusses property management. The discussion continues through to chapter 118, which acts as a summary and checklist.

A good place to start is to distinguish *property management* from *rental management.* Property management involves tasks that need to be performed whether a property is rented out or not, whereas rental management refers to tasks that are performed in relation to rental guests. Therefore, "property management" refers to the following:

Garden maintenance. This involves the general maintenance and upkeep of landscaping and gardens. It is thus typically associated with villa management. It includes trimming plants and trees, weeding flowerbeds, mowing lawns and replacing plants. In the case of condominiums or other properties within a development, garden maintenance is usually part of the management company's duties and billed as part of the common area management fees.

Swimming pool cleaning and maintenance. Managing a swimming pool generally includes five elements: pool cleaning; replenishing water levels due to evaporation or leakage; the purchasing and application of pool chemicals; inspection and maintenance of the pool pump system and filters; inspection and repairs to the pool (such as loose tiles or grout).

Pest control. As discussed in chapter 55, pest control is an essential element in the management of a tropical property, if you don't want the property to be eaten by termites or to become a home for a hundred other varieties of insects. Pest control tends to be a service included within the scope of common area management for managed developments and apartment complexes. However, do not automatically assume the service includes pest control *inside* your property, which is a privately owned space.

Security. If your property is a condominium unit, it is usual for the management company to provide security for the building. For a stand-alone property, it is wise to consider some form of security, such as an alarm system, CCTV or on-site security guards. The key concept is that any security solution needs to be *practical.* If you have CCTV or a webcam linked to the Internet, you might be able to watch as someone enters your property and starts to rob it, but then what? Likewise, sensor lights and alarm systems might act as a deterrent in some cases, although to be practically effective alarm systems must be linked to a quick response unit – a service provided by some private security companies. Due to the issue of practicality, the best solution is often low tech: an on-site security guard (to reduce costs, it is possible to engage a security guard only for the 12-hour night shift).

Airing the property. If a property is not occupied, the property must be periodically aired to prevent mould and musty smells. Property management companies usually offer "unoccupied services", which typically includes the cleaning and airing of a property on a weekly basis.

Property inspection and maintenance. Even when unoccupied, a property (and its systems, equipment and appliances) needs to be periodically inspected in order for faults to be rectified and for the property to be maintained in good condition. This includes checking the exterior of the property for weather related damage and the interior for leaks after heavy rain. If repairs are needed, contractors must be engaged and supervised while work is carried out.

Payment of utility bills. Property owners need to make arrangements for the payment of utility bills, which are commonly payable on a monthly basis, including electricity, water, telephone, Internet, cable or satellite TV. This is particularly important for non-resident owners. The payment of utility bills is a standard service offered by most property management companies.

Collection and forwarding of mail. If you are using your property's address for any purpose (for example, if it is the correspondence address stated in legal contracts), it is necessary for mail to be collected and forwarded on a regular basis. Again, this is usually a service provided by property management companies.

Wastewater management. If wastewater is collected in septic tanks, these need to be checked periodically and emptied if necessary. Naturally, this is more applicable to a tenanted property, although it is relevant to property management.

Common area management and maintenance. If a property is part of a condominium or managed development, management fees for the upkeep and maintenance of common areas are payable whether or not the property is rented out (and for this reason it is mentioned here).

Below is a summary of the tasks falling under the ambit of property management:

PROPERTY MANAGEMENT
Garden maintenance
Swimming pool cleaning & maintenance
Pest control
Security
Airing the property when not in use
Property inspection & maintenance
Payment of utility bills
Collection and forwarding of mail
Waste water management
Common area management & maintenance

The second step is to identify the tasks related to the *rental management* of a property (as distinct from *property management*). The following is a summary of the key services associated with short-term rental management (many of these services are not required in relation to long-term rental, or are required only on a limited basis):

Prior to arrival. So that the property is at a comfortable temperature and in a state of readiness for the arrival of guests, it is common for air-conditioners to be switched on and for last minute checks to be performed to make sure all plumbing, air-conditioning, electrical systems and appliances are functioning properly.

Meet and greet. It is standard practice for rental guests to be met at their point of arrival, which is usually the airport, by a (Thai) person holding a sign bearing the guests names.

Airport transfer. Arranging for guests to be transported from the airport to the rental property is a standard requirement for most short-term rentals. Usually airport transfer (to and from the property) is included in the rental rate; sometimes it is provided at an additional cost.

Guest reception. Upon arrival at the property, it is common to welcome guests with some sort of refreshment or "welcome drink". Luxury property owners (or more thoughtful property owners) also arrange fresh flowers, essential oils and soft music for guest arrivals. Remember, most short-term rental guests have travelled halfway around the world to get to the property.[324]

Welcome pack. It is good practice for a selection of basic provisions (tea, coffee, milk, bread, sugar, fruit, bottled water, juice, beer, etc) to be provided so guests don't immediately need to go shopping. Guests also appreciate arriving at a property to find a well-stocked fridge (or at least something in the fridge!). If provisions are provided, they should demonstrate some level of cultural

---

[324] It should be recognised that the manner in which guests are welcomed also has an indirect impact on complaints. If guests are sincerely and warmly welcomed on check-in, they are less likely to complain about minor issues; if they do feel the need to complain, they usually do so in a cordial manner. If guests are not warmly welcomed (for instance, their baggage is dumped on the pavement and the driver promptly disappears), complaints tend to be made in a more adversarial manner and as a deliberate means to elicit some form of compensation.

sensitivity; for instance, if guests are Korean or Japanese, instant noodles and green tea are generally preferred instead of coffee and biscuits. Ideally, these provisions should comprise a shopping list that has been individually tailored in advance to meet the requirements of the guests (this can be provided complimentary or as an additional service).

Property orientation. A qualified person should be on hand to "introduce" guests to the property. This is generally a familiarisation tour of the property and includes the operation of appliances, entertainment systems, safes, and how to access the Internet. The person conducting the introduction should also provide details concerning the frequency of cleaning, the changing of linen and removal of rubbish. In addition, the person should be able to answer any questions the guests might have about the local area; recommend restaurants and tours; and advise guests about things they should be aware of. Remember, guests are typically strangers to the area they are staying in, so local information is often appreciated. I am reminded of the instruction recently given to guests upon arrival at a luxury villa: "Please don't leave your shoes outside!" The guests were surprised because the normal request is to remove shoes before entering. The reason was soon discovered: ignoring the advice, one guest left his shoes outside on the mat and they promptly disappeared, taken by a street dog![325]

Information portfolio. It is common to leave a booklet on the coffee table, which contains essential information and commonly-asked questions, such as instructions how to operate air-conditioning systems, entertainment systems and appliances; instructions how to use the internet together with the password; any rules and regulations related to the property and common areas; emergency contact numbers; and information about the local area, including restaurants, bars and excursions.

Inspection and inventory control. An inspection and inventory should be conducted with the guests (at both check-in and check-out) to ensure the items noted in the inventory list (see *Rental agreements,* chapter 117) are present and everything is in working order. This ties in with the payment and refund of a security deposit (an inventory list with "replacement values" should form part of the rental agreement).

Collection of deposit. If the security deposit has not been paid in advance together with the rental payment, it should be collected from the guests at the time of check-in.

---

[325] In this case, the owner of the shoes took things in good humour, although if it had been a guest flying in straight from the office wearing Gucci shoes or their best pair of Jimmy Choo's, it could have ended badly!

Meter readings. If utility bills are to be paid by guests according to usage, meter readings need to be taken at check-in and check-out (ideally in the presence of the guests to avoid disagreements). The meter readings should be noted in the rental agreement or in a separate document referred to by the rental agreement.

Housekeeping. Housekeeping is one of the key components of rental management. It involves the cleaning of the property and the changing of bed linens and towels on a regular basis for the duration of the rental period. When engaging a management company, it is important to pay attention to the details of the housekeeping service; due to the vast differences in standards between management companies (and among the different staff of a chosen management company), it is important to confirm with each management company what cleaning duties are *specifically* included so there are formal standards against which the quality and comprehensiveness of cleaning can be assessed. It is also necessary to agree on the frequency and timing of housekeeping services to ensure they correspond with the rental contract (short-term or long-term) and the preference of the guests. Long-term tenants might not require cleaning services or might require only weekly housekeeping, while short-term vacation guests might expect the property to be cleaned and towels and linen changed on a daily basis. These details need to be agreed in advance with the management company and included in the rental agreement with guests because rates charged by management companies naturally differ depending on the frequency of cleaning (such as daily, weekly or twice each week). In other words, if a weekly rate has been agreed with a management company and guests subsequently request housekeeping on a daily basis, the management company will adjust rates accordingly, which will affect your profitability. Another detail to consider is whether the property owner or the management company is responsible for supplying towels and linen. If the management company supplies towels and linen, this will be reflected in the fee structure. As a rule of thumb, there needs to be a *minimum* of three sets of towels and linen per person: one in use, one in storage, and one in the laundry at any given time.

Laundry. While the laundering of towels and linen is often part of the housekeeping service, it is listed separately because the service is sometimes arranged by a specialist cleaning company (some companies collect and deliver to the property).

Removal of rubbish. One of the cleaner's tasks is usually to remove rubbish from the property and place it in a bin for government collection. The task is noted separately because rubbish must sometimes be taken away from the property to a separate collection point.

Amenities. Some property owners or management companies provide guests with a full range of luxury soap, shampoo and super soft toilet tissue; while others provide a measly wafer of soap that disappears after a single use and a few sheets of the cheapest toilet paper left on the roll by the previous guests. The range and quality of amenities provided for rental guests is entirely up to you. Just remember, the cost of good quality amenities is usually only a tiny fraction of the rental rate but is disproportionately appreciated by guests.

"Pre-emptive" maintenance. Rental properties need to be regularly inspected to ensure all systems (plumbing, electrical, air-conditioning) and appliances are functioning properly. The objective is to make sure that if any maintenance or repairs are necessary, they can be carried out when the property is unoccupied. Problems should not be left for guests to discover for two reasons: first, because of the inconvenience caused to guests and, second, to avoid requests for refunds or discounts, which is common if a property fails to meet expectations and guests are disturbed by technicians.

Emergency contact. If any systems, equipment or appliances are discovered to be faulty by guests, or in the event of an emergency, there should be an emergency contact person (ideally more than one) who is able to solve problems. It must also be established whether the person is contactable 24-hours or only during office hours. Details should be provided to guests in advance, or upon arrival. There is a disparity in expectations between short-term vacation guests and long-term tenants; the former generally expect things to be fixed immediately or within the same day of a fault being discovered, while the latter tend to be slightly less demanding.

Key management. Key management is a responsible job, which involves handing over the keys to guests, ensuring there are a sufficient number of keys for the number of guests, and getting keys back from guests at the end of their stay. It is also a security related task, whereby keys must be held securely when the property is unoccupied and records need to be kept of the personnel that have copies of the keys in order to perform their duties. Locks also need to be periodically changed.

Below is a summary of the tasks generally falling within the ambit of rental management:

RENTAL MANAGEMENT
Prior to arrival
Meet and greet
Airport transfer
Guest reception
Welcome pack
Property orientation
Information portfolio
Inspection & inventory control
Collection of deposit
Meter readings (if applicable)
Housekeeping
Laundry
Removal of rubbish
Amenities
"Pre-emptive" maintenance
Emergency contact
Key management

116
Additional services

The third step is identifying the additional services you might want to include as part of the "rental package" in order to differentiate your rental property (or services that you will provide as "optional extras"). Examples might include the following:

Food delivery. Property owners and rental management companies often provide menus from local restaurants that have agreed to deliver food to the property.

In-house chef. Many rental agents offer in-house chef services for breakfasts, lunches or dinners, or for special meals upon request. Guests are usually charged a set fee for the services of the chef, plus the shopping bill for food and drinks.

Car rental. Car (or motorbike) rental is the most popular additional service for rental guests, especially for properties that are not within walking distance of beaches and amenities. Alternatively, when guests are not comfortable with driving in Thailand, a car and driver is often requested. If you own a car and plan to make it available for the use of rental guests, make sure the car insurance covers commercial use. In many cases, it is better to make arrangements with a professional rental company (with comprehensive insurance), which means guests can sign contracts directly with the rental company.

In-house massage is another service often requested by rental guests.[326]

Concierge. Concierge service is a popular requirement, especially for non-English speaking guests. A concierge is a person who is at hand to assist guests during their stay for arranging car hire, tours, excursions, restaurant bookings, or just to act as a translator.

Tours and excursions. Some rental guests prefer to pre-arrange tours and excursions before their arrival in Thailand. Alternatively, leaflets and tour information can be provided inside the property (some property owners or concierges view this as an opportunity to earn additional income through referral fees).

---

[326] Although for owners that are concerned with getting oil on bed linen, it is often better to recommend a local spa!

Baby sitting. The services of a reliable babysitter are sometimes requested. This can either be provided at an outside location or a babysitter can come to look after children at the rental property.

Grocery shopping and delivery. This is a useful service to offer to rental guests who prefer not to spend their precious vacation time in a supermarket.

Guest laundry. The laundering of towels and linen is generally covered under housekeeping; however, the laundry of guests' personal items is usually a separate and additional service.

Live-in staff. Larger luxury rental properties often have separate accommodation for staff. Indeed, a live-in maid (chef or property manager) is expected in certain segments of the rental market.

Offering additional services

With reference to the services mentioned above, there are three general options:

Firstly, services can be offered as part of the rental package to add value and differentiate your property from competitors. For instance, you might decide to offer a rental rate that includes the services of a concierge, an in-house chef, car rental, personal laundry and a free massage with a local spa.

Secondly, services can be offered as optional extras. If properly planned, they might also provide an opportunity to earn additional income apart from rental revenue.

Thirdly, if you don't plan to provide any of these services, it is always helpful to have relevant contact information available for guests so they can contact service providers directly.

Below is a summary of the most commonly requested additional services:

ADDITIONAL SERVICES
Food delivery
In-house Chef
Car rental
In-house massage
Concierge
Tours & excursions
Baby sitting
Grocery shopping and delivery
Guest laundry
Live-in staff

117
Marketing, bookings and administration

The fourth step is to identify the tasks involved in marketing a rental property, together with the management and administration related to accepting bookings. This generally includes the following:

Marketing. When you list a property with property rental agents, you benefit by piggybacking onto established marketing channels where your property is advertised to potential customers and matched with relevant enquiries. Any costs related to the marketing of your property are usually included in the agreed commission rate[327]. If you plan to *directly* market your rental property, it is necessary to plan and implement your own marketing strategy, utilising channels such as flyers, print advertising, Internet marketing or database marketing (see chapter 120, which discusses marketing in more detail).

Website. If your property is marketed through rental agents, your property will appear as a listing on their websites. On the other hand, if you market your property directly, a website is usually a key requirement. However, a website is not enough by itself; potential clients need to be directed to your website using techniques such as Search Engine Optimisation (SEO), Google Adwords, blogs, articles, database marketing, or through the use of traditional marketing methods.

Answering enquiries. Prior to the confirmation of a rental booking, potential guests usually request additional information about the property or its location or, if making a booking through your website, they often just want to make contact with a human being before parting with their money. It is therefore necessary for someone to be responsible for timely communication.

Keeping a booking calendar. Booking calendars are essential tools for potential customers when choosing between rental properties; they also reduce the number of enquiries that are solely concerned with availability. It should be an easy task to find a suitable calendar on the Internet that can either be downloaded or attached to your website. Alternatively, an on-line calendar can be built into your website by a web designer. When a rental booking is confirmed, it is important that calendars are updated by blocking out the relevant dates[328]. It is

---

[327] Unless a special advertising campaign highlighting your property is planned, in which case a contribution to marketing costs might be expected.
[328] Especially for direct rental websites that have an *auto-confirmation* function.

also common practice for rental agents to request your property to be put "on hold" or "reserved" while they work with their clients to confirm the details of a rental booking or allow time for payment to be transferred. The booking calendar must therefore be capable of managing both reserved and confirmed dates.

Screening tenants. With long-term tenancies in developed property markets, it is common for potential tenants to be screened by rental agents. Credit checks are made and references are requested from previous landlords before a tenant is accepted. For short-term vacation rentals, since payment is usually made in full in advance, the "screening of tenants" usually takes the form of placing restrictions on certain types of guests, such as groups of university student or stag parties (you get the idea!) These restrictions need to be clearly stated in marketing materials.

Confirming bookings. Once the details of a rental booking have been agreed, the booking needs to be confirmed with some form of rental agreement. Guests need to be made aware of the relevant terms and conditions *before* entering into a binding agreement, together with any management rules and regulations that apply to the property or common areas. With most website bookings this happens automatically, so it is especially important to ensure any terms and conditions (see chapter 121) are incorporated into the online documentation.

Accepting deposits and payments. A system needs to be set up to receive payments and deposits, and for refunds to be made.[329]

Rental agreements. To ensure bookings are made on a professional and legal basis, and to avoid misunderstanding, a rental agreement should be drafted to reflect the specific circumstances of each booking (see chapter 121). Ideally, the rental agreement should also include an inventory list, which is a list of each item in the property, together with a replacement value (in the event of breakage or the "disappearance" of items). These documents need to be considered in conjunction with the payment of a security deposit, an inspection of the property (upon check-in and check-out) and the refund of money (see below).

Coordinating property and rental management services. When a rental booking is confirmed, it is necessary to communicate the dates, arrival time and guest details to those responsible for property and rental management services, in order for the property to be prepared in advance and for the coordination of airport transfers.

---

[329] Professional tax advice should be sought in relation to taxation on rental income.

Bookkeeping and accounting. Detailed records of all payments made and received in relation to a rental property need to be kept to assist with the preparation of accounts and the payment of taxes on rental income (see chapter 123). There are numerous qualified accounting firms that can prepare accounts and submit them on your behalf to the relevant authorities.

Dealing with complaints. If you are consistently renting out your property, complaints are inevitable. This is certainly an area where the 80/20 rule applies![330] No matter how good your property or how far you go to make guests happy, guests will complain and complaints need to be dealt with. The best way to *prevent* complaints is to be honest about the details of your property in marketing materials. In other words, don't misrepresent facts such as size, quality standards, location, distance from the beach, or the fact that there is ongoing construction on both sides of the property! In addition, misunderstandings and disagreements can be avoided by having sufficiently detailed rental agreements, and by engaging a professional management company to maintain the property and provide faultless guest services. When you have done all that is possible to provide guests with an exceptional experience and still complaints are received, it is simply a matter of taking action to deal with them in the most efficient, courteous and professional manner possible. The vast majority of complaints fall into three categories: guests don't like the property (or location) and want to be moved to another (which may or may not be possible); technical problems, whereby an appliance, equipment or system is not working properly; or service is deemed to be sub-standard, whether it relates to housekeeping and cleaning, laundry or car hire. With the majority of rental business conducted via the Internet, bear in mind when dealing with complaints that it doesn't take much effort for a guest to post a derogatory comment on a travel blog or to email a complaint to a website where your property is listed.

Refunding money or security deposits. As a rental property owner, it is necessary to establish procedures for refunding money. In addition to the advance payment of rent, guests should pay a security (or damage) deposit. The security deposit is then refunded after guests vacate the property, assuming the check-out inspection does not reveal any damage or missing items. If damage has been caused to the property, the amount involved needs to be discussed and agreed (with reference to the "inventory list"), whereupon the security deposit is refunded less an appropriate deduction. In addition, with regard to complaints, whether a problem is satisfactorily resolved or not, the question of a refund often arises. In most cases, rental guests request a discount in consequence of a justified complaint; while in other cases, guests have decided to seek a discount and are

---

[330] In this case 80% of the problems are created by 20% of customers.

searching for a reason to justify it! Whatever the reason, rental property owners must be prepared to refund money when necessary to resolve disagreements.

Below is a summary of the tasks generally associated with the marketing, bookings and administration of a rental property:

MARKETING, BOOKINGS & ADMINISTRATION
Marketing
Website
Answering enquiries
Keeping a booking calendar
Screening tenants
Confirming bookings
Accepting deposits and payments
Rental agreements
Coordinating property and rental management services
Bookkeeping & accounting
Dealing with complaints
Refunding money or security deposits

118
Who is responsible for each task?
(Essential)

The previous four chapters have identified the main tasks associated with property and rental management. The fifth step, therefore, is to decide which services are required and who will be responsible for providing them. It is also helpful at this stage to confirm the costs involved.

> **Important tip:** Choosing who will manage and take responsibility for each task is the most important part of the process. Management is key. If a property is professionally managed, it is instantly recognisable: guests will be happy, your life will generally be made easier and your rental property will be profitable. If a rental property is poorly managed, it is equally noticeable: guests will complain, your level of stress will be elevated and profits will suffer! In short, the professionalism of those appointed to take charge of rental management can make or break a rental property.

The importance of professional management

To help illustrate the importance of professional property management, here are three *real life* examples:

- Example 1. The staff hired to clean and maintain a swimming pool hadn't turned up for a week, during which time the water level had dropped by ten centimetres (the pool was no longer an infinity pool; more of a *finity* pool!) and the water had turned a murky green colour. This is discovered on the morning of the guests' arrival and there is not enough time to fix the problem (additional water must be delivered by truck[331] and the earliest possible delivery is the following afternoon; and chemicals must be added to clean the water, whereby three days are needed before the water is safe for swimming again). The guests arrive and are horrified to find algae in the pool of the luxury villa they have paid 18,000 Baht (US$ 600) per night in advance for a much-needed one-week annual holiday and then realise the pool will be "out of order" for half their holiday. After arriving from a 12-hour flight, the lead guest immediately calls the rental agency (and

---

[331] Truck water is common for properties that are not on the government water supply network or that do not have the own deep-water wells.

the property owner) to demand their money back in full. Eventually, because it is high season and alternative accommodation is difficult to find at short notice, the guests settle for a 50% discount and, in their disgruntled state, spend the remainder of the holiday venting their dissatisfaction and complaining about minor problems. [Accounting note: monthly cost of pool cleaning service = 4,000 Baht (US$ 130), loss of rental revenue = 63,000 Baht (US$ 2,100)].

- Example 2. The management company engaged to manage a luxury villa has not performed regular *proactive* inspections. They are also very busy and, as a consequence, have only sent staff to clean the property late in the afternoon on the day of the guests' arrival. When housekeeping staff open the storeroom, it is discovered that all the towels and linen smell of mould due to the high humidity and because they have been sitting there for several weeks. As there is not enough time to send the towels and linen to the laundry before guests arrive, the maids decide to put mouldy sheets on the beds and mouldy towels in the bathrooms. After a long flight, the guests arrive late at night, tired, and just want to shower and go straight to bed … only to find the towels and bed linen smelling like putrid fungus. The booking has been made directly with the villa owner who, due to the time difference, gets woken up by a call in the middle of the night by justifiably irate customers (who demand a discount).

- Example 3. A honeymoon couple arrive after a long-haul flight to their private villa and notice the beautiful Jacuzzi in the master bathroom. As soon as the concierge has left and they are alone, they turn on the taps, strip off their clothes and jump in the Jacuzzi. An hour later, they are snuggled up on the sofa in the downstairs living room when they feel water dripping on them. The drips grow in frequency. They manage to jump up just as the ceiling collapses onto the sofa under the weight of a Jacuzzi-sized wall of water. It was later discovered that the outlet pipe under the Jacuzzi had been incorrectly fitted and the management company had failed to perform proactive maintenance (which should include checking the plumbing systems and equipment to ensure everything is in proper working order). The guests had to be moved into a hotel while repairs to the ceiling could take place. (Ok, so this last story has been slightly embellished but it is "loosely based" on real events!)

At least the point has been made: if a property is not properly managed, things will quickly come off the rails and guests will not be shy to complain. Professional, competent property management companies (and individuals) are the key to ensuring guests have an unforgettable experience (for the right reasons) and maximising rental revenue.

In relation to rental property management, the most common complaints relate to:

1. Poor, inattentive or inadequate cleaning of the property
2. The frequency of changing towels and bed linen
3. Plumbing problems
4. The response time in relation to fixing problems

With regard to housekeeping and cleaning, if a guest checks into a hotel that has not been properly cleaned or where equipment or appliances are not working, the guest is typically moved to another room, with apologies but no loss of revenue. However, if rental guests arrive at your property to find it is not clean or things are not functioning properly, what are the alternatives? Unless you own another property that is both comparable and unoccupied, guests must either reluctantly put up with things or find alternative accommodation. Putting up with things is normally accompanied by a complaint and a request for compensation, while finding alternative accommodation usually translates into a total loss of revenue or, worse, *it ends up costing you money.* In addition, if the booking is through a rental agent, guests will complain to the agent who, in turn, will be reluctant to promote your property in future, which translates into future loss of revenue! This does not take into account the emotional disappointment suffered by guests; in cases where guests have worked all year and looked forward to their one annual vacation, any disruption or service that falls short of expectations has the potential to ruin their holiday and cause a disproportionate reaction.

Furthermore, and as previously mentioned, it doesn't take much time or effort for a guest to post a less than flattering comment on a travel blog or rental website, which can affect future enquiries and, in the case of direct rental property listings, could result in your listing being removed from a site. With the vast majority of initial searches for rental properties being conducted via Internet, this does not assist your marketing objectives.

In short, the success of a rental property depends on the quality of property and rental management; to underestimate this point is the first step to failure. It is unfortunate when property owners view property management as a cost rather than an investment, which is a profound mistake.

Management structure

It is also necessary to consider the various conceptual approaches to apportioning management tasks and services. There are four basic approaches:

1. Full property and rental management companies.

The most straightforward and "hands-off" solution is to appoint one company to manage everything; the whole gamut of property management, rental management, the provision of additional guest services, together with the marketing and administration associated with rental bookings (in other words, all the tasks mentioned in chapters 114 - 117).

Some professional property management companies have the resources to provide such a comprehensive service. In such cases, property owners need only to specify minimum and maximum rental rates, whereby the management company will only accept enquiries falling within the specified rate band and will not bother the owner with further correspondence (except a monthly statement of account). However, while this approach suits some property owners, it sometimes lacks the flexibility required to maximise occupancy and rental income.

Important tip: Property owners that are not resident in Thailand should be aware of the unscrupulous practice where management companies (or staff of the management company) rent out properties without the knowledge of the owners and pocket the money. I am familiar with several cases where property owners have arrived in Thailand for a holiday and, without notice, have turned up at their property to find it occupied by rental guests. This has happened to properties that are not even on the rental market but are being managed for non-resident owners. To combat this, some owners employ a manager to keep their eye on the management company!

2. Dividing tasks according to specialisation.

An alternative (and perhaps the most common) approach is to appoint a management company to provide property and rental management services (the tasks noted in chapters 114 - 116), while engaging another company (or companies) to market the property and manage bookings. Indeed, it is unusual to find a company that is expert at both property management *and* marketing. It is far more common for a company to focus on providing property and rental management services *or* marketing; rarely do they excel at both (many of the most proficient property marketing companies do not provide property management services). Companies that do provide good results in both tend to have two separate departments, one specialising in property management, the other in marketing. The other so-called "full-service" companies typically enter the market to provide property management services, then add a website and start answering rental enquiries. Thus, rather than having the relevant expertise and achieving superior results in both areas, the result is usually good property management and low occupancy.[332]

Getting superior results in both property management and rental bookings often requires engaging companies that specialise in each area; thus, one company provides property management services and *several* other companies are engaged to market the property (and pass bookings to the property management company).

3. Assigning tasks separately.

A third approach is to separately appoint companies or individuals to manage the various different tasks and services. For instance, a specialist pool company might be engaged to clean and maintain the swimming pool; a landscaping company might be engaged to maintain the garden; a pest control company is engaged to spray the property each month; while another company is engaged to provide security. In addition, a management company is engaged to provide cleaning and housekeeping, an individual is engaged for maintenance and property repairs, while another is employed to arrange meet-and-greet, airport transfer, welcome drinks and guest orientation. Then various rental agents are appointed to market the property, while a bookkeeper is hired to manage payments, deposits and refunds.

Obviously, with this approach, there are numerous companies and individuals to coordinate, which requires a far greater level of involvement on behalf of the property owner. Indeed, the more tasks are divided, the more involvement and coordination is required and, for this reason, it tends not to be a viable solution for non-resident owners. In addition, for the property to operate successfully, each of the service providers needs to work together in a consistent and seamless manner. For instance, if one person is responsible for meet-and-greet and airport transfer, while another person is responsible for key management, guest reception and property orientation, the staff involved need to work together to coordinate the check-in of guests. Suppose there is a flight delay and guests arrive late; who will be responsible for communicating this information and rescheduling the various tasks?

4. Self-property management!

The most "hands-on" approach, and one that is certainly not for the faint of heart,

---

[332] Most companies specializing in property management often have a vague clause in their engagement contract to use only *best endeavors* to promote property rentals.

is managing a property yourself,[333] hiring out only the services of a specialist nature that you are unwilling or unable to do. Naturally, this is only an option for those resident in Thailand.

Costs

The issue of costs must also be taken into consideration. Each of the four different management structures mentioned above has a different cost structure. For instance, some full-service property and rental management companies might end up taking 35-50% of your rental revenue; other property management companies charge a fixed fee each month or a fixed fee for each service required, while others charge a set fee plus a percentage of rental income. Some rental agents take 10% commission; others want 20%.

The successful operation of a rental property requires a fine balance between providing a professional service to keep guests happy and actually making a profit (also bearing in mind the issue of taxes on rental income, see chapter 123). Therefore, depending how you decide to apportion the various rental management tasks and services, it is important to compare and evaluate costs at this point.

While noting the cost of each service, it is also a useful exercise to separate *fixed costs* and *variable* costs. Fixed costs are basically the costs you must carry whether or not the property is occupied, while variable costs accrue only when the property is rented out, i.e. such costs depend on occupancy. Therefore, fixed costs generally include the tasks mentioned in chapter 114 under the category of "property management", while the tasks listed in chapters 115 - 117 generally fall under the category of variable costs (unless staff or a management company has been engaged on a fixed monthly retainer to manage the property irrespective of occupancy).

It is also an interesting exercise to consider total monthly *fixed* costs in relation to the average daily rental rate. For example, suppose total fixed costs are 30,000 Baht (US$ 1,000) each month and the average rental rate per night is 10,000 Baht (US$ 330), fixed costs are therefore equivalent to three nights rental revenue. Variable costs should be covered automatically by rental income. In other words, this calculation gives you the number of nights per month you must rent out the property to cover fixed costs. In effect, it gives you a *breakeven* point.[334]

---

[333] Consideration must be given to an appropriate company structure and the issue of a work permit.
[334] It is not a precise breakeven point calculation because a proportion of the rental rate goes towards covering the variable costs.

Checklist

The following charts are a summary of chapters 114 - 117, listing all the tasks mentioned in relation to property management, rental management, the provision of additional guest services, and the marketing and administrative tasks associated with rental bookings. These charts are a useful property rental management checklist for noting the companies or individuals responsible for providing each service, together with the associated fixed or variable costs.

PROPERTY MANAGEMENT	Who is responsible?				Costs?	
	Self	Third-party	Property Management Company	Rental Management Company	Fixed	Variable
Garden maintenance						
Swimming pool cleaning & maintenance						
Pest control						
Security						
Airing the property when not in use						
Property inspection & maintenance						
Payment of utility bills						
Collection and forwarding of mail						
Waste water management						
Common area management & maintenance						
TOTAL:						

RENTAL MANAGEMENT	Who is responsible?				Costs?	
	Self	Third-party	Property Management Company	Rental Management Company	Fixed	Variable
Prior to arrival						
Meet and greet						
Airport transfer						
Guest reception						
Welcome pack						
Property orientation						
Information portfolio						
Inspection & inventory control						
Collection of deposit						
Meter readings (if applicable)						
Housekeeping						
Laundry						
Removal of rubbish						
Amenities						
"Pre-emptive" maintenance						
Emergency contact						
Key management						
TOTAL:						

ADDITIONAL SERVICES	Who is responsible?				Costs?	
	Self	Third-party	Property Management Company	Rental Management Company	Fixed	Variable
Food delivery						
In-house Chef						
Car rental						
In-house massage						
Concierge						
Tours & excursions						
Baby sitting						
Grocery shopping and delivery						
Guest laundry						
Live-in staff						
TOTAL:						

MARKETING, BOOKINGS & ADMINISTRATION	Who is responsible?				Costs?	
	Self	Third-party	Property Management Company	Rental Management Company	Fixed	Variable
Marketing						
Website						
Answering enquiries						
Keeping a booking calendar						
Screening tenants						
Confirming bookings						
Accepting deposits and payments						
Rental agreements						
Coordinating property and rental management services						
Bookkeeping & accounting						
Dealing with complaints						
Refunding money or security deposits						
TOTAL:						

119
Setting rental rates

When setting rental rates for your property, there are a number of factors that need to be considered; while chapter 111 discussed the differences between short-term and long-term rentals, the principles remain the same for both.

The process of setting rental rates should incorporate the following seven issues:

1. Research
2. Advice of agents
3. Pricing strategy
4. Seasonality
5. Occupancy and yield analysis
6. Consistency
7. Flexibility

Important tip: While these issues should be taken into account when setting rates, the *key* point is that the market ultimately decides what rates should be. When selling a property, if the asking price is too high there will be little interest; similarly, if the rental rates you publish are too high, there will be few enquiries. Recognise that there is a "price ceiling". You will know when you hit it because enquiries will stop! Remember, you must meet the market; it is the market that decides and you must take indicators from it.

1. Research

When considering rental rates for your property, the starting point is to do your homework, which means conducting research on comparable properties. The key word here is *comparable:* it is necessary to identify and evaluate properties with the same or similar attributes in regard to location, distance from the beach, floor area, number of bedrooms, sea views, construction quality, and standard of furnishing.

The most efficient method is to perform an Internet search of property rental websites using the attributes of your property as the search criteria, and to evaluate the results. Other useful resources include local property agents, local property publications, and rental websites where properties are listed directly by property owners (i.e. not through rental agents).

Research should also include hotel rates. This might sound odd because hotels are a different market to private property rentals. However, hotels of a similar standard offering similar rates are direct competitors to your rental property. From the perspective of a potential guest, the choice of vacation accommodation is often between a (luxury) hotel villa and a private villa; or a choice between a hotel room and a private apartment. It is therefore wise to consider the rental rate of your property in terms of "cost per room", which helps you to compare your property with hotel rates. For instance, if your property has three bedrooms and the nightly rate is US$ 300, the cost per room is US$ 100. For comparison, if three couples are travelling together on holiday, they could book your property or three hotel rooms for the same cost.

Generally speaking, the more research you conduct, the better the feel you will have for the market, together with an understanding of the rates that are achievable for your property.

2. Advice of agents

There is a difference between *listed* rental rates and *actual* rental rates; the former being the rates advertised by property owners and rental agents, while the latter are the rates actually confirmed when bookings are made. Published rates, depending on the channel, are usually flexible in that potential guests often communicate with the property owner or agent to negotiate discounts or special rates prior to booking. This needs to be born in mind when considering rental rates for your property. In other words, just because the advertised rate for a comparable property is US$ 600 per night, does not mean it is booked at that rate. This is where rental agents can be helpful. Rental agents have their fingers on the pulse of the market because they are familiar with published rates and, because they process bookings, they also know the *actual* rates at which properties are booked. In other words, they are familiar with the *market rate* for rental properties.

It is also necessary to consider rental rates in conjunction with occupancy levels (see point 5 below). For instance, if the rental rate is set at 12,000 Baht (US$ 400) per night, it might be possible to achieve an occupancy level of 50%, while a rate of 10,000 Baht (US$ 330) per night might achieve 60-70% occupancy. This is an area where the advice of rental agents can prove to be invaluable.

Important tip: When seeking the advice of rental agents, it is necessary to be aware of each agent's commission structure. Agents tend to work on one of two main commission structures: either a percentage commission of the rental value (usually between 10-20%) or a mark-up on top of the rental rate, whereby a rental rate is confirmed with the owner, the agent then determines their own (higher) rate and pockets the difference. With the former, it is technically in the interests of the agent to advise owners to set a *higher* rental rate, while with the latter commission structure it is in the interests of an agent to get the owner to agree to the *lowest* possible rate.

3. Pricing strategy

Once you have an understanding of the rates that are achievable for your property, it is necessary to consider a pricing strategy. It should be understood that the lower the rates, generally the higher occupancy you will achieve, and vice versa, all other things remaining equal. Thus, fundamentally, the option exists either to market your property at a higher rate, with the attendant possibility of low occupancy; or at a lower rate with the likelihood of higher occupancy. If your property is new to the rental market, it might be wise to enter the market with lower rates and then increase the rates over time as occupancy levels increase. Indeed, if you are focussed on the general market where there is fierce competition, it might be necessary to accept lower rates to confirm bookings. Alternatively, if you target your property at a particular niche market where there is little competition, higher rates might be achievable.

Another strategy is to differentiate your property from others by advertising rental rates, which are inclusive of various services that are usually excluded, such as car hire, in-house chef or concierge. The flip side of this strategy is the adoption of a "bare bones" pricing strategy, i.e. advertising rates that exclude some of the "standard" services, such as housekeeping, airport transfer or utilities, which then become optional extras. Such a strategy allows you to grab the attention of potential rental guests, although it could backfire once the "extras" become apparent. Therefore, when using this strategy, it is important to ensure the exclusions are clearly advertised. This also applies to service charges or taxes; some owners add a 10% service charge and 7% government tax to published rental rates.

Perhaps the most effective strategy is to set rates at a reasonable level, then use special promotions to attract bookings (see the section on promotions in chapter 120).

4. Seasonality

It is uncommon to find properties that advertise the same rental rate throughout the year. Just like hotels (and most other tertiary markets), rates are usually seasonally adjusted according to demand. In other words, rates are generally lower during "low season" (where supply exceeds demand) and higher during "peak seasons" (where demand exceeds supply).

To design a rate schedule that reflects seasonal demand, it is necessary to research the generally accepted dates for "low", "middle", "high" and "peak" seasons in the resort area where your property is located, and adjust rates accordingly (bearing in mind they should remain competitive with comparable properties for the same periods). To provide an example, here are the advertised rates for a three-bedroom villa in Koh Samui:

Season	Rental Period	Daily Rate
HIGH	16 Jan - 30 Apr	325 USD
MID	1 May - 30 Jun	300 USD
HIGH	1 Jul - 31 Aug	325 USD
MID	1 Sep - 31 Oct	300 USD
LOW	1 Nov - 14 Dec	250 USD
PEAK	15 Dec - 15 Jan	400 USD

5. Occupancy and yield analysis

It is useful to analyse rental returns and yields at various occupancy rates. The following spreadsheet takes the seasons (high, mid, low and peak) and calculates the number of days that fall within each season. It then estimates the rental rates for each season and reduces the rates by 25% to allow for (estimated) property management costs. Different occupancy rates are then applied – 40%, 50% and 60% – to estimate annual rental revenues[335]. Finally, based on a property value of 20M Baht (US$ 665,000), the yield (see chapter 10) is automatically calculated based upon the rental income generated at each occupancy level.

These calculations are useful for purposes of cash flow forecasting; however, more importantly, they demonstrate the impact of different occupancy levels on total rental revenue. Many property owners focus excessively on nightly rates and fail to appreciate the significance of occupancy levels on annual income. Looked at in another way, if your property is rented out continually all year with one-week

---

[335] In reality, rental income calculations for peak seasons are normally based on higher occupancy levels (such as 70%), while rental income calculations for low seasons are generally based on lower occupancy (such as 40%). These calculations were omitted to simplify the chart. For reference, *conservative* investors often base their figures on renting out a property for 100 days of the year, which is approximately 27% occupancy.

rental bookings with a one-day gap between each check-in and check-out, the occupancy rate is 88%[336]. If, however, the one-day gap becomes a four-day gap (between each check-in and check-out), occupancy falls to 64%.[337]

Important tip: The objective of rental property owners should not be the maximisation of rental *rates;* instead, it should be the maximisation of *income* through the interplay between rates and occupancy.

---

[336] ((365/8) x 7)/365) x 100
[337] ((365/11) x 7)/365) x 100

Rental Analysis (Property Value 20M BHT)

Season	Date from	Date to	Days	Nightly Rate (BHT)	Rate less 25% Mgmt Costs	Number of days at % occupancy			Net Rental Income (excl. taxes)		
						40%	50%	60%	40%	50%	60%
High	07/01/2011	22/04/2011	106	15,000	11,250	42	53	64	477,000	596,250	715,500
Low	23/04/2011	30/06/2011	69	12,000	9,000	28	35	41	248,000	310,500	372,600
High	01/07/2011	31/08/2011	62	15,000	11,250	25	31	37	279,000	348,750	418,500
Low	01/09/2011	14/12/2011	105	12,000	9,000	42	53	63	378,000	472,500	567,000
Peak	15/12/2011	06/01/2012	23	18,000	13,500	9.2	12	14	124,200	155,250	186,300
TOTAL			365			182.5	237	292	1,506,600	1,883,250	2,259,900

Yield: 7.53% 9.42% 11.30%

510

6. Consistency

When working with rental agents, it is often best to set rental rates, provide them to each agent and then confirm that each agent is listing the property at the same rate[338]. Pricing consistency is prudent because the easiest way to upset rental agents is if they find your property listed at a lower rate with one of their competitors. In fact, rental agents can lose their credibility if a customer is in the process of confirming a booking (or has already confirmed a booking) and then discovers the same property published on another website at a better rate.[339]

If you market your rental property through your own website or list directly with property rental sites, *while at the same time* working with rental agents, it is also prudent to maintain price consistency. A rental agent's business model is to earn a commission on the rental rate where the commission is included in the published rate[340]. However, some property owners market their rental properties directly and deduct the commission from the rental rate, which allows them to publish a lower rate. Such a strategy might deter rental agents from working with you; indeed, if they find that you are directly marketing the property at a lower rate, agents might stop actively promoting your property. A policy of consistency on published rates might therefore be considered "agent-friendly". Thus, if you market your property directly and list with rental agents, it is wise to advertise the same rates.[341]

However, a consistent pricing policy with reference to rental rates does not mean you cannot negotiate or offer "promotions" (see chapter 120); it simply means that consistency is maintained on a *formal* level to avoid disagreements with agents and confusion among potential customers.

7. Flexibility

Being flexible is often the key to achieving higher occupancy levels, which usually translates into higher overall rental revenue. Flexibility can be introduced into the rental strategy in a number of ways, most obviously is in relation to rental rates. While this might appear to contradict the requirement for consistency discussed above, what this means is simply being flexible *in negotiations* when

---

[338] Unless you have agreed with agents to use a "mark-up" pricing strategy.

[339] Often, if a client finds a lower published rate for the same property, they assume the rental agent is cheating them.

[340] In some cases, international agencies use a multi-level network of agents and must therefore share commission with other agents lower in the network.

[341] Indeed, some rental agency contracts specify that "to ensure competitive pricing, the rates listed on the property owners website or though other channels or agents *must not be lower* than the rates provided".

enquiries are received (not publishing different rates). Remember, there is no contradiction between having a *consistent* pricing strategy *and* being flexible. It is possible to maintain *formal* consistency through published rates, and at the same time to be flexible with rates upon receipt of enquiries.

For instance, if a potential guest likes your property but doesn't quite have the budget, flexibility on price can help to confirm bookings and fill in "occupancy gaps" (gaps in the rental calendar between confirmed bookings). All too often I have seen owners list their rental properties with agents where minimum and maximum rates are agreed; if a rental enquiry is then received that is slightly under the minimum rate, it is declined, which often means the property sits empty earning zero revenue, rather than being flexible on rates to capture the revenue. Rate flexibility should also extend to assisting rental agents when they have a customer with a lower budget than the published rate. If you are willing to reduce your rates to help an agent to confirm a booking (and make money), they will more actively promote and recommend your property to other customers, safe in the knowledge that they have the support of a property owner who is willing to be flexible.

In addition to being flexible on rates, it is also possible to introduce flexibility through special offers such as "last minute deals", free nights ("pay 3 stay 4") and discounts for returning guests. Alternatively, flexibility can be introduced without reducing rates by including "free of charge" additional services such as car rental or an in-house chef. It is also possible to pass on these special offers in a consistent and systematic manner through the network of rental agents.

Summary

When setting rental rates for your property, there are a number of factors that need to be considered, including:
- Research on *comparable* properties (including hotels).
- The advice of rental agents who are familiar with the *market rates* for rental properties.
- Pricing strategy, such as entering the market with low rates and increasing them over time as occupancy levels increase.
- Designing a rate schedule that reflects seasonal demand.
- Occupancy, particularly with regard to the objective of maximising *income* through the interplay between rates and occupancy.
- A policy of consistency on published rates.
- Being *flexible* in order to achieve higher occupancy levels.

120
Marketing

There are many different ways to market your property. Some are conventional, while others are creative and unconventional. How the issue of marketing is approached is purely a matter of choice and ingenuity, and how much effort you are prepared to put in to rent out your property.

The importance of marketing (and the quality marketing materials) cannot be underestimated. Some people go to the trouble of building beautiful luxury villas that remain unoccupied due to poor marketing or due to a lack of understanding of the marketing function. Indeed, some people's idea of rental marketing is fixing a placard on the outside of a property and hoping their target market is among passers by![342]

Others confine themselves to the traditional route of listing properties through rental agents with established marketing channels; while others try a combination of approaches, which might include building a website and marketing the property directly. The latter increases the amount of involvement, although it can be more profitable because paying commissions to agents is avoided. Indeed, when designing a marketing strategy for a rental property, it is the relationship between these interrelated issues – marketing channels, profitability and involvement – that needs to be considered.

Without going too deeply into the technical details and psychology of marketing strategy, the following discussion is aimed at providing a basic checklist of tasks for anyone new to property marketing. If the plan for renting out your property is solely to list your property with rental agents, the task is relatively straightforward and involves just five actions, which are discussed in turn:

1. Photography
2. Text
3. Selecting agents
4. Agency agreements
5. Staying on top of things.

---

[342] This can vex property agents who go to the trouble of marketing the property and confirming a rental booking, and then potentially lose repeat business because guests can now contact the property owner directly.

It should be noticed that the first four of these tasks could be performed by the appointed rental agents, with negligible involvement on your part. However, as the following discussion makes clear, you might prefer to get involved!

After the five basic tasks, the discussion continues with:

6. Websites
7. Internet marketing
8. Rental booking websites
9. Other forms of marketing
10. Promotions

1. Photography

Top quality photography is a *crucial* component of the property marketing process.

With the sophistication of modern digital technology, it is possible to take half-respectable pictures with pocket-sized cameras or iPhones and upload them immediately to websites at virtually no cost. Why hire a photographer? Or why not just leave photography to the rental agents? However, while these quick and easy solutions are tempting, taking snapshots or leaving marketing photography to agents with no formal photographic training is a mistake. Quite simply, photos sell properties. Properties presented in the best light with professionally taken photographs get rented first; an average property with top photography will attract more rental enquiries than a high-end property that has been poorly photographed. Here is a firsthand example from a luxury property rental agency:

Among numerous properties listed on a rental website were two luxury villas in Phuket within the same price range. The first received very few bookings, although each time customers returned from their holiday they gave the villa rave reviews and planned to return to the same villa the following year. The second villa generated a disproportionately higher level of interest but each time it was booked, without exception, customers returned to complain the villa was not as good as it had been portrayed; indeed, many claimed that it had been "misrepresented". On one occasion guests arrived at the villa, immediately called the agent and demanded to be moved to another villa (which is not an easy task for a rental agent during the peak season). When the manager of the rental agency flew to Phuket for an inspection, the reason became clear: the first villa had been poorly photographed, while the second villa had been "creatively" and professionally photographed.

While this is not meant to encourage "creative photography", the message is clear: photography is one of the key elements of a property marketing strategy and significantly impacts the number of enquiries generated. Properties that have been professionally photographed generate more enquiries and superior profits; those marketed with average photography generate average returns. In other words, you will be doing a property (and your rental business) a disservice by taking photographs with a pocket camera or leaving it to be photographed by property agents with no professional training. Therefore, don't cut corners on photography: hire the best photographer you can afford. Money spent on photography should fall under the category of "investment", not "cost".

With regard to fees, while photographers cannot always be judged by their rates, a photographer's fees are often an indication of their professionalism and rates can vary significantly; some "photographers" charge 1,500 Baht (US$ 50) per property, others charge 35,000 – 60,000 Baht (US$ 1,160 – 2,000) per property. What accounts for this difference?

At one end of the scale, the so-called "photographer" arrives with a small digital camera and wanders around taking exterior shots and "holiday snaps" of each room. At the other end of the scale, professional photographers arrive with "props" such as wine glasses, flowers and fruit to enhance the shots, and lighting equipment to present a property in its best light. They might also use models to "inspire the imagination". In addition, a professional photographer will return to the property at different times of the day (and on several different days) to take pictures in different lighting conditions such as late afternoon, just before sunset and with the property lit in the evening. Furthermore, it is standard practice for professional advertising photographs to undergo "computer post production" where images are digitally "cleaned" and digital touch-ups are used to enhance lighting, colours and tones.

In the context of marketing, it pays to remember that while photographs might be taken in a fraction of a second, they can last for years of marketing use. Most importantly, in the high speed Internet marketing environment where you have just moments to catch peoples' attention, they create the critical first impression for potential rental guests browsing through rental websites. In addition, especially if you have a newly completed property, it pays to spend good money to have the property photographed in its "as new" condition because, once it has experienced rental use, it will no longer be in pristine condition (until the first renovation!).

Important tip: Instead of letting rental agents wander through your house to take "happy-snaps", it is more intelligent to arrange for your property to be professionally photographed and to supply each agent with a CD of professionally taken images.

"Virtual tours" – panoramic 360-degree interactive visual tours – of a property are also becoming widely used and provide potential guests with the experience of actually walking through a property. These are a product offered by select photographers. Using a particular photographic technique, together with a special software programme that "knits" pictures together to avoid perspective distortion, it is possible to create a three-dimension virtual "tour" of your property. This is one way to set your property apart from others (that are depicted only by two-dimensional photography). It also addresses the hesitation of rental guests by "showing them around" the property before they confirm a booking; in other words, "what they see is what they get". It also helps to reduce "cognitive dissonance" (and complaints) upon arrival.

2. Text

While photographs create the first (and often decisive) impression of a rental property, the accompanying text enhances that impression. For instance, there is a difference between:

"Five bedroom villa located on the beach with sunset views..."

And:

"Wake up to the sound of waves rolling gently onto the beach and watch glorious sunsets from the pool deck of this stunning five bedroom villa..."

When writing advertising text for a resort property, you should ideally be trying to give potential guests a feel for actually staying in the property (instead of a description). There is a significant emotional element involved in the decision-making process for vacation rentals. Therefore, avoid listing features in an overly factual manner: *"... three bedrooms, dining room, swimming pool, balcony",* which is more suitable for an engineering magazine. Instead you should be focussing on benefits and engaging the emotions in a tasteful manner:

"... take a refreshing dip in the infinity pool and dine under the stars on the moon-terrace with tantalising dishes served by our talented chef".

With marketing text, it is also necessary to keep in mind the people most likely to rent your property and speak directly to them. For instance, if you are targeting families with children, be sure to include key selling points such as: *"safe environment for children to play".* If, on the other hand, you are targeting young revellers, use phrases such as: *"close proximity to bars, nightlife and entertainment areas".*

It is useful to remember that while rental agents might be professionals in their field, it doesn't naturally follow that they are expert copywriters or that they have had training in writing effective advertising text. In fact, many agents follow the same standard format – hardly a recipe for superior results. The truth is that the quality of text, and whether or not it inspires potential guests, directly influences the number of enquiries and bookings for your property. It can mean the difference between guests competing to book your property and receiving no enquiries at all, especially in a competitive rental market.

No one should care more about renting out your property and maximising rental revenue than you, the property owner. Therefore, if you have a particular talent for creative and inspiring writing, it is often better to write your own text than to leave the task to a rental agent; if you don't have a talent, engage someone who does. Make the effort to supply text to the rental agents, instead of leaving the profitability of your property in their hands. In other words, get involved because you are ultimately responsible for the results! It also saves agents time and effort, which is appreciated. Finally, if agents insist on writing their own text, be sure to review and approve it before it is published.

3. Selecting agents

There are numerous rental agents in each of the main resort areas and property owners need to choose carefully which ones they work with. In addition to selecting agents on the basis of professionalism and reputation, it is necessary to determine each agent's strategy in terms of market coverage and specialisation. For instance, one agent might be particularly strong in the luxury market segment and weak in the lower price ranges (it would be a waste of time listing your 3 million Baht (US$ 100,000) condominium with an agent whose target market is the super rich), while other agents might promote to the general rental market or specialise in niche markets such as weddings, corporate events or seminars.

Market specialisation is key factor. While most agents focus on the English speaking market, which includes European and American tourists and expats living throughout Asia, others focus on German, Swedish, Korean and Russian speaking markets. Property owners need to consider the various different geographical markets not only to increase market coverage but, most importantly, because high and low seasons are different for each country and are therefore complementary in terms of annual occupancy.

Important tip: Europeans have summer vacations in July and August, while high season for Korean honeymoon couples is September to December and March to June. Christmas for Europeans and Americans is on the 24th or 25th of December, while for Russians it is 7th January. New Year for most of the world is January 1st, while for the Chinese it is either at the end of January or the beginning of February (depending on the lunar calendar). Considered together, a global marketing strategy is one way to balance rental bookings throughout the calendar year.

While many rental agents profess to have a global marketing strategy, most tend to have a particular geographic focus; indeed, if a rental agent is exclusively English speaking, how can it effectively cover the Russian or Chinese markets?[343] In addition, while most agents claim to use a wide range of marketing channels and strategies, each tends to have its own particular field of expertise; for instance, some have a predominantly Internet-based marketing strategy that relies on sending emails to a database; others have an established base of loyal customers; while others rely on walk-in customers (usually those with offices in central locations with busy foot traffic).[344]

Useful tip: To ascertain which rental agents have the most successful Internet marketing presence, go to the search engines[345], type in "property rentals Phuket", "villa rentals Samui" or "apartments for rent Pattaya" and see which companies appear at the top of the search results.

In addition to rental agents in Thailand's resort areas, listing with international property rental agents can also prove to be an effective strategy. These can be Internet-based rental agents or agents located in the country of origin for an important target market. The best strategy is to list your property with several agents that specialise in your type of property and price segment and that, collectively, provide you with the widest possible market coverage.

If, on the other hand, you plan to engage a sole property agent to provide full property and rental management services, it is essential to ensure the company has a strong rental-marketing department.

4. Agency agreements

When working with rental agents, it is important that some form of "agency agreement" is in place between property agent and property owner (see chapter 121), which sets out the respective obligations of both parties, including the commission rate. Most importantly, if you plan to engage multiple agents, make sure the contracts do not contain a clause that grants any one agent an "exclusive

---

[343] Unless local sub-agents have been appointed.
[344] Some agents focus purely on rental properties located in one resort area, or even a specific area within a resort area, relying only on foot traffic.
[345] Such as www.google.com or www.yahoo.co.uk

agency" for your property. If any property agent insists that you sign a "standard agency agreement", check the details carefully to ensure the agent is working on a non-exclusive basis.

5. Staying on top of things

Once photography and text have been supplied to the rental agents, and agency agreements have been signed, it does not mean you should sit back and forget about your rental property. When an agent has been engaged, it is necessary to check your property listing to make sure all the details are correct. For instance, a friend wondered why he had received no enquiries for his modest two-bedroom villa, until he discovered the person in charge of inputting data at the rental company had made an error and used the rates from a luxury beachfront property!

Property owners should remain in regular contact with each agent to get feedback and fine-tune the marketing strategy. To get better results, for instance, it might be necessary to modify the offer or adjust the rates (see previous chapter). Alternatively, special promotions can be communicated through agents to increase occupancy (see "Promotions" below). Taking an active interest also demonstrates to agents that you are serious about results and that you are keen to assist agents with their enquiries. With regard to communication, if an agent contacts you to discuss rates, availability or to confirm a booking, responses need to be as close to "real-time" as possible. Agents tend to promote properties whose owners are quick to respond to enquiries. For this reason, rental property owners should consider using a Blackberry or iPhone for emails, or appointing a secretary to deal efficiently with enquiries.

> **Important tip:** If you are easily contactable and able to give immediate replies, agents will promote your property ahead of others because they know they can get a deal done (any delay is an opportunity for their competitors to offer alternative accommodation or for their clients to change their mind). If, on the other hand, an agent must wait a day or two to receive a response, your property will soon find its way to the bottom of the recommended list.

6. Websites

If you are content to leave all of your property marketing to rental agents, then you don't need to read any further. However, if you prefer not to be entirely dependent on rental agents; or if you believe the investment in time and money required to directly market a rental property will be more (cost) effective than paying commission to rental agents, there are countless methods that might be employed.

One place to start is with a well designed and user-friendly website. It is even possible to build a simple website yourself using one of the many on-line website building programmes, many of which are free[346]. Websites have come a long way from being mere information providing portals. A property rental website should provide an on-line calendar to allow potential guests to check availability without having to send an email. Ideally, your website should also include a "virtual tour" of the property and an online payment system to allow customers to pay deposits and confirm bookings immediately.

Rental property owners that are slow to respond to enquiries or where international telegraphic transfer is the only method of payment (which typically take several days to be received) often lose bookings (without being aware of it) to property owners with online payment processing systems. For reference, there are two types of online payment system: "online payment systems" where currencies are used for commercial payments, and "payment processing systems" that allow payments to be made with credit cards. Three commonly used systems are Paypal, Worldpay and Paybyweb.[347]

If you are working with agents as well as promoting your property directly through your own website, bear in mind the policy of "agent-friendly" pricing mentioned under "Consistency" in chapter 119.

7. Internet marketing

Having your own website without some level of Internet marketing is like waving your arms in the middle of a Shakira concert to attract attention. In other words, unless someone knows where you are, they are not going to notice you. Similarly, a website will not attract much attention unless you bring or "drive" traffic to it. This can be done in a variety of ways.

The most basic method is Search Engine Optimisation (SEO), which is optimising your website to assist search engines (such as Yahoo and Google) to pick up and prioritize your site when returning search results. There are many different ways to optimise your site, for instance, through the words chosen as a domain name or URL[348], the text and "keywords" used on each page, the number of pages, the number of links to other websites, the frequency with which the website is updated, and many other ways Internet marketing wizards have discovered that reach beyond the limits of my comprehension. For those without the requisite knowledge, the normal course of action is to pay someone to do it, although make

---

[346] For instance, www.weebly.com
[347] www.paypal.com, www.worldpay.com, www.paybyweb.com
[348] The URL or "Uniform Resource Locator" is the address of a specific Web site on the Internet.

sure you are getting results for your money; in other words, make sure your site is returned within the top five or six search results for particular word searches.

Another common way to drive traffic to a website is to use paid for advertising, such as Goodle AdWords or "pay-per-click", which are the sponsored links appearing next to search results. More creative ways to bring people to your website include blogs, listings on property and travel-related forums, posting articles, and social networking sites such as Facebook and Twitter[349]. Database marketing – mailing to email addresses on a database list – can also work well if properly targeted and professionally implemented. For instance, special offers or newsletters can be sent out regularly to those who have voluntarily submitted their details to your website, or to databases that have been purchased, provided they are of sufficient quality (and most are not).

However well designed and marketed your website might be, it must be said that it is difficult to (cost effectively) compete for Internet traffic with the websites of rental agents. It is much like David against Goliath: a website with one rental property competing for traffic with websites featuring hundreds of properties[350]. The challenge is compounded because rental agents typically have a larger budget for Internet marketing and are able to spread marketing costs over a larger number of properties, which is more cost effective than marketing a website with a single property.

8. Rental booking websites

An alternative means to market your rental property is to list the property directly on "owners" rental websites[351], which are basically platforms for owners to directly offer their properties to travellers, whereby the platform provider handles the optimisation and promotion of the site. In other words, the property owner is responsible for uploading text and images to create a listing (which is a time consuming task), while the service providing company brings traffic to the site[352]. It could therefore be considered a hybrid between having your own website and listing your property with an agent; you have your own pages within a website where potential guests can browse through competing offers, while enquiries are forwarded directly to the respective property owners.

In terms of marketing, the key to success with such sites is the same: sharp

---

[349] www.facebook.com, www.twitter.com
[350] Websites with more pages and more information are ranked higher by search engines.
[351] For instance, http://www.tripadvisor.com/BusinessListings or www.holidaylettings.co.uk
[352] The company charges either a listing fee or a commission on the value of rental bookings.

photographs and well-written text[353]. However, perhaps of equal importance is the manner in which a property is differentiated from others by promotions and special offers, such as complimentary spa treatments, early bird specials or free nights. Efficient response times to enquiries is another key issue, together with the ability of guests to "auto-confirm" bookings without having to correspond with owners.

Finally, it should be noted that price points are crucial, particularly for the type of customer that browses the Internet to compare alternative offers and who prefer to book holiday accommodation directly with property owners.

9. Other forms of marketing

Most of the discussion so far has been concerned with Internet marketing, primarily because of its dominance as a marketing and business medium. However, there are numerous other (traditional) marketing channels that could be used to attract tenants, such as paid-for advertising in local magazines, newspapers and in-flight magazines, or leaflets and flyers distributed to restaurants, bars and local businesses.

However, with print advertising, it is necessary to keep two things in mind: first, this form of advertising tends to be comparatively expensive (less cost effective) unless it is tailored and targeted to a particular market niche. Dropping thousands of leaflets from a plane is only cost effective for wartime propaganda purposes; to be viable in a commercial context, advertising must be considered in terms of cost per confirmed booking (or enquiry generated). Second, print advertising in local publications and locally distributed leaflets is effectively marketing to people already in Thailand (or in the case of airline magazines, on their way to Thailand) and the majority of people in Thailand already have their accommodation booked. This means you are marketing to the few who have travelled without a pre-arranged booking or those who might have a confirmed hotel reservation for a few days and thereafter plan to move into a rental property (or to those who are planning to return to Thailand for their next vacation, which is a long response lead-time).

In addition to print advertising, there are many other creative ways to market a rental property. For instance, it is possible to orchestrate a package deal with a travel agent or make a special offer for employees, friends or family of a club or organisation. Alternatively, a rental property could become a retreat for the top management of a corporation or promoted as a prize for the best performing

---

[353] Properties must also meet the requirements of rental guests in terms of location, size, design, etc.

salespeople; or the property could be endorsed by way of a joint venture with a wedding planner. If the result is just one booking from each new idea, it doesn't take long to boost occupancy. Indeed, each successful method adds another piece to the puzzle: a few months long-term rent through the use of local print advertising, a number of "short-term" weekly rentals via rental agents, several direct bookings through a website, some gaps in the rental calendar filled through creative marketing, and soon the rental property will be providing a reasonable return on investment.

10. Promotions

Special promotions are one of the most effective ways to fill in occupancy "gaps" in the rental calendar and to generate additional rental income. Based on the premise that an empty property is dead money, it is preferable to have tenants in your property paying US$ 200 per night than having a property sit empty at a published rate of US$ 400 per night! Using special promotions to fill occupancy gaps could also be considered a means to cover overheads (the fixed monthly costs associated with property management), which has the long-term impact of increasing overall profitability in combination with rental bookings at the full-published rate. Remember, profit is simply revenue minus costs (and taxes) so any confirmed booking at a reasonable rental rate should assist profitability[354]. In addition, the higher the occupancy rate, the more attractive a property appears as a *business* upon resale.

There are numerous promotions that can be used in the context of a rental property. One method is to offer lower rates for "reduced occupancy". For example, if your property has three bedrooms, it is possible to "lock-off" one or two of the rooms and offer the property with one or two-bedroom occupancy at a reduced rate. This can be justified by the fact that with reduced occupancy, electricity bills tend to be lower (mainly through lower use of air-conditioning), cleaning and laundry bills are similarly reduced and there is the indirect benefit of reduced wear and tear.

With vacation rentals, the generally accepted practice is for short-term rental rates to *include* utility bills, and for long-term rates to *exclude* utility bills (which are paid according to metered usage). This leaves the possibility of stripping out the utility costs from short-term rentals and offering special (short-term) rates that do not include utility bills, i.e. "short-term rates plus bills". In this way, you guarantee receipt of an amount that is sufficient to cover overhead costs, while guests cover the unknown sum represented by utility bills.

---

[354] Provided it is not offset by wear and tear.

Another method of promotion is to offer "low season" rental rates or special "weekend" or "weekday" rates. Alternatively, reduced rates can be offered for specific dates, according to the gaps in the rental calendar; in other words, it is a targeted means to fill gaps between confirmed rental bookings.

Other promotions include "last minute" special offers, which might help to rescue occupancy rates by filling the gap before the next confirmed booking. At the other extreme is the "early bird" promotion, which is a marketing creation to encourage guests to confirm bookings and pay deposits before a certain deadline. Alternatively, lower rental rates or discounts can also be offered to returning guests.

Another popular promotion is to offer free nights for bookings that exceed a pre-determined length of stay; for instance, "one free night for each five nights booked", "pay 3 stay 4" or "pay 7 stay 9". If you prefer not to give away free nights, consider including free services or "complimentary extras" such as car rental, spa treatments, excursions or boat trips.

For quick reference, here is a summary of the promotions mentioned above:

- Low rates for reduced occupancy
- Special low season offers
- Special weekend or weekday rates
- Special rates for specific dates
- Short-term rates "plus bills
- Last minute special offers
- Early bird promotions
- Discounts for returning guests
- Free nights
- Complimentary extras or services

Summary

- Top quality photography is a key component of the property marketing process, which creates the critical first impression for potential rental guests.

- The quality of advertising text, and whether or not it inspires potential guests, directly influences the number of enquiries and bookings for your property.

- Property owners need to choose carefully which rental agents to work with in terms of market coverage and specialisation.

- When working with rental agents, it is important that some form of agency agreement is in place, which sets out the respective obligations of the parties.

- When an agent has been engaged, property owners should remain in regular contact to get feedback and demonstrate a commitment to assist agents with their enquiries.

- When setting up your own property rental website, it should incorporate an availability calendar and an on-line payment system.

- If you have your own website, it is necessary to drive traffic to it using methods such as Search Engine Optimisation and "pay-per-click" advertising.

- Owners direct websites are a hybrid between having your own website and listing your property with an agent.

- The effectiveness of traditional marketing channels, such as magazine advertising, must be considered in terms of cost per confirmed booking.

- Special promotions are one of the most effective ways to fill in occupancy gaps in a rental calendar.

121
Rental agreements

Many people rent out their properties in Thailand by confirming the rate, agreeing dates and receiving payment, without any formal contract being signed. This works well ... until a problem arises, whereupon there is nothing in writing to clarify the basis of the rental and nothing to refer to that might help settle a dispute. The purpose of a rental agreement, therefore, is to formally set out all the details that have been agreed, and to act as a point of reference in the case of misunderstanding or disagreement. For this reason, a rental agreement should be used each time a property is rented out, whether on a short-term or long-term basis.

From a commercial point of view, a balance needs to be struck somewhere between a rental contract that is excessively detailed and onerous to the point of scaring a would-be tenant, and a contract that lacks sufficient detail to provide an adequate basis for resolving disagreements.

Important tip: To ensure the terms and conditions of a rental agreement are binding, they should be brought to the attention of the guest (and agreed by signing) prior to payment being made. In other words, if the guest has transferred payment, and the terms and conditions of the rental are sent afterwards, the guest could claim they are not binding since the contract had been constituted before he became aware of the terms and conditions.

Rental agreements need to be professionally drafted to suit the individual circumstances of the rental and the property. Contracts for long-term tenancies and short-term rentals differ in their content, although the basic structure is the same; once drafted, however, it should be possible to use the agreement as a template for subsequent rentals by changing only the unique details of the booking (such as names, dates, rental rates and services provided).

The main points that should be covered by most rental agreements are detailed below:

Contractual clauses

Parties to the agreement. On behalf of the guests, the rental agreement is usually signed by the "lead guest" or by two or more of the guests acting jointly; the agreement should make the lead guest (or guests) responsible for the behaviour of all guests staying at the property. As a property owner, professional tax and legal advise should be sought in regard to the most suitable entity for entering rental agreements, bearing in mind the issues of liability and taxes on rental income (see chapter 123). Addresses and contact numbers should be stated and passport copies should be attached to the agreement.

Location of the property: The rental agreement should state the name and address of the property, together with a description of the property including area, number of rooms, room sizes, bed configurations, swimming pool size and depth, and any other descriptive detail that is considered relevant.

Rental period. This should comprise the date of arrival and date of departure, together with the total number of days, weeks or months.

Arrival and departure times. It is advisable to state the earliest check-in time and the latest checkout time in case consecutive bookings require customers to be checked in and out on the same day. It is common for checkout to be prior to 12 noon (or 10am), while common check-in times are 2pm or 3pm. These times can be used in the absence of specific check-in and check-out times being requested by quests (although in practice it is usual to accommodate guests' actual arrival and departure times).

Rental rate. The daily, weekly or monthly rental rate should be stated, together with the total rental value, i.e. the number of days, weeks or months multiplied by the daily, weekly or monthly rate.

Payment schedule. The schedule for payment is an important detail. It is common to request a deposit to confirm the booking, followed later by the balance. The deposit is commonly 15% - 30% of the total rent, and is usually payable within 3-5 days of confirming availability or signing the rental agreement.[355] The balance is usually payable in full 30-60 days prior to the date of arrival.[356] It follows that if a booking is made less than 30 days before the date of arrival, full payment in advance should be requested. If the agreement relates to long-term rental on a monthly basis, rent is normally paid on the first day of each month for the duration of the term. The payment schedule is important due to its relationship to cancellations and refunds (see below). It is additionally important because

---

[355] Sometimes a higher deposit is requested for bookings made for peak seasons (such as 50% of the total rental value), which must be paid within 48 hours of confirmation of availability, i.e. there is a shorter "on hold" period. This is to guard against the potentially greater loss of revenue due to peak season cancellations.

[356] Again, while 30 days is common for low season bookings, 45-60 days is more common for peak season bookings.

rental properties are often put "on hold" (for the requested dates) pending receipt of payment, which means the property cannot be booked by another party until the hold status expires.

Account details and currency. If payment is to be transferred to an account, sufficient details of the bank account should be provided to enable an international telegraphic transfer[357]. It is also important to state the currency and, if the payment currency is different from the currency in which the rental rate is denominated, the exchange rate needs to be stated. The issue of bank charges also arises and is typically addressed by specifying "payments to be remitted free from all bank fees and charges".

Services included. The agreement should include details of the services agreed. This includes services that are standard, and those that are optional or provided upon request (refer to chapters 115 - 116). For instance, "the rate includes cleaning services and change of linen each 3 days, airport transfer to and from the property (for the number of guests registered on the booking), daily breakfast and personal laundry. The more detail included, the less scope for misunderstandings.

Utilities. If utilities and services (electricity, water, satellite TV) are included in the rental rate, this needs to be stated. If they are additional and payable according to usage, this should be specified, together with the unit rates.[358] In addition, the agreement should refer to the procedure for confirming meter readings at both check-in and checkout. A separate document is often used at check-in to note the meter readings, which is signed and accepted by the guest (the same document is typically used to confirm the number of keys provided, together with a replacement cost in the event that keys are lost).

Maximum number of guests. It is a matter of prudence to state the maximum capacity of the property or the maximum number of guests (including children) that may reside at the property, corresponding to the rental rate. This is to prevent the property being booked by two guests who then arrive at the property with twelve friends (with the consequence of extra cleaning, higher utility bills and additional wear and tear). One approach is to request the name of each guest in advance who become "registered" guests. If the management company later finds additional "unregistered" guests residing at the property, the agreement can provide the option of requesting them to vacate the property or increasing the rental rate (at your discretion).

---

[357] Usually bank name, bank address, account name, sort code, account number, SWIFT code, BIC code.

[358] If guests are made aware of their responsibility for utility bills, but are not aware of unit rates, it can result in disagreement at the time of checkout.

Security deposit. It should be standard practice to take a security deposit to cover the cost of any damage[359] or breakages during the rental term (not normal wear and tear) or to cover utility bills. It is also necessary to outline the procedure for taking and returning deposits. For instance, the "damage deposit" could be paid in advance by bank transfer together with the rental payment, and returned in the same manner at the end of the rental period; or it could be paid separately to the property manager upon arrival and returned in the same manner (less the cost of breakages!). As the return of the security deposit is dependent on whether damage or breakages have occurred, to function properly and fairly it needs to work hand-in-hand with inspections upon check-in and check-out, together with an "Inventory Checklist of Furniture, Fixtures and Appliances" (see below). With regard to the amount of a security deposit, for short-term rentals such as 7-14 days it is common to request one or two days rent or 25% of the rental value. For long-term rentals on a monthly rate, one or two month's rent is typical.

Inventory Checklist of Furniture, Fixtures and Appliances. Upon check-in, a walk-through inspection of the property should be conducted with the guests to inspect furniture, fittings and appliances and to ensure their proper working condition. The inspection should be accompanied by a checklist of items, which describes each item and provides a "replacement cost". Once the inspection is complete, the inspection report should be signed. Upon checkout, another walk through inspection should take place and in the event of any damaged or "missing" items, the appropriate amount as set out in the checklist should be deducted from the security deposit. In the case of major damage, such as smashed windows or explosions caused by fireworks detonating indoors (real life example), the rental agreement should provide for "a reasonable amount to cover the cost of repair and, if it exceeds the amount of the security deposit, the additional cost will be payable on demand".

Cancellation. The rental agreement must provide a procedure for cancelling (or changing) a booking, together with a system for the calculation of any cancellation charges. This clause usually works hand-in-hand with the payment schedule. For instance, one method is to specify a cancellation charge of 20% if a booking is cancelled more than 60 days before the arrival date; a 50% cancellation charge if the booking is cancelled between 30-60 days prior to arrival; and a 100% cancellation charge if the booking is cancelled less than 30 days before arrival (i.e. the full rental payment is forfeited). As a property owner (or agent), cancellation charges are designed to compensate for loss of revenue if another booking cannot be secured for the same dates, especially at short notice. Alternatively, the rental payment received can be credited for future use of the

---

[359] Including any "excessive cleaning" required for upholstery or rugs.

property (for the same number of days) within a certain specified period after the date of cancellation, such as twelve months. The cancellation clause should also cover the issue of payments not being received by the scheduled date, in which case the property owner should *reserve* the *right* to follow the procedure for cancellation. In addition, it should cover instances where guests vacate the property before the end of the rental period without mutual agreement.

> **Important note:** Cancellation by the property owner should also be covered, such as in the case of natural disaster, severe interruption of services, or where the property is otherwise rendered unusable. Ideally the property owner should reserve the right to terminate the agreement and return money without interest or penalty. Alternatively, the property owner can "endeavour to locate an alternative property for the guest".

Rules and regulations. If your property is situated within a development or condominium block, there are usually rules related to visitors and the use of common areas. These rules should be incorporated back-to-back into rental agreements (usually as an appendix) to avoid discrepancy and instances where tenants find themselves in breach of rules they are unaware of. If the property is not part of a development, it is wise to include some general terms and conditions related to the use of the property, for example, *no pets* or *no smoking inside the property.*

No assignment. A "no assignment" clause should be included in the agreement to prevent guests subletting the property, except with the express written consent of the owner.

No Alterations. It is wise to include a clause expressly prohibiting alterations, decorations, additions or improvements to the property without the express written consent of the owner (unauthorised alterations or additions could therefore be considered "damage"). This is generally more relevant for long-term tenancies although it is worthwhile including in all agreements.

Repairs and maintenance. A clause outlining that the property owner (or property manager) will be responsible for "all repairs and maintenance" prevents tenants from attempting their own repairs (which if not done professionally could necessitate more expensive repairs!). If repairs are attempted (and things are made worse), they can therefore be treated as "damage".

Disclaimer. It is prudent to include some form of disclaimer, which removes or "disclaims" responsibility and liability for events that are beyond your control as a property owner. Such events should include the breakdown of the supply of water, or electricity, or of the swimming pool filtration system. This clause is especially important in Thailand with its local standards and conditions, poor infrastructure and frequent interruptions in the supply of electricity (particularly in less developed and remote locations). Indeed, as this section is being written, both electricity and water supply systems have been down for more than three days due to a tropical storm (and this is not a remote location but a major resort destination!). Civil disturbances, acts of government, fires and natural disasters such as earthquakes, storms and floods, which affect the normal operation of the property or rental services (or destroys the property and renders it uninhabitable) should also be covered (these are generally referred to as *force majeure*[360] events). A disclaimer does not mean you will not use best endeavours to quickly rectify problems; it just means that you cannot accept responsibility for the events and their consequences. In addition, it is necessary to protect yourself to the fullest extent possible against claims arising from accidents or injury related to the use of the property.

Valuables. If security safes are provided in the property, guests should be instructed to use them for their valuables. Most rental agreements also contain a clause stating that "valuables left at the property are left at the guest's own risk and that the property owner shall not be responsible for any loss".[361]

Insurance. It is a good idea to advise guests to obtain comprehensive travel and medical insurance to cover cancellation,[362] loss or damage to personal property, and evacuation and repatriation on medical grounds.

Liability for third parties. If rental guests invite or allow other persons into the property, it should be made clear that damage or theft of property by third parties will be the sole responsibility of the guests.

Complaints. There should be a defined procedure for making and dealing with complaints.

Sale of the property. If you are planning to sell the property (at the same time as renting out the property), there are two issues to consider: the issue of honouring confirmed rental bookings after sale and transfer, and the issue of viewings by

---

[360] French for "superior force", it is a common clause in contracts that essentially frees parties from obligation upon the event of an extraordinary event beyond the control of the parties.

[361] If a security company has been engaged to provide security for the property, or if security is one of the services provided by the management company, it is crucial to check the terms, conditions and, most importantly, liability of the security company and management company in the event of theft.

[362] Sometimes comprehensive cancellation insurance covering the entire party is stated as a condition of the contract.

potential purchasers when the property is occupied[363]. In relation to sale of the property, the agreement should contain a clause to the effect that "the property owner shall have the right to sell the property and shall make every effort to ensure all terms and conditions of this agreement shall be applicable to the new owner". In relation to viewings, the rental agreement should allow "agents the right during reasonable hours and upon prior notice to enter the property for the purpose of conducting viewings". These clauses are specifically designed with the interests of the property owner in mind. However, it should be noted that any viewing conducted while guests are in residence, especially for short-term rentals, are a disturbance and should be kept to an absolute minimum[364] (indeed, due to the disruption, some guests might not find such a clause acceptable).

Contractual relations

The points noted above are suitable for inclusion in most standard agreements between property owners and rental guests. In the case where a rental agent (or management company) manages the booking process, agents will generally use their own rental contract (which the property owner should review). The rental agreement will therefore be between an agent and the guest, rather than between the property owner and the guest. The chart below shows the two alternate contractual relationships.[365]

---

[363] Since resort property buyers are typically on vacation and therefore have limited time, it can present a difficulty asking potential buyers to wait for guests to checkout before a viewing can be arranged.

[364] It is advised that only "qualified" viewings should be accepted, i.e. only parties that have expressed a *specific* interest in your property, as opposed to "general property introduction tours".

[365] It is also possible for more than one rental agency to be involved in the chain.

The rental agreement exists either between the rental agent (or management company) and the guest, or the property owner (landlord) and the guest. In the former case, therefore, a separate agreement should exist between the property owner and the rental agent to cover commission rates[366] and the roles and responsibilities of each party. This agreement is referred to as an "Agency Agreement" or "Partner Agreement". In such cases it is also important that the terms and conditions discussed in this chapter (in relation to rental agreements between property owners and guests) are included in the property description and booking confirmations used by the rental agents. It is the property owner's responsibility to communicate this information and ensure its proper implementation, otherwise there could be a conflict between the agent's terms and conditions and those desired by the property owner.

Important note: In cases where a rental booking is confirmed through a rental agent and then the guest makes a subsequent future booking directly with the property owner, the owner often has a residual liability to pay commission to the agent. This is usually provided for in an Agency Agreement by wording such as: "commission is payable where the rental period is arranged by the rental agent, or is directly arranged with the owner or owner's representative *after introduction of the client by the rental agent,* which includes repeat bookings".

As mentioned in the previous chapter, if you are planning to engage multiple agents, it is important to ensure none of the agreements contain a clause that grants any of the agents an "exclusive agency" for your property. If a property agent insists you sign their company's standard agreement, be sure to check the details carefully.

It is also necessary to read the terms and conditions of rental agreements in conjunction with any agreement that has been entered into with a management company. I recall an instance where a property owner had engaged a management company to manage the property and a rental agent to promote the property, whereby both contracts granted the parties (the management company and the rental agent) the exclusive right to arrange car rental and excursions for the guests (bearing in mind this is an additional source of income for both companies). Upon the arrival of one group of guests, the rental agent was busy selling excursion packages and car rental to the guests when he noticed an information display had been placed in the property by the management company to promote their own excursions and car rental. Disagreement ensued and both parties complained to the property owner who then had to get involved to keep the peace and renegotiate the contracts!

---

[366] These usually range between 10% – 20%.

Summary

- The purpose of a rental agreement is to formally set out all the details that have been agreed between the property owner and the guest, and to act as a point of reference in the case of misunderstanding or disagreement.
- When a rental booking is confirmed through an agent, a separate agreement should exist between the property owner and the agent to cover commission rates and the roles and responsibilities of each party.
- If you are planning to engage multiple agents, it is important to ensure none of the agreements contain a clause that grants any of the agents an "exclusive agency" for your property.

122
What to do after a booking is confirmed?

When a rental booking has been confirmed, there are several things that need to be done. Many of these are plain common sense, however, procedures should be put in place so their operation becomes systematised.

If a full service management company has been engaged to manage both your property and rental bookings, most of the tasks should happen automatically, without involvement on your part (except checking your bank balance!). If, on the other hand, a rental booking has been received through an independent rental agent (or made directly between the guest and property owner), details of the booking need to be communicated to those responsible for managing the property and for providing services to the guests. The management company generally needs four pieces of information:

1. Guest names
2. Date and time of both arrival and departure
3. A detailed list of services to be provided
4. Any other comments or special requests related to the booking

If property management services and the provision of guest services have been allocated among several different companies or individuals (see chapter 118), each service provider needs to be given the relevant information[367]. It might also be necessary to follow up again with the personnel involved nearer to the arrival date to ensure everything is arranged.

In addition to providing information to property and guest management staff, it is also necessary for certain information to be provided to the guests; information that is not publicly disclosed but is instead divulged to guests upon receipt of full payment. This information usually includes:

1. The address and directions to the property
2. The contact details for local staff, such as property managers, drivers or key holders.
3. Emergency contact numbers.
4. Useful local information, such as restaurants, entertainment areas and tourist attractions (although this is often provided in the guest information folder at the property).

---

[367] This is why the approach of dividing management and services requires a higher degree of involvement on the part of the property owner.

123
Taxes on rental income

Many foreign property owners remain blissfully unaware about the taxes on rental income. Sometimes this is genuine "unawareness"; other times it is deliberate – if you don't know about taxes, you don't need to pay them, right? However, when the tax authorities come calling, ignorance of the law is not generally considered a defence (although it might get you a bit of sympathy!).

Rental income derived from property situated in Thailand is taxable income, although the level of taxes payable differs depending on the property ownership structure (i.e. whether it is owned personally, or by a Thai or offshore company).[368] This chapter outlines the tax implications for each type of ownership, with Land and House Tax discussed separately at the end.

Personal name

For foreign individuals owning Thai property in their personal name, all rental income is taxable, regardless of the individual's nationality, residence status or whether rent is received within or outside of Thailand. Foreign individuals earning rental income in Thailand have a duty to file a personal income tax return in Thailand.[369]

Rental income is subject to personal income tax at the rate of 10 - 37% (see chapter 94), which is calculated on a person's net income after deduction of expenses and allowances. The allowances are quite substantial; for instance, property owners are permitted a standard no questions asked 30% deduction for expenses against rental income[370] and the first 150,000 Baht of personal income is tax-free.

If a property is rented to a Thai company, 5% withholding tax should be deducted from rental receipts (rather than relying on taxpayers to voluntarily file tax returns and declare their income, the Thai revenue department relies heavily on withholding taxes imposed at source, for obvious reasons). The 5% withholding tax then acts as a tax credit against personal income on the tax return.

There is no withholding tax if the property is rented to a person.

---

[368] For this reason, taxation on rental income should be a consideration in the choice of ownership structure.

[369] In some cases, Thai law contains provisions that deem managers or agents responsible for filing tax returns on behalf of a foreign individual and for the payment of taxes.

[370] There is also the option of claiming *actual* expenses incurred, although supporting documentary evidence is required (and corporate tax provisions governing the deduction of expenses will apply).

Thai company

When a Thai company owns a property and earns rental income, the rental income is subject to corporate income tax at the rate of 15 - 30%.

However, in the case of a Thai company, if the rental income received for the property is considered below market value without reasonable grounds, the tax authorities have the power to assess the company for tax on the amount that the property could reasonably be rented out for under ordinary circumstances. For this reason, rent paid to a company should reasonably reflect market value in order to avoid a possible tax assessment based on "deemed" income. In other words, a *nominal* rent will not suffice.

If the property is rented to another Thai company, 5% withholding tax should be deducted from rental receipts, although there is no withholding tax if the property is rented to a person.

Foreign company

If a foreign company is the registered owner of a property, its liability to Thai income tax depends on whether or not the company is "carrying on business in Thailand", which in turn depends on how the property is managed[371]. It also depends on the source of the rental income, i.e. whether funds are remitted from Thailand or from abroad. For instance, if a foreign company is *not* carrying on business in Thailand, tax is 15% of gross income; while corporate tax rates of 15 - 30% apply to income received by a foreign company that *is* carrying on business in Thailand.

A 15% withholding tax applies to funds that are remitted from or within Thailand[372] (in the case where a foreign company is *not* carrying on business in Thailand, the 15% withholding tax is considered a final tax in that the revenue department takes 15% of the gross revenue and no more questions are asked).

The chart on the following page provides a general summary of the taxes on rental income:

---

[371] Section 76 of the Revenue Code says that if a foreign company has an employee, a representative or go-between to carry on business in Thailand and thereby derives income in Thailand, the foreign company is deemed "carrying on business in Thailand" (source BDO Richfield Advisory Limited, www.bdo-thaitax.com)

[372] For this reason, there might be tax savings on rental income if rent is not paid from or within Thailand.

Property ownership	Tax on rental income
Personal name	10 - 37% personal income tax on rental income (whether paid within or outside Thailand), with an allowed standard deduction of 30%. 5% withholding tax if rented to a Thai company (tax credit against Personal Income on tax return).
Thai company	15 - 30% corporate income tax, although the Revenue Department has the power to assess rent at "market value". 5% withholding tax if rented to a Thai company.
Foreign company	15% of gross income if rental income is paid from or within Thailand to a foreign company not carrying on business in Thailand. 15 - 30% corporate tax rates apply if income received by a foreign company carrying on business in Thailand. 15% withholding tax if funds are remitted from or within Thailand.

House and land tax

Saving the discussion of land and house tax till last does not mean it is an insignificant tax. Indeed, *if land and house tax is properly and strictly implemented*[373] it could become a significant part of a property's tax liability and owners therefore need to consider their liability for filing the relevant tax return.[374]

According to the Land and House Tax Act 2474, if you own property in Thailand (land, houses, buildings, structures), which has been used in the last year for commercial purposes – including rental properties and vacation properties – Building and Land Tax is payable each year at the rate of 12.5% of the yearly rental value of the property.

The yearly rental value is calculated according to the lease agreement or the annual value *assessed* by the Land Department, whichever is higher (an "assessed value" means the amount of money that may reasonably be gained from the property each year *if* the property is rented out).[375] In other words, if the property is rented out, the actual rent received will act as the tax base; if it is not rented out, a "deeded" amount is used to collect the tax.

The only exemptions are vacant properties or owner-occupied properties. With regard to "owner-occupied", this does not include directors of companies; companies (whether Thai or foreign) are considered separate entities and cannot avail themselves of the residency exception (therefore, when buying property through a Thai company for vacation use, the tax authorities still expect a reasonable rent to be paid in return).

Responsibility for the payment of house and land tax is the owner or lessor (if the owner or lessor is a company, the company is generally liable to pay the tax). In cases where the owner of the land is not the same as the owner of the villa or building on the land, the law provides for the tax liability for both land and building to pass to the building owner. This is also the case with leasehold interests, where the freehold owner can pass the liability for house and land tax to the lessee (leasehold owner) through the terms of the contract (most freehold property owners prefer not to have a 12.5% hole eating into their rental revenue

---

[373] House and Land Tax is a "local tax" in that it is collected not by the Thai Revenue Department but by the local municipality to be used for maintaining and developing the area under its jurisdiction.

[374] Local government complacency cannot be depended upon in perpetuity.

[375] A new tax proposal aims to collect tax on the official appraised asset value instead of the rental value (at the rate of 0.5%) according to BDO News "Thailand: 2011 Property Tax Update" www.bdo.co.th

and therefore try to pass the tax liability to the lessee). To achieve this, a clause similar to the one below is used[376]:

> *"The lessee agrees to pay to the Lessor any and all taxes, if any, beginning with taking possession of the property and during the term hereof which may be levied upon or assessed against the property..."*

[376] See "Housing Building Tax" at www.thailandlawonline.com

Conclusion

Congratulations for making it to the end!

I sincerely hope the information in this book has been useful to readers. In fact, if only one distinction or piece of information has served to better protect your investment, the whole exercise has been worthwhile.

However, one thing should be clear in Thailand: success is not a given. To do things properly – whether you are buying, building or renting out a property – there is a lot to know, things are not straightforward and many traps await unsuspecting buyers. The challenges associated with operating in Thailand are always obvious in retrospect, although to be successful we need to be aware of them and take steps to avoid them *beforehand*. Being proactive, being prepared and performing thorough due diligence are thus essential elements of a safe investment.

Therefore, if you decide to buy property in Thailand's resort areas, don't commit the error of making an impulse purchase. Instead, protect yourself by performing thorough research before you enter into an agreement, take appropriate expert advice at each stage of the process, and approach the process sequentially. Never be tempted to save costs by cutting corners and if at any time things don't feel right, don't be afraid to walk away from a deal.

Foreign buyers often exercise a lower standard of care than they would when purchasing property in their home country. Don't be among them. Thailand can be a difficult place both to purchase property and conduct business; for this reason a *greater* degree of awareness is necessary.

The following quote was written in the context of the global economy; however, it is equally appropriate to the situation of purchasing property in Thailand:

> *"These are very interesting times, times that will favour the prepared and the bold, and be catastrophic for those who are neither prepared nor bold."*

> (Rick Rule)